In euägl̃ · ß̃m · Marcũ · cap̃ · 16 ·

Euntes in mũdũ vniuersũ predicate euãgeliũ oĩ
creature, 2c ————— vbĩs ·

· Mar · 16 ·

· Mathei · 24 · c̃ ·

Et predicabitur hoc euãgeliũ regni in vniuerso orbe
in testimoniũ omnibus gentibus · 2c̃ · /Glosa · s ·

· Math · 24
Nicol · de lyra ·

(Et predicabitur euãgel · regni) i · euãgeliũ xp̃i q̃d mtroduc
cit ad regnũ celeste 2c̃ · (in vniuerso mũdo) q̃ eñ ante
destructionẽ ciuitatis per tytũ et vespasianũ in tribᵘ p̃tibᵘ
orbis · s · Asia /Affrica et europa predicatũ sit euãgeliũ
xp̃i patet sic · /Diuide eñ petro fides p̃dicata est · i italia
2c̃ · q̃ req̃rat si placet · ——————

· Sequitur i eãdẽ glosa ·

(In testimoniũ oibus gentibus) quasi dicat · ad hoc p̃
dicanda e fides in vniuerso orbe · vt testimoniũ xp̃i
audiretur in oĩ genere · s̃m q̃ dictũ fuit ap̃lis actuũ
p̃ · / Eritis m̃ testes m̃ ierusalem : et iudea : et sama
ria et vsq̃ ad vltimũ terre · ——————

· Actuũ · i ·

℔ Sequitur ·

Considerandũ q̃ alia est predicatio euangelij futura i
omnibus gentibus : q̃tũ ad efficentiã · sc̃ q̃ omnes gē
tes recipient fidem xp̃i · Et hoc erit in cõsumatione
seculi · s ·

Nicol · de lyra ·

· Nota ·

Quoniam oritur q̃stio /quo modo p̃dicatus fuerit
euangeliũ xp̃i · p̃ totũ orbem vl quo modo maneat
adhuc p̃dicandũ · req̃rat el Tostado sr̃ matheu ·
cap̃ᵒ xxuij · q̃stioẽ · xlvij · p̃ totũ · 2c̃

· el Tostado ·

THE
Libro de las profecías
OF
Christopher Columbus

An *en face* edition

✠ Translation and commentary by
Delno C. West
AND
August Kling

University of Florida Press
Gainesville

Columbus Quincentenary Series

Copyright 1991 by the Board of Regents of the State of Florida.
Printed in the U.S.A. on acid-free paper.
The University of Florida Press is a member of University Presses of Florida,
the scholarly publishing agency of the State University System of Florida.
Books are selected for publication by faculty editorial committees at each of
Florida's nine public universities: Florida A&M University (Tallahassee),
Florida Atlantic University (Boca Raton), Florida International University
(Miami), Florida State University (Tallahassee), University of Central Florida
(Orlando), University of Florida (Gainesville), University of North Florida
(Jacksonville), University of South Florida (Tampa), University of West
Florida (Pensacola).

Orders for books published by all member presses should be addressed to
University Presses of Florida, 15 NW 15th Street, Gainesville, FL 32611.

Library of Congress Cataloging-in-Publication Data

Libro de las profecías. English.
    The Libro de las profecías of Christopher Columbus: an en face
edition / translation & commentary by Delno C. West and August
Kling.
        p.   cm. — (Columbus quincentenary series)
    Translation of: Libro de las profecías.
    Includes bibliographical references (p.   ) and index.
    ISBN 0-8130-1054-3 (acid free paper)
    1. America—Discovery and exploration—Spanish.   2. Columbus,
Christopher—Religion.   I. Columbus, Christopher.   II. West, Delno
C., 1936–   .   III. Kling, August, 1927–   .   IV. Title.   V. Series.
E117.L5313   1991
970.01'5—dc20   90-19549
                                                                              CIP

The preparation of this volume was made possible in part by a grant from the
Division of Research Programs of the National Endowment for the
Humanities, an independent federal agency.

This book is dedicated to our wives
Jean West and Marjory Kling

"In bonds of love united, man and wife,
Long, yet too short,
They spent a happy life."

Joseph Hall, Bishop of Norwich, 1574–1656
Elegy on Sir Edward and Lady Lewkenor

✠ Illustrations

Contents

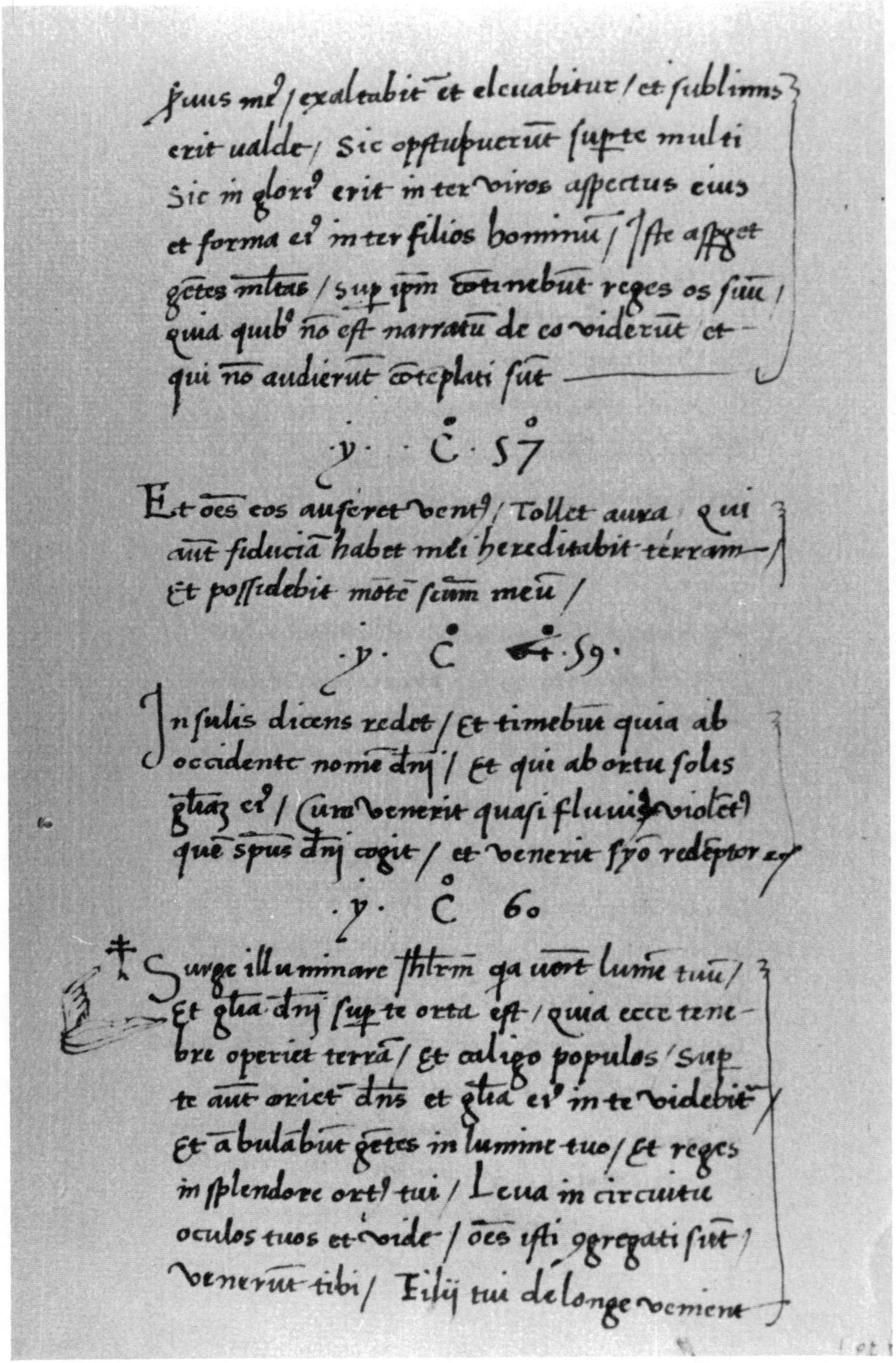

filius me / exaltabit et eleuabitur / et sublimis
erit ualde / Sic opstupuerut sup te multi
Sic in gloria erit inter viros aspectus eius
et forma ei inter filios hominu / Iste asperget
getes mltas / sup ipm cotinebut reges os suu /
quia quib no est narratu de eo viderut et
qui no audierut coteplati sut ————

y · č · 57

Et oes eos auferet ventus / Tollet aura / qui
aut fiducia habet mei hereditabit terram ——
Et possidebit monte scūm meu /

y · č · 59 ·

In sulis dicens redet / Et timebut quia ab
occidente nome dni / Et qui ab ortu solis
gltiaz ei / Cum venerit quasi fluuius violet
que spus dni cogit / et venerit syo redeptor ey

y · č · 60

† Surge illuminare jhtrm qa uenit lume tuu /
Et glia dni sup te orta est / quia ecce tenebre operiet terra / Et caligo populos / sup
te aut oriet dns et glia ei in te videbit
Et abulabut getes in lumine tuo / Et reges
in splendore ortus tui / Leua in circuitu
oculos tuos et vide / oes isti ggregati sut /
venerut tibi / Filij tui de longe venient

Figure 1: Manuscript page from the hand of Ferdinand Colón

Preface

✠ This coauthored book is unusual in that the two authors have never met. I had been studying the *Libro de las profecías* since 1984 when I learned through the National Endowment for the Humanities staff that August Kling was working on a translation of that document before his death in the spring of 1986. Subsequent conferences with Mrs. Marjory Kling led to an agreement to coauthor this book using Dr. Kling's translation and notes. Although I never met Dr. Kling, I came to admire his abilities as a researcher and linguist, and his insights into the Admiral of the Ocean Sea's spirituality.

Born on 26 July 1927 in Schenectady, New York, August J. Kling was educated at Wheaton College, Princeton Theological Seminary, McGill University, and the Universities of Mexico, Edinburgh, Paris, and Vienna. Although a longtime parish pastor, early in his professional career he developed an interest in the lives of prominent scientists who were noted Christians. These studies led him to focus on the life and work of Christopher Columbus, whose extant documents, especially the *Libro de las profecías*, reflect a deep Christian commitment. In 1984 Kling left the parish ministry to devote full time to his research interests.

Both authors owe many debts to colleagues and sponsors of this project. Both wish to thank the National Endowment for the Humanities, Division of Texts and Translations, for grant funds to complete this project and Dr. James McCord and his excellent staff, Kate Levan and Patricia Calvo, at the Center of Theological Inquiry, Princeton, New Jersey, for financial, moral, and intellectual support. Also, I would like to thank my university for continued interest in this project expressed by sabbatical leave, released time from teaching, and funds from its Organized Research Committee.

Further, I wish to express my deep thanks to academic friends who helped with this project. Dr. Francisco Morales Padrón was always available to share his incredible knowledge of Columbus and the New World Encounter and eventually presented me with a gift of the newly published exact facsimile of the *Libro de las profecías* (Collección tabula Americae, Madrid, 1984). Drs. Juan

Gil and Consuelo Varela have been special friends and strong supporters of this project who were always willing to share ideas and their vast knowledge of the Columbian sources. Dr. Christian Zacher read the earliest draft and made many helpful suggestions. Dr. E. Randolph Daniel, Dr. Teofilo Ruiz, and Dr. Leonard Sweet read the manuscript later and added further counsel and advice. Dr. Michael Gannon, and the editors and staff of the University Presses of Florida have been an excellent team to work with in seeing this task to publication.

As always, without the support of one's family, scholarly activity is impossible. We express our greatest gratitude to our wives and children.

Delno C. West

✠ Abbreviations

Quotations from primary source material are designated by brackets [ ] which refer the reader to the following collections of sources:

Ferdinand	Ferdinand Colón, *The Life of the Admiral Christopher Columbus*, translated by B. Keen (New Brunswick, 1959).
Las Casas	Bartolomé de las Casas, *Historia de los Indias*, edited by A. Carlo (Mexico City, 1951).
L.P.	*Libro de las profecías:* Page numbers refer to the text and the translation in this study.
Raccolta	*Raccolta di documenti e studi pubblicati della R. Commissione Colombiana per quarto centenario della scoperta dell'America* (Roma, 1892–94). Material edited or written by C. de Lollis unless otherwise indicated.
Varela	Consuelo Varela, *Cristóbal Colón: Textos y documentos completos* (Madrid, 1984). Used whenever possible.

1

Introduction

Saint Peter stepped out upon the water, and to the extent that his faith remained firm, he walked upon it. Whoever finds so much faith as a grain of mustard seed will be obeyed by the mountains. Knock and it must be opened unto you. No one should be afraid to undertake any project in the name of our Savior, if it is a just cause and if he has the pure intention of His holy service. [L.P., 111]

✠ A small ship, battered by storms, returned to the harbor of Palos on 15 March 1493. It brought news of a voyage across the Sea of Darkness, and that news drew back the veil that had concealed from each other the people of the two halves of the world. The opening up of the Western Hemisphere marked the beginning of an era that will reach its five-hundredth anniversary in 1992. The return of Christopher Columbus from his first voyage of discovery, and the rapid spread of his printed report throughout Europe in 1493, began an interaction between the Old and New worlds that continues to this day. The event was not only the discovery of a New World but a new beginning in a new age for the civilization of the old world.

As in most things human, these new experiences were both daylight and darkness with all the subtle shadings in between. Interaction became colonialism. The helping hands of missionaries were less strong than hands grasping for gold. The early, friendly meetings between discoverers and discovered soon fell victim to exploitation, mutual infection with diseases, and the horrified recognition of cannibalism and ritual slaughter practiced by many of the New World peoples and slavery and genocide practiced by many from the Old World.

But for all of that, the unveiling of a New World marked a new beginning in a new age for both halves of the world. The era continued to be one of discovery and development. Each new generation was amazed by these changes and developments. The future seemed to be shaped by recapitulations of the return of the ships *Niña* and *Pinta* through threatening storms with news of some advance on an unexpected frontier, an advance that would change lives and solve some incredibly stubborn problems but at the same time create a score of new ones.

1

Christopher Columbus is one of the best-known world heroes. People everywhere know his name and some facts about him. His memory, invoked by paintings, statues, monuments, geographical names, biographies, poetry, and stories, is surpassed by only a few other leaders of world history. But our purpose is to call attention to something more significant about Christopher Columbus than his fame as the discoverer who opened up a frontier and gave the world a new beginning and a new age.

Christopher Columbus was a man with a vision. The vision came first, long before it reached fulfillment in the discovery. It was strong, patient, and unwavering in the face of human opposition and ridicule. It was undaunted by obstacles and unknown dangers. Only after long years of single-minded dedication came at last a discovery.

The magnitude of the discovery, with its incalculable, unfolding implications, brought down on the Discoverer a series of pressures, compromises, errors, conflicts, and frustrations that were far more harmful to his health and happiness than the problems of the earlier years when he promoted his vision with so little success. In this, too, the great Discoverer was typical of the age he began. His vision was followed by his discovery and both were tremendously successful, but they did not add up to a success story. They did open a new era of human development, but not all agree on how warmly to view this as human progress. Yet, human development must be seen as inevitable and positive. Just as records are there to be broken and problems to be solved, so frontiers beckon individuals who have a vision of something new. Christopher Columbus was a man who had a dream, kept the faith, and ran the full course from vision to discovery.

Our purpose is to present for the first time in English the book by which Christopher Columbus explained his vision to his king and queen. He called it a *Notebook of authorities, statements, opinions and prophecies on the subject of the recovery of God's holy city and mountain of Zion, and on the discovery and evangelization of the islands of the Indies and of all other peoples and nations.* Library catalogers labeled it *Libro de las profecías*, the *Book of Prophecies.*

The reader will recognize in the title that the vision of Columbus was one of a missionary and a crusader. This theme is present in writings that survive from every period of his life, in notes written on the margins of books he owned that are dated as early as 1481, and in letters to a wide range of people throughout his lifetime. After 1501, he often signed his name *Xp̄o ferens*, or "Christ-bearer," and he often spoke and wrote of his spiritual vision as that of a missionary and crusader destined to lead the way to new lands and set in motion the events of a new age. His contemporary biog-

raphers agree in recognizing this vision and the spiritual discipline of his life. They do not agree, however, in their perceptions of the struggle of the visionary "Christ-bearer" in his responsibilities as Viceroy and Lord High Admiral when he became enmeshed in the tragedy of conflicting interests of native peoples he discovered, the Spanish sovereigns he served, and sailors and colonists he attempted to govern.

All the world knows the story of the discovery of Christopher Columbus; few know the story of his vision. By 1492, technical advances and intellectual abilities had made the time ripe for crossing the Ocean Sea—some argue that if Columbus had not done it, someone else soon would have. But one important ingredient was missing: a vision so strong that nothing could deter its holder from the attempt. The vision and the discovery should be considered as having an important connection. The discovery was of a material reality of things perceived by the senses. The vision was a spiritual reality, something only later observed by the Discoverer's senses. Visions, prophecies, hopes, values, ideals and goals are similar spiritual realities. Our purpose here is to obtain a clearer understanding of the vision and the discovery as two complementary and interacting realities in the life and work of the Genoese explorer. He was a seer of an ever-unfolding vision of the meaning of what he had discovered, the destiny of the new world in ages to come.

Christopher Columbus was a careful student of the Bible. He studied it systematically together with the opinions of learned scholars and commentators who were held in the highest regard in his day. The focus of the Discoverer's interest was the prophesied latter-day enlargement of the Christian Church which would take place through the discovery and evangelization of all the world's nations and tribes, with the consequent renewal and enrichment of Christendom. Although aided by the commentators, he interpreted the Holy Scriptures himself with confidence, claiming that he had the direct illumination of the Holy Spirit in his study of the sacred text. Columbus said and wrote that the divine guidance he received through the Bible not only generated the vision for all of his voyages to the New World but also supplied his motivating drive and sustained him through his trials and dangers. He professed to believe implicitly in his own special vocation as the "Christ-bearer," a missionary discoverer, divinely called and equipped for the task of announcing a new era of foreordained expansion and renewal for all Christendom. The *Libro de las profecías*, compiled by Christopher Columbus to substantiate each of these claims in minute detail, is surely the world's most unique notebook of an individual's personal Bible studies.

Reading the journals and letters of Columbus, one becomes aware

of a saga somewhat like a journey through the mists of creation. This awareness is appropriate, given the uniqueness of his voyage that linked the two great halves of the hitherto separated world in history and development. But Columbus was also at home in the vicinity of what he believed to be the terrestrial paradise. He was somehow at ease and unharried through the Homeric struggles of his thirteen months shipwrecked and marooned; he seems somehow to have celebrated his chains of imprisonment as did St. Paul. Step by step, the Discoverer seems aware of playing out a role on a stage that held the whole world and all of its history. Bishop Bartolomé de las Casas, his earliest biographer, caught the spirit of the Admiral from reading the sources of the enterprise and recognized that major changes in historiographical and religious thinking were taking place as a result of the discoveries: "I believe it surpassed them [the discovery over other world historical events] in quality and quantity because it was founded on the glory of the divine name, the expected improvement of the holy Catholic faith, and the conversion of infinite souls" [Las Casas, p. 39]. The Bishop of Chiapas understood Columbus's sense of millenarian hope and providential mission as expressed through his many documents, his articulation of his own apocalyptical relationship to history as a way to find meaning in events.

This understanding is basic to the way we must deal with the *Libro de las profecías*. Scholars have paid slight attention to this work that was so important to the Discoverer himself. There are many reasons for their refusal to devote serious attention to it: it has been an embarrassment to devotees of the first American hero because it conflicts with the view of Columbus as a scientific explorer and symbol of technological advancement. Furthermore, the complete text has remained virtually inaccessible except to multilingual scholars who happen to have access to one of the 560 copies of the 1892–94 edition of the *Raccolta di documenti e studi pubblicati della R. Commissione Colombiana*, the pages of which we found uncut in the copy available in the rare book room of the Firestone Library at Princeton University in 1984. Any true understanding of Columbus must take seriously his plan, intent, and achievement in the *Libro de las profecías*. His views were those of an avowed providentialist, but those views give us a fundamental way to understand his motives and his beliefs.

The following chapters provide background and suggestions for how to read the *Libro de las profecías* and its fascinating glimpses into the Discoverer's powerful vision of an eschatological hope, the prophesied expectation of new and wonderful things for all people in all places of the inhabited earth. Special attention is given to the intellectual and cultural background of Columbus, his associa-

tion with churchmen, especially Observantine Franciscans, apocalyptic thought in Spain on the eve of the discoveries, and other writings by the Admiral and his contemporaries that relate to the genuineness of his spirituality and religious vocation.

The *Libro de las profecías*, dictated by Columbus and compiled under his direction, is a notebook of Bible studies, a working file of source materials intended for use in his continuing study of and meditation on the Bible. Ultimately, he planned to compose from these notes a lengthy apocalyptic poem to be presented to the Catholic monarchs of Spain. The notebook contains a selection of biblical passages dealing with his areas of special interest: the City of God, the discovery of islands and peoples, the mission to evangelize all the nations of the earth. The themes and many of the specific quotations from Bible prophecies had, Columbus claimed, held his attention for many years and had nurtured his plan of discovery.

The immediate purpose for the compilation of this particular notebook was, the Admiral said, to remind King Ferdinand and Queen Isabella that the discovery had been "simply the fulfillment" of all the prophets had foretold and to encourage the monarchs to expect the fulfillment of other prophecies in which the Bible foretells "great events for the world" [L.P., 111]. The notebook was not intended to be read as a continuous narration or discourse. It was a collection of fragments of inspiration, sparks of light to kindle thoughts of hope, understandings of faith, glimpses of an unfolding divine plan for the future course of world events. Our description of the use of the Bible by the Discoverer is not a theological critique of his assumptions or methods. It is rather an attempt to understand what he was writing and to appreciate what it meant to him, and then to set his study and use of biblical prophecies in their context as a major factor in the direction and motivation of his historical work of exploration and discovery.

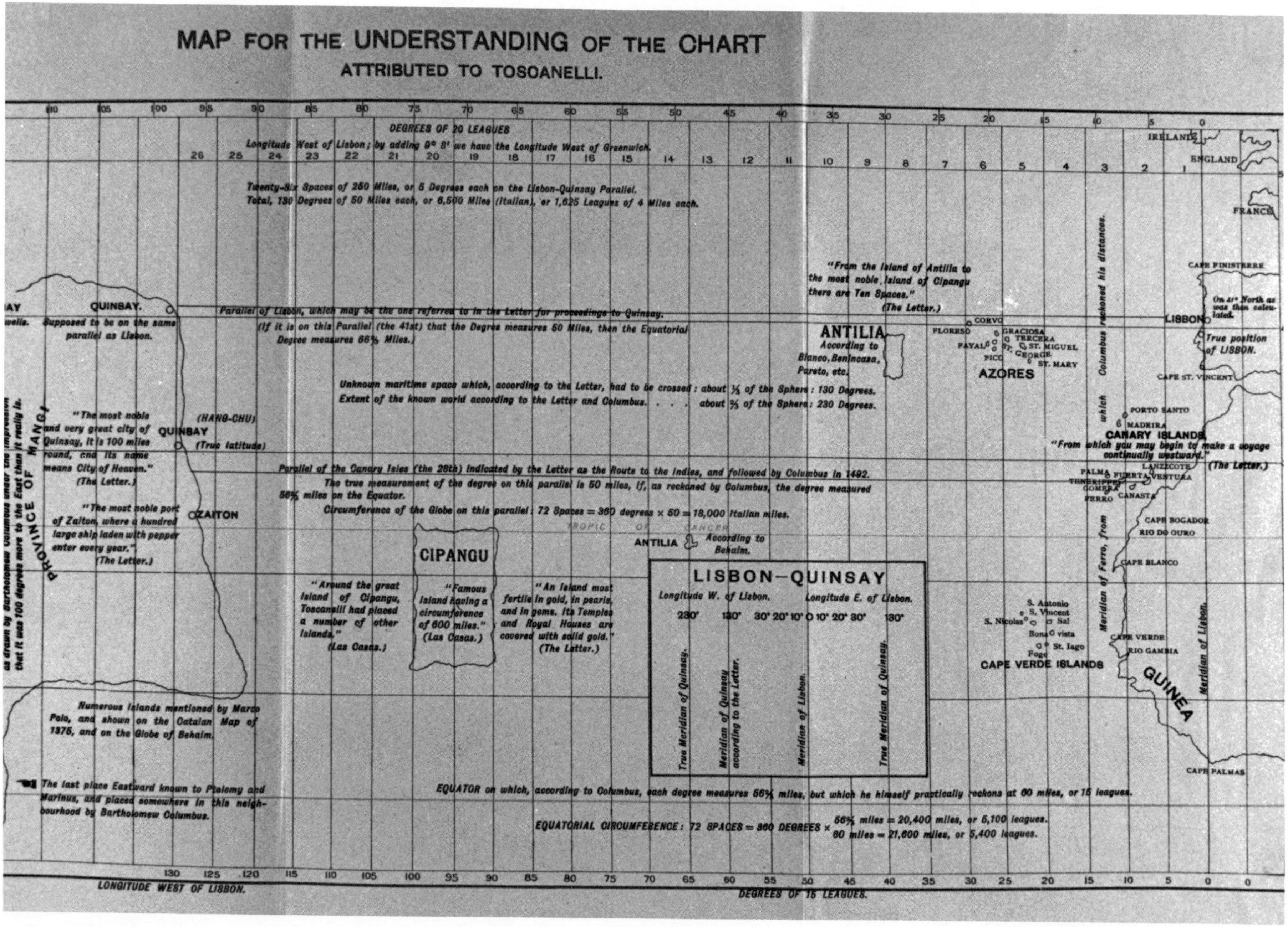

Figure 2: Vignaud's reconstructed chart of Toscanelli's map

2

Intellectual and Cultural Background of Christopher Columbus

God, who teaches the hearts of men effortlessly and without the clamor of words, and who art a present help in every time of need, give understanding. For we are not learned in literature, but we take up this task in thy power. For blessed is the man who learns from thee, Lord, whom thou teaches from thy law. We therefore pray thee to cause us to understand the things that are written by the spirit in words and books and prophecies concerning thee and thy holy place. Amen.

[L.P., 101–2]

The third voyage of Christopher Columbus was intensely devoted to the Holy Trinity. Its object was to find the suspected southern continent, named for the legendary Paria, and to claim that continent for the Spanish monarchs. Since the continent was calculated to be farther south than islands already discovered, Columbus's plan was to sail due west from a point off Cape St. Ann in Guinea (10 degrees latitude). Miraculously, the first landfall appeared on the horizon on 31 July 1498 as three mountains, confirming his destination. He named the landfall Trinidad. Sailing into the Gulf of Paria, he encountered the powerful Orinoco River and knew from its force that he had found a continent. Upon further exploration, and due to irregularities in magnetic and celestial observations, he concluded not only that he had found a continent but that he had arrived near the site of the biblical Terrestrial Paradise. Finding the location of the Terrestrial Paradise had long been one of his goals, and he thanked God for the privilege of its discovery.

Afraid to enter such sacred ground (which he believed to be only a few miles inland) and pressed for time, he charted the location and made straight for Hispaniola and his colony at Santo Domingo. Mismanagement of the colony weighed heavily on the Admiral; it had caused him great personal agony as well as increasing criticism at the Spanish court. He had left the colony under the administration of his brothers, Bartholomew and Diego, and they had failed to manage effectively either the native Indians or the growing num-

ber of Spanish immigrants. Their mismanagement eventually ended in a mutiny led by the Alcalde, Francisco Roldán. Continuous rumors of discontent and poor supervision reached the Spanish court, and Columbus hoped to return to Hispaniola to take action before the monarchs stepped in and resolved the problems themselves. He was too late. Unknown to him, the monarchs had already dispatched Francisco de Bobadilla to Hispaniola with titles and power as chief justice and royal commissioner. Bobadilla was to investigate rumors of injustices and seek equable solutions for the colony. Instead, he sided with the colonial dissidents, arrested Columbus and his brothers, and returned them to Spain in chains. Christopher Columbus wore his chains like a martyr, refusing the offer of the ship's captain to remove them. For the rest of his life, the Admiral kept and displayed the chains as symbols of his persecution by enemies of his enterprise.

Chained, humiliated, and disgraced, Columbus returned to Spain from his third voyage at the end of November 1500. Awaiting an audience with the monarchs to clear himself and his brothers of Bobadilla's charges and possibly to persuade them to finance a fourth voyage, Columbus accepted the invitation of a friend, the Carthusian monk Gasper Gorricio, to stay at the monastery Nuestra Señora Santa Maria de las Cuevas across the Guadalquivir from Seville. It was here, as he awaited his appointment with Ferdinand and Isabella, that he began to collect materials and to organize the *Libro de las profecías*. This project had long been on his mind as a means of explaining fully the religious significance of his enterprise. He worked on the notebook for several months.

One of the most striking aspects of the life of Christopher Columbus was his self-awareness as a man of destiny.[1] He viewed himself as the chosen and appointed messenger of God, predestined to open the way for evangelization and colonization of lands newly discovered by himself on behalf of the household of God. But his destiny did not end with the predetermined evangelization and colonization of the New World. That was to be only a prelude to the military recapture of Jerusalem by the Spanish, when the Holy Temple would be rebuilt in the last days, enabling the assemblage of Christians from a converted world. Columbus's self-awareness as a man of destiny appears everywhere in his writings. It had such a central place in his spirituality that his contemporaries also regarded him in the same light, causing both to view the voyage of discovery an eschatologically important juncture in world history. Historiographically, to him and to others, the discovery of new lands and peoples was elevated to equal importance with the Creation and the birth and passion of Christ and thus rapidly changed the standards of emphasis in the sequence of world history.[2]

Columbus was an optimist who sold the Catholic sovereigns of Spain, the pope, and the European public his visions of renewal, recovery, and expansion. His rhetoric promoted an age of dreams. His natural optimism was nourished by biblical eschatology. Through the windows of prophecy, he saw to the West the gold-domed palaces of Cathay or Cipangu, but in reality it was Jerusalem he was seeing. It was the "civitas Dei" in the profoundest sense that drove the Admiral forward. For Columbus, prophetic vision became an agenda for confident involvement.

The Admiral of the Ocean Sea was not driven on to what he called the "enterprise of the Indies" by the mere love of adventure and desire for fame and fortune. From the beginning he had in mind a vision of the other side of the world. Much has been written about what he and others thought was there. To Columbus, the important question was not what was there but what would it mean to Christendom, especially Spain, to have access to and passage through those unknown parts of the globe.

A prophetic vision begins to take shape early in the notes in the margins of his reference books. In the margin of *Historia rerum ubique gestarum* by Aeneas Sylvius Piccolomini (Pope Pius II), a note written in 1481 provides the first evidence of Columbus's apocalypticism. His eschatology reaches its final expression in an addition to the *Libro de las profecías* in 1504 [L.P., 227]. In the years between, he refined the apocalyptic vision of his enterprise and the expected results of its success in the texts, letters, marginal notes, reports, and diaries that he wrote. He quoted scores of ancient and medieval writers and made extensive use of Scripture. The *Libro de las profecías* was a summary of related eschatological ideas that constantly flooded his mind during his long career.

During the past five hundred years, most of our attention has been centered on Columbus's scientific theories. His religious beliefs either have been ignored or have taken second place to secular interests. Yet, science and religion were integrated in his mind to produce the vision he held. Biblical truths held an equal place with scientific knowledge, and he thought theological study to be as important as cosmological or geographical theory.

It is clear from many surviving documents that five sources of knowledge were important to Columbus's enterprise: scientific conceptions from ancient Greeks and Romans supplemented by works from Jewish and Arabic scholars; facts and prophecy from the Bible; teachings of the church fathers; interpretations of medieval theologians and cosmographers; and practical information gleaned from conversations with people from all walks of life.

Felipe Fernández-Armesto has called our attention to Columbus's contribution to the solution to the general Renaissance problem of

explaining the Atlantic ocean "space." He has stated that the Admiral's voyage marked "a moment of definition in the growth of awareness of the Atlantic 'space' and, therefore, in the modification of men's traditional image of the world."[3] Ancient and medieval scholars whom Columbus studied had different ideas about the size of the earth and the ratio of land surfaces to oceans. There was never any debate over the shape of the earth since men had known it to be a sphere long before the Christian era. Rather, arguments centered on the disposition on the globe of land and water surfaces, whether there were habitable zones south of the equator, and if so, whether the equator could be crossed to reach those areas. There was serious speculation about the possibility and advisability of sailing "under the earth." Debates over distances, wind and current patterns, logistics, and possible undiscovered islands and mainlands were the issues with which Columbus had to deal to sell his proposal to monarchs and learned committees in both Portugal and Spain.

J.R.S. Phillips has shown with rich erudition that exploration in the fifteenth century was a new phase of European expansion dating back at least to the twelfth century and the Mongol invasions. As a result of continued and increased contact between Europe and Asia, the "European world view" by 1400 was a mixture of theories, exotic tales, classical scholarship, and thirteenth- and fourteenth-century reports from travelers.[4]

Columbus absorbed cosmology from Cardinal Pierre d'Ailly (1350–1420), the learned chancellor of the University of Paris. In his copy of *Imago mundi*, the Admiral made 898 notes in his own handwriting. These postilles rarely argue with the Cardinal or contradict what he says. Rather, they highlight the text with key words which guide Columbus back to a particular idea, or they are a cross reference to other sources or an elaboration on d'Ailly's text. In some places, the annotations overwhelm the text. Pierre d'Ailly was an encyclopedist who recorded in the *Imago mundi* all he could find out about the world in the early fifteenth century. Further, he added treatises to his book on specific topics relating to such interests as geography and astrology. Much of his material was borrowed wholesale from Bishop Nicholas d'Oresme (1325–82), dean at Rouen, and from the Franciscan scholar Roger Bacon (c. 1220–c. 1294) of Oxford and Paris, who learned cosmology and the sphere of the earth from John of Holywood (d. 1244) and Robert Grosseteste (1175–1252). Columbus's vision was thus deeply rooted in the cosmology and geography of the Middle Ages. The sharp discontinuity by which many historians and biographers separate him from his medieval roots is a fiction.

It is clear from his notes in the margins of his reference books that Columbus argued for a smaller earth and much less ocean

surface than there actually is [*Raccolta,* pt. I, vol. 2, p. 376, note 23]. Many parts of the unknown world, he believed, contained islands and mainlands with a smaller ocean covering the rest of the globe than that conceived by ancient scholars. Columbus based his arguments on passages found in Pierre d'Ailly's *Imago mundi,* which in turn was grounded on the compilations of Roger Bacon's *Opus maius.* His scientific data were further supported by references to unknown lands found in scriptural passages.

In one of the most heavily annotated parts of Columbus's copy of the *Imago mundi,* chapter 8, the Bacon-d'Ailly conclusions are based on ancient geographers and philosophers and supported by the Apocryphal Esdras (2 Esdras 6:42).[5] The summary of the theory is that the length of a degree at the equator is 56 2/3 land miles. Based on this figure, Columbus estimated that he could reach Asia by sailing westward approximately 2,500 miles from the Canary Islands to Japan. Thus, his idea of size is a medieval picture of the world, not the developing Renaissance picture held by those authorities whom he had to convince at both the Portuguese and Spanish courts. In a marginal note, Columbus combines his experience with that of the theory presented in d'Ailly's short treatise, *Epologue mappae mundi,* found in the opuscula attached to the *Imago mundi:*

> Note that frequently when sailing south from Lisbon to Guinea, I purposefully studied the course, as captains and mariners do, and I later took the altitude of the sun with the quadrant and other instruments, several times, and I found them [the readings] to agree with Alfragan that the length of a degree is 56 2/3 miles. . . . Therefore, we can state that the circumference of the earth at the equator is 20,400 miles.   [*Raccolta,* pt. I, vol. 2, p. 407, no. 490]

This vision of Columbus was the last installment of an ancient and medieval hypothesis that portrayed a vast ocean filled with countless islands and possibly a large undiscovered continent symmetrically equivalent to Europe, Asia, and Africa. Roger Bacon had presented the medieval summary of suspected islands and mainlands in the unknown world. Pierre d'Ailly had relied upon this information in *Imago mundi,* which Columbus read so faithfully. In the geographical section of his *Opus maius,* Roger Bacon presented information derived from ancient geographers and thirteenth-century travelers. As a result, Bacon insisted upon the habitability of the southern hemisphere. He suggested the possibility of sailing westward from Spain and insisted that the Sea of Darkness (i.e., the Atlantic Ocean) was smaller than believed.[6]

There is no way of knowing when and where Christopher Columbus conceived the idea of sailing across the Ocean Sea to reach

Asia. It was not a new idea, but it was dismissed as impossible and undesirable by many in the fifteenth century. (Even his motives for doing so were mixed and obscure in their priorities — scientific, economic, political, and mystical. This study is basically concerned with the mystical, but we recognize that other motives were just as strong and frequently influenced him.) Columbus seemed to have got the idea young in life from his experiences as a seaman and from living with his wife at Santo Porto. Once the seed of the idea was planted in his mind (which he believed was done by God), he began to build a scientific case to prove its feasibility.

Columbus often clouded his theories, knowledge, and objectives for reasons of secrecy. Mystery surrounds the man and his enterprise even five hundred years later. It is arguable, for example, whether his main intent was to reach Asia. It was his stated objective, but his extant writings show that he was convinced that he would find islands and maybe a mainland that were unclaimed or capturable. It is not likely that he planned to become Viceroy over China since everyone knew that China was an advanced civilization with a powerful government. Yet he made sure that the *Capitulations of Santa Fé*, which authorized the first voyage, empowered him to claim unknown islands and mainlands for the Crown and that he would administer them for the monarchs and share in their wealth. Nor was Columbus alone in his search for Atlantic islands. The chief interest of Atlantic explorers, as attested by numerous requests to the Portuguese king for charters of exploration in the fifteenth century, was a quest for islands. Columbus was certain that there were islands, and maybe a continent, between Spain and Asia. Both practical evidence and geographical theory supported this probability. Ferdinand Colón, his son and biographer, lists this as one of his father's primary motives:

> The Admiral's third and last motive for seeking the Indies was his hope of finding before he arrived there some islands or land of great importance whence he might better pursue his main design. . . . This being so, he argued that between the end of Spain and the known end of India, there must be many other islands and lands.
>
> [Ferdinand, p. 23]

The practical evidence was everywhere for a dedicated searcher to find. Artifacts had washed ashore in times past in the form of carved wood. Flora of unknown origin, and outside the taxonomy of Europe, was found in the sea and occasionally on the beaches of the Atlantic islands near Europe. Even human bodies with "broad faces" like the Chinese had been found. Columbus himself had seen these while in Galway. And, there were the innumerable stories of mariners sighting islands and lands to the west. English and

Scandinavian sailors had sailed the northern part of the Atlantic for centuries and told stories of lands to the west of Iceland and Greenland. Maps and ocean charts frequently placed mythical islands, such as the Brendan chain and the Antilles, in the Atlantic.[7]

Studies of ancient and medieval geographers and travelers confirmed Columbus's suspicions, and Seneca had predicted the discovery of lands beyond Thule (Iceland). Columbus quoted this famous passage from Seneca's *Media* twice and translated it into Spanish once in the *Libro de las profecías*.[8] Marco Polo, Columbus's travel guide to the East, described how Asia was coasted by a large ocean and reported that the ships of the great Khan traveled far out into the sea to trade with the peoples of distant wealthy lands. The evidence pointed to an ocean between Europe and Asia which contained islands and possible mainlands which could be had.

Launching an exploratory expedition across the Ocean Sea would be expensive. Only a major government could fully afford such an enterprise, and only a major government could enforce claims to discovered lands. In order to gain financing and political backing, Columbus knew that he had to convince government leaders, ultimately monarchs, who relied on their scientific advisors to recommend action. He had to assemble convincing data and arguments to persuade men of varied backgrounds of the worthiness of his enterprise. Thus, he built his case on scientific knowledge and theory, his practical knowledge of the sea, and on biblical prophecy. In the end, it was the arguments based on biblical prophecy (and possible commercial gain) that tipped the scales in his favor when the pious Catholic monarchs chose to endorse and finance his enterprise against the advice of their academic advisors.

We have made the point that Columbus relied heavily upon ancient and medieval cosmology to form his vision of what was across the Ocean Sea and what constituted the size, shape and content of the world. His practical understanding of that ocean, however, was much more a product of the Renaissance and relied primarily upon the new cartographic thinking being developed at Florence, Italy. No one seriously questions Columbus's admiring use of Paolo dal Pozzo Toscanelli's work in the field of geography.[9]

Paolo Toscanelli was a medical doctor by profession, but, typical of fifteenth-century educated Florentines, his intellect ranged far beyond the ills of the human body into the fields of mathematics and cartography. Through his studies and discussions with other Renaissance scientists, Toscanelli came to understand that combining Ptolemy's gridding system with perspective geometry might be adaptable to the cartography of the Ocean Sea. Such a combination would allow measurements in the absence of landmarks. The gridding method gave metric coherence, allowing mariners with a grid-

scaled map to sail grid distances in any direction and to return following the same method.

Intellectuals in Renaissance Florence had achieved a sense of terrestrial space by the third quarter of the quatrocentro. A mental image of the habitable globe had emerged in which the Ocean Sea was an integral part of the earth instead of an uncrossable barrier. The sea was seen as a navigable ocean linking continents, a highway with island "rest stops" between Europe and Asia. Making the Ocean Sea an intercontinental waterway was a remarkable intellectual achievement that grew out of new geographical speculations in mid-century Florence.

The impetus for the concept of a navigable Ocean Sea, which was itself an integral part of the global environment, grew out of Italian-Byzantine discussions that took place in 1439 at the church council called in Florence to reunify the Christian faith. Gemistos Pletho, the Byzantine geographer and recent editor of Strabo's geographic theories, led symposia with interested Florentines, including Toscanelli, on Strabo's and Ptolemy's major theories.[10] These discussions not only filled in theoretical gaps of knowledge about coastal Asia but also related ancient theory to contemporary knowledge about the area that had been brought back by merchants, missionaries, and other travelers. The Florentine interest was primarily commercial, but for Renaissance scholars the information brought the area of coastal Asia into sharper intellectual focus.

Intellectual speculation became visual identity, however, when Italian cartographers applied developing Renaissance artistic methods to map making. Maps came to portray a global unity hitherto unknown. A leading proponent of both new geographical ideas and cartography was Paolo Toscanelli.

In 1474, the Canon of Lisbon, Fernam Martins de Roriz, attended the funeral of Toscanelli's friend and mathematical collaborator, Nicholas of Kues, at Todi. Martins was in charge of the Portuguese navigation committee sponsoring exploration down the African coast. These efforts had been hampered by a navigational crisis: as they sailed farther south, the Portuguese lost their primary guidance point, the pole star. Thus, Martins was greatly interested in the developments of geographic theory in Florence and in Toscanelli's system of cartography. He asked the elderly doctor to prepare a summary for the Portuguese king.

On an endleaf of his copy of the *Historia rerum ubique gestarum*, by Aeneas Sylvius Piccolomini, Columbus reproduced, in his own hand, the letter sent from the famous Florentine physician and geographer to Fernam Martins, Canon of Lisbon and councilor to the king of Portugal [*Raccolta*, pt. I, vol. 2, p. 364; pt. I, vol. 3, plate LXIII; and part V, pp. 571–72].

What was important in the Toscanelli correspondence, besides the fact that Toscanelli's data supported Columbus's measurements of a short distance to the Orient, was the new, cartographic idea of visual space that was continuous and relative to the fixed eye of the individual observer. Toscanelli explained:

> The straight lines, therefore, drawn lengthwise [vertically] on the chart, indicate distance from east to west, but those which are transverse [horizontally] show the spaces from south to north. . . . From the city of Lisbon in a direct line to the westward, to the most noble and very great city of Quinsay, there are 26 spaces marked on the chart, each one containing 250 miles. . . . This space is a third part of the whole sphere. . . . But from the island of Antillia [supposedly an island beyond the Canaries], which is known to you, to the most noble island of Cippangu [Japan], there are 10 spaces. . . . Thus there are not great spaces of the sea to be passed which are unknown.   [*Raccolta*, pt. I, vol. 2, p. 364]

The art historian Samuel Edgerton has studied Toscanelli's new concept of visual space and its influence upon Renaissance science, especially cartography: "What Toscanelli demonstrated to Martins and hence to Columbus was that once the surface of the earth was conceptually organized into a rectilinear grid, it took on a new sense of conformity. It was no longer to be thought of as a heterogeneous assemblage of frightening unknowns."[11] Edgerton points out that Toscanelli was the leading Ptolemaic expert of his time and that his chart, known to Columbus, was based upon Ptolemy's grid of the earth. The importance of the geometric grid was that it gave to the sphere of the earth a geometric continuity. All locations could be fixed in relation to one another by coordinates, and, by extension, unknown sites could be brought into harmony and proportion to the whole. As Edgerton concluded, "Whatever the configuration of a grid-divided surface, the observer is able to comprehend all of its continuity as long as he can relate to the side of at least one undistorted, modular square which represents the true unit of measurement for judging the whole."[12]

Such thinking led to significant changes during the Renaissance in architecture and painting as well as cartography. Although Vignaud was mistaken in his study of the influence of Toscanelli upon Columbus, we have included Vignaud's reconstruction of how Toscanelli's map may have looked. The map is lost but likely was taken by Columbus on his first voyage. Using such a map, Columbus was able to visualize the Ocean Sea as a sea-link between continents and to conceptualize the earth as a series of grids. The practical application of this information was for Columbus to sail from grid to grid to accomplish his goal, a psychological encouragement of

incalculable importance. Writing to the Renaissance Pope Alexander VI, a man of learning who was likely familiar with the new cartography, Columbus expressed his voyage exactly in these terms: "I had gone ten lines into the other hemisphere" ("Yo anduve dies líneas del otro emisperio") [Varela, p. 311].

Biographers of Columbus have always referred extensively to his discussions with learned commissions of mathematicians and theologians in the courts of Portugal and Spain. They have mentioned a few details of his citations of biblical references in those discussions. Yet we are left with the impression that this use of the Bible was not a systematic study, only a grasping for some authority by which to reinforce views formed and goals adopted on grounds other than study of the Bible. The possibility exists that the Genoese explorer meant precisely what he said and was speaking sober truth in his intensely autobiographical letter to the Sovereigns which he included in the *Libro de las profecías:* "The Holy Spirit . . . encouraged me with a radiance of marvelous illumination from his sacred Holy Scriptures" [L.P., 105]. The reports of his earliest biographers and correspondents are consistent with this view, and evidence of serious studies of biblical prophecy and learned commentators and interpreters of those prophecies by Columbus prior to 1492 bears proof of the validity of his statement. As will be shown later, such proof existed as early as 1481 in the postilles to Columbus's copy of Piccolomini's *Historia*. And, even though they cannot be dated, further proof exists in the postilles to Pierre d'Ailly's *Imago mundi*, which the German paleographer, Fritz Streicher, believed were written between 1480 and 1483.[13]

There are scores of biblical prophecies announcing the future unveiling of unknown lands and future contact with unreached peoples on which Columbus relied to make his spiritual case. A summary of this search for biblical sites composes Part III of the *Libro de las profecías*. In these texts, he found prophecies announcing unknown islands and peoples, future worldwide missionary endeavors to extend the kingdom of Christ, future world unity in the worship of God, and future treasures and offerings from distant lands to enrich the house of God and the Church of Christ. The vision Columbus developed while contemplating these prophecies included higher levels of human happiness, longevity, prosperity, liberty, social progress, and new technology.

It was rare for laymen to read the Bible in the fifteenth century. It was unique for a layman to be a careful exegete of Scripture. Yet, the Admiral gives a clear presentation of how he interpreted Scripture in the *Libro de las profecías*. He began his notebook with a definition of his hermeneutical presuppositions by declaring that he always followed the standard medieval exegetical tool, the *Quad-*

riga as taught by St. Thomas Aquinas [L.P., 101]. The *Quadriga* developed out of early Christian attempts to justify literary styles within both the Old and New Testaments by formalizing a fourfold sense in Scripture: the literal, the allegorical (what is believed), the anagogical (what is hoped for), and the tropological (moral lessons).[14] Columbus chose a simple statement from the *Decretis* of Jean Gerson to explain:

> The literal teaching tells facts;
> The allegory tells what you should believe;
> The moral interpretation tells how you should act;
> The anagogy tells where you are going.   [L.P., 101]

He then gives an example of this system using the word "Jerusalem" for his interpretation, a common example used by exegetes and poets (e.g., Dante) in the Middle Ages. Jerusalem literally is the earthly city where pilgrims travel, but allegorically, it indicates the church in the world. Tropologically, Jerusalem is the soul of every believer, and anagogically the word means the heavenly city, "the celestial fatherland and kingdom." The Admiral then offers a prayer seeking guidance in understanding Scripture in this manner. The prayer is followed by a short discourse on grammar and its relation to exegesis in which he demonstrates that verbs in the past tense are sometimes used to indicate the present or the future.

Columbus concludes his statement on exegesis by turning to Nicholas of Lyra (*Glossa ordinaria*) in order to expand his hermeneutics into a system of twofold literal meanings. In this way, he can see concordance in Scripture by accepting the idea that events that happened in the Old Testament prefigured events that happened in the New Testament. Quoting Nicholas, Columbus promised his readers that he would be guided by the concept that "in these cases there is a twofold literal meaning, and the one is more important than the other when it fulfills more perfectly the thing that was predicted" [L.P., 103]. This statement is then explained by two examples.[15]

Scriptural study led Columbus to many conclusions, as we will see. Since the Holy Bible was the source of all knowledge to men in the fifteenth century, it was to Columbus, then, an important source of geographical information. Explorers do not go forth and probe about. They search for definite objects which they believe to exist based on the geographic information they have. Such information can be empirical or nonempirical.[16] Columbus had what we would call a "spiritual map" in his mind as well as a physical map when he undertook each of his four voyages. The "spiritual map" included those imagined areas of the world mentioned in the Scriptures either lost after antiquity, or predicted to be found in the

"last days" of the history of the world. From a literal interpretation of Genesis, for example, he actively sought the Terrestrial Paradise. The location of the biblical garden he believed had been concealed until his day. Some authorities held that it had washed away during the great flood described in the Old Testament; many others argued that it survived because of its location atop a mountain. Typically, medieval *mapaemundi* placed Asia and the East to the top of the map, and, according to Columbus's favorite sources, paradise was "eastward of Eden." The Terrestrial Paradise existed outside the known world, beyond Asia, in the unknown ocean surrounding all land masses. Paradise could be found because it was perceived as a real location, but eschatologically, it would not be located until near the end of time.[17]

On his third voyage, Columbus believed that he was sailing those uncharted waters on the outer fringe of Asia. It was a part of his destiny that God showed him the location of the site of the Terrestrial Paradise when he at last found the continent of South America. His suspicions were confirmed as he observed the simultaneous natural phenomena of strong river currents, magnetic variation, and celestial disparity. In an effort to understand the unknown forces at play, Columbus reasoned that he had arrived near the highest part of the earth where the Garden of Eden should be located. A few miles inland, he stated, one would arrive at the bulge of a "pear-shaped" earth on top of which was to be a promontory "like the nipple on a woman's breast." On top of the "nipple" was the legendary site [Varela, pp. 215–16].

The encounter with the Terrestrial Paradise was no casual affair for Columbus, nor were his conclusions about it spontaneous. The notations in his copy of d'Ailly's *Imago mundi* demonstrate a long concern with the Terrestrial Paradise, and they are specific. He writes next to d'Ailly's topographical description of Asia, "The Terrestrial Paradise is there [on a mountain in the Orient]" [*Raccolta*, pt. I, vol. 2, p. 376, note 19, and p. 401, notes 397–99]. His report of its location was supplemented by references to Pierre d'Ailly, St. Isidore, Bede, St. Ambrose, and Duns Scotus as well as by scriptural references to the Book of Ezra. And he remained convinced. In his letter of 1502 to Pope Alexander VI, he described his voyages and stated, "I believed and I still believe what so many saints and holy theologians believed and still believe: that there in that region is the Terrestrial Paradise" [Varela, p. 311].

Columbus frequently insisted that his "enterprise of the Indies" was the fulfillment of prophecy rather than the result of mere reason and study.[18] This conclusion was not affected by his encounter with the mainlands of South America or Mesoamerica or by his failure to confirm that Cuba was what Marco Polo had described as Ci-

pangu (Japan). These were lands newly discovered, peoples newly reached, and there were prophecies already at the point of fulfillment. These prophecies were of great and wonderful things from God that would cause rejoicing for Christendom and for all the world.

Mistakenly, scholars have portrayed Columbus as a man of unusual learning for an unlettered seaman and son of a cloth merchant. His father in reality was a well-to-do businessman with considerable civic duties in the city of Genoa.[19] The single most important unresolved question concerning the life of the Admiral of the Ocean Sea is that of his education. We know almost nothing about when he learned to read and write or where he gained the knowledge he displayed in his writings. It is safe to conclude that most of his learning was self-taught and that he became a serious student only after settling in Lisbon after 1476. He may have gained some basic skills when he was a child. Professor Desimoni has shown that the weavers of the St. Steven's quarter in Genoa, where Columbus's father kept his home and shop, had established a school for their children.[20] There is no evidence that Christopher Columbus ever attended this neighborhood "grammar school," but if he did, the curriculum likely would have given him elementary preparation for a twofold use of Latin. The first aim of the school would have been the preparation for the daily practice of religion, i.e., *pietas literata*, followed by instruction in the daily practical use of the language as it applied to the community of merchants, for letter writing, record keeping, and other business transactions. Nevertheless, such instruction would have made Columbus functionally literate.

He was a born student, however, who loved to read and learn, and he was a natural observer. Von Humboldt was impressed by Columbus's natural intelligence in conceiving the voyage and then systematically planning it.[21] Somewhere a foundation in reading, language, science, analysis, and how to classify knowledge and calculate math was acquired by the young man. One of his most notable characteristics was his ability to catalog physical and natural science and offer, on occasion, rational explanations for unfamiliar phenomena. For example, he examined and reported on various island and continental landmasses, the physiognomy of vegetation, the habits of animals and birds, and the variations in magnetism.

An example of these skills was demonstrated early, during Columbus's first voyage to the New World. On 17 September 1492 he encountered the magnetic phenomenon of declination. Such variation probably had been observed on earlier voyages by the Vikings or the English, but Columbus's log is the first to leave a written record of the occurrence. While passing through the area of zero

variation, the pilots noticed that the compass needle had drifted to the northwest from the polar star. Needless to say, some of the sailors panicked until Columbus reassured them, "This is because the star which appears, moves and the needle does not." He had concluded that the North Star was circling the North Pole.[22]

Perhaps most important were his bibliographical skills. He knew where to look for answers to his questions. The same could be said for his brother Bartholomew. They both had the same interests in cosmology, cartography, and geography. Although Ferdinand says that his father had studied at the University of Pavia, there is no record of his having been there. Ferdinand either wished to glorify his father on this point, or he mistook the University of Pavia for the alley in Genoa named Vicolo Pavia, where the weavers had established the school for their children.[23] The matriculation records at the University of Pavia are well preserved, and several searches by scholars have failed to produce his name. Moreover, matriculation at the University of Pavia during the period given by Ferdinand conflicts with other known events in Christopher Columbus's life that place him elsewhere.

Also, his command of Latin was not at a university level and definitely demonstrated that he strengthened it and began to use it more seriously after learning Spanish.[24] If he had studied at the University of Pavia, Latin would have been his "natural" written language. It was not. Spanish became the language in which he wrote all his letters and most of his postilles. The *Libro de las profecías* was composed in Latin for a definite purpose, because of its religious nature, and many of the postilles are in Latin. He only used his native Italian language twice. The problem was that Genoese Italian was not a written language in the fifteenth century. Columbus, however, did attempt to compose one postille in it. A poorly written Italian postille, consisting of Spanish and Portugese corruptions, exists in a notation to his copy of Pliny's *Historia naturalis*. All the rest of the postilles in that document are Spanish translations of the Italian text he used.

The other example of Columbus's attempt to write in Italian is an interesting note added to the *Libro de las profecías*. On folio 58a, he wrote a note on the Psalms at the bottom of Father Gorricio's text. The most arresting feature of this note is that it illustrates a humanistic sophistication not usually associated with the Admiral. The text exhibits characteristics of northern Italian humanism in its calligraphy, syntax, and spelling. The hand conscientiously formed rotund letters, and the syntax is complicated in its rhetoric. The note begins with a small "d" followed by an elaborate capital "D." The preposition "de" is used instead of the more common "di," and the Admiral incorporated humanistic spellings (e.g., double

consonants) where appropriate. He clearly corrected his spellings, as in "Salmista," which he changed to the more "correct" northern Italian humanistic "Psalmista." The note was probably added after the compilation of the manuscript was finished. Before he died, Columbus was attempting to gain some knowledge of a more cultivated Italian language than his native Genoese. The care he took with presenting this one passage, to make it "correct" by humanistic standards, shows that he wanted to make an important remark and do so in a form of Italian that would complement the Latin in which he chose to present divine prophecies.[25]

When and where Columbus learned to read and write, make mathematical calculations, and analyze sophisticated scientific, historical, and theological works remain a mystery. He intensified his studies while waiting in Spain for backing from the monarchs. He saw from the beginning that he would have to debate leading intellectuals; he thus read everything he could in his effort to present his case effectively. He must have prepared very well, for he impressed contemporaries with his deportment and confidence before learned commissions. Even though he lost every debate, his presentations so impressed the Spanish monarchs that they could never bring themselves to give an unqualified "no" to his proposal. His deportment was that of a man well prepared and well versed to argue his theses with numerous citations from respected sources at his fingertips.

His favorite scientific source, as indicated above, was the French cardinal, Pierre d'Ailly. The *Imago mundi* was a translation with additions of the thirteenth-century work of that name by Gantier de Metz. D'Ailly probably finished his edition in 1410 and it was printed at Louvain around 1480. Pauline Watts has demonstrated Columbus's heavy dependence upon this source as well as on the attached *opuscula*. She has detailed how d'Ailly, a diligent encyclopedist, opened other authoritative and influential ancient and medieval authors to Columbus. D'Ailly was particularly concerned with relationships among history, astronomy, and theology.[26] Columbus's second favorite source, but the book he probably read earliest, was Aeneas Sylvius Piccolomini's *Historia rerum ubique gestarum,* printed in 1477. Other books in his library are listed below.

Columbus wanted to give the impression of being an educated man, when in reality he was an unlettered man with superior intellect and genius. He knew it. The letter to the monarchs attached to the *Libro de las profecías* shows that he was always a little overwhelmed by his understanding of a large body of knowledge that encompassed Scripture, cosmography, natural science, history, geography, and theology. With little formal education but with an ability to grasp complex ideas, he sought an explanation for his

ingenuity. He came to believe that God had given him a special gift of understanding, or *spiritualis intellectus*.

To Christopher Columbus, the foundation to all learning was the Holy Bible. He believed, as most men of his day did, that all knowledge is explicitly or implicitly set forth in the Bible and that every effort should be made to understand the message contained in Holy Scripture. Ancient philosophy and science had long ago been deemed aids to understanding the hidden meaning of Scripture, and their use had been legitimatized by the church fathers. Columbus lived at a time when a wider body of ancient literature was coming available though important late medieval translations of Greek and Arabic texts.

The earliest datable product of the systematic study of Columbus's search for scientific knowledge about the world also includes his interest in prophecy. In 1481, on a blank space in his copy of the *Historia rerum ubique gestarum*, he recorded the words "desde el comienç del mundo fasta esta era de 1481, son 5241 años" ("from the beginning of the world to our year 1481, there are 5241 years") [*Raccolta*, pt. I, vol. 2, p. 368, no. 858].

The larger part of the *Libro de las profecías*, and the principal source material of the vision of Columbus, was the Bible. He referred to his dream as "a radiance of marvelous illumination from His sacred Holy Scripture." It was the hundreds of biblical references to distant "islands of the sea," "lands far off," nations who "have not heard" because of their location far beyond the boundaries of the known world that inspired him. It was the scores of biblical prophecies that announced the future unveiling of those unknown lands and future contact with those unreached peoples that sustained him. It was the prophecies of future contact with those unreached peoples and the prophecies of future worldwide extension of the kingdom of Christ, of future worldwide unity in the worship of God, of future treasures and offerings from distant unknown lands to enrich the house of God and the church of Christ that motivated him.

A list of the biblical passages quoted by Columbus and the ancient and medieval authors known to him, either directly or indirectly through other sources, is truly impressive. The Admiral was much better "read" than we had thought. Such a list shows a knowledge of scholars from three cultures—Christian, Jewish and Moslem—and from many eras. The list of these sources is fairly complete: the vast number of documents that survive written or used by Columbus precludes that the list is definitive.

These lists, of course, are misleading. Columbus did not read all the authors he quoted or mentioned. D'Ailly's *Imago mundi* contained passages from many of the writers listed here, and Colum-

✠ Scriptures Quoted by Columbus

Genesis	Daniel	Baruch
Exodus	Hosea	Judith
Deuteronomy	Joel	Matthew
I Kings	Amos	Mark
I Chronicles	Obadiah	Luke
II Chronicles	Jonah	John
Esther	Micah	Acts
Psalms	Habakkuk	Romans
Ecclesiastes	Zephaniah	I Corinthians
Solomon	Zachariah	II Corinthians
Ezra	Esdras	I Thessalonians
Jeremiah	I Maccabees	II Thessalonians
Ezekiel	Ecclesiasticus	II Timothy
Isaiah	Wisdom	Hebrews
Apocalypse		

✠ Ancient Authors Quoted by Columbus

Aristotle	Julius Caesar	St. Augustine
Eratosthenes	Flavius Josephus	St. Ambrose
Strabo	Marinus of Tyre	St. Gregory
Ptolemy	Diodorus	St. Isidore
Seneca	Julius Capitolinus	St. John Chrysostom
Solinus	Ovid	St. Jerome
Plato	Pindar	Aristotle

✠ Medieval Authors Quoted by Columbus

St. Thomas Aquinas	Alfonso de Zamora	Peter Comestor
Jean Gerson	Ahmed-Ben-Kothair	Ibn-Roshd (Averroes)
Francis de Meron	Breviary (anon.)	John Holywood
Nicholas of Lyra	Bede the Venerable	Duns Scotus
Pierre d'Ailly	Walfridus Strabo	Albumazar
King Alfonso X	Pope Pius II	The Sybil
Johannes Muller	Paolo Toscanelli	Roger Bacon
Joachim of Fiore	John Mandeville	Aquila
Merlin	The Koran	Marco Polo
Alfraganus (al-Farghani)	Almanach	Rabbi Samuel de Israel de Fez
Avicena	Alphonsus Tostatus Episc Abulensis	Nicolas Secundinus

bus's copy of Plutarch's *Lives* gave him excellent summaries. There is no evidence that Columbus actually read much beyond the few books he owned in order to explore farther the ideas of authors listed in his own reference library. He did have access to larger libraries, however, in the monasteries where he stayed. After he died, his books were incorporated into Ferdinand's great personal library. Ferdinand gave his library to the cathedral chapter of Seville, where it was neglected and plundered. Out of some 15,000 books and manuscripts, only about 2,000 survive to form the nucleus of the present-day Biblioteca Colombina located in the Seville Cathedral. Extant books known to have been owned by Christopher Columbus are the following:

- Pierre d'Ailly, *Imago mundi*, printed at Louvain between 1480 and 1483. This text contains 898 postilles.
- Aeneas Sylvius Piccolomini (Pope Pius II), *Historia rerum ubique gestarum*, printed at Venice in 1477. This text contains 861 postilles.
- Marco Polo, *De consuetudanibus et conditionibus orientalium regionum* (Latin summary *Il Milione* done by Francesco Pipino), printed at Antwerp in 1485. This text contains 366 postilles.
- Pliny, *Historia naturalis* (translated into Italian by Cristoforo Landino), printed at Venice in 1489. This text contains 24 postilles.
- Plutarch, *Las vidas de los ilustres Varones* (translated into Castilian by Alfonso de Palencia), printed at Seville in 1491. This text contains 437 postilles.
- *Concordantiae Bibliae Cardinalis S.P.*, an anonymous fifteenth-century concordance, undated. No postilles but marginal markings to highlight important scriptural passages.
- St. Antoninus of Florence, *Sumula confessionis*, printed in 1476.
- A fifteenth-century palimpsest containing Seneca's *Tragedies*.
- Abraham Azcuto, *Almanach perpetuum, cuius radix est annun*, 1473. Folios copied by Columbus's hand and others in looseleaf "notebook" form.

These books survive. Paolo Taviani believes at least two other books were owned by Columbus: John Mandeville, *Travels* (probably in a Latin translation), and Julius Capitolinus, *De locis habitabilibus*. He bases his claim on Andrés Bernáldez's observations that Columbus was reading these books while a guest in the Bernáldez home. And, from the postilles, one notices that Columbus either owned or had access to the *tablas Alfonsinas*, which he used for the numerous astrological calculations in the *Libro de las profecías*. The Alfonsine tables were based on the eleventh-century observations of the Arabic Cordovan scholar Arzachel, reworked and updated by scholars at the court of Alfonso X from 1262 to 1272.[27] Other books bought later in life, after the first voyage, or books suspected to

have belonged to Columbus are Albertus Magnus, *Philosphia naturalis*; Ptolemy, *Geography*; Giovanni da Genova, *Catholicon*; and St. Isidore, *Ethymologie*.[28]

The Admiral was a prolific writer himself. Varela has published an up-to-date list of those items believed authentic. Included in his extant writings are these:

- Over eighty letters, memoranda, supply lists, and miscellaneous documents, which have survived in their entirety or in fragments.
- The *Diario* or logbook of the first voyage, which survives only in a copied form.
- Lengthy letter descriptions of the third and fourth voyages.
- The *Libro de las profecías*.
- The *Book of Privileges*.
- A Will and Testament.
- Over 2,000 marginal notes to the books he owned, ranging from one-word entries to lengthy commentaries.

Other works written by Columbus that have not survived include:

- Numerous maps and charts drawn by him or with his brother Barthomew. One map of the northern coast of Hispaniola survives in the Biblioteca Colombina, but its authorship remains debatable. Columbus drew a "plainsphere" on a blank page to his copy of *Imago mundi*. The pen and ink drawing titled "Triumph of Columbus," which is attached to the Nicoli Oderigo correspondence in Genoa, has been attributed to Columbus by several scholars, including Henri Harrisse. That drawing was more likely done by a sixteenth- or seventeenth-century artist. It carries a sample of Columbus's signature, but the style of the picture is baroque.
- A navigation table, "Declaracion de la tabla Navigatoria" (mentioned by Antonio Rodriguez de Leon Pinelo, *El Paraiso en el Nuevo Mundo*, ed. R. Benenechea [Lima, 1943], pp. 369–70). Pinelo wrote in 1650.
- A book sent to the monarchs and "read secretly by them" (Harrisse cites from a letter to Columbus from the monarchs dated 5 September 1493).[29] It is unclear whether Columbus composed this book or sent a book he owned to the king and queen.
- *The Book of the Second Voyage* (used by and quoted from in Ferdinand's biography, chap. iv, p. 12).
- "A work written in the style of Caesar's *Commentaries*," mentioned by Columbus in his letter to Pope Alexander VI [Varela, p. 311].
- In a postille to the *Imago mundi*, Columbus refers, in a cross reference to himself, to possible scientific notebooks he may have kept: to "my papers on the sphere" [Raccolta, pt. I, vol. 2, p. 386, note 160].
- H. Harrisse, *Notes on Columbus*, lists a treatise, "On the Discovery

of the Arctic Pole," which he says is mentioned in Columbus's letter to Dona Juana de la Torres.[30] We have not found this reference.

• "Treatise on the Five Habitable Zones" [Las Casas, p. 49].

Columbus was a man of action, but he was also somewhat "bookish." He had an insatiable desire for knowledge in the fields related to his dreams, for he knew that he had to have both a theoretical base and a practical one for his enterprise. He spent extended periods of time in Franciscan convents and in the Carthusian monastery outside Seville. The two most logical places where he could have had access to good libraries were the monasteries of Santa Maria de la Rábida and Nuestra Señora Santa Maria de las Cuevas. Santa Maria de la Rábida had been converted from a Moorish fortress to a Franciscan convent during the thirteenth century. Its reputation as a center of learning was well known by the fifteenth century. The convent, however, was plundered in 1837, when all religious houses in Spain were suppressed by the liberal government, and its library and archives were scattered.[31] The well-endowed monastery of Nuestra Señora Santa Maria de las Cuevas was founded in 1400 by Archbishop Goñzalo de Mina. By the late fifteenth century, its library was estimated to have had approximately ten thousand items. Yet, that library, too, has been scattered without any record of what was held there.[32] It was while he lived in this monastery that Columbus directed the work on the *Libro de las profecías*. Its library deteriorated from neglect in the sixteenth century.

Spanish monastic libraries, including La Rábida and Las Cuevas, have not been adequately surveyed for their medieval, especially their prophetic, holdings.[33] In Franciscan libraries, one would find books relating to preaching: Bibles, Bible commentaries and exegeses, homiletical works, postils, *florilegia*, and *exemplorum*.[34] Carthusian libraries would have focused more on the writings of the church fathers and medieval theologians. After the fifteenth-century monastic reforms led by Cardinal Ximenes, all monastic libraries would have been encouraged to collect more books.

Surviving lists of other Spanish library holdings or lists that have been compiled in modern times indicate an attraction to eschatological thought similar to that throughout Europe. Spain, with its victories against the Moors, its Inquisition against heretics, its expulsion of the Jews, and its nationalistic aspirations expressed by unification of the kingdoms of the Iberian peninsula, naturally turned to prophetic texts to seek eschatological explanations for its successes. The invention of printing increased the distribution of such texts. It became popular to publish anthologies of prophecy as well as the texts of important prophetic writers. Compendiums or collations

of prophetic authors were especially popular with new presses, for example, the *Refundicio compendiada de la summa concordiae Veteris et Novi Testamenti di Joachim.*[35]

Another example of such anthologies was the production in 1495 or 1496 of a collection of miscellaneous sermons and treatises on prophecy by the publishing house of Pablo Hurus at Zaragoza. The collection contained two important apocalyptic texts known to Columbus: Martin Martinez de Ampriés, *Libro del Antichrist,* written around 1493, and the older *Epistolas de Rabi Samuel.*[36] Ampriés summarized prophetic writings from many sources and concluded that the theme of a world struggle between the forces of Antichrist (backed by Jews and Moslems) and Christendom would soon take place. The Spanish monarch would play a major role in leading Christendom to victory. The monarch would then organize a world-wide missionary thrust which would cause the rapid conversion of all peoples to the Christian faith, followed by a golden age.[37]

Christopher Columbus's strong ties with the Franciscan order placed him within their circle of mysticism, and the circumstantial evidence is strong that he was member of the Third Order of St. Francis. His association with Franciscans at La Rábida and elsewhere brought him into contact with apocalyptic enthusiasts of the Observantine reform, which was at its peak in the late fifteenth century.[38]

From the death of St. Francis onward there were groups of Friars Minor who wished to follow a vocation that they believed was outlined in the *Rule* of 1223, which had been approved by Pope Honorius III. Shortly after the death of St. Francis, however, the *Rule* had been relaxed by papal decree. But, regardless of papal approval to the contrary, individuals chose the most austere life possible and believed themselves to be a divinely inspired elect whose role was the *renovatio* of the evangelical life in the last age of the world. The influence of the Calabrian Abbot Joachim of Fiore upon their thinking is well known as it was expressed by various important dissidents in Italy and France. Many scholars have been keen to declare the same influence upon fifteenth-century Spanish Franciscans, yet one can scarcely find a direct quotation from Joachim of Fiore's writings in the literary works associated with the order in that country.[39] On the other hand, the lingering undercurrent of Joachim's dynamism of sacred history is present in fifteenth-century Spanish Franciscan attitudes about themselves and the mission of their order. Confusion arises when one tries to distinguish such a Joachite eschatology from other, more general apocalyptic expectations in this period.

The Observantine movement began in Spain through a series of independent reforms in Santiago, Castile, and Aragon.[40] In 1388,

Rodrigo Martín of Lara was allowed to retire with a few companions to a hermitage across the border in Portugal to follow a strict interpretation of the *Rule* of St. Francis. Other hermitages followed, and in 1392 the Province of Santiago was established. More houses were founded in the early fifteenth century, bringing the total to eleven. In 1390, Pope Clement VII permitted Observantine houses to be built at Manzarera and Chelva in Aragon. In 1403, the hermitage of Santo Espiritu de Monte in Murviedro (Valencia), led by the famous Joachite-Franciscan, Francisc Examenis, was authorized by Pope Benedict XIII. In 1421, Pope Martin V allowed Santo Espiritu de Monte and other nearby Observantine houses to form a Custody. In Castile, Observantine houses began to appear around the turn of the fifteenth century, and by 1415 there were more than a dozen. Santa Maria de la Rábida joined the movement in 1412. By 1461 the reform reached the Canary Islands (and possibly the Madeira Islands).[41]

These reforms were a protest against nonfeasance in the Order of Friars Minor. Just like the dissidents in fringe orders before them, the Observantines wished to observe exactly the *Rule* of St. Francis as approved by Pope Honorius III in 1223. Much of their inspiration was drawn from the Spiritual Franciscans of earlier years whose links to the Joachite movement were well established.[42] Franciscan fringe groups, many of which were connected directly or indirectly to the Spiritual Franciscans, had existed in Spain from the earliest years of the order. According to inquisition records, individuals and groups within these fringe elements who held apocalyptic beliefs were frequently labeled as "Joachite."[43] The persistence of these groups in following a rigorous observance of the *Rule* of 1223, both within the order and outside of it, eventually led to major reform by the late fifteenth century. The desire to live the simple life taught by St. Francis in the most austere way attracted diverse characters in the fifteenth century, such as Juan of Guadalupe, leader of the Discalced movement and reformer of Franciscan convents in Extremadura; John Pérez, Guardian of La Rábida and friend to Columbus; and Cardinal Ximenes, the most powerful churchman in Spain. The appointment of Francis Ximenes de Cisñeros as Provincial for the Castile Province in 1492 intensified the reform movement which ended in the domination of the Observantines in that region. With his elevation to Archbishop and Chancellor of the state in 1495, Ximenes extended his reforms to all Franciscan convents.

Spain has a rich eschatological heritage from three religions: Christian, Moslem, and Jew. Spanish apocalypticism has not received much study by scholars, nor has anyone attempted to explain how eschatological thought from these three religions influenced

thinking in the fifteenth century. Christopher Columbus felt free to pull from all three sources and cannot be identified with any particular group or movement. The *Libro de las profecías* is a composite of many influences but has visible influence of Joachite and pseudo-Methodian origins. The draft structure of the *Libro de las profecías* is divided into an Introduction and three parts. Columbus gave credit to Joachim of Fiore, the Sybils, Merlin, and the pseudo-Methodius for his inspiration, but he limited his citations, with few exceptions, to the most impeccable authorities: the Church Fathers and well-respected medieval and contemporary theologians. His exegetical methods were orthodox and his conclusions conservative. He did not criticize the church, the state, or society; instead he advocated the strongest possible eschatological role for the existing church and state. The overall themes of his collection were that an important stage of prophecy had been fulfilled with the discovery of new lands and new peoples and that the eschatological clock was ticking away. The next steps, he tells his monarchs, must soon begin, for the world would last only another century and a half. First the gospel message must be spread on a global scale; second, Jerusalem must be captured by the Spanish monarch and the Holy Temple on Mt. Zion must be rebuilt. These accomplishments would usher in the last days and the biblical chronology relating to them.

Columbus gave a prominent place to Joachite eschatology in the *Libro de las profecías*. The famous Calabrian abbot is given as a reference in the postilles and cited by the Admiral in the *Libro de las profecías* a total of seven times. The citations are duplicative. Two of these references are postilles to Pierre D'Ailly, *De Concordia Astronomie, Vertitatis et Narrationis Historice*, four are included in material found in the *Libro de las profecías* (two of these are copied from D'Ailly and two are the same quote from a letter no longer extant from Genoese ambassadors at the Spanish court), and one is a reference to the same ambassadorial letter in the so-called *lettera Rarissima*.

Twice Columbus attributes a quotation to Joachim in the *Libro de las profecías* which he believed to have been authentic but was not. The citation foretold that the Spanish monarch was to lead Christian forces to recapture Jerusalem. It is likely that the missing ten pages, f. 67v to 77r, purposefully removed very early from the manuscript, focused on Joachite eschatology. These folios comprise the introduction to Part III of the handbook, "De futuro. In novissimis." Columbus began this third period of prophetic history with Jeremiah 25, in which a warning is issued to listen to the message of His servant to spread God's message throughout the world "to all the people" including those yet unknown. The warning continues that "God has been sending His messages to you [the king]. I have faithfully passed them on to you, but you have not listened." The

passage goes on to say that God has sent his prophets many times, but the king refused to heed their words. One last chance will be offered for salvation to all nations when the king stands before the Holy Temple in Jerusalem and announces God's word to all the world. Columbus follows the warning with reference to the letter brought to the Spanish monarchs in 1492 by Genoese ambassadors calling for them to lead a new crusade:

> Not undeservedly or without reason, I call earnestly to your attention, most noble sovereigns, some very important things that are to be observed, since indeed we did read that Joachim the Abbot of Southern Italy has foretold that he is to come from Spain who is to recover again the fortunes of Zion.   [L.P., 239]

The first major subdivision for this part of the *Libro de las profecías* Columbus labels in large letters: ABBAS IOACHIM. It is here that ten leaves have been cut out and removed from the document. Because of this mutilation, we will never know the extent of Columbus's knowledge of Joachim of Fiore's writings or the pseudo-Joachite literature.

Speculation as to the origin of the quotation attributed to Joachim of Fiore by the ambassadorial letter has centered on two documents. De Lollis, Bloomfield, and McGinn believe that the citation came from the *Oraculum Turcicum*, a late medieval apocalyptic treatise which called for the appearance of a "last world emperor."[44] Milhou and Watts have proposed a similar late medieval text, *Ve mundo in centum annis.*[45]

We know, however, that Columbus exhibited subtle Joachite-Franciscan influences throughout his life and writings. He adored the Trinity and relied heavily upon the guidance of the Holy Spirit. He firmly believed that he had been given the gift of spiritual intelligence, he expected a new age (i.e., a New Heaven and a New Earth), and he divided the *Libro de las profecías* into three parts of prophetic history.

It could be argued that any or all of these general ideas were universal apocalyptic beliefs and not necessarily Joachite. The influence of the Calabrian abbot and his disciples in the thinking and life of Columbus was present in the more subtle, underlying current of Joachimism. As Marjorie Reeves has pointed out, Joachim's originality was to work out a threefold pattern of history, yet incomplete, as the work of the Holy Spirit would illuminate a final age of history: "Joachim gave historical happenings a unique importance, linking past, present, and future moments of time with transcendental purpose. It invited the casting of roles in the final acts of the drama. Above all, it opened up the prospect of new human agencies called to participate in the last decisive works of God in

history. The backcloth of apocalyptic drama gave enhanced stature to actors in history."[46]

The Abbot Joachim of Fiore (d. 1202) was the most important late medieval apocalyptic writer. Departing from traditional Augustinian thought, Joachim placed the Sabbath Age of the world within human experience by creating a threefold division of history. In the coming Third Age or *status*, the third member of the Trinity, the Holy Spirit, would illuminate mankind in the final stage of history, creating a period of peace and understanding.[47] Joachim's mind held an amalgamation of central themes, but none was so compelling as the meaning of history. Simply put, he envisioned history as a development from patterns and symbols based on the two testaments, each of which he divided into seven concordant patterns. Extending from the dual procession of the Two Testaments, he perceived a three-*status* dynamic and organization of history in which the salvation of the world progressed from creation to an expected age of grace in the future. Each age was guided by a member of the Trinity, but they were interrelated as each new age received its germination from the fructification of the last. In the last age, a renewed church would be composed of a reformed people devoted to the contemplative life.

The influence of Joachim's followers is more apparent in the late fifteenth century than the thought of the abbot himself. Interest in the Calabrian writer's ideas, however, was growing strong, as illustrated by the appearance of Joachim's major works and several spurious writings in print for the first time between 1516 and 1577. Joachim's followers from the thirteenth century on altered and debased his ideas when other strains of apocalyptic thought were grafted onto his themes. It was from these pseudo-Joachite sources that fifteenth-century Franciscans, and thus Columbus, created a medley of apocalyptic lore from which emerged a general feeling of anticipation that important eschatological events were about to occur.[48]

After the death of St. Francis, the Order of Friars Minor underwent considerable change, mostly toward a more relaxed interpretation of the mendicant life. Reaction was immediate as small groups sprang up, especially in the Italian March of Ancona, wishing to retain the simple life of poverty. The sources give us little exact information about these developments, but by the middle of the thirteenth century the leadership of the order was in open conflict with the so-called spiritual party of friars.[49] In their opposition to the leadership of the order, many spirituals turned to the writings of Joachim of Fiore to legitimize their stance, believing themselves to be the "new spiritual men" predicted by the Calabrian abbot to lead the world into the Third Age.[50]

Passionate Joachite-Franciscans and their disciples throughout the late thirteenth and fourteenth centuries recast Joachim's original ideas to meet contemporary needs and combined the Calabrian Abbot's thought with other apocalyptic theories. This new mosaic of apocalyptic thought centered on events near to the end of time which emphasized the salvation of all the world, the recapture of Jerusalem, and the rule by a leader who could combine the powers of both church and state.[51]

Early Spiritual Franciscan thinkers such as Angelo Clareno focused their attention on the evangelical life outlined by the Gospels and exemplified by St. Francis. Promoting the *vita apostolica* as taught in the *Rule* of 1223, they called for a strict adherence to poverty, humility, and renunciation. Joachim of Fiore's theories lent justification to their cause. The Clareni were dealt the harshest discipline and eventually ousted from the Order of Friars Minor. They continued as a fringe group until they were officially reinstated in the order in the wake of the Observantine reform in 1473 by order of Pope Sixtus IV. Unable to conform even to the stricter Observance, however, they were ousted again in 1486 and placed under episcopal jurisdiction by Pope Innocent III.[52]

The best summary of Spiritual Joachite-Franciscan ideas was produced by Peter John Olivi in the late thirteenth century. A promising student at Paris, Olivi finished his studies and returned to Provence as a lector. Olivi would exercise extraordinary influence over Spanish Franciscans and Franciscan fringe orders in the following centuries. His *Expositio super regulam,* a commentary on the Franciscan *Rule* of 1223, and his *Postilla super apocalypsim,* a Joachite treatise, became especially respected by the Observantine reformers who had the former printed in 1511.[53] The *Postilla* was heavily excerpted into the treatise *De statibus ecclesie secundum expositionem apocalypsis,* which was translated into the Catalan language and became an important fourteenth-century Spanish text.[54] Further influence of Olivi in Spain can be found in the writings of his disciple Ubertino da Casale. Ubertino da Casale's popular work, *Arbor vitae crucifixae Iesu,* circulated Olivi's ideas in a readable form. Numerous copies survive in Spain, and it was translated into Castilian for Queen Isabella.[55]

The effective Spanish conduit for Spiritual Franciscan Joachimism, however, was Arnold of Villanova, court physician at Aragon. He had become acquainted with Peter Olivi at Montpellier while both were teachers there. His position at court gave him a particularly respectable and lasting audience in Spain. He wrote treatises in both Latin and Catalan on eschatological topics showing the imminence of Church renewal by the chosen elect, the Spiritual Franciscans, as well as a political eschatology advocating the rule of

Christendom by "one pastor and one shepherd."[56] Many of Arnold's ideas were condemned by the Inquisition at Tarragona in 1316, but his eschatological thought had already made its mark upon Spanish thinkers.

Another French Joachite who made a lasting impression on Spanish apocalypticism in the fourteenth century was Jean de Roquetaillade.[57] He presented a threefold plan of eschatology that included the appearance of a world leader in the form of an enigmatic king from the line of Charlemagne, the immediate conversion of Jews and infidels, and a millennium in which political power would transfer to Jerusalem where the mysterious emperor would rule jointly with an angelic pope. Working out of Jerusalem, the elect (i.e., the Franciscan Order) would carry the Gospel to the rest of the world. The most widely known work by Jean de Roquetaillade in Spain was *Vade mecum in Tribulatione,* which was translated into Castilian and circulated widely throughout Iberia.[58] Although Jean de Roquetaillade pictured a French king as the great leader who would drive out the Moslems and capture Jerusalem, Spanish apocalyptic writers soon reserved this role for the Spanish monarchs, a belief that Columbus mistakenly attributed directly to Joachim of Fiore.[59]

Italian and French Franciscan Joachimism also filtered into Spain through Franciscan fringe orders which in turn drew from the Spiritual Franciscan movement. The apocalyptic thought generated from the Spiritual movement was influencing important Spanish thinkers by the late fourteenth and early fifteenth century. Two of the most potent Spanish writers affected were Prince Peter of Aragon (son of James II of Aragon), who became a Franciscan later in life, and Fray Francisc Examenis.

After a distinguished career at the royal court, Peter entered the Franciscan Order soon after his wife died in 1358. Peter was attracted to apocalyptic thought, and in 1377 he wrote *Exposició de la visió damunt vita* in which he copiously cited Jean de Roquetaillade and the pseudo-Joachim, *super Hieremiam.* The *super Hieremiam* was written in the early thirteenth century as an anti-imperial treatise against Frederick II. Peter concluded that in the near future, the king of Aragon would conquer all of Spain, attack and capture all the Moslem lands, and enter Jerusalem victorious. Thus would begin a fifteen-year reign of peace and harmony at the end of which the Antichrist would appear initiating the events of the last times.[60]

Fray Francisc Examenis, head of the reform hermitage at Santo Espiritu, was a more classical Joachite who wrote two treatises, *Apparatus de triplici statu mundi* and *Vida de Jesuchrist.* Following chronological patterns drawn from Joachim of Fiore, he envisioned a *princeps mundi* who would appear in the sixth era of the second

age. This mighty ruler would conquer many islands and subjugate many nations, rule all of Christendom, and capture Jerusalem. Shockingly, however, he would reveal himself for what he really was, the last vestige in a series of antichrists before the final Antichrist. Examenis was an extremely popular writer, and his works were copied as late as 1477.[61] Examenis and his group of followers were early advocates of a strict adherence to the *Rule* of 1223. Unlike other reformers, however, they did not mistrust learning or consider unlettered simplicity a degree of poverty. Many Aragonese reformers, unlike their counterparts elsewhere, believed intellectual activity necessary for sound and successful reform.[62]

Added to these infusions of Joachite apocalypticism was the immense influence of the Lullian tradition in Spain. A member of the Third Order of St. Francis, Ramon Lull had also studied at Paris in the late thirteenth century. A contemplative and a visionary, Lull flirted with the ideas of Joachim, among others, and his literature was standard reading throughout Iberia. Not a radical himself, his mystical essays were fused with radical Franciscan thought which encouraged apocalyptical thinking in Spain.[63]

In the late fifteenth century the Spiritual Franciscan Joachite position was taken by the popular John Alamany in his *Venguda de Antichrist.* Continuing the themes of Francisc Examenis and Jean de Roquetaillade, John Alamany predicted that a "new David" would rise up against the Moors, evil powerful men, and bad clerics. This monarch would lead a crusade through North Africa and Egypt toward Jerusalem, where he would rebuild the temple. A great war would then ensue against the Antichrist in which the "new David" would capture all the world and be recognized as the "last world emperor." The "new David," according to John Alamany, was to be the Spanish monarch.[64]

The idea of a last world emperor, a mighty monarch in the last days, became increasingly popular during the late fifteenth century in Spain. It is a role Christopher Columbus gave to King Ferdinand, as we shall show later, and Columbus saw himself as the agent of the new David who had discovered the resources that would enable the Spanish monarch to fulfill his destiny. The concept of a last world ruler was not a part of Joachim of Fiore's original scheme. Instead, it developed from an marriage of Joachite thought with the pseudo-Methodius which had reached European apocalyptic circles much earlier. This text, written in the seventh century, probably from Jewish messianic sources, appeared in Byzantium almost immediately and was translated into Latin and spread to the West in the eighth century. Eventually the treatise was translated into several vernacular languages and printed early and often. For example, there were ten editions between 1470 and 1475, and

an especially beautiful edition was published by M. Further in 1498 which contained woodcuts by Sebastian Brant.[65]

The general theme of the last world empire was based on the Book of Daniel in the Old Testament, the pseudo-Methodius, and selected patterns of Joachite thought. The theory developed a series of world kingdoms culminating in the messianic fifth monarchy. The popularity of the theme in Spain can be demonstrated in the late fifteenth century when it became incorporated into a number of apocalyptic works.[66]

As noted earlier, Spanish libraries have not been adequately surveyed for their late medieval holdings. Copies of Joachim of Fiore's *Liber de Concordia novi et veteris Testamenti* survive in Spain, and there are copies of the continuously compiled *Liber de summis Pontificibus* and *Liber de Provincialibus Presagiis*. And the major works of the above-mentioned Joachite-Franciscans are extant.

It is likely that Columbus had access to one of the numerous compendiums since his handbook ranges across so many authors. A remarkable example of these collations, due to its illustrations of *figurae*, concord charts, and pope prophecies, was the *Summula sue Breviloquium super Concordia novi et Veteris Testamenti*. Written between 1351 and 1355 and recopied at least until 1488, the *Breviloquium* has been described by Lee, Reeves, and Silano as a "revised Joachimism to fit the times."[67] This important manuscript was a synthesis of Joachite thought containing parts of Joachim's *Liber de Concordia Novi et Veteris Testamenti*, excerpts from other genuine writings by the Calabrian abbot, plus pseudo-Joachite and Joachite literature. The evidence demonstrates its author's thorough familiarity with the works of Peter John Olivi, Arnold of Villanova, and Jean de Roquetaillade.

The *Breviloquium* was a message to the Spanish that Aragon and Catalonia would rise up under a new Zorobabel who represented the fourth beast and the eleventh kingdom (from the seed of the eagle, which was identified as Rome). The new Zorobabel would recapture Jerusalem and usher in a period of "silence" during which the temple would be rebuilt. Finally, this priest-king would join church and state, bring peace and justice to all the world, convert the Jews and infidels, and launch a worldwide mission to gather all "the sheep together under one shepherd."[68]

These are the traditions from which Columbus developed the *Libro de las profecías*. Late-fifteenth-century amalgamations of apocalyptic thought from a variety of sources put down in popular collations of texts, which he had read or heard about, guided his thinking. He told Father Gorricio that the genre in which he wished to issue the final product of his handbook was a long apocalyptic poem [Varela, p. 285]. Using this literary form was popular when

addressing prophecy to the Spanish monarch. One of the more interesting collections of Spanish prophetic poetry is found in the *Cancionero de Baena*, written for the young King John II of Castile upon his crowning.[69] Collectively these poems promoted the idea that the monarchy of Spain was destined to destroy its enemies and rule as the universal monarchy over Christendom. Charles Fraker has presented in-depth studies of several of these, including the work of the Sevillian poet Gonçalo Martínez de Medina.[70] Martínez is interesting because he relied on the Spanish *Profecias de Merlin* and the *Vade mecum in tribulatione* by Jean de Roquetaillade. The poet identified the Spanish monarch as the one to destroy the enemies of Christendom and push on to the capture of Jerusalem. Much of the poem is given over to criticism of the different estates of society — clergy, nobles, and others. The king, the poet advocates, should reform the church and the state, reorganize Christian society, promote the spread of the gospel message, and rule over a "new" Christendom.

✛ Notes

1. The most recent summary of Columbus's self-vision is by L. Sweet, "Christopher Columbus and the Millennial Vision of the New World."

2. See, for example, Francisco López de Gómara, *Hispania Victrix. Primera y segunda parte de la historia general de las Indias*, t. 22, p. 156. This popular account of the New World proclaimed the discovery the "greatest event since the creation of the world except for the birth and death of our Savior."

3. F. Fernández-Armesto, *Before Columbus: Exploration and Colonization from the Mediterranean to the Atlantic, 1229–1492*, p. 252.

4. J. Phillips, *The Medieval Expansion of Europe*, pp. 228–29.

5. *Raccolta*, pt. I, vol. 2, "Postille ai trattati de P. d'Ailly." For a detailed account of the layer of sources encountered by Columbus in this text, see P. Watts, "Prophecy and Discovery: On the Spiritual Origins of Christopher Columbus's 'Enterprise of the Indies,'" pp. 83–84. In a lengthy note after postille no. 23 in *Imago mundi*, Columbus justifies his use of the aprocryphal Esdras as a prophet. He cites the acceptability of Esdras to St. Ambrose, St. Augustine, Peter Comester, and Francis of Meron (*On the Truth*) and then concludes, "From this results a notable fact, namely that Esdras was a prophet and that his prophecies, even though they were not canonical, were still authentic" [*Raccolta*, pt. I, vol. 2, p. 377].

6. G. Sarton, *Introduction to the History of Science*, 2:958.

7. For substantial evidence known to Columbus, see S. Morison, *Admiral of the Ocean Sea: A Life of Christopher Columbus*, 1:82 ff.

8. For a brief history and analysis of this passage from Seneca, see G. Moretti, "Nec sit terris ultima Thule (La profezia di Seneca sulla scoperta del Nuovo Mondo)," pp. 95–106.

9. The only serious challenge to the authenticity of Columbus's knowl-

edge and use of Toscanelli's ideas was made in 1902 by Henry Vignaud, *Toscanelli and Columbus: The Letter and Chart of Toscanelli.* Vignaud's book caused much research into the topic, leading most scholars to believe that Vignaud was wrong in his conclusions. The arguments and their bibliography can be found in P. Taviani, *Christopher Columbus: The Grand Design,* pp. 399–402.

10. T. Goldstein, "Geography in Fifteenth-Century Florence," pp. 18–19. For a full account of Pletho and his symposia at Florence, see two articles by M. Anastos, "Pletho and Strabo on the Habitability of the Torrid Zone," and "Pletho, Strabo and Columbus."

11. S. Edgerton, "Florentine Interest in Ptolemaic Cartography as Background for Renaissance Painting, Architecture, and the Discovery of America," p. 275.

12. Ibid., p. 287.

13. F. Streicher, "Las notas marginales de Colón en los libros de Pedro Alíaco, Eneas Silvio y Marco Polo, estudiadas a la luz de las investigaciones paleográficas," p. 49. For a complete summary of Streicher's paleographic studies of Columbian writings, see his "Die Kolumbus-Originale: Eine Palaographische Studie," pp. 196–249.

14. G. Evans, *The Language and Logic of the Bible: The Earlier Middle Ages,* pp. 114–22, gives a history of the *Quadriga* in Western theology.

15. Such a twofold literal meaning became increasingly important during the Reformation. See H. Oberman, *Forerunners of the Reformation: The Shape of Medieval Thought,* p. 286.

16. For the process of envisioning geographical phenomenae, see J. Wright, *Human Nature and Geography,* p. 266. See also J. Gill, *Mitos y utopías del Descubrimiento,* pp. 50–56, on Columbus's search for the mines of Solomon and the site of Ophir.

17. An interesting study of Columbus's ideas about the Terrestrial Paradise within the context of world religions is by S. Fasce, "Colombo, il Paradiso terrestre e Mircea Eliade," pp. 199–206.

18. J. Perez de Tudela y Bueso, *Mirabilis in Altis,* p. 249 ff., effectively argues the prominent role of the search for the Terrestrial Paradise in Columbus's grand project: "No en su Terce Viage, sino ya al regresar del Primero, proclanó, proclanó Colón que venía del Paraíso Terrenal. . . . Como patente es también su cavilación preveo sobre il Paraío, a tenor del apostillado de su mano sobre Ailly y Eneas Silio" (pp. 417–18).

19. *Raccolta,* pt. II, vol. 3, C. Desimoni, "Questioni Colombiane," p. 82 ff.; *Raccolta,* pt. II, vol. 1, L. Belgrano and M. Staglieno, "Documenti relativi a Cristoforo Colombo e sua famiglia," pp. 84–164. See also *Citta di Genova,* "Colombo," p. 124 ff.

20. *Raccolta,* pt. II, vol. 3, C. Desimoni, "Questioni colombiane," p. 29; and G. Balbi, "La scuola a Genova e Cristoforo Colombo," pp. 31–36. See also A. Agosto, "In quale 'Pavia' studió Colombo?" pp. 131–36, who argues that Columbus attended the monastery school in the modern-day section of Genoa known as "Paverano." Attendance at the monastery school would better explain the Admiral's ability to grasp complex mathematical and scientific concepts because of its more "scientific" curriculum.

A more general study of what merchant sons might have studied in the fifteenth century is in P. Grendler, *Schooling in Renaissance Italy: Literacy and Learning, 1300–1600*, especially the chapter "Girls and Working-Class Boys in School."

21. A. von Humbolt, *Cristóbal Colón y el descubrimiento de América*, pp. 20–22.

22. For a complete study see, N. de Vaudrey Heathcote, "Christopher Columbus and the Discovery of Magnetic Variation."

23. That Ferdinand wished to present his father as a classical hero can be seen from his notations to his father's copy of Plutarch, *Las vidas de los ilustres Varones*, trans. Alfonso de Palencia (Seville, 1491). Although Christopher Columbus owned this book, all of the 437 notations are in the hand of Ferdinand. Our assumption is that Ferdinand studied this source as a guide in writing his biography of his father.

24. R. Pidal, "La lengua de Cristóbal Colón." S. Pittaluga, "Il 'vocabulario' usato da Cristoforo Colombo (Una postilla all 'Historia rerum' di Pio II e la lessicografia medievale)," argues that Columbus's Latin notes show unusual erudition well grounded in classical and late medieval usage.

25. For a study of Italian humanistic script, see W. Ullman, *The Origin and Development of Humanistic Script*.

26. Watts, "Prophecy and Discovery," p. 86.

27. Taviani, *Christopher Columbus*, p. 174.

28. Ibid., p. 450.

29. H. Harrisse, *Notes on Columbus*, p. 164.

30. Ibid.

31. J. Coll, *Colón y la Rábida*, pp. 66–67. The entire convent was plundered, including tiles, roof timbers, bricks, pavements, orchards, trees, and gardens.

32. B. Cuartero Huerta, *Historia de la Cartuja de Santa Maria de las Cuevas de Sevilla y de su filial de Cazalla de la Sierra*, 1:24, 2:702. Columbus lay buried there until 1509. The monastery was converted into a ceramics factory in the early nineteenth century, and it has sat vacant for most of the twentieth century.

33. P. Borigas i Balaguer, "Profecies Catalanes dels segles xiv–xv: Assaig bibliogràfic," pp. 3–49, presents a model survey of Catalonia, but it is limited to archives in Catalunya, Madrid, Barcelona, and Carpentras.

34. J. Lenhart, *History of Franciscan Libraries in the Middle Ages*, p. 182.

35. Balaguer, "Profecies Catalanes," p. 26.

36. Bibliotheque National, Paris, Rés. D. 6201.

37. Ibid., chapter xxvii.

38. A. Milhou, *Colón y su mentalidad mesiánica en el ambiente franciscanista español*, pp. 42–44, and J. Gil, "Los franciscanos y Colón," p. 101.

39. In 1933, R. Ricard, *La 'Conquete spiritual' du Mexico*, made cautious suggestions as to a limited extent of Joachim's influence. Guarded speculation continued in the works of J. Maravall, "La Utopía político-religiosa de los franciscanos en Nueva España," and in M. Bataillon, "Evagélisme et millénarisme au Nouveau Monde," pp. 25–36. Twenty years later, J. Phelan, *The Millennial Kingdom of the Franciscans in the New World*, demon-

strated stronger ties of Joachite eschatology to New World Franciscan chroniclers than previously believed. He was supported by the work of G. Baudot, *Utopía e historia en México.* Recent studies have relied on these earlier works plus strong circumstantial evidence to advocate full-blown Joachite influences upon fifteenth- and sixteenth-century Spanish Franciscans. Two of the more notable are L. Weckmann, "Las esperanzas milenaristas de los franciscanos de la Nueva España," and Milhou, *Colón y su mentalidad.*

40. L. Iriarte, *Franciscan History,* pp. 65–66.

41. For data relating to establishments see, M. Bandin, "Introducción a los orígenes de la observancia en España. Las reformas en los siglos xiv y xv," pp. 943–45.

42. M. Reeves, *The Influence of Prophecy in the Later Middle Ages: A Study in Joachimism,* pp. 229–30.

43. J. Pou y Martí, "Visionarios, Beguinos y Fraticelos Catalanes, siglos xiii—xv," 18 (1922): p. 22.

44. M. Bloomfield, "Recent Scholarship on Joachim of Fiore and his Influence," p. 38; B. McGinn, *Visions of the End: Apocalyptic Traditions in the Middle Ages,* p. 346; C. de Lollis, *Raccolta,* p. 83.

45. Milhou, *Colon,* p. 379; Watts, "Prophecy and Discovery," p. 95.

46. M. Reeves, "The Development of Apocalyptic Thought: Medieval Attitudes," p. 51.

47. Standard studies by Reeves and McGinn should lead to lengthy bibliography about Joachim. See Reeves, *Influence of Prophecy,* and B. McGinn, *The Calabrian Abbot: Joachim of Fiore in the History of Western Thought.* For a wide range of reprinted Joachim studies, see D. West, *Joachim of Fiore in Christian Thought: Essays on the Influence of the Calabrian Prophet.*

48. A. Castro, *Aspectos del vivir hispánico: espiritualismo, mesianismo y actitud personal en los siglos xv al xvi,* pp. 22–26, quotes several fifteenth-century Castilian texts expressing such impulses.

49. J. Moorman, *A History of the Franciscan Order,* p.288.

50. Reeves, *Influence of Prophecy,* p. 191 ff.

51. Although these ideas originated from the circle of Spiritual Franciscans, they were popularized with the production of the pseudo-Joachite *Liber de Fiore* and the *Liber de summis Pontificibus.*

52. P. Severi, *L'ordine dei frati minori. Lezioni storiche* 1:77–78.

53. The *Expositio super regulam* was printed as part III in *Firmamentum trium ordinum intitulatur* (Venice, 1511). For a background to Olivi's apocalypticism, see R. Manselli, *La 'Lectura super Apocalypsim' de Pietro di Giovanni Olivi: Ricerche sull'escatologismo medioevale,* and D. Burr, "Olivi, Apocalyptic Expectations, and Visionary Experience."

54. Pou y Martí, "Visionarios," 18 (1922), pp. 29 ff. A. Vidal, "Un ascete du sang royal: Philip de Morque," p. 396, has detailed the influence of Olivi on the fourteenth-century circle of reformers led by Philip of Majorca.

55. F. Callacy, "Les idées mystico-politiques d'un Franciscian spirituel," p. 727. L. Oliger has analyzed the importance of Ubertino to the Observantine movement in "De relatione inter observantium Quaerimo-

nias constantienses (1415) et Ubertini Casalensis quoddam scriptum."

56. R. Manselli, "La religiosità di Arnaldo da Villanova," p. 59.

57. J. Bignami-Odier, *Etudes sur Jean de Roquetaillade (Johanes de Rupescissa),* is still the authority on his life and thought.

58. K. Pietsch, "The Madrid Manuscript of the Spanish Grail Fragments."

59. For a detailed account of how this idea was transferred from France to Spain, see Pou y Martí, "Visionarios," 21 (1924):351.

60. H. Lee, M. Reeves, and G. Silano, *Western Mediterranean Prophecy: The School of Joachim of Fiore and the Fourteenth-Century Breviloquium,* pp. 83–84.

61. J. Webster, "Nuevas apotaciones a los estudios Examinanos-Francisc Examenis, OFM: su familia y su vida,"

62. Baudin, "Introducción," p. 600.

63. J. Careras y Artau and T. Careras y Artau, *Historia de la filosofiá española: filosofía cristiana de los siglos xiii al xv,* pp. 42–43.

64. R. Alba, "Acerca de Algunas particularidades de las Comunidades de Castilla tal vez relacionadas con el supriesto acaecer terreno del milenio igualitario," p. 180.

65. McGinn, *Visions of the End,* p. 302.

66. The standard study is E. Sackur, *Sibyllinische Texte und Forschungen. Pseudo-Methodius Adso und die triburtinische Sibylle,* esp. pp. 53–56. A more modern treatment of the textual migration is by P. Alexander, "Byzantium and the Migration of Literary Works and Motifs: The Legend of the Last World Emperor." Also see Reeves, *Influence of Prophecy,* p. 295 ff., and McGinn, *Visions of the End,* pp. 33–35, 43–45, 184–87, 275–85.

67. Lee et al., *Western Mediterranean Prophecy,* p. xi.

68. For the modern textual edition of the *Breviloquium* and for this reference see ibid., p. 319. For Columbus's reference to one flock and one shepherd, see L.P., p. 405.

69. Marquis of Pidal, ed., *Cancionero de Baena,* The best survey of these is C. Fraker, *Studies on the Cancionero de Baena.*

70. Pendal, ibid., no. 335; C. Fraker, "Prophecy in Gonçalo Martínez de Medina."

3

The Piety and Faith of Christopher Columbus

For the islands wait for me, and the ships of the sea in the beginning: that I may bring thy sons from afar. [Isaiah 60:9a, L.P., 251]

✠ Taken together, the depth of Columbus's life of learning, his association with religious houses, and his sense of personal destiny made him an exceptionally pious man. In seeking to identify his religious nature, we have concluded that he is best viewed as an "evangelical" Christian—not in the modern sense of the word "evangelical" but in the sense of the Catholic tradition and church of the times. His "evangelicalism" sprang from an affinity with the Franciscan Order and its ideology of mission. In his letter to the king and queen, which accompanied the *Libro de las profecías*, we see the marks of a spiritual experience that changed his life, but he gives us no details, only the effect. It was almost a religious vocation:

> I am only a most unworthy sinner, but ever since I have cried out for grace and mercy from the Lord, they have covered me completely. I have found the most delightful comfort in making my whole aim in life to enjoy His marvelous presence. [L.P., 111]

Christopher Columbus looked to the Bible to find messages from God. He expected, and he experienced, that the message would be made clear by the illuminating agency of the Holy Spirit enlightening not just one text but the entire divine word in Scripture. The Discoverer insisted that he was but a human instrument and that God had called him to do a task and equipped him for it. The discovery of the New World was an event foretold by prophecies; the Discoverer was an agent of that divine plan. He was a participant in the action; but in a deeper spiritual sense, he was also a spectator of the great and mighty things that God had purposed to accomplish:

> With a hand that could be felt, the Lord opened my mind to the fact that it would be possible . . . and he opened my will to desire to accomplish the project. . . . The Lord purposed that there should be something miraculous in this matter of the voyage to the Indies.

41

. . . But afterwards it all turned out just as our redeemer Jesus Christ had said, and as he had spoken earlier by the mouth of his holy prophets. This is the way we really should believe that the other matter will turn out [i.e., crusade]. If what I have said is not already sufficient to recommend such belief, I submit the gospel texts in which he said that all things would pass away, but not his marvelous Word, and he also said that all things must be fulfilled that were said by him and written by the prophets.   [L.P., 105–7, italics ours]

These words from the *Libro de las profecías* describe a pattern of religious experience that we recognize as having much in common with devout Christians of many traditions and in many periods of history. The documents surrounding the life of Christopher Columbus support the fact that he was the kind of person he claimed to be. His way of life and his dealings with all sorts and conditions of people, both in close relationships and in casual acquaintance-ships, was generally consistent with that kind of profession of reli-gious faith.

The most severe critic of Spanish religious practices in the six-teenth century was the Dominican Bishop of Chiapas, Bartolomé de las Casas (1474–1566).[1] Las Casas knew Columbus personally, having met him in 1493, and had access to the Admiral's papers and family. He had gained firsthand experience in the New World by settling in Hispaniola in 1502. Thus, he did not hesitate to criti-cize the Admiral's ineptness as a colonial administrator and his igno-rance in matters of law and government, which were Las Casas's own areas of specialization. Writing about Columbus many years after his death, Las Casas was still awed by "the most outstanding feat man has ever seen [i.e., the discovery]" [Las Casas, p. 329]. He recalled his own first impression of Columbus in Seville and Barcelona after the return from the first voyage in 1493:

I saw them in Seville. . . . The news spread over Castile like fire that a land called the Indies had been discovered. . . . They flocked from all directions to see him; the roads swelled with throngs come to welcome him in the towns through which he passed. . . . The monarchs were very anxious to see him. They had organized a sol-emn and beautiful reception to which everybody came. The streets were crammed with people come to see this eminent person who had found another world, as well as to see the Indians, the parrots, the gold and other novelties. . . . The highest nobility . . . beaming with happiness and anxious to greet the hero of the exploit that had caused so much rejoicing in all of Christendom. Finally, Colum-bus reached the royal stand. He looked like a Roman senator: tall and stately, gray-haired, with a modest smile on his dignified face. . . . Columbus then told them quietly about the favors God had granted the Catholic kings. . . . He described some customs of the

Indians and praised them as simple and gentle people ready to receive the Faith, as could be seen from the Indians present. . . . The King and Queen heard this with profound attention and, raising their hands in prayer, sank to their knees in deep gratitude to God. The singers of the royal chapel sang the "Te Deum laudamus" while the wind instruments gave the response and indeed, it seemed a moment of communion with all the celestial joys. Who could describe the tears shed by the King, Queen and noblemen? What jubilation, what joy, what happiness in all hearts! How everybody began to encourage each other with plans of settling in the new land and converting people! [Las Casas, pp. 323–24]

After a lifetime acquaintance with the Admiral, his work, his personal papers and library, his family, and his reputation among his contemporaries, Las Casas concluded that Columbus was an exceptionally devout and pious man.

Rather than analyze the depth of Columbus's religious beliefs, or consider his intense piety as a guiding force in his life, biographers have extracted passages from his religious expressions, especially the *Libro de las profecías*, to conjure up all sorts of theories about his origins. He has been pictured as a Byzantine exile or, most often, a "converso" Jew. The former theory is most easily discounted. All of his sources were Western, and he evidenced no interest in the learned Greek expatriates, their circles, or their literature, although these were circulating prominently in Italy. With the exception of St. John Chrysostom, which he read in Latin translation, he had little interest in the Greek fathers. Nor was he familiar with Byzantine science. The Greek studies of Pico della Mirandola, Marsilio Ficino, and Erasmus were printed and circulating, but Columbus made no mention of them. Pletho, the greatest Byzantine geographer of the fifteenth century, had introduced Strabo's works to Florence in 1439, which caused Renaissance scholars, including Paolo Toscanelli, to reconsider their geographic theories. Columbus preferred Strabo to Ptolemy, yet he did not read Pletho. There is no evidence that he spoke or read any Greek. His use of an occasional word in that language, including that in his signature, was common among Western commentators. There are "familiar lapses" only into Portuguese and Spanish in the Columbus documents; there are no lapses into Greek.[2]

Any careful reading of the *Libro de las profecías* also lays to rest the fanciful theory that Christopher Columbus was an unavowed Jew searching for a Western homeland for the Jewish people. This view has been made possible simply because only short citations from the manuscript have been previously available. Columbus was an ardent Christian who would have all Jews converted to Christ, and the sooner, the better! He saw their refusal to acknowledge

the Messiah as a refusal to obey God and the gospel. With St. Augustine, he viewed this as a sinful rejection of the true Messiah and a refusal to obey the truth.

The principal attempt to prove that Columbus was a "converso" Jew was made by Salvado de Madariaga. Writing in 1940, he says in describing the letter to the king and queen that accompanied the *Libro de las profecías:*

> This evangelical tendency towards essentials rather than forms and authority was characteristic of the "converso" turn of mind. . . . Colón . . . in his letter to the King and Queen betrays the "converso" . . . brings in the Jews at once, as if subconsciously eager to break the monopoly of truth which the Christians believe they hold: "I say that the Holy Ghost works in Christians, Jew, Moors and all men of any other sect and not merely in the learned, but in the ignorant." Far less bold statements than this were to lead "Conversos" to the stake during most of the sixteenth century. This view was revolutionary and a foretaste of the Reformation; he rushed in where angels will have their wings singed in the next generation. But he is already a protestant; and this particular flavour of his religious faith provided yet another indication of his Jewish origin. . . . The central piece of this Book of Prophecies is the letter of Rabbi Samuel Jehudi, of Morocco, written in 1068, urging the Jews to be converted to the "law of Christianity.". . . There is one item in this anthology of biblical texts and comments which deserves special attention. Colón is discussing Psalm II of David and reports that Rabbi Solomon, in his comments on this psalm, says that "our masters," i.e., Jewish rabbis, held it to apply to Christ. The whole discussion on which Colón enters here reveals a mind mainly centered on the "converso" position—the man whose original faith has been Jewish and whose present faith is Christian. Thus, referring to Rabbi Solomon, he writes: "He calls heretics the 'Conversos' from Judaism to the Catholic faith who reasoned against the others who had remained in their infidelity, on the basis of that Psalm." And again: "Which is evident according to learned men converted from Judaism."[3]

Madariaga is correct in identifying the "apocalyptic" element in Columbus's *Libro de las profecías.* But, he incorrectly brings this element to focus on the situation of the "conversos" of the fifteenth and sixteenth centuries and overlooks the true focus of Columbus (following such perfectly orthodox interpreters as St. Augustine, Pierre d'Ailly, and Nicolas of Lyra) on the original tension of primitive Christianity as it arose among the "conversos" of the early Christian centuries. Madariaga claimed:

> It is always in this mental region that we find Colón: the border-line between the two faiths. The problem of the converted Jew, but also

the problem of the Jew who remains unconverted. His mind is always watching the lost brethren, wondering whether they will ever follow him into the fold of the true faith, which he honestly and sincerely holds, yet with an inevitably Jewish flavour, with that sense of "promise," of "mission," and of "apocalyptical catastrophe" which the Jews took over and always take over into Christianity.[4]

The use of the Bible by Columbus, especially the prophecies of the Old Testament, was a Christian use of Jewish materials. Columbus faced squarely the central, essential question dealt with at such length by St. Paul, the gospel writers, the church fathers and Christian teachers of all ages. Before making any use of those prophecies, it was first necessary to establish their relevance for Christians, precisely because Christians are not "children of Abraham according to the flesh" but have been grafted into the covenant people at the point at which the Jewish people rejected the Messiah, and the Gentiles have become "children of Abraham according to faith," by receiving and believing in the Messiah. Thus, the prophecies of the Old Testament, in announcing future events concerning the people of God, have been interpreted by all traditional Christian writers following St. Paul and the church fathers as having a clear focus of completion in the people of the New Covenant, the Christian church. Prophecies concerning the temple point to a household of faith; prophecies concerning Jerusalem refer often to·the "City of God" or earthly people of the Messiah in the sense intended by St. Augustine in his book by that name; prophecies concerning Zion often refer to the kingdom of God as an era of the rule of Christ in a "Peaceable Kingdom," of "novus ordo seculorum" dealt with in the writings of St. Augustine and his interpreters.[5]

Madariaga based his case in large measure on folios 62 and 63 of the *Libro de las profecías.* Here Columbus copied a long quotation from Nicholas of Lyra, who in turn had cited St. Augustine and St. Paul along with Rabbi Solomon. The main point is that the New Testament writer interprets Psalms 2:6–8 as a prophecy literally referring to Christ the Messiah as "greater than the angels," which was regarded by St. Augustine and Nicholas of Lyra as the true literal meaning of the prophecy. Nicholas of Lyra accepted this interpretation, and added the supporting facts that (1) "the ancient teachers of the Hebrews understood this Psalm as referring to the Messiah in its literal meaning," (2) "for the purpose of a response to the heretics Rabbi Solomon and other later Hebrew scholars interpreted the Psalm as referring to David," and (3) it "is obviously fabricated that this Psalm should be interpreted as referring to David in its literal meaning," since "the ancient Hebrew scholars expounded this Psalm as referring to the Christ" [L.P., 237].

In this passage, Columbus was faithfully pursuing the theme that he announced at the beginning of the *Libro de las profecías*, namely, applying the hermeneutical insights of great teachers in his study of the Bible. His whole point in this section is that the Messianic prophecy found in Psalms 2:6–8 should not be viewed as a mere figurative, allegorical interpretation, not even as a "twofold literal meaning" of the kind indicated by Nicholas of Lyra" [L.P., 103], "not on a mystical interpretation, but on the literal, just as Augustine says" [L.P., 237].

Far from evidencing the veiled Jewish self-awareness of Columbus, as Madariaga would have us believe, this and other material in the *Libro de las profecías* shows the Discoverer to be interpreting biblical prophecies entirely in the tradition of St. Augustine and the other church fathers and exegetes.

Christopher Columbus was a man of sincere spirituality and a deep personal Christian faith. The sources all speak of his near monastic discipline and exemplary Christian character at every stage of his life. Undoubtedly he was ambitious and austere, and he may have appeared arrogant and detached in his well-known scheming and grasping for gold and power. Yet he wrote Pope Alexander VI offering to finance an army to conquer the Holy Lands for Christendom; he extracted from Queen Isabella a promise to employ the gold of the Indies for the expansion of the church; he was an entrepreneur whose chief aim in life was to be an instrument by which prophecies would be fulfilled. The astounding ends are fully adequate to explain all the means he used to pursue them, and the opposition and misunderstanding he aroused.[6]

Two letters written to the king and queen demonstrate that his spirituality and religious motivations remained constant over the years. In the letter written aboard the *Niña* during the homeward passage to Luis de Santangel (but meant to be read to the king and queen), and forwarded on 4 March 1493 from anchorage near Lisbon, we hear Columbus's praise of God and his missionary fervor:

> The Eternal God, our Lord, who gives to all those who walk in his way victory over things which appear impossible; and this was notably one. . . . So, since our Redeemer has given this triumph to our most illustrious king and queen, and to their renowned realms, in so great a matter, for all of this Christendom should feel joyful and make great celebrations and give solemn thanks to the Holy Trinity with many solemn prayers for the great exaltation which it will have in the salvation of so many peoples to our holy faith.
> [Varela, p. 146]

The style and content remain unchanged in his letter written to the monarchs that accompanied the *Libro de las profecías* a decade

later. In this letter, Columbus presented the most profoundly autobiographical religious reflections to come to us from his pen [L.P., 105–11]. He recalled his career from "a very early age," his earnest prayers and studies relating to his "desire . . . the fire that burned within . . . to sail from here to the Indies." He described his motivation, his acquisition of skills, and his unique intuitive understanding as divine gifts from "the Lord who opened my mind," from "the Holy Spirit who encouraged me with a radiance of marvelous illumination from his sacred Holy Scriptures."

He reminded the sovereigns of the seven years when all who spoke of his project "denounced it with laughter and ridiculed me." He claimed that through these trials, "continually . . . the Scriptures urge me to press forward." The very trials proved that "the Lord purposed there should be something miraculous in this matter." This enterprise could not fail because it turned out "just as our redeemer Jesus Christ had said . . . by the mouth of his holy prophets." He would present (in his *Libro de las profecías*) a selection of these prophecies as evidence not only for the divine support of the voyages of discovery but also for further wonderful developments for the church, the Household of God.

Admitting that he was a self-taught layman, he quoted Scripture to show that God encouraged "exalted statements" by "persons who never studied literature." Columbus traced for the sovereigns a divine plan for past and future history of the world, revealed "in the Old Testament by the mouth of prophets, and in the New Testament by our Savior Jesus Christ." He supported his interpretations by quoting St. Augustine, Cardinal d'Ailly, and the learned King Alfonso and by referring to "many revered teachers and theologians." He pointed out that "before the consummation of this world," the Scriptures prophesy that "the Gospel must now be proclaimed to many lands," and many other "great events for the world." He claimed that "a particular prophecy . . . applies particularly to my experience, and it refreshes me and makes me rejoice every moment when I think of it." He is "a most unworthy sinner," who has "cried out for grace and mercy from the Lord" and has found "most delightful comfort" in enjoying "His marvelous presence." His "journey to the Indies" was "simply the fulfillment of what Isaiah had prophesied, and this is what I desire to write in this book so that the record may remind Your Majesties, and so that you may rejoice." Other great prophecies concerning the City of God remained to be fulfilled: "You may be certain that there will be success. . . . our Savior's promises are reliable." Whoever "finds so much faith as a grain of mustard seed" will find that "He is a gracious Lord, who desires people to do things for which He makes himself responsible."

There can be no doubt that Columbus was a devoutly pious man whose mysticism was intimately integrated with his thoughts and actions. Throughout his journals and letters, we find him constantly in prayer, invoking the names of Christ, Mary, and the saints and solemnly giving praise to God. His spirituality fed his ambition and that spirituality was at the heart of his *idée fixe*. Casare De Lollis, the editor of the *Raccolta*, observed that "from the beginning he dignified his grand undertaking in his own eyes and those of others, expecting that its effect would be to facilitate the complete triumph of the Christian faith."[7] He fervently believed that he was inspired and favored by God, that he had been chosen to do a "great work": that he was a man of destiny, divinely inspired in thought and action. He met the long years waiting for approval and financing with patience and sustained optimism for he "knew" that the Spanish monarchs, who had been titled the "Catholic Monarchs" by the pope, would be moved to action by God just as he had been. Unlike many laymen of his day, he read his Bible, the church fathers, and past and present theologians. He must have carried a Bible or a collection of Scriptures with him as he constantly quoted or paraphrased Scripture during his voyages; on one occasion he is said to have appeared on deck with a Bible in hand to exorcise a waterspout.

As a lay Christian, Columbus showed a special devotion to the Order of St. Francis and the Seraphic founder's teachings (as those teachings were understood in the fifteenth century), including a deep attraction to the doctrine of the Immaculate Conception. He demonstrated a special love for Jesus and the Virgin and, through her, a total devotion to the Trinity.[8] He knew that the Holy Spirit guided his every move and enabled his mind to grasp all that it needed to penetrate the Ocean Sea. His confidence in himself and his abilities are second only to his confidence in divine guidance. He and his crew worshipped daily aboard ship, and whenever they disembarked on the voyages special prayers and services were said.

The Admiral summarized his special calling in the letter he wrote to King Ferdinand and Queen Isabella describing his fourth voyage. Columbus relates a vision he had as a young man in which the Holy Spirit said these words to him:

[God] caused your name [i.e., Columbus] to be wonderfully resounded through the earth . . . and gave you the keys of the gates of the ocean which are closed with strong chains. [Varela, pp. 322–23]

He never lost sight of this commission. His voyages were always undertaken in the name of the Trinity. Whenever he faced danger, unusual difficulty, or unknown phenomena, he resorted to religious

vows, promises of pilgrimage, and penance. There is no record in any of his writings or in those of his contemporaries that he was given to cursing or irreverence of any form. The record speaks of an extraordinarily religious man set apart by his piety. His son, Ferdinand, described him:

> In eating and drinking, and in the adornment of his person, he was very moderate and modest. . . . He was so strict in matters of religion that for fasting and saying prayers he might have been taken for a member of a religious order. He was so great an enemy of swearing and blasphemy that I give my word I never heard him utter any other oath than "by St. Ferdinand." [Ferdinand, p. 9]

The driving force in his life was a deep spiritual belief in the providential nature of his enterprise:

> Who can doubt that this fire was not merely mine, but also the Holy Spirit who encouraged me with a radiance of marvelous illumination from his sacred Scriptures, by a most clear and powerful testimony from the forty-four books of the Old Testament, from the four Gospels, from the twenty-three Epistles of the blessed Apostles — urging me to press forward? Continually, without a moment's hesitation, the Scriptures urge me to press forward with great haste.
> [L.P., 105]

Others, too, saw his accomplishments as guided by the hand of God. Bartolomé de las Casas proclaimed that "divine Providence chose him to accomplish the most outstanding feat ever accomplished in the world until now." Later, in the *History of the Indies*, the humanitarian bishop of Chiapas laments his inadequacies in his efforts to describe the meaning of Columbus's discoveries:

> Many times I have wished that God would inspire me again and that I had the eloquence of Cicero to extol the indescribable service to God and to the whole world which Christopher Columbus rendered at the cost of such pain and dangers when he so courageously discovered the New World with skill and expertise. . . . My limited knowledge and poor eloquence causes me to think that the results of Columbus's labor speak better for itself. . . . Here in a few words stands greater principles worthy of prime consideration above all others. Is there anything in the world comparable to the opening of the tightly shut doors of an ocean that no one dared enter before? . . . But since it is obvious that at that moment God gave this man the keys to the awesome seas, he and no other unlocked the darkness, to him and to no other is owed for evermore everything that exists beyond those doors. . . . He showed the way to the discovery of immense territories . . . whose peoples form wealthy and illustrious nations of diverse peoples and languages . . . and of all the sons of Adam . . . they are now ready and prepared to be brought to the knowledge of their Creator and the faith. [Las Casas, p. 328]

His son confirms this belief that his father

> was chosen for his great work by Our Lord, who desired him as his true Apostle to follow the example of others of his elect by publishing His name on distant seas and shores, not in cities and palaces, thereby imitating our Lord himself. [Ferdinand, p. 3]

There can be no doubt that Columbus and his contemporaries saw the discoveries from the perspective of deep religious belief. On every island the Admiral had his men erect a large wooden cross, and at many points in the adventure he called upon divine intervention with a spirit of unquestioning expectation that God would intervene to take direct control of the situation at hand.

Fortunately, many written accounts of the manner and spiritual life of the Discoverer have been preserved, written by persons who had occasion to observe him personally or knew him by reputation. Ferdinand described his father as a deeply religious man of intense faith and disciplined life, an exemplary Christian who was strict and regular in all religious observances, who never cursed and always paused for prayer before writing a letter or undertaking any venture. The court correspondent, Peter Martyr, reported the Admiral in similar terms. Jaime Ferrer, the Catalan jeweler, geographer, astrologer, lapidary, and advisor to the Spanish monarchs, called him "an apostle and ambassador of God."[9]

In the year 1516, the learned Bishop Agostino Giustiniani, also a native of Genoa, published the *Polyglot Psalter* with parallel columns for the text of the Psalms in Hebrew, Arabic, Greek, Aramaic, and Latin. As he reached the point of his commentary on Psalm 19:4, "their message reaches out to all the world," he used the occasion to write a lengthy marginal note reporting on the life and work of his compatriot, Christopher Columbus:

> At least in our times, when by the marvelous attempt by Christopher Columbus, a Genoese, an almost new world has been discovered and added to Christendom. And, indeed, since Columbus frequently declared himself to have been selected by God that through him this prophecy might be fulfilled. . . . Having accomplished these marvelous navigations and returning into Spain, Columbus fulfilled the work of the prophetic declaration.[10]

This is an interesting statement by a churchman who did not know the Admiral, probably had not read anything written by the Discoverer except maybe the letter of 1493 announcing the discovery which by 1516 had been translated into Italian and distributed widely, and had probably gleaned most of his information from other Genoese who had known Columbus. The Genoese bishop was a writer of vast learning and illustrious reputation who was well qualified to pronounce the judgment of a younger contemporary

upon the life and work of a fellow citizen of Genoa. Such judgment would not have been given lightly. Agostino was born in 1470, when Columbus was about age nineteen, to a seafaring family that may have actually employed Columbus as a seaman for travel to the island of Chios. He entered the Dominican Order in 1487, taught Oriental languages in Lombardy, and was appointed Bishop of Nebbio on the Island of Corsica in 1514. Agostino was the first to print the Scriptures in so many languages in a polyglot version. He was invited to open a course in Oriental languages at the University of Paris by Francis I, and from there he went to England and was recognized by King Henry VIII, Sir Thomas More, and other English scholars.

It is not likely that Agostino had any knowledge of the *Libro de las profecías* since, if such were the case, he probably would have referred to it in his tribute to the Discoverer's life and achievements. It is significant, however, that Agostino, one of the leading Bible scholars of his age, wrote so effusively about the life and work of the Admiral as a fulfillment of prophecy. The interruption of the text for a commentary, and an insertion of the Admiral's biography at the point where he reached one of Columbus's favorite Psalms, was important; it lent a measure of credibility to the ideas of Columbus on the subject of his understanding and exegesis of biblical prophecies. At the very least, it speaks well for the favorable reputation Columbus enjoyed as a man who "frequently declared himself to have been selected by God that through him this prophecy might be fulfilled."

One of the more curious depictions of the Admiral's religious piety surfaced in 1670 when the papers of Nicolo Oderigo were given to the Genoese archive. Oderigo had been ambassador to the Spanish court, a close friend of Columbus, and he was one of the persons the Admiral chose to keep copies of his so-called *Book of Privileges*. Attached to a letter written by the Admiral to the ambassador was the drawing titled "Apotheosis of Columbus." Some scholars, including Harrisse, have attributed the pen and ink drawing to Columbus himself because of the signature along the margin.[11]

The drawing shows the Admiral seated with "Providence" in a vehicle crossing the Ocean Sea. Both are holding the sail with their feet firmly planted on a globe. *Monstri superati,* such as envy and ignorance, are being plowed under by the vehicle pulled by "constancy" and "tolerance." The vehicle is being pushed along by "religion." Overhead, the journey is being encouraged by figures representing "victory," "hope," and "fame."

The drawing is obviously from a baroque artist, not Christopher Columbus. The signature was likely added later, as the note next

to it states that the signature is an example of how the Admiral signed his name. More important, the drawing is an allegory drawn in the sixteenth or seventeenth century to portray the religious nature of the discovery and the piety of the Discoverer. For some reason, someone wanted to demonstrate visually the Admiral's reputation as a man of piety.

We would offer two theories as to why this drawing was made. It could have been a sketch for a proposed float in a royal procession. Three times in the sixteenth century Spanish monarchs visited Genoa, and each was given a procession.[12] More likely, it was a sketch for a proposed fresco by Lazzaro Tavarone (1556–1641). Tavarone was a well-known decorator of palaces in Genoa who had studied in Spain with Cambiaso. One of his most popular fresco themes was events surrounding Christopher Columbus. The drawing is similiar to his style and technique.[13]

Columbus's religious nature could be paradoxical. On one level we find superstition, on the other an intellectual understanding of his relationship with the Godhead. When it came to day to day interaction with the Deity, Columbus resorted to commonly held practices of Spanish popular piety. But when it came to analyzing his mission, he sought a deeper meaning and thus turned to Scripture and its interpretation by famous scholars.

Two examples of his superstitious religious nature will suffice. One of the interesting aspects about the first voyage is that, although it took place during the hurricane season, no severe storms were encountered in the Caribbean. On the return trip of the first voyage,

however, a tremendous storm blew up on 12 February near the Azores. The wind and the sea were the worst experienced by any of the crew in all their years at sea.[14] In order to calm his crew, and himself, Columbus assembled them on deck to pray and to make vows for safety. The storm was so bad that the Admiral feared that his ship would go down, so he wrote a lengthy account of his first voyage; he had it placed in a wax-sealed wine cask and tossed it into the sea in the hope that someone would find the cask and carry the news to the monarchs in case he was lost at sea. They prayed collectively and individually, but the storm grew more intense. When prayers failed to abate the storm, Columbus suggested that they draw lots to chose one of their members to go on pilgrimage to Santa Maria de Guadelupe in Extremadura if they returned to Spain safely. Beans were placed in a hat with one bean marked with a cross. Columbus himself drew the crossed bean.[15] The storm continued and the Admiral suggested another drawing for another pilgrimage, this time a journey to Santa Maria de Loreto in Italy. Pedro de Villa, a seaman, drew the crossed bean. The fury of the storm increased and yet another pilgrimage was suggested, this time to Santa Clara de Moguer. Again, Columbus drew the crossed bean, and he tells us how proud he was that God expected more from him than the others. The storm raged on. In a final effort, the officers and crew fell to their knees and cried in unison to the Virgin, loud enough to be heard above the storm, for her intercession. They promised to go in procession, barefooted and dressed only in shirts, to the nearest shrine dedicated to her upon reaching any land. Finally, that evening, the storm weakened and land was sighted to the northeast [Varela, pp. 126–27]. Some days later, on 3 March, off the coast of Portugal, another storm struck, and again the crew drew lots to go on pilgrimage, this time to the shrine of Santa Maria of La Cinta in Huelva. Again, Columbus proudly drew the crossed bean [Varela, p. 134].

An incident that we believe to be apocryphal, but indicative of how Columbus's piety was perceived by others, was recorded as occurring during the fourth voyage. The fleet encountered a huge waterspout with severe tornado proportions. As the fearsome spout approached, the story goes, Columbus chose to exorcise it to protect his fleet. He stood on the deck and read from the Gospel of John about Jesus calming the tempest in the Sea of Galilee off Capernaum. Then, grasping the Bible in his left hand, he drew his sword and traced a sign of the cross in the sky followed by a circle to encompass the fleet. The spout passed between the ships without damage to anything or anyone [Ferdinand, p. 246].[16]

Columbus claimed two visions during his lifetime. One was prophetic. He believed that the Holy Spirit had spoken to him, saying

that his name would be proclaimed throughout the world. He does not specify when or where this happened, only that it was "in my youth." In his mind, he connected it to his success in discovering the New World [Varela, pp. 322–23].

The second was a vision given to him on 6 April 1503 as words of comfort and encouragement. He was off Veragua anchored at the mouth of the Belén River. He and his crew had spent several weeks building a new colony named Santa Maria de Belén, and he was preparing to return to Spain. There had been trouble with the Cacique Quibian, who had vowed to massacre the Christians. Columbus was alone on his flagship while the others were upriver gathering supplies of food and water for the long trip home. A storm blew up, causing much concern for the Admiral as he worried that the anchors would give way and the ships would be driven to shore by the winds and breakers. As he was worrying about this possible catastrophe, he heard shots and cries from upriver and then total silence. That evening bodies of his sailors began floating down the river. He realized that he was surrounded by hostile Indians and that all of his men probably were dead. The Admiral fell into deep depression and fear that his mission and his life were over. In his words:

> I was outside and all alone. . . . there was no hope of rescue. . . . I climbed in pain to the highest point of the ship and called in tears and trembling to your Highnesses' mighty warriors in all four corners of the earth for strength, but none of them answered me. At length, groaning with exhaustion, I fell asleep, and I heard a most merciful voice saying: "O fool, so slow to believe and to serve your God, the God of all! What more did He do for Moses or for his servant David? He has had you in His care from your mother's womb. When He saw you a grown man, He caused your name to resound most greatly over the earth. He gave you the Indies, which are so rich a section of the world, and you have divided them according to your desires. He gave you the keys to the gates of the Ocean which were held with such great chains. You were obeyed in many lands and you have won a mighty reputation for yourself among Christians. What more did He do for the people of Israel when He led them out of Egypt, or for David, that shepherd boy whom He made a king of the Jews? Turn yourself to Him and acknowledge your sins. His mercy is infinite. Even your old age will not prevent you from achieving great things for His domains are many and vast. Abraham was more than a hundred years old when he begot Isaac. And Sarah, was she a girl? You cry for help with doubt in your heart. Ask yourself who has afflicted you so grievously and so often — God or the world? The privileges and covenants which God has given you will not be taken back by Him. Nor does He say to them that have served Him that He meant

it otherwise, or that it should be taken in another sense; nor does He inflect torments to show His power. His way is to fulfill his promises with increase. Thus have I told you what your Creator has done for you and for all men. He has revealed to me some of those rewards which are waiting for you for the many toils and dangers which you have endured in the service of others.

I heard all this as if in a trance. The message was so positive that I could find no reply. All I could do was to weep over my sins. Whoever it was that had spoken, ended by saying: "Fear not, but have faith. All these tribulations are written on tablets of marble and there is a reason for them."   [Varela, pp. 322–23]

On the intellectual level, Columbus's theology and beliefs reflected the influence of reform-minded Franciscans. We find him attracted not only to Observantine ideology but possibly to the "recogimiento" movement, which flourished among the Franciscans in Spain after 1480.[17] The "recognimiento" emphasized internal spiritual experiences in which the worshipper sought God by looking into the inner self. Through such spiritual exercise, one could attain union with God. In traditional Franciscan fashion, Christopher Columbus perceived that God had chosen to reveal himself to an unlearned and "lesser one" in society. Through internal spiritual experience, Columbus believed that he understood fully what God expected from him and would show him how to accomplish that expectation. Combining interunion with God, as taught by the recogimiento, with Spiritual Franciscanism, the Admiral believed, as mentioned in the first chapter, that the Holy Spirit imparted *"spiritualis intellectus"* to the elect so that they might discover unknown truths. He acknowledged that he had spent hours studying the theories of experts, years at sea accumulating the seamanship necessary to lead a fleet across the Ocean Sea, and lengthy discussions with men of all backgrounds about the far Atlantic; but even so, his success, he strongly believed, was due entirely to the gift of understanding given to him by the Holy Spirit.

The gift of understanding, *spiritualis intellectus,* in Christian thought, enables the recipient to penetrate revealed truth, and it intensifies one's faith so that all things ultimately are seen through faith.[18] Columbus wished to leave no doubt that he had received the charismatic gift of *spiritualis intellectus* which enlightened his mind to enable him to understand the hidden mysteries of prophetic texts, to gain practical and intuitive abilities in navigation, and to comprehend cosmography and related sciences intellectually. As he put it,

I have had business and conversation with learned men among both laity and clergy, Latins and Greeks, Christians and Moslems, and many others of different cultures. I prayed to the most merciful Lord

concerning my desire, and he gave me the spirit and intelligence for it. He gave me abundant skill in the mariner's arts, an adequate understanding of the stars, and of geometry and arithmetic. He gave me the mental capacity and manual skill.   [L.P., 105]

Virgil Milani has argued that Columbus was attempting to stress a deeper meaning for "intelligence" at this point and that he could have implied a shade of meaning found in St. Augustine whenever the church father referred to intelligence of or from God.[19] We would argue that Columbus spoke of a charismatic gift of understanding given by God.

In chapter 2 we demonstrated the influence of the Order of Friars Minor, especially the Observantine reform, on Columbus's intellectual growth. At the expense of some redundancy, we will now investigate ways in which Franciscan piety colored his religious life. When and where contact with the Order of Friars Minor first occurred, and what its ultimate meaning might be to the life of Christopher Columbus, is still being debated among historians.[20] When he lived on the island of Porto Santo, there was a Franciscan friary nearby and he could have associated with the friars there. Sustained contact with the order, however, began in 1485 when he appeared at Santa Maria de La Rábida with his son Diego. Why he chose to stop at the convent is unknown. It is plausible that he knew of the convent from earlier contacts with Franciscans near Porto Santo or in Portugal. Such an immediate detour, even though somewhat out of his way to Huelva, fit his normal pattern of visiting the nearest church to hear Mass following a long journey. And, it could be that he wished a place to rest for himself and young Diego before attempting to locate his sister-in-law, Violante Moniz Perestrello, who had married Miguel Muliart. The Muliart family lived in Huelva.

The popular picture of Columbus standing hat in hand to beg bread and water for the young Diego is unlikely. Franciscan houses served as rest stops for travelers and normally provided food and overnight lodging. In any case, the stop was one of the most fortuitous made in the Admiral's life as he was received by Fray Antonio de Marchena, Custos of Seville sub-Province, who was probably at the convent on his periodic visitation. Fray Antonio de Marchena was a well-known astrologer (astronomer) and intellectual whose fame had established him at the royal court. This was to be Columbus's first opportunity to discuss his ideas and conclusions about the Ocean Sea with a sympathetic scholar well versed in Renaissance science. It is believed that he stayed at La Rábida for five months discussing his plans in infinite detail with Fray Antonio and the other brothers.

Columbus and Fray Antonio became fast friends and allies for

the rest of their lives. Fray Antonio de Marchena rose through church administration to become Vicar Provincial of the Castile Province and an influence at court when Columbus needed friends before the king and queen. He arranged for Columbus's first meeting with the Queen by providing him with a letter of introduction to Father Hernando de Talavera, Queen Isabella's confessor. The important role played by Fray Antonio can be seen in the tribute Columbus gave the learned friar after many years of dealing with the court:

> In all this time every mariner, pilot, philosopher and every other man of learning deemed my enterprise to be false; never did I get help from anyone except Father Antonio de Marchena, barring that from God. . . . Everyone regarded it [his enterprise] as folly except Father Antonio de Marchena.   [Varela, p. 243]

Altogether, Columbus spent five months at the Observantine reform house of La Rábida, which boasted a good library and an observatory on the balcony. That Columbus was willing to discuss his ideas in such detail with anyone at this point indicated the immediate trust and respect he had for Fray Antonio. Columbus had just left Portugal where he had petitioned King John II to finance his voyage and was turned down. More disheartening, King John appeared to have doublecrossed Columbus by sending his own ships on an expedition to discover a route across the Ocean Sea. With the possible exceptions of King Ferdinand and Queen Isabella, Fray Antonio de Marchena seems to have been the only person to whom Columbus revealed his entire plan after leaving Portugal. He cautiously held back key facts and observations to protect his enterprise. Given Columbus's thirst for knowledge and the intellectual stimulation of a recognized scholar of Fray Antonio's caliber, we can assume that he continued to research his plan in the convent library during the five months spent at La Rábida.

The other great friend and supporter Columbus found at La Rábida was Fray John Pérez, prior of the convent. It is unlikely that Fray John was present at La Rábida in 1485, but he was such a supporter by 1491 that he intervened after the last rejection of Columbus's scheme by the monarchs and was instrumental in causing them finally to approve the project. Fray John had been Queen Isabella's confessor before Father Hernando de Talavera, and he was a noted leader in the Observantine reform movement. Besides using his political influence for Columbus, Fray John seemed to have been Columbus's preferred priest and religious counselor. It was Fray John who performed Mass on 2 August 1492 before the first voyage, and it was he who led the procession the next day down to the harbor in Palos and made the blessings over the kneel-

ing sailors before they boarded ship for the New World. Upon returning from his first voyage, Columbus spent two weeks at La Rábida discussing his adventure with Fray John Pérez. He likely had long conversations about the conversion of the Indians, for on the second voyage Fray John was invited along by the Admiral to assess the missionary needs in the newly discovered islands.

There is no direct evidence that Christopher Columbus ever joined the Third Order of St. Francis (Tertiaries). But Alain Milhou and others have made a convincing case based upon circumstantial evidence found in the sources.[21] The most famous eyewitness account of Columbus exhibiting any sign of membership in the Third Order is by Andres Bernáldez, who stated that Columbus "arrived in Castile in the month of June, 1496 dressed as an Observantine Friar of the Order of St. Francis and resembling one in appearance, little less than in his dress, with the cord of the Order, which he wore for devotion."[22] According to legend, he was buried in Franciscan robes.

The distinguishing feature of the lay fraternity was the wearing of the Seraphic cord either externally or under one's clothing. Men and women of all social classes and occupations sought lives of holiness through the lofty ideals of St. Francis. According to the modern Franciscan historian Lazaro Iriarte, "the environment in which this evangelical holiness developed . . . invariably crystallized into apostolic or charitable projects."[23] In Spain, attraction to the order swelled from the fifteenth century onward: "There came in time a moment when St. Francis reigned as the supreme luminary over the whole of Spanish society: kings, bishops, generals, scholars, and artists thought it an honor to call him 'our seraphic Father' . . . and to be buried in his robes."[24]

In the preface letter to the *Libro de las profecías,* Columbus uses Franciscan ideology to explain his qualifications as an exegete of prophecy. He notes in typical Spiritual Franciscan fashion that learning and worldly stature have little to do with God's choice of those who receive His revelations. Using the text from Matthew, where Christ tells his followers that the Father has hidden certain things from the "wise and prudent" and will reveal them in the future to the *parvuli,* "little ones" [L.P., 107], Columbus fully justifies his role in eschatology. Spiritual Franciscans from the earliest times had pointed to this passage of Scripture as evidence for their cause. To them the Father had begun to disclose full knowledge through St. Francis ("the little one") and would continue to do so to those who followed the Seraphic saint in a strict adherence to his *Rule.*[25] Columbus was awed by the thought that God had revealed a new heaven and a new earth through him, and the admiral was further

humbled in the belief that God now chose to explain the prophetic future to follow those discoveries through his pen.

Columbus in his own writings showed a special devotion to the Trinity, Christ, and Mary of the Immaculate Conception. These special devotions were so pronounced that they are also noted by others who wrote about the Admiral. Devotion to the Trinity was popular among the Franciscans, especially among those reformers with historical ties to Spiritual Franciscanism who adopted the Joachite three-age scheme based on members of the Trinity. After the first voyage, for example, Columbus wished all to praise the Holy Trinity for his discovery. In his letter of 15 February 1493 to Luis de Santangel announcing the discovery, he stated, "All of Christendom should . . . make great celebrations and give solemn thanks to the Holy Trinity." Another symbol of this devotion is to be seen in the Admiral's signature, which takes the form of a triangle (see conclusion of this chapter). By the third voyage, his devotion had become an obsession; he dedicated the entire voyage to the Trinity and vowed to name the first new land sighted after it.

Columbus approached the Trinity through Jesus and Mary.[26] He frequently began his correspondence by scrawling across the top of his letters the phrase JESUS CUM MARIA SIT NOBIS IN VIA. That was his prayer for the recipient. As was typical of all sailors, it was to the Virgin that Columbus appealed whenever frightening storms arose at sea. His adoration of Jesus and Mary is clearly seen on the first voyage when he named the first landfall San Salvador (Holy Savior) and the next island sighted Santa Maria de Concepción. A special devotion to Jesus would naturally follow an attraction to the Franciscan way of life, which featured above all a basic Christocentrism of a literal imitation of Jesus' words and deeds.

The doctrine of the Virgin of Immaculate Conception was not yet dogma, nor was it considered heresy. The Franciscan Pope Sixtus IV in 1477 and 1480 had permitted a liturgical office of the Conception, and he twice forbade either side debating the issue to make any accusations of heresy. His support led to renewed outbursts of adoration of Immaculate Conception in Spain. The doctrine was most fervently promoted and defended by the Franciscan Order in the late fifteenth century. Duns Scotus, the Franciscan scholar at Oxford, had removed theological obstacles to the belief in the fourteenth century, and the Order of Friars Minor took up her cause because their ardent Christocentrism placed her immaculate form at the central place of honor.

The Franciscans were not the only ones supporting the cause for the adoption of a dogma that recognized Immaculate Concep-

he would find the lost mines of Solomon which the authorities believed to be in the Far East. Such a notion was not farfetched, since fifteenth-century science held that the origin of gold, and thus the most abundant supply, would be at the equator. The object of the third voyage was to find the undiscovered continent of Paria which was to the south along the equator and likely contained Solomon's mines as well as the site of the Garden of Eden [Varela, pp. 264–65].

The rich mines were not found on the third voyage as anticipated. But on the last voyage, he and his men stumbled onto the richest field of gold yet discovered in the area of Veragua, and he immediately made the connection with the rich mines of Aurea made famous by King Solomon. He believed that he was on the rim of the mother lode and a few more miles inland would put him at the heart of Aurea. Thus, he digressed in his account of the fourth voyage:

> David in his will left three thousand quintals of gold from the Indies to Solomon for the cost of the Temple buildings, and according to Josephus it came from these same countries. Jerusalem and Mount Zion are to be rebuilt by the hand of a Christian [king]: thus God says through the mouth of His prophet in the fourteenth Psalm [v. 7]. The Abbot Joachim has said that he who rebuilds it must come from Spain.
>
> [Varela, p. 327]

Columbus continued his digression by offering his services to aid in this rebuilding but definitely not as the new David. That role he gave to his king. He was to be a privileged collaborator with the Spanish monarch in the salvation of the world, the recapturing of Jerusalem, and the rebuilding of the temple.

That Columbus should pick Ferdinand as the new David shows the Admiral's familiarity with prophecies currently popular in Spain. Arnold of Villanova had adjusted Joachite predictions regarding the new David to identify him as the Spanish king.[30] The Merlin prophecies, printed sometime before 1500 in Spain, identified the Spanish monarch with the new David.[31] And, the letter sent by the ambassadors of Genoa to the Catholic monarchs, from which Columbus quoted, called for the Catholic monarchs to reconstruct the "casa del Monte Zion" [L. P., 111, 239]. Furthermore, a letter had been sent out by Don Rodrigo Ponce de León to all the noblemen in Aragon and Castile in 1486, just after Columbus first arrived in Spain, which promoted the theme of the new David.[32]

The letter of Ponce de León reached back to the pseudo-Isidore prophecies of the destruction and reconstruction of Spain. The pseudo-Isidore prophesied that the destruction of Christian Spain

by the invasion of the Moors in the eighth century had been God's punishment for a chosen people who had sinned. The prophecy tells of a day in the future when a Christian king (from the line of the Visigoths) would raise up and drive out the Moors, unify the country, and eventually extend his hegemony over all of Christendom.[33] In his letters, and in the *Libro de las profecías*, Columbus consistently reminds the king that he, Columbus, will raise the funds to enable the Spanish monarchs to capture Jerusalem. In his letter to Pope Alexander VI (dated 1502), the Admiral, in his frustration with the Spanish monarchs, even volunteered to lead a force to the Holy Land himself (but in their name) and outlined to the pope the number of troops and horses needed for the crusade [Varela, p. 312].

The secret of the Ocean Sea had not been penetrated earlier because God wanted it hidden until He was ready. Columbus believed that God had chosen him, a humble servant, as the vehicle through which the last great mystery would be revealed—a new land to gain for Christ and his sovereigns. A new world had been unveiled to which the Gospel message must be sent, a new world which was the source of Solomon's gold to be used to finance the recapture of Jerusalem and the rebuilding of the temple. Just as John the Baptist was the precursor who announced Christ to the ancient world, Columbus was the messenger to the New World.[34] He was so sure of these events that he believed that the end times would begin within 150 years [L.P., 109].

One of his favorite Scriptures was Psalms 18:5 (RSV 19:4): "Yet their voice goes out through all the earth, and their words to the end of the world." He quoted this passage five times in the *Libro de las profecías* and paraphrased it elsewhere in his writings. The leading points in the *Capitulations of Santa Fé*, drawn up before the first voyage, and the first item of his *Instructions* issued by the monarchs for the second voyage, reflected Columbus's discussions with the monarchs concerning his mission. Both of these documents command him to lay claim to unknown islands and continents and to spread the Gospel of Jesus Christ to the peoples who lived there.

Due to the success of the first voyage, strong, related scientific and theological theories had been disproved. According to many ancient scholars, Aristotle among them, people in the opposite hemisphere, the Antipodes, were unreachable because of the torrid zone which separated the two hemispheres. Since God had established this uncrossable barrier, it was believed by many that any people inhabiting those regions could not be sons of Adam, nor could they receive the gospel message promised "to all the nations." Thus, speculation about their appearance tended to produce grotesque and misformed beings. St. Augustine responded to the problem by

guessing that the opposite hemisphere was entirely ocean, and the weight of his conclusions settled the issue for many. The more modern ideas of Bacon/d'Ailly gave the region land forms without declaring them inhabited or uninhabited.

Columbus rejected those who held that the gospel would not be preached there. In a marginal note to the *Imago mundi*, he stated that without doubt people lived beyond the equator and they must be brought the message of Christ [*Raccolta*, pt. I, vol. 2, p. 376, notes 20, 23]. Columbus found the region to contain land inhabited by beings not unlike those in Europe, Africa, and Asia. Thus, they must have been the sons of Adam and needed the gospel preached to them. This is why Christopher Columbus found his role as the messenger of the New Heaven and the New Earth so important. God had selected him for an apostolic mission of grave importance.

Ambitions to spread the gospel and capture the Holy Land were long-held objectives of the Friars Minor, originating with St. Francis himself. To the Spiritual Franciscans, this came to have eschatological meaning as well.[35] As the messenger of the New Heaven and the New Earth, salvation of the Indian peoples was constantly on Columbus's mind [L.P., 229 ff.]. Over and over in his journey diaries, memoranda, letters, and in the *Libro de las profecías*, he returned to this theme and desire. In his first description of the Indians (12 October 1492), he proclaimed their readiness for the Gospel: "for I knew that they were a people to be delivered and converted to our holy faith rather by love than by force" and "I believe that they would easily be made Christians." Three days later he returned to this theme: "I cannot find that they have any religion, and I believe that they would be speedily converted to Christianity for they have a very good understanding" [Varela, pp. 30, 34]. Ferdinand, using his father's notes, makes the curious observation that the light seen by Columbus on 11 October, which "flickered like a little wax candle," had religious significance. The light, sighted shortly before the landfall at San Salvador, Ferdinand believed foretold of his father's new world mission: "the Admiral, who had first seen the light amid the darkness, signifying the spiritual light with which he was to illuminate those regions" [Ferdinand, pp. 58–59].

In his letter to the sovereigns, dated 29 May 1493, Columbus called for the establishment of a church and for an abbot and monastic missionaries to be sent to the Indies in order to convert the Indians. To pay for missionary activities, he suggested that a 1 percent assessment be placed on all gold taken from the islands and set aside for this work [Varela, p. 179].[36] The monarchs were pleased and receptive to the suggestion to begin missionary activities but made no move toward funding. In their first "instruction"

to Columbus for the second voyage, they direct that missionary activity should be a high priority:

> Wherefore, desiring the expansion and increase of our Holy Catholic Faith, their Highnesses charge and direct the Admiral, Viceroy and Governor that he strive and work to win over the peoples of the said islands and mainland by all ways and means to our Holy Catholic Faith.[37]

Jaime Ferrer, who showed unusual religious and scientific interest in Columbus's voyages, put the Admiral in the role of "Apostolo y Ambajado de Dios."[38] To Pope Alexander VI, Columbus showed his awareness of these commands and expectations when he stated that his guiding prayer in life was "I hope Our Lord to reveal His Holy name and His Gospel throughout the world." Furthermore, failing to extract the necessary resources from the Spanish monarchs, Columbus makes the same appeal to the pope:

> Now, most blessed Father, I beg your Holiness for my consolation and in regard to other aspects of this holy and noble enterprise, that you give me the aid of several priests and religious that I know to be suitable for this purpose [propagation of the faith], and by means of an Apostolic Brief, order all the superiors of any one of the orders of the Carthusians, of the Jeronymites, of the Minors and Mendicants, that I, or whoever I delegate, may choose up to six of them, to carry out their work wherever it may be necessary in this enterprise, because I hope in our lord to reveal His Holy Name and Gospel in the world.   [Varela, p. 312]

As the messenger of the New Heaven and the New Earth, Columbus saw his duty as twofold: he was to open the way for missionaries to bring salvation to the rest of the world, and he was to find gold in such great quantity that his sovereigns "within three years would undertake and prepare to go and conquer the Holy Places" [Varela, p. 101]. As James Cummins has observed, "In his mind, the whole 'empresa de Indies' was only a means to that predestined end: the New World was to redeem the Old City."[39] Columbus, the visionary, clearly had an idea from the beginning of launching a crusade. It was a primary argument he made before the Catholic monarchs when seeking their support:

> I declared to your Highnesses that all the profit of my enterprise should be spent in the conquest of Jerusalem. Your Highnesses smiled and said that it pleased you, and that even without this [profit] you had that strong desire.   [Varela, p. 101]

And later, in the *Institución de Mayorazgo,* or Deed of Entail, he reminded the King and Queen of this same purpose,

At the moment when I undertook to discover the Indies, it was with the intention of petitioning the king and the queen, our Sovereigns, that they might resolve to expend the potential revenues occurring to them from the Indies for the conquest of Jerusalem. Indeed, it is the thing which I have asked of them.   [Varela, p. 197]

Fulfilling the medieval idea of freeing the holy places had an unusual attraction to the Spanish monarchs. Politically, their success in unifying the peninsula had relied upon crusade ideology as they drove the Moors from Spain. Following the capture of Granada, they were universally seen as the leaders destined to continue that crusade across North Africa into the Holy Land. Columbus can be credited with changing those plans by turning their attention toward the west instead of the south and east.

A crusade mentality in Spanish military activity on the peninsula went back to the mid-eleventh century. The ideology turned to legal status when the Spanish monarchs' crusading zeal in the *reconquista* of the Iberian peninsula led to the so-called *patronato real,* a series of special papal dispensations to Spain in its struggle against Islam.[40] Papal support intensified in the fifteenth century under the pontificates of Nicholas V, Calixtus III, and Sixtus IV. The key document was the papal bull *Orthodoxie fidei propagationem,* thereafter popularly called the "Bull of Granada," granted to Ferdinand and Isabella by Innocent VIII in 1486. After a long preface on the propagation of the faith, the salvation of barbarian nations, and the repression of infidels and praise to the Catholic monarchs for their endeavors up to that time in doing these things, Innocent VII conceded:

This we gladly confer and as a reward of their crusade made them rulers, guardians and keepers of the lands they conquer and the people there resident . . . they may possess and control the churches, monasteries, and other ecclesiastical benefices and occupied territories regained by them in the enterprise to which they consecrated themselves by vow.[41]

Not stopping with what was already captured, the pope then included all future territories gained through a continuous crusade:

We confer the full right of patronage and of presentation of suitable persons to the Apostolic See for the cathedral churches . . . the monasteries and conventional priories in the lands thus far acquired . . . or that will, by them or their successor be acquired . . . as it may come to pass in the future.[42]

Similar authority had been granted to the king of Portugal by Nicholas V and Calixtus III by 1454 in the Portuguese king's quest to extend his realm into Africa. Thus, ecclesiastical responsibilities

for both monarchies were well established within the known boundaries of Europe and Africa.

But if crusading zeal was to continue into the new lands found far to the west in the Ocean Sea, a clearer definition of each country's ecclesiastical rights and responsibilities had to be made. Immediately upon Columbus's return from the first voyage and on the heels of his announcement, Pope Alexander VI was contacted to extend royal patronage to the Indies.[43] Four bulls were forthcoming in 1493 that collectively established the famous line of demarcation between Spain and Portugal. The bulls rest heavily upon a demand that the monarchs in each country spread the gospel. Edwin Sylvest's studies of missionary activity in the New World have shown that such activity grew out of a century of crusading spirit which, in turn, kept that crusading spirit alive.[44]

King Ferdinand not only had papal permission to propagate the faith and establish ecclesiastical control of the church in the lands he conquered; he also had inherited the titles "Patron of the Holy Places" and "King of Jerusalem." It had been the houses of Aragon and Anjou, his ancestors, who aided the Franciscans in establishing convents in the Holy Land and provided protection to pilgrims traveling to the holy places. Robert of Anjou and his wife, Sancha of Mallorca, established these convents in 1333, and Pope Clement VI gave to them the title "Patron of the Holy Places." This title passed from Sancha to Pedro IV of Aragon in 1343. Later, King Alphonso V took the title "King of Jerusalem" when he captured Naples. "King of Jerusalem" was a Hohenstaufen title dating back to the rule of Frederick II. Finally, the title was confirmed and reissued to King Ferdinand and his successors in 1510 by Pope Julian II.[45] Maria Doussinague had made an exhaustive study of Spanish crusade ideology and enthusiasm in the fifteenth century. In order to encourage this enthusiasm and dream, Pope Innocent VIII gave the Spanish rulers rights to all crusade taxes they could collect after 1485.[46] Columbus, who was well aware of the desires of his monarchs and knew of the pope's encouragement, wrote Pope Alexander VI in 1502 to assure him that "this enterprise [voyages] was undertaken with the objective of employing the profits from it in restoring the Holy Temple to the Holy Church" [Varela, p. 312].

Besides a political climate favorable to crusade mentality, the crusade ideology of Christopher Columbus also had to do with his geographical-historical-religious imagination. With this imagination, he developed a geoeschatology to describe the relationship between geographic lore and theology of the last times.[47]

The Admiral's urgency for a new crusade intensified after the third voyage when he believed that he had found the Terrestrial

Paradise, the Garden of Eden. The search for the Terrestrial Paradise was much on his mind from the beginning as can be seen in numerous postilles to the works of Piccolomini and d'Ailly [Raccolta, pt. I, vol. 2, pp. 299, 376, 379, 401, 438–39]. Such subjective, nonempirical lore was important to him in establishing his exploration agenda and goals and frequently affected his behavior.

The connection between locating the Terrestrial Paradise and launching a crusade to Jerusalem had fundamental geoeschatological significance to Columbus. In Christian historiography, the chronology of human events is the road between the Garden of Eden in Genesis and the New Jerusalem in Revelations. Hermeneutically, Eden is both the ideal of the first time and the eschatological goal of the end time. Furthermore, in late medieval theory, Eden was located in precise and perfect antipodal balance to Jerusalem. Eden was the exact center of one hemisphere while Jerusalem was at the exact center of the other.[48]

The geoeschatology of the drama of salvation made the two sites the alpha and omega of the history of mankind. History began in Eden in perfect righteousness and in a perfect environment. But Eden was also the geographic site of man's first sin; thus, Adam was evicted from it by God and sent to the opposite of Paradise, that is, to Jerusalem on the other side of the world.

To Columbus, then, the finding of the geographic site of the Terrestrial Paradise meant human history was coming to an end. The two geographic areas had to be brought together, both had to be in the hands of the Christians for Christ's return. Since the king of Spain now held dominion over the Terrestrial Paradise, it was only logical and prophetic fulfillment for him to hold dominion over the city of Jerusalem as well. By controlling the "centers" of both hemispheres of the earth, he would truly be the expected "last world emperor" predicted in a variety of prophetic sources. The recapture of the House of Zion was an essential part of Columbus's chronology of "last times."

The *Libro de las profecías* shows Christopher Columbus intensely committed to the cause of crusade but with inspiration drawn from biblical prophecy instead of the realities of political power. Instead of a crusade moving eastward across North Africa to recover the Holy Land, Columbus promoted a move westward that he believed was the prophesied path to the Holy City. According to the Admiral's interpretations of Scripture, discovery, evangelization, and the development of New World resources should precede a crusade to Jerusalem. The great reconquest of the Holy Land would be accomplished from the abundant logistical provisions supplied from the New World. As he stated in his letter to Pope Alexander VI, "This enterprise was undertaken with the object of employing the profits

from it in the cause of [restoring] the Holy Temple of the Holy Church" [Varela, p. 312]. It was this view that focused his attention on gold and on population centers. It was an ambition to provide tremendous wealth for new undertakings of Christendom that drove the Admiral. In a sense, he was right, for the Europeanization of the Western Hemisphere outflanked Islam in the long run and ushered in a new age.

We cannot deny that the Admiral wanted a comfortable income for himself and his heirs, but the primary motivation in his quest for gold was spiritual. On many occasions, he clearly stated that any gold found should be used first and foremost to propagate the faith and to launch the final crusade to Jerusalem. In a letter describing the fourth voyage, he defined his spiritual and temporal obsession for the metal. "Gold is most excellent," he said, "Gold constitutes treasure, and he who possesses it may do what he pleases in the world, and may also attain to bring souls to Paradise" [Varela, p. 327]. Statements such as "I do not wish to delay but to discover and go to many islands to find gold" [Varela, p. 35] or "Our Lord in his goodness guides me so that I may find this gold" [Varela, p. 94] occur with disturbing frequency in his writings. Such singlemindedness in his search has caused students of the great Admiral to conclude that he was greedy. But his search went beyond a materialistic craving. Gold had religious value as it was the means by which he could carry out his divine mission. The metal took on eschatological meaning to the Admiral when he wrote about the gold he found in Veragua. Science and Scripture merge in his mind at this point. Science held that the greatest source of gold was at or near the equator. Queen Isabella was aware of this speculation and asked her scientific advisor, Jaime Ferrer, to write to Columbus to inform him about the latest scientific theories regarding the location of precious metals. Ferrer, who turned out to be a kindred spirit to both the Queen and her Admiral, spent most of his letter analogizing Columbus's mission to that of the Apostles, especially the Apostle Thomas. But he ended his letter with the advice which the Queen had requested and placed gold into a religious context:

> Sir, it is indeed certain that the temporal things *in suo genere* are not evil or repugnant to things spiritual when we make good use of them, however, and [when used] for such purpose that God created them . . . the Queen, our Lady, commanded me to write to you of my knowledge . . . and I say that it is within the equinoctial regions where great and precious things, such as fine stones and gold [will be found].[49]

Ferrer based his theory upon observation that large amounts of precious metals had been found in areas where people lived near

the equator and had dark skins. Science could only speculate about the geophysics of gold by applying naive anthropological information, but his line of thought was important and would eventually lead to a paleocentrical theory in which gold and other metals would naturally collect near the equator due to the spin of the earth.

Better proof "existed," however, for Columbus in the Old Testament's historical record. The most abundant source for gold in world history had been the mines of Solomon, long ago lost but presumed to be in the Far East near the equator. Sources show that Columbus had long researched possible locations for gold and that he was convinced that King Solomon's mines were somewhere on the outer edge of Asia. Aeneas Sylvius Piccolomini (Pope Pius II), in his *Historia rerum ubique gestarum*, placed them in the Orient, and Columbus highlighted this opinion in his copy of that book [*Raccolta*, pt. I, vol. 2, p. 366, note 857]. An argument made in a short treatise by d'Ailly placed them in the distant southeastern extremity of Asia; the Admiral added a postille cross-referencing his statement to d'Ailly's *Imago mundi* and to his own notes, i.e., "my papers on the sphere" [*Raccolta*, pt. I, vol. 2, p. 386, note 166]. When he finally found gold in some quantity at Veragua, he declared that he was close to the fabled Ophir and Mount Sopora. After quoting Josephus and several Old Testament texts, he convinced himself that he was near the famous mines. He digressed in his letter of 1503 which described the fourth voyage:

> Josephus says that this gold [of Solomon] was found in Aurea. If so, I declare that those mines of Aurea are a part of these in Veragua which . . . are at the same distance from the pole and at the equator. . . . David in his will left Solomon 3000 quintals of gold from the *Indies* to aid in the building of the Temple and, according to Josephus, it was these same regions. Jerusalem and Mount Zion are now to be rebuilt by Christian hands.   [Varela, p. 327, italics ours]

Thus, to Columbus, God had shown David and Solomon where to find the gold necessary to build the temple; now God had shown Columbus those same regions in order that the proceeds be used by the Spanish monarchy to rebuild that same temple.

Jerusalem held a special allegorical significance to Columbus just as it did for many. To him, it was more than a place on the map, and it was the example that first came to mind for him to explain exegetical method at the beginning of the *Libro de las profecías*. Jerusalem to Columbus was the Jerusalem of St. Augustine, a symbol standing for an expanded future reality, a socio-moral standard, and a trend that operated through all ages of history. To think about Jerusalem was to think about history, to learn principles that have meaning for conduct of elect people of every age, to glimpse God's

future plans as disclosed to prophets. The Bible refers to the holy city in all these ways and encourages thought about the jeweled and golden house of many mansions seen by John. Ultimately, Jerusalem represented the unity and peace of the whole people of God.

Jerusalem was the goal of conquest, the mark of shame, the fretful evidence of defeat and humiliation and much more. The crusades were the endeavor that more than any other program gave unity and cohesive purpose to European Christendom, the collective venture that gave dynamic identity to Christian Europe as a civilization. They represented the coming of age of the new world that emerged from the devastation that swept over the old Christian world that had gathered about Jerusalem, Antioch, Alexandria, Ephesus, and other eastern centers. Jerusalem was not just a city and a principle. It was a powerful political symbol, a rallying cry understood by every Western Christian of whatever language.

We conclude this chapter on the piety and faith of Christopher Columbus by analyzing his famous signature. The themes of Columbus's Christian piety come together in his curious and unique signet. The pyramid of letters and punctuation marks never varied, but he would sometimes replace X̅p̅o̅ FERENS with "el Almirante" or "Virey." He never explained the meaning of this signet, but he did express his desire that his progeny continue using it. It is probably safe to say that the pyramid formation of the signature represents the Trinity. Many students of Columbus and his enterprise have since tried to decipher it. Endless speculation has twisted the monogram in every direction. It has been read forward and backward

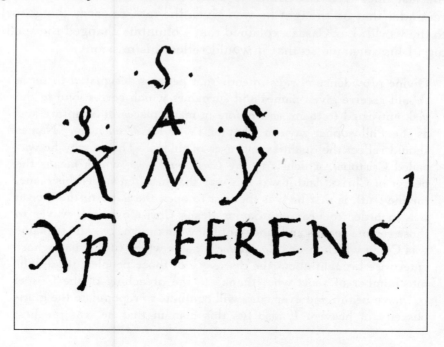

and from an inverted position. Thacher listed eight possible meanings for the signature, and the four most popular in the vast literature on Columbus are as follows:[50]

SERVUS
SUM ALTISSIMI SALVATORIS
XRISTE MARIA YESU
(I am the servant of the most exalted Saviour
Christ, Mary, Jesus)

SALVO
SANCTUM ALTISSIMUM SEPULCRUM
XRISTE MARIA YESU
(I shall save the Holy, most high sepulcher
Christ, Mary, Jesus)

SERVIDOR
SUS ALTEZAS SACRAS
XRISTE MARIA YSABEL
(The servant of the most exalted majesties
Christ, Mary, Isabella)

SUM
SEQUAX AMATOR SERVUS
XRISTI MARIAE YOSEPHI
(I am follower, devotee and servant of
Christ, Mary, Joseph)

Regardless of the meaning he attributed to the letters and dots, the last line, Xp̄o FERENS, is Graeco-Latin for his name and a reminder that he thought he was given the task to carry the gospel to the world. Las Casas explained that Columbus changed the spelling of his surname so that it would reflect his mission:

> Divine providence always intends that persons designated to serve should receive given names and surnames which correspond to the task entrusted to them, as we note in many places in Scripture and as the Philosopher says in Chapter IV of his *Metaphysics*, "Names should reflect the qualities and uses of things." This is why he was called Cristobal, which is to say *Christum Ferens*, which means the bearer of Christ. And it was this way that he often signed his name, for the truth is that he was the first to open the gates of the Ocean Sea in order to bear our Savior Jesus Christ over the waves to those remote realms and lands until now unknown. . . . His surname was Colon which means *repopulator*, a name which fit the man whose enterprise brought about the discovery of those peoples, those infinite number of souls who, thanks to the preaching of the Gospel . . . have begun and every day will continue to repopulate the glorious city of heaven. It also fits this man in that he was the first

to bring people from Spain . . . to found colonies, or new populations; which once established amid the original inhabitants . . . should constitute a new . . . Christian Church and a happy republic.

[Las Casas, p. 28]

Ferdinand confirms Las Casas's interpretation:

Reflecting on this, I was moved to believe that just as most of his affairs were directed by a secret Providence, so the variety of his name and surname was not without its mystery. . . . The Admiral's name foretold the novel and wonderful deed he was to perform. If we consider the common surname of his forebears, we may say that he was truly Columbus or Dove, because he carried the grace of the Holy Ghost to that New World which he discovered, showing those people who knew Him not Who was God's beloved son, as the Holy Ghost did in the figure of a dove when St. John baptized Christ; and because over the waters of the ocean, like the dove of Noah's ark, he bore the olive branch and oil of baptism, to signify that those people who had been shut up in the ark of darkness and confusion were to enjoy peace and union with the Church. . . . And if we give his name its Latin form, which is Christophorus Colonus, we may say that just as St. Christopher is reported to have gotten that name because he carried Christ over deep waters with great danger to himself, and just as he conveyed over people whom no other could have carried, so the Admiral Christophorus Colonus, asking Christ's aid and protection in that perilous pass, crossed over with his company that the Indian nations might become dwellers in the triumphant Church of Heaven.   [Ferdinand, p. 8]

Thus to contemporaries and to posterity he wished to be remembered as *Christum Ferens*, the Christ Bearer. Just as his legendary namesake, St. Christopher, had been ordered by Christ to plant his staff beside his hut so that it would be covered with fruit and blossoms in the morning, Columbus planted the cross of Christ in the New World so that it, too, might bear fruit and blossoms.

If, as we have claimed above, Columbus saw himself as the messenger of the New Age who bore the Gospel across the sea to those who had not known of it, and if that message blossomed to fruition to rejuvenate the Christian faith, then the typology which he had in mind for himself was that of a new John the Baptist. The Admiral's admiration for the precursor of Christ is expressed by a poem copied into the *Libro de las profecías* [L.P., 237]. John the Baptist was the last prophet of the Old Testament and the messenger of the New Testament. He paved the way for Christ's mission during the First Advent as Columbus would pave the way for the Second Advent. Although we hesitate to add to the confusion of interpretations surrounding Columbus's signet, another is possible.

SALVO
SANCTUM ALTISSIMUM SEPULCRUM
XRISTE MARIA YOANNES
(I shall save the holy, most high sepulcher
Christ, Mary, John [the Baptist])

There is no evidence that he used this signet until after the turn of the century, nor is it likely that he added X$\overline{po}$ Ferens until even later [Varela, p. lxxi]. The symbolism of the signature is plain enough as it included all the themes of his religious and eschatological beliefs: his devotion to the Trinity, his adoration of Christ and Mary, the hope to recapture Jerusalem, and his role as the messenger of a New Heaven and a New Earth.

The primary instruction and concern of the second voyage was the salvation of the souls in the lands Columbus had discovered. It was so ordered by the monarchs, who encouraged Columbus to take missionaries with him as well as colonists. The naming of major islands encountered on this trip was symbolic of this mission and of his role in spreading the Gospel. The first island he named Dominica because it was sighted on Sunday, but he then proceeded with appellations that honor either the Virgin or great missionary saints — Santa Maria de Guadalupe, Santa Maria de Monserrate, San Martin, San Jorge, San Anastasia. Then he names in succession, San Cristobal, Santa Cruz, and San Juan Bautista.

In summary, Christopher Columbus looked upon himself as a man of destiny who had been given a charismatic gift to understand Scripture, navigation, maps, winds, tides, astronomy, cosmography, mathematics and related sciences. His understanding of his mission, or enterprise, was drawn from the Bible or proved by the Bible, and he knew that he was opening up new lands rich with gold and other valuables. He believed himself a chosen person working for the good of all Christendom in opening up the rest of the world to the gospel message. He knew that he would be misunderstood and maligned, but he accepted that as the lot of a divinely chosen person. He thought himself a precursor who would open the ways and set the standards for the conquest and appropriation of new lands, and he believed most strongly that proper utilization of those new lands would enable the Spanish monarchs, and all Christendom, to recapture the Holy Temple in Jerusalem.

The chief concern of Christopher Columbus was not what men would think of him but what God would think of him. His earliest biographers reveal this character clearly by trying to relate him to Old Testament characters. The apparent inconsistencies in his story and action are not so much weaknesses and lapses as his own attempts at accommodation to political realities in a world in which his particular kind of motivation was rare and difficult to engage. He was a man of vision, dreams, hope. All of these goals

were unintelligible to many of his contemporaries and to nearly all of his biographers and readers in the succeeding five hundred years. But the goals were perfectly clear in the light of his biblical sources and world events as seen through the eyes of prophecy.

✝ Notes

1. Bishop las Casas was named the "Apostle of the Indies" because of his obsession with ending the Spanish tyranny in the New World. Las Casas denounced Spain's greed for gold and power as a moral aberration that would lead to the nation's moral, economic, and political suicide, inviting divine judgment for the destructive exploitation of the Indies.

2. The most recent claim that Columbus was Byzantine Greek is from R. Durlacher-Wolper, "The Identity of Christopher Columbus." This unresearched article has Columbus an exiled member of the Palaeologus family who came from the isle of Chios. Durlacher-Wolper offers no proof for the claim.

3. S. de Madariaga, *Christopher Columbus: Being the Life of the Very Magnificent Lord Don Cristóbal Colón*, pp. 360–61. Sweet, "Christopher Columbus," pp. 376–78, effectively argues against Madariaga's thesis.

4. Maderiaga, p. 362.

5. On the problem of Columbus's meaning of the term "Casa Santa," see J. Gil, "Colón y la Casa Santa." Gil is the most creditable modern scholar who holds to the belief that Columbus was a converso Jew. He does not advocate that Columbus had some sort of secret Jewish agenda, such as finding a homeland for exiled Spanish Jews, but rather reasons that Columbus's Jewish origins combined with his Christian beliefs to produce an eschatology from both sources. See Gil, *Mitos y utopías*, pp. 206–17, for this argument.

6. The only challenge to the sincerity of Columbus's piety that we know about was made by William Gillett and Charles Gillett, "The Religious Motives of Christopher Columbus," pp. 18–19, where the Gilletts claim that "in these extracts [from the sources] we fail to find anything which necessitates or justifies the suppositions of those who imagine that we must incorporate religious motives with those of material advantage." It is difficult for us to understand what "sources" the Gilletts were reading since religious motives stand out so strongly in all of the Admiral's writings.

7. *Raccolta*, pt. I, vol. 2, "Illustrazione al Documento XXXII," p. lviii.

8. For Christopher Columbus's devotion to the Virgin see, I. Bengoechea Izaguine, "La Virgen Maria en la vide y la obra de Cristóbal Colón."

9. See copy of Ferrer's letter in J. Thacher, *Christopher Columbus*, 2:369.

10. A. Giustiniani, *Polyglot Psalter*, note D.

11. C. Markham, *Life of Christopher Columbus*, p. 223, also believes this to be drawn by Columbus, proving that the Admiral had "a bold, free touch, and some artistic feeling."

12. In 1507, King Ferdinand was received at Savona by Louis XII of France. In 1529, King Charles V entered Italy at Genoa on his way to receive the crown of the Holy Roman Empire. And, in 1545, King Philip II visited Genoa on his way to Germany and the Low Countries.

13. See examples of his frescos and drawings in L. Ragghianti, "Lazzaro Tavarone disegnatore," or M. Newcome, "Drawings by Tavarone."

14. D. Ludlum, "Early American Hurricanes, 1492–1870," p. 2, demonstrates that this was not a hurricane but a "well-developed example of extra-tropical cyclonic storms."

15. This is the first connection of the famous Lady of Guadelupe with the New World. Within a hundred years, she would become the patron of Mexico, revered throughout the Americas. On his second voyage, Columbus named the first island he discovered "Dominica" because he sighted it on a Sunday. The second, however, he named "Santa Maria de Guadalupe" in honor of the Extremadura apparition.

16. The oral tradition of Columbus's exorcism is found in A. Herrera Tordesillas, *Historia general de los hechos de las Castellanos*, I, lib. V, chap. 3.

17. Andrés Martín, *Los Recogido: Nueva vision de la mistica española (1500–1700)*, pp. 12–13.

18. P. Mulhern, "Gifts of the Holy Spirit," 7:99–100. *Spiritualis intellectus* was promised in Isaiah 11:1–3 and given to the Apostles at Pentecost. The church fathers saw this and other gifts as special aids for Christians to use against evil. St. Thomas Aquinas believed that all gifts from the Holy Spirit were supernatural aids to enable the receiver to achieve natural perfection. In the later Middle Ages, *spiritualis intellectus* was claimed by many individuals and groups. The importance of *spiritualis intellectus* to the Spiritual Franciscans, for example, who greatly affected Columbus's ideas through their influence upon the Observantine reform movement, was primary, as it validated their claims to be the new spiritual men predicted by Joachim of Fiore. The Spiritual Franciscans believed that the age into which the world was entering would be illuminated with a true form of *spiritualis intellectus*. See Reeves, *Prophecy in the Later Middle Ages*, p. 210 and E. Benz, *Ecclesia Spiritualis*, pp. 128–31.

19. V. Milina, *The Written Language of Christopher Columbus*, pp. 129–30.

20. See E. Barzan, "Los Franciscanos y Colón," for a detailed list of proven and possible contacts with the Franciscan Order.

21. Milhou, *Colón y su mentalidad mesiánica*, pp. 42–51, summarizes the problem.

22. A. Bernáldez, *Historia de los Reyes Catolicos Don Fernando y Doña Isabel* I, ser. 1, pt. II, p. 78.

23. Iriarte, *Franciscan History*, p. 491.

24. Ibid., p. 493.

25. Benz, *Ecclesia Spiritualis*, p. 42. See also D. West, "The Reformed Church and the Friars Minor," p. 274.

26. Bengoechea Izaguine, "La Virgen Maria," pp. 427–28.

27. Fray Gorricio wrote this sometime between 1491 and 1505. For a description of this treatise, see M. Serrano y Sanz, *El archivo colombino de la Cartuja de las Cuevos. Estudio histórico y bibliográfico, Cristóbal Colón y descubremiento de América*, p. 676.

28. "Cometi viaja de nuevo al cielo y mundo que fasta entonçes estaba oculto." This is the first time he recognizes his discovery as a "New World."

29. A. Roselly de Lorgues, *L'Ambassadeur de Dieu et le Pape Pie IX*, p. 381.

30. Pou y Martí, "Visionarios," p. 54

31. Alba, "Acerca de Algunas," p. 176. See also P. Balaguer, "La visión de Alfonso X y las 'profícias de Merlin'."

32. *Historia de los hechos de Don Rodrigo Ponce de León, Marqués de Cádiz*, t. 106, pp. 247–48.

33. Alba, "Acerca de Algunas," p. 200.

34. In the *Breviloquium*, the writer places John the Baptist as announcer of the Joachite Second Age and St. Francis as the announcer of the Third Age and initiator of the sixth *tempus* in the history of the church: *Summula seu Breviloquium super Concordia novi et veteri Testamenti*, ff. 16r and 34r.

35. D. West, "Medieval Ideas of Apocalyptic Mission and the Early Franciscans in Mexico," p. 297.

36. Anastos dates this memorandum as April 1493 in S. Morison, ed. and trans., *Journals and Other Documents on the Life and Voyages of Christopher Columbus*, p. 199. This date is based on Las Casas, chap. 77, who says that it was written before Columbus left on the second voyage. Thacher, 3:98, agrees, as does de Lollis, *Raccolta*, 1:136. Varela, who has made the most recent study of Columbus's letters and memoranda, places it after the second voyage.

37. Morison, *Journals and Other Documents*, p. 204.

38. Thacher, *Christopher Columbus*, 2:204.

39. J. Cummins, "Christopher Columbus: Crusader, Visionary and Servus Dei," p. 45.

40. W. Shiels, *King and Church: The Rise and Fall of the Patronato Real*, p. 4.

41. Ibid., p. 66.

42. Ibid.

43. H. Linden, "Alexander VI and the Demarcation of the Maritime and Colonial Domains of Spain and Portugal, 1493–1494," p. 2.

44. E. Sylvest, *Motifs of Franciscan Mission Theory in Sixteenth-Century New Spain Province of the Holy Gospel*, p. 13.

45. S. Eijan, *Hispanidad en Tierra Santa-Actuacion diplomatica*, pp. 30–38.

46. M. Doussinague, *La politica internacional de Fernando el Catolico*, p. 723. See also G. Gaztambide, *Historia de la Bula de la Cruzada in España*, pp. 672–74.

47. J. Wright, *Human Nature and Geography*, p. 266, coined the term "geotheology" of which "geoeschatology" is an aspect. See also Sweet, "Christopher Columbus," pp. 380–82, on the eschatological importance of Jerusalem to Columbus.

48. C. Singleton, "Stars Over Eden," p. 5. Dante located Eden in the southern hemisphere as far as geographically possible from Jerusalem.

49. Thacher, *Christopher Columbus*, 2:366.

50. Ibid., 3:456.

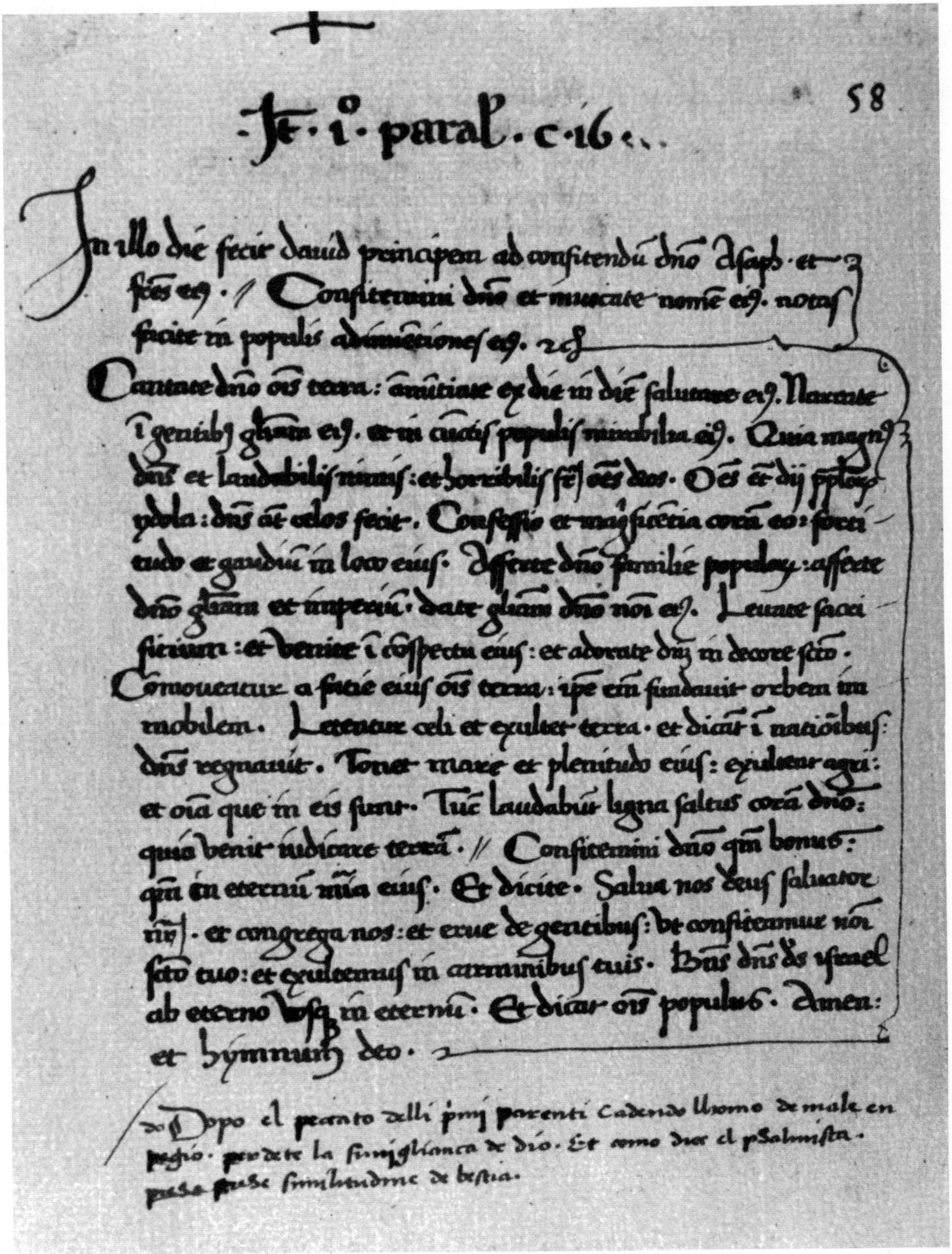

Figure 5: Manuscript page with note written by Columbus in humanistic Italian

4

The Libro de las profecías: Its History and Meaning

The winter and spring of 1501–2 were extremely busy for the Admiral of the Ocean Sea. He had been returned to Spain in chains after his third voyage, and his health was deteriorating because of rheumatoid complications. Of some eighty-five extant letters and memoranda in his hand, a full 20 percent, or twenty-one, were written during these months. They display the range of his interests and activities at the time. He was actively trying to clear himself of the charges brought by Bobadillo, at the same time preparing for his fourth voyage and compiling his *Book of Privileges* in an effort to guarantee that those rewards, titles, and commissions granted by the monarchs would be granted to him and to his heirs. On top of these activities, he was actively compiling the *Libro de las profecías*. Both the *Book of Privileges* and the *Libro de las profecías* are in handwritings different from his own, showing that he was guiding their production while concentrating his energies on immediate problems.

Gerald Weissmann, director of the Division of Rheumatology at the New York University School of Medicine, has studied the symptoms of Columbus's various maladies and concluded that he suffered from Reiter's syndrome, a severe form of rheumatoid arthritis. Reiter's syndrome is diagnosed "by a triad of arthritis, uveitis, and urethritis: inflammation of the joints, eyes and terminal urinary tract."[1] Reconstructing a case history of Columbus's illness and comparing it to known case histories of the disease, Weissmann demonstrates that the malady became so crippling by 1502 that special contraptions had to be built aboard ship for the Admiral, that he was frequently bedridden and had to be carried ashore on occasion. The syndrome can be acquired from intestinal bacteria, although some indirect evidence of modern cases may suggest venereal spread as well. Whether he died from one of the complications of Reiter's syndrome or some other cause cannot be established without autopsy, but, as is well known, he did die shortly after his fourth voyage in 1506 at the young age of fifty-five.

Reiter's syndrome would not have affected Columbus's mind. Some of his most important biographers have claimed that disease caused him to sink into some sort of stupor, thereby turning his

attention to biblical prophecy.[2] But what it would have done is incapacitate him for weeks at a time and make research and writing extremely difficult. He had to have friends and relatives help in the compilation of the *Libro de las profecías*.

We have little reason to question that the manuscript was compiled between 13 September 1501 and 23 March 1502. Most of the text is reliably dated by the correspondence between Columbus and Father Gaspar Gorricio attached at the front of the collection. Internal references also confirm the dates. Some notes were added to blank sections, such as the events of the eclipse of the moon on the night of 29 February 1504, while Columbus was marooned in the bay he called Santa Gloria on the island of Jamaica.

The complete manuscript of the *Libro de las profecías* has 84 folios, of which some sheets have been removed and a few left blank. There are nine blank sheets, or 4.5 folios, three sheets, or 1.5 folios, with only one sentence on the page, and 14.5 sheets, or 16.5 folios, removed. Attached at the beginning of the manuscript are letters between Columbus and Father Gorricio, and added to the end of the manuscript is a page containing a long poem and further scriptural references to be worked into the text. The bound manuscript is preserved in the Biblioteca Columbina in the Cathedral at Seville, Spain.

The title, *Libro de las profecías*, is a misnomer given the manuscript from the earliest listings. The actual incipit reads:

> Incipit liber s[ive manipulus de au]ctoritatibus, dictis, ac sentiis, et p[rophetiis circa] materiam recuperande sancte civitatis, et montis Dei Syon, ac inventionis & conversionis insularum Indie, et omnium gentium atque nationum, ad Ferdinandum et Helysabeth etc. reges nostros hyspanos.   [L.P., 101]

A more descriptive, more accurate, and less confusing title would be "Handbook, or Notebook of Prophecies." It is best described as a working manuscript in which the Admiral was collecting sources and ideas for a long apocalyptic poem. He clearly stated in a letter to Father Gorricio, dated from Granada on 13 September 1501, that he intended to revise the materials and turn them into poetic form ("para después tornarlas a rever y las poner en rima") [Varela, p. 285].

The manuscript was first mentioned in a letter from Columbus to his friend the Carthusian monk Father Gaspar Gorricio, in which the Admiral asked the monk to read the compilation and edit and add references where necessary. Father Gorricio's answering letter indicates that little was changed in the original manuscript. Reference to the *Libro de las profecías* is next found in an inventory of Don Diego's property and then cataloged as item number 2091 in

Don Ferdinand's library. The text is mentioned as a source by both Ferdinand in his biography of the Admiral and by Bishop Bartolomé de las Casas in his history. It was carefully described in detail by the principal librarian of the Biblioteca Colombina, D. Diego Alexandro de Galvey, in 1766 in a letter to a colleague, D. Juan Manuel de Santander.[3] This letter shows the manuscript to be identical to that which we have today. It was described and recataloged by la Rosa y Lopez in his *Biblioteca Colombina catálogo de sus libros impresos* in 1888.[4]

Although seen and mentioned by early scholars such as Navarrete, Harrisse, and Irving, it was not used.[5] The first printing of the text was by Cesare de Lollis in the *Raccolta di Documenti e studi pubblicati dalla R. Commissione Colombiana* in 1892. Most recently, the document has been printed in exact facsimile in the Colección Tabula Americae, edited by Professor Francisco Morales Padrón. The facsimile is accompanied by a Spanish translation of the text by D. Francisco Alvarez Seisdedos, the first translation into any modern language.[6]

The basic parts of the notebook were written in the hands of Columbus's thirteen-year-old son, Ferdinand, and Father Gaspar Gorricio. More specifically, Father Gorricio's hand begins the book with notes on scriptural exegesis. A passage copied from Nicholas of Lyra *Glossa ordinaria*, "on Daniel, Chapter 8," follows to furnish an example of the foregoing hermeneutical suggestions. This hand is unidentified. Then follows, or has been inserted later, the famous letter to the Catholic monarchs, designed to accompany the notebook, which explains its content and Columbus's eschatological beliefs. This letter we believe to be written by the Admiral himself.

After the letter to the monarchs, the next several folios (6b–15a) are in the hand of Father Gorricio, with the small exception of a poem added to the end of folio 12a by an unknown hand. Folios 15b–20b are in an unknown hand with interspersed textual comments and marginal notes by Columbus himself. The handwriting of Father Gorricio continues at folio 21a–22a. Folios 22b, 23a and 23b are blank pages. Folio 24a–28b are in the same hand as 15b–20b. Father Gorricio again writes the text from folio 29a through folio 30a. Up to this point, the material in the *Libro de las profecías* consists of general biblical references and passages from church fathers and famous theologians. These collected references and passages announce and describe Columbus's twofold eschatological purpose: the evangelization of the whole world and the recapture of Zion by the Spanish monarchy.

The essence of the *Libro de las profecías* begins on folio 30b in the section entitled "Concerning What Has Already Taken Place" ("De Preterio"), that is, what has taken place in relation to the two

themes. The section begins with Ferdinand's hand and concludes on folio 53b. Two more blank pages separate this section from the next, which begins on folio 54b, again written by Ferdinand, and entitled "On the Present and the Future" ("De Presenti et Futuro"). Ferdinand's hand abruptly ends on 57b, and the section is continued by Father Gorricio on folio 58a (at the bottom of this page is the statement by Christopher Columbus written in Italian). Folio 58b contains a poem in an unknown hand followed by one and a half blank pages. The text picks up again on folio 59b with the famous passage from Seneca's *Medea* written and translated into Spanish by Columbus himself. The rest of this page contains two more notes by Columbus listing eclipses of the moon, one in 1494 and the other in 1504.

After Columbus's notes, on folio 60a, Father Gorricio again begins the text of this section and continues through folio 62a. (Columbus, however, added a note at the end of folio 61b.) Folio 62b is a passage copied from Nicholas of Lyra's *Glossa ordinaria* by an unknown hand. Folios 63a–66b are missing from the notebook. Folio 67b begins the third section of the notebook and is entitled "Prophecies of the Future. The Last Days." ("De Futuro. In Novissimus.") One half of folio 67b has been cut out, and the next ten sheets are missing. Folio 77a has a short poem inserted at the bottom of the page by an unknown writer, then Father Gorricio's hand continues this section, beginning on folio 77b and going to the end of the manuscript. The end sheets, folio 83b–84b, are in the hands of Columbus, Ferdinand, and Father Gorricio: 83b contains lists of donations Columbus wished to make, 84a is blank, and 84b lists more Scripture references and a long poem written in both margins.

The excised sheets between folios 67b and 77a have presented a mystery to Columbus scholars for a long time. One early reader in fact wrote across f. 77a: "Mal hizo quien hurto de aqui estas hojas porque era lo mejor de las profecias deste libro" ("An evil deed was done by whoever ripped from here these sheets because it was the best of the prophecies of this book").

The third section is introduced by the entire twenty-fifth chapter of the prophecy of Jeremiah, which predicted the coming destruction of Jerusalem and glimpses the wider horizon of final, universal divine judgment upon all the nations. Then follows a fascinating reference to other prophecies of an age of restoration prior to the final judgment as interpreted from the Bible by Joachim of Fiore. Columbus cites evidence that Joachim taught that the age of renewal, the restoration of Zion, was to begin in Spain. At precisely that point, the next nine and one half sheets are missing. We shall probably never know what the missing pages contained or who

removed them. They may have been cut out by the Admiral himself, or by his heirs.

We can only offer possible explanations for the removal of the sheets: (1) The comments and compilations on these pages were objectionable to persons who were able to cut and remove the sheets. This possibility may have been especially strong if the passages here relied heavily upon the Calabrian Abbot Joachim of Fiore, for his teachings and those of his followers were suspect during the Inquisition in Spain. Such an act of mutilation could have been done by the inquisitors themselves in their attempts to suppress ideas viewed as dangerous heresies following the publication of Luther's *Babylonian Captivity of the Church*, or the sheets might have been removed by relatives or friends of the Admiral so that he would not be accused of adhering to strange doctrines. (2) One of his sons, his grandson (Luis), or other descendants removed the material because it was believed to be damaging to their lengthy court cases over the Admiral's titles, rights, and privileges. (3) Government censors seeking to suppress potentially revolutionary writings among the papers of an influential national hero might have destroyed the pages, but this is not too likely because we know that the sheets were missing before 1766. (4) Bishop las Casas, the last known person to have used the text, may have destroyed the section if it contained comments derogatory to Indian peoples. He was the most outspoken advocate for Indian rights before the Spanish courts, and if a Columbus document contained material damaging to his case he might have removed it. (5) The manuscript may have suffered the same fate that modern library books do by readers who remove pages for their own use. The books in the cathedral library were not well protected and suffered much damage during the sixteenth and seventeenth centuries.

So many hands working on the notebook has led to endless confusion about its meaning and purpose. We propose, however, that the entire project was being directed and overseen by the Admiral himself. Evidence for this is that he inserted his own notes and comments where he wished, on page bottoms and in the margins to the copied text.

Inserted at the beginning of the manuscript folios are letters between Columbus and his friend, collaborator, and fellow Italian Father Gorricio, a Carthusian monk. The letter dated 13 September 1501 from Columbus to the monk explains his intent in the *Libro de las profecías*, that is, to revise it and compose a poem from it, but he had not had time to complete his work. He sought Father Gorricio's help as a reader, asking him to add anything the monk thought relevant. The letter is torn and incomplete. There follows the response of Gorricio from his monastery at Las Cuevas, dated

23 March 1502. Father Gorricio had had six months to review the material. We quote in full the letter as it clearly states the extent of collaboration by Father Gorricio:

> My most noble and distinguished Lord: In my other letter, I reported to your lordship having received your letter and book of prophecies and opinions and authorities relating to the matter of Mt. Zion and Jerusalem and the peoples of the islands and all nations. As I am able with my inadequate intelligence, since you command, I have worked at it as best I was able, especially since it is such a sacred project, hoping to be instructed and to have my understanding awakened in things to the service of the Lord our God, and for the benefit and honor of our Sovereigns and the whole of the Christian religion. *Thus, by the grace of the Holy Spirit, and guided by the work of your lordship which presented me with the abundance of so many and such true authorities, opinions, statements and opinions,* I have interposed and added a few remaining items, as one who reaches for the leftovers on the branches of the olives and the grain. Thus, with your original material, as well as the crumbs, I am very content, and in this way I have been introduced to a subject very remote from my own studies. In this I find great pleasure, praying to Our Lord that he would fulfill "what he has spoken by the mouth of the prophets." May it please his infinite mercy to do this, and to carry forward the holy desires of your lordship, just as your noble person has called to our undeserving attention the islands of the Indies and the mainland. My lord, the little that I have added, and intermixed, your lordship will find in my handwriting. I send the whole work back again for correction by your spirit and prudent. . . . I have not attempted to reorganize the opinions, or the subjects, far less the . . . historical material, but I have inserted some rules and opinions of the doctors on the subject, by which any careful reader may be instructed and have clarified the doubts that may occur to him. Throughout I have been as brief as I could, by referring back to the originals and also by avoiding the offense of writing too much, especially as I have recognized that in the material your lordship prepared, and in what I added, if there is not a most abundant supply of authorities, and prophecies for the expressed purpose . . . books of the Old and New Testaments, nor all the holy fathers and doctors have written, then may it please the Lord to give the spirit with the will and desire for the task, and that will suffice. If you lordship instructs anything further, in this as in other matters, you know you will find me ready and waiting. Done in this his holy house of Las Cuevas, the twenty-third of March, the year 1502.

> [*Raccolta*, pt. I, vol. 2, pp. 75–76. italics ours]

There is little reason to doubt that the *Libro de las profecías* is an authentic work by the explorer. As Father Gorricio stated in his letter, the conception of the work was Columbus's, as was the

scope, the outline, the method, and the selection of most of the material. As to whether the whole purpose of the book and its conclusions are authentically his, we need only point out that these are stated in the "Letter from the Admiral to the King and Queen," inserted in the text. The work as a whole is exactly what he titled it: *"liber sive manipulus"*—a book or a collection, sheaf, armful of interpretations and prophecies. The *Libro de las profecías* presents related selections of biblical data, with carefully chosen representations of highly respected interpretations. The letter to the monarchs presents the Navigator's own conclusions arising from his practical experience and personal faith, assisted by the written material as an instrument to bring to focus divinely revealed truth on the subjects that interested him. Columbus presumes, with emphasized professions of his own humble origins and unworthiness, to exhort and counsel his king and queen. He does not simply urge conclusions or ideas supported by reasons. He presents a full selection of biblical quotations, along with highly respected interpretations, and urges that this material be allowed to inspire and to inform the personal faith and inner processes of spiritual experience of the sovereigns. The *Libro de las profecías* is a sermon, in a sense, and its author is the preacher and messenger of "great events for the world" to be accomplished by those who have "so much faith as a grain of mustard seed," and who may, like Columbus himself, "be certain that there will be success" because God "makes himself responsible" for the fulfillment of the prophecies he has disclosed in the Bible.

Historians and biographers have told and retold the story of the life and accomplishments of Christopher Columbus using more or less the same original documents. Most have viewed the *Libro de las profecías* as genuine but as a kind of relatively unimportant excursion into fanaticism that occurred late in the explorer's life.[7] Others attempting to prove that Columbus was a converso Jew have seen the *Libro de las profecías* as a kind of *auto da fé*. The manuscript was seen as a demonstration of something less than entire sincerity, intended to convince the sovereigns and the world of his orthodox Christian beliefs. At the same time, they have contended, he cryptically advanced the interests of the race and religion of Jews persecuted and displaced by the Inquisition. Still others, with more apparent credentials and credibility, view the work as a characteristic product of his complex mind and personal ambitions of grandeur, festooning his titles and his discoveries with grandiose decorations of the most extreme sort. Yet others have accepted the document as authentic and have recognized that it reveals its author as he really was, in his early life as well as in later years: intensely medie-

val and mystical in his deep spirituality, resolutely tenacious in pursuing his mystical concepts.

The *Libro de las profecías* has not exerted much influence in the affairs of men. It has lain unstudied and unread in the Biblioteca Colombina. There was slight interest in the document after Navarette published it in a condensed form in 1825. Washington Irving knew of it and used it for his *The Life and Voyages of Christopher Columbus*. The real discovery of the document, however, was in France with the reappraisal of Columbus's missionary work. Count Roselly de Lorgues in a series of articles and books called attention to the Christian piety of Columbus at the encouragement of Pope Pius IX and sought to persuade the church to make the Admiral a saint.[8] Roselly's many studies inspired León Bloy's *Le Revelateur du globe*, which in turn served as the source for Paul Claudel's popular play, "Le Livre de Christophe Colomb."[9]

The only scholarly influence exerted by the *Libro de las profecías*, that we can find, was on the writings of the nineteenth-century French historian Edgar Quinet. He cited the *Libro de las profecías* in his *La Christianisme et la révolution française* and in *La Révolution religieuse du dix-neuvième siècle*. He found powerful ammunition in the writings of Christopher Columbus for his theme of *l'ideé de l'Eglise universelle*, a church that would encompass the entire world and one that would find its regenerated strength in the New World.[10]

As stated, Christopher Columbus compiled his *Libro de las profecías* during the years 1501–2, adding some notes and possibly enlarging the work as late as 1505. Systematic Bible studies, however, were a lifelong pursuit of the Admiral. The earliest biographers, and his own contemporaries, recognized him as a student of biblical prophecies and a man of disciplined religious vocation. The *Libro de las profecías* was the end result of many years of study and contemplation.

Among the handwritten notes, or postilles, on the margins and blank pages of one of the earliest volumes in the personal library of Christopher Columbus, we have found clear evidence of an earlier, smaller version of the *Libro de las profecías* bearing the date 1481. Columbus was at that time thirty years old, and both his use of the Bible and his plan for a voyage of discovery are already discernible in the notes. The volume bearing these notes, preserved today in the Biblioteca Colombina at Seville, was printed in Venice in 1477. It is his copy of Aeneas Sylvius Piccolomini (Pope Pius II), *Historia rerum ubique gestarum*. Four postilles written in the clear hand of Columbus on the blank pages at the end of Piccolomini's treatise form the essence of the later *Libro de las profecías*.

The first of these postilles on biblical sources is headed by the

title *"Auctoritates in brevia"* and reads as follows from the Piccolomini volume.

SUMMARY OF AUTHORITIES

They shall lift up their voices in praise; when the Lord shall be glorified, their rejoicing shall sound across the sea. Give glory to God because of these teachings, as the name of the God of Israel is among the islands of the sea. We have recognized his praises coming from the uttermost parts of the earth, the song of triumph of his Righteous one.   [Isaiah 24:14–16]

Once every three years the king's (Solomon's) fleet would sail to Tharsis, with the servants of Hiram, and from there they would bring back gold, and silver, and ivory, and apes, and peacocks.

[II Chronicles 9:21]

Ours is a God who, before time began, accomplished his saving work to be in the middle of the earth.   [Psalm 73 (74): 12]

Note that this should be understood as "in the middle of the land of promise."   [*Raccolta*, pt. 1, vol. 2, p. 365, no. 855].

These quotations deal with three subjects to appear later in the *Libro de las profecías:* the remotest ends of the earth, the islands of the sea, waiting to be taught the name of the Lord and to learn to glorify him; the ships of Solomon, which made journeys every three years to bring back great wealth; and God's arranging for his saving work to take place in the middle of the lands, that is, the promised land.

The second of the series is entitled *Aurelii Augustini De Civitatte Dei libro 17 capitulo 24 quod Esdras fuit propheta.*

AURELIUS AUGUSTINE, *CITY OF GOD*
BOOK 17, CHAPTER 24
THAT ESDRAS WAS A PROPHET

During all the time after the Jews returned from Babylon, following Malachi, Haggai and Zachariah who were prophesying then, and Ezra, there were no more prophets until the advent of the Savior, unless you count Zachariah the father of John and Elizabeth his wife, who were so close to the birth of Christ, and after his birth the aged Simeon, and the aged widow Anna, and John himself who was the last of all, who as a young man did not actually predict that Christ was to come, but instead pointed out the unrecognized Christ as an act of prophetic recognition. Because of this the Lord said, "The law and the prophets were until John." Also with these five instances of prophecy known to us in the Gospels, should be included the Virgin Mother of the Lord, who prophesied before John the Baptist. The reprobate among the Jews did not accept their prophecy, but it was accepted by the countless Jews who did believe the Gospel. Indeed at that time Israel was divided into

two parts, a division that the prophet Samuel in the days of King Saul predicted would be permanent. Now Malachi, Haggai, Zachariah and Ezra were received as the last in the authoritative canon also by the reprobate Jews. Their writings are like the writings of the others, those few people in the great multitude who prophesied and who wrote the things preserved as authoritative canon. The many things among their predictions that refer to Christ and his Church, I will not write in this work, but with God's help in the next book, which will be more suitable, lest here we should be burdened with too many more details.

[Raccolta, pt. 1, vol. 2, p. 366, no. 856]

This is a list of the canonical Hebrew prophets of the period after the return of the Jews from exile in Babylon. Augustine states that he will show that many of their prophecies (as also the other prophets) refer to Christ and his church. This theme will be a central one in the *Libro de las profecías*.

The third of the series Columbus titled: *Josepius De antiquitatibus libro 8 capitulo 3.*

FLAVIUS JOSEPHUS, *ANTIQUITIES OF THE JEWS* BOOK 8, CHAPTER 3

The king (Solomon) then also built many ships in the Egyptian Channel of the Red Sea, at a place called Ezion Geber, not far from the Greek city that is now called Beronica. At that time the kingdom of the Jews was in its pristine condition, and they had the assistance of the technology of Hiram of Tyre for constructing the ships. For he sent many navigators and other specialists in maritime sciences, whom he commanded to navigate with their provisioners to the place then called Ophir, which is now called the Gold Country, which is in India, to gather gold there, and after collecting four hundred talents, they were to return again to the king.

In those days, the kings brought back from the place called the Gold Country precious stones and pine timbers, to be used for the strengthening of the temple and for the royal palace and for instruments of music. And he used this to make zithers and nablas, for singing before God the hymns of the Levites. The things that were brought back in those days were superior in both beauty and quantity to all that was ever brought back to the king in any other time. In no way can what is sold today at a good price as pine wood be compared with that wood; it had the same round piney knots, but it was much clearer and extremely beautiful. I mentioned this as one who knows something about the true quality of pine. Now for the purpose of an accurate reminder of that king, I think we should indicate the quantity of the gold brought back to him in those times, which was by weight six hundred and sixty six talents, not including that which the merchants bought, or what

the kings sent as a gift to the coparch of Arabia. The gold was sufficient to make two hundred lances, which were of six hundred shekels; he also made three hundred shields, each one having three minas of gold, and placed them in the house which was called the Forest of Lebanon, along with whatever other items of gold and precious stones were necessary for banquets. And while he made all these things in a single order from the craftsmen, he also directed that other gold vessels be crafted more slowly. The gold and the silver were not sold and bought, but there were many ships that the king commissioned to sail to the sea of Tharsis, so that they would penetrate into the interior land of the nations, and so that they could buy all kinds of things, and then bring back to the king the goods purchased and the gold and silver, including some elephants, and peacocks, and apes. The sea journey outward and homeward required three years. The illustrious fame of the king spread about all the provinces, disclosing his power and his wisdom everywhere, so that all the rulers everywhere desired to see him personally, because of the unbelievable things that were said about him, and by making very rich gifts they demonstrated their great interest concerning him. Therefore they sent to him aromatic spices, and carts and horses, and asses and mules, all of which pleased the king because of their quality and beauty. (And the rest as it is in the text.)   [*Raccolta*, pt. I, vol. 2, pp. 366–67, no. 857]

Josephus described the voyages of Solomon's fleet, assisted by Phoenician technology, to the "land of gold" called Ophir, located in India. He described the immense riches brought back from those lands so distant that the voyages were made once every three years. This idea was elaborated further in the *Libro de las profecías*, combining with the interpretation of the Old Testament prophecies as referring to Christ and the church. Prophecies of the restoration of Zion and Jerusalem are thus considered to predict the future wealth, glory and peaceable kingdom of Christ and his church.

The fourth of the series is headed by the title *Esta es la coenta de la criacion del mondo segondo lo Judios*; the language of this postille is Spanish with strong traces of Portuguese.

THIS IS THE CHRONOLOGY FROM THE CREATION OF THE WORLD ACCORDING TO THE JEWS

Adam lived 130 years, and then fathered Seth. Seth lived 105 years, and then fathered Enos. Enos lived 90 years, and then fathered Cainan. Cainan lived 70 years, and then fathered Malalchel. Malalchel lived 65 years, and then fathered Enoch. Enoch lived 65 years, and then fathered Mathusalen. Mathusalen lived 187 years, and then fathered Lamech. Lamech lived 182 years, and then fathered Noah. Noah lived 500 years, and then fathered Seth, and Seth was one hundred years old when the flood came. Thus, from the creation

of the world to the flood were 1656 years. Seth lived two years after the one hundred mentioned above, and after the flood he fathered Arphaxad. Arphaxad lived 35 years, and then fathered Sala. Sala lived 30 years, and then fathered Heber. Heber lived 34 years, and then fathered Phalech. Phalech lived 30 years, and then fathered Reu. Reu lived 35 years and then fathered Saruch. Saruch lived 30 years, and then fathered Abraham. And from the flood to the birth of Abraham are 295 years, and, according to the Jews, there are 292. Abraham lived one hundred years and then fathered Isaac. Isaac lived. . . .

From the birth of Isaac until they went out from Egypt, 400 years. And after they left Egypt until the first Temple was constructed, 480 years. And after the first Temple was constructed until its destruction are 410 years. And after the first Temple was destroyed until the return from the captivity in Babylon makes 70 years, and then was begun the second Temple. And the second Temple lasted 400 years. And from the birth of Abraham until the second Temple was destroyed 1088 years. And from the destruction of the second Temple, according to the Jews, until the present, this being the year of the birth of our Lord 1481, there are 1413 years, and from the beginning of the world until this year 1481, there are 5241 years . . . the world . . . 5244. [*Raccolta,* pt. 1, vol. 2, pp. 368–69, no. 858]

Beginning with Adam, Columbus lists the antediluvians for a total of 1,656 years, followed by the patriarchs, adding 400 years for the captivity in Egypt, then 480 years to the completion of Solomon's Temple, next 410 years to the destruction of the Temple, followed by 70 years of Babylonian captivity, then 400 years continuance of the second temple until it was destroyed. Columbus summarized that from the birth of Abraham until the destruction of the second temple were 1,088 years; then, according to the Jews, from the destruction of the second temple until now, "being the year of the birth of Our Lord 1481," is 1,413 years. Thus, "from the beginning of the world to our year 1481," are 5,241 years. Twenty years later, on folio 5a of the *Libro de las profecías,* Columbus presented another chronology, "according to the calculation by King Alfonso, which is considered to be the most exact," listing 5,343 years from Adam until the "Advent of our Lord Jesus Christ," making the new total for the year 1501 (the date of that writing) to be 6,845 years.

As a student of biblical prophecies, the Admiral was obliged to establish reference points in the chronology of the historical portions of the Bible, including the times when the prophets wrote, so as to be able to use their prophecies to extrapolate to the later ages of the world. In this preliminary attention to the chronology of Bible history, he followed precisely the same pattern that would

be used later by other great discoverers who were careful students of Bible prophecies, such as Isaac Newton, Johannes Kepler, and Blaise Pascal, not to mention such earlier interpreters of Bible prophecies as St. Augustine, Roger Bacon, Joachim of Fiore, and Pierre d'Ailly.

Taken together, the four postilles form an exact and complete outline of the plan that was executed in 1501–2 in the compilation of the *Libro de las profecías*. The first issue to be met in the manuscript is the "fourfold interpretation of the Bible," by which the meaning of the "Holy City and Mount Zion" are explicitly extended to include the entire experience of the Christian church from the spiritual life of the individual Christian to the glorification of the innumerable multitude in heaven. This is exactly the interpretation given to Zion and to Jerusalem by St. Augustine, Nicholas of Lyra, and Pierre d'Ailly, who were the principal mentors of Columbus in his study of the Bible. The *Libro de las profecías* was an improved and enlarged version of a collection of "authorities, statements, opinions and prophecies" that the Discoverer had clearly in mind and was written for ready reference in the year 1481.

The postilles in the margins of the books the Admiral owned and the *Libro de las profecías* serve as bookends around his mind and his discovery. To begin with, he cited these books and the items he had transcribed on their page margins constantly in his speeches and debates before the monarchs and their advisors, those whose support he was seeking for his enterprise. He had to persuade them of the things he believed and the importance of those ideas with intense conviction. Thus, the "authorities, statements, opinions and prophecies" were necessary. They had to have more convincing authority than a Genoese navigator no matter how good a mariner he was. The notes on the pages of Piccolomini's *Historia* were the Discoverer's depositions before the councils as he would convince them of things he believed to be true and urgent for the well-being of Christendom. The door stood ajar, as by the hand of providence from remotest ages prophesied, and it was urgent that the opportunity be gratefully accepted and not passed by. In his interminable wrangles with the expert advisors in the court of John II of Portugal and the Catholic sovereigns of Spain, Columbus was constantly referring to the opinions of his authorities on cosmology, navigation, and the Bible. There is no reason to doubt that items carefully selected from the Bible and listed as "Summary of Authorities" on the fly-leaves of one of his principal sources of authoritative cosmological information were anything other than a listing of evidence in support of his voyage of discovery. There can be little doubt that Columbus's systematic study of Bible history and prophecies began at least as early as 1481, concurrently to forming his great

plan. The *Libro de las profecías* of 1501–2 was but one further elaboration of the Admiral's studies of the Bible and church theologians when once again his credibility was questioned.

Columbus's study of Bible prophecies is not a mere amateur's interest, not a hobby. His studies were intensely practical as well as mystical, and just as he was a responsible, careful mariner, he was a visionary evangelist. In his own words, he explained that his journey across the ocean was made not by the aid of maps or the mathematics of navigation but by the light of Bible prophecies [L.P., 105]. Columbus compiled prophecies because he had dedicated his life and his talents to the service of Christ, whose evangelical call was a controlling reality in his life to the extent that contemporaries viewed him as a latter-day apostle of the Christian faith. He was a careful compiler and one who showed great reverence for the material he collected. His breadth of understanding and keenness of selection and interpretation was commendable for a layman. The Admiral first extracted a large body of material from many portions of Scripture, bearing on all aspects of the things that interested him. He did not jump to conclusions, so as to be overly selective, but covered a wide spectrum of prophetic previews of subjects. He did not take the opinion of any single commentator or follow the interpretations of any school such as the Joachite tradition. He searched for the best commentators and recorded various opinions. He did not hesitate to assume that he would be able to interpret the material himself. He had formed a general vision and then dealt with such particulars as the location of the origin of the gold of Ophir. In the *Libro de las profecías*, we see Columbus's mind at work. We see him using the assistance of collaborators but clearly providing the vision and the leadership himself.

✠ *Notes*

1. G. Weissmann, *They all Laughed at Christopher Columbus: Tales of Medicine and the Art of Discovery*, p. 13. See also E. Braunwald et al., *Harrison's Principles of Internal Medicine*, pp. 1436–37. Physicians recognize two forms of Reiter's syndrome, either of which could have applied to Columbus: the postvenereal and the postdysenteric. The disease manifests itself in several painful ways and can lead to permanent disability in some cases.

2. D. West, "Wallowing in a Theological Stupor or a Steadfast and Consuming Faith: Scholarly Encounters with Columbus's *Libro de las profecías*," pp. 45–56. Filson Young, for example, stated in *Christopher Columbus and the New World of His Discoveries*, p. 146, that Columbus was having "mental hallucinations" in his later years. M. André, *La Véridique aventure de Christophe Colomb*, p. 259, calls him "quite mad" and a "possessed and hallucinated being."

3. British Library, Add. 13.984.

4. De la Rosa y Lopez, *Biblioteca Colombina. Catálogo de sus libros impressos*, pp. 51–52.

5. West, "Wallowing in a Theological Stupor," p. 50. Henri Harrisse called the notebook a "deplorable lucubration which we sincerely hope will never be published" in *Notes on Columbus*, p. 84.

6. Cristóbal Colón, *Libro de las profecías* (Colección Tabula Americae, Madrid, 1984).

7. For a full account of the attitudes of biographers and historians toward the *Libro de las profecías*, see West, "Wallowing in a Theological Stupor."

8. Count Roselly de Longue's culminating effort was his *Mémoire pour solliciter la béatification of Christophe Colomb*.

9. For the background to Claudel's play see, E.T. Dubois, "Léon Bloy, Paul Claudel and the Revaluation of the Significance of Columbus," pp. 131–44.

10. Both are contained in E. Quinet, *L'Ultramontanisme, Oeuvres complètes*, pp. 180, 182, 200, 263–64, 338–40, for example. Quinet used the partially edited text from the recently completed Columbus sources by Fernández de Navarrete, *Colección de los viages y descubrimientos*. For a recent and superb study of nineteenth-century apocalypticism and literature which devotes several pages to Quinet including his use of the *Libro de las profecías*, see M. Reeves and W. Gould, *Joachim of Fiore and the Myth of the Eternal Evangel in the Nineteenth Century*, pp. 77–83.

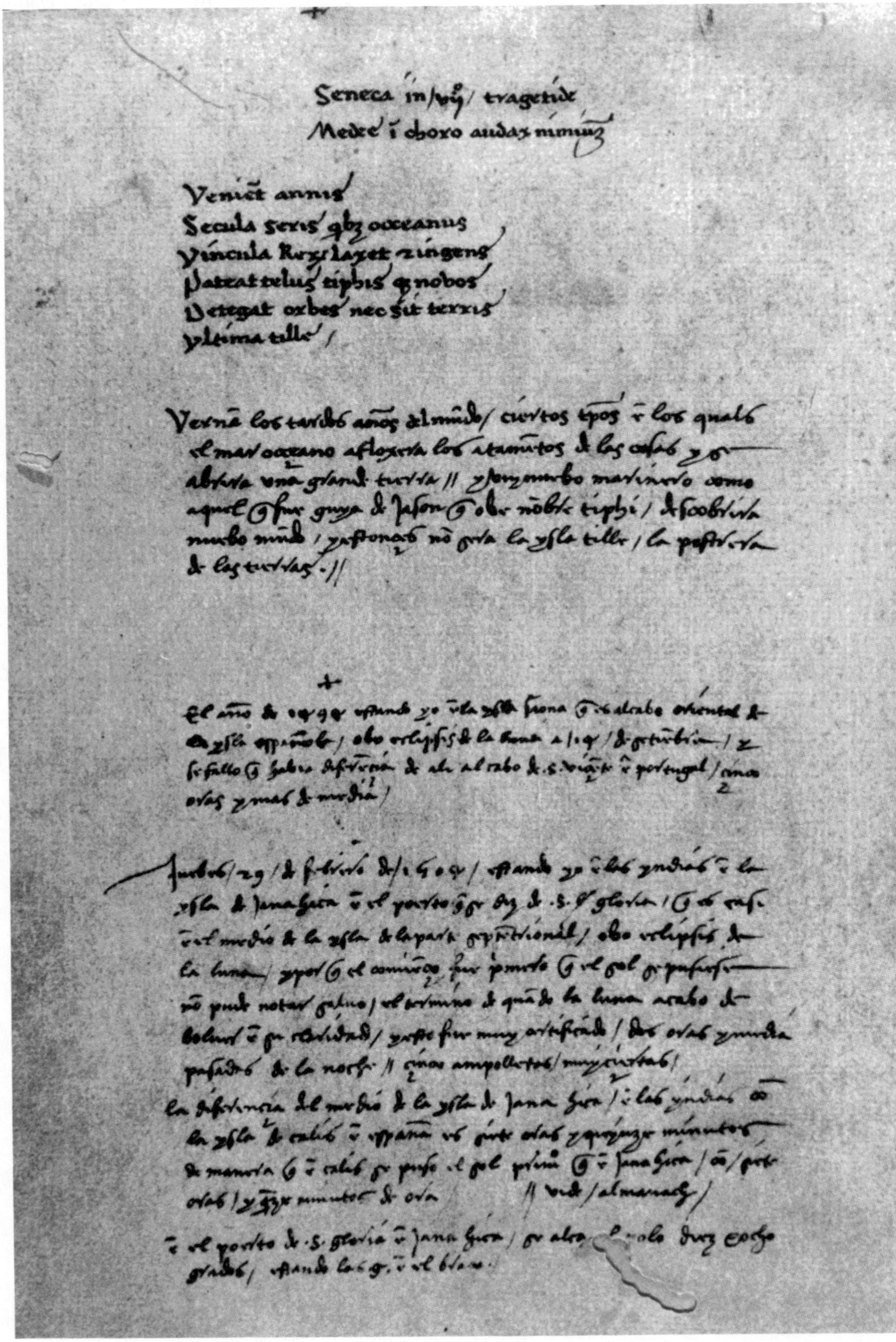
Seneca in /vij/ tragedie
Medee i choro audax nimium

Veniet annis
Secula seris quibus occeanus
Vincula rerum laxet et ingens
Pateat telus tiphisque nobos
Detegat orbes nec sit terris
Ultima tille /

Figure 6: Manuscript page from the hand of Christopher Columbus

Libro de las profecías

Book of Prophecies

A Note on the Translation of the Text

✠ The *Vulgate textus receptus* has served as the basis for most of the quotations from the Bible found in the *Libro de las profecías*. The notable exceptions are those appearing in citations from the works of St. Augustine (which used an earlier Latin version) and "citations" from writings attributed to "Rabbi Samuel" (which used yet another version). The transcription of the Vulgate text is often faulty, with minor omissions and errors that seldom represent significant variations in meaning but that seem to reflect a copyist's lack of training and experience. We would argue these faults as grounds for concluding that the collaboration of Father Gaspar Gorricio (known otherwise to have been a skilled writer) was actually as limited as he claimed in his letter of 23 March 1502.

In translating the Latin text, we have followed the citations from the Bible as they appear in the *Libro de las profecías* without attempting to make emendations, since the purpose of this work is to present the understanding of these texts as perceived by Columbus. Questions of biblical criticism involving the source of the readings used and the many textual errors that appear were dealt with in a cursory way by de Lollis as he prepared the diplomatic transcription, heliotype facsimiles, and editions of this work in 1892–94.

The vocabulary and style of the translation have been patterned after the Douay Version of the Bible because it presents to contemporary readers an impression nearest in English to that of the Vulgate in the time of Columbus.[1] Where the meaning of words and the understanding of sentence constructions seemed to require greater clarity, we have adapted vocabulary and style from Monsignor Knox's translation of the Bible.[2] In some cases where it seemed appropriate, we have used vocabulary from the English Authorized Version, or the Revised Standard Version, to translate Vulgate Latin expressions in words more familiar to contemporary readers.

Numbers identifying chapter and verse refer to the Latin Vulgate and Douay Versions of the Bible. Where variant numbers for chapter and verse appear (such as Psalms) in brackets, these are noted "AV" to indicate the English Authorized Version. Wherever Colum-

bus and his copyists indicated a chapter number, we have included the verse numbers also, though it should be understood that these verse numbers did not exist in 1502 but were first used later in that century. Where Columbus referred to a book of the Bible without using a chapter number, we have inserted the number in brackets.

We have used ". . ." to indicate omissions. At the end of many Scripture texts, Columbus added the symbol "&c." as an indication that the context would shed additional light on the relevance of the passage to his particular use of it. We have preserved these references as they appear. At the end of some Scripture quotations, Columbus added the words "&c. per totum" as an indication that the entire passage, or that which follows to the end, sheds a particularly rich light on his use of it. We have translated this as "&c. to end." On a few occasions, Columbus added at the end of scriptural texts, "&c. per totum capitulum." We have translated these as "&c. throughout whole chapter."

The *Libro de las profecías* was being compiled by several aides to the Admiral. Consequently, he annotated the work in his typical fashion with marginal remarks, which serve as an index or further elaborate on the text. Marginal notes have been included at approximately the same location as in the original manuscript. Columbus's system of highlighting passages with a finger pointing from a hand drawn in the margin is also included.

Material in brackets represents an occasional contextual insertion not in the original text or in the the edition published by de Lollis. Material in parentheses was present in the text as printed in 1892. It should be pointed out that the text of 1892 expanded countless abbreviations of the manuscript and clarified many doubtful readings.

✦ *Notes*

1. *Douay Bible* (Douay Bible House, New York, 1944).
2. R. Knox, *The Holy Bible, a Translation from the Latin Vulgate in the Light of the Hebrew and Greek Originals* (New York, 1956)

Outline of the
Libro de las Profecías

I. Introduction of Themes, 100–169
   A. Exegetical System and Authorities
   B. Letter to King and Queen
   C. Long listings of Scripture from Psalms which deal with Columbus's two major themes: salvation of the world and recapture/rebuilding of Holy Temple
      1. Highlights [by drawing hand with finger pointing to selected text]: Ps. 46, "God shall reign over all nations"
      2. Highlights: Ps. 47, Importance of Zion
   D. Prayers for prophetic guidance
   E. Quotation from St. Isidore on kinds of prophecies and prophetic vision
   F. Quotations from Rabbi Samuel
      1. Gentiles as chosen people and owners of the Holy Temple
      2. Gentiles from all the earth. Emphasis on unknown parts of world converted in last days
      3. Highlights: People of all nations will convert and gather at the Holy Temple in Jerusalem
   G. Quotations from St. Augustine
      1. All nations (and islands of the Gentiles) will worship him
      2. Worship by all nations explained
      3. Columbus says that he gets his strength from Isaiah 51:7–8 and his "role" from Ps. 2:7–8
      4. The city of Jerusalem as City of God
      5. Importance of Astrology
      6. Inheritance of Gentiles
      7. Ends with Mark 16:15–16 and Matthew 24:14, "Go ye into the world"
   H. "Go ye into the world" explained
      1. Gloss from Nicholas of Lyra
      2. Columbus comments: Gospel has been preached to three parts of the earth by the Apostles, now should be preached to the fourth part
      3. Highlight: Final preaching at the end of the age with reference to Alfonso Tastato
      4. Highlight: Matthew 28:18–20
      5. Gloss from Nicholas of Lyra
      6. Comments from St. Augustine with highlight of "all to be saved"

       7. Pierre d'Ailly, Astrology and Chronology of Last Things
          a. End of Moslem faith
          b. Antichrist
          c. Chronology 1 day=1,000 years
          d. Holy Lands and Holy Temple
          e. Last days sequence from pseudo-Methodius which ends with the capture of Jerusalem
       8. d'Ailly/pseudo-Methodius sequence supported by
          a. Texts from Isaiah
          b. Highlight: Is. 11:10–12, "People of the world will assemble"
          c. Highlight: Is. 55:5, "Behold I have given him" (probable reference to King of Spain)

II. Part I: Concerning What Has Already Taken Place, 169–217
    A. Theme: Ancient greatness and fall of Jerusalem
    B. Texts: Related Old Testament Scriptures
    C. Highlights: Isaiah 44, 57, and 60 texts prophesying rebuilding of Jerusalem and the Temple
    D. Marginal notes beside Daniel 11 and Daniel 12: advent of Antichrist and consummation of the age

III. Part II: On The Present and Future (Immediate Future), 217–238
    A. Theme: Salvation of all the nations
    B. Old Testament texts
    C. Poem on theme of "Last Days" with comments
    D. Seneca, *Medea* verse and Columbus translation of it into Spanish
    E. 1504 Note about eclipse
    F. New Testament texts with glosses from Nicholas of Lyra
    G. Commentaries and glosses from St. Augustine, St. John Chrysostom, and St. Gregory
    H. Highlights: Matthew 15, "A people which I knew not hath served me," and highlight of Columbus's own commentary regarding conversion of all nations
    I. Gloss by Nicholas of Lyra
    J. Ends with poem "Joy in the Birth of St. John the Baptist"

IV. Part III: Prophecies of the Future. The Last Days, 238–255
    A. Introduced by entire chapter 25 of Jeremiah which predicts the restoration of Jerusalem prior to the final judgment
    B. Pseudo-Joachim quote that restoration and age of renewal will come from Spain
    C. Next ten pages cut out of text
    D. Scriptural islands and unknown lands now found: Tharsis, Ophir, Chitim
    E. Highlight: Isaiah 42:3–4, "the islands wait for his law"

V. Fly Leafs of Manuscript, 256–259
    A. Payments to be made to individuals and monasteries
    B. Lengthy poem
    C. Additional Scripture to be worked into the notebook

Incipit liber s[ive manipulus de au]ctoritatibus, dictis, ac sententiis et p[rophetiis circa] materiam recuperande sancte civitatis, et montis Dei Syon, ac inventionis & conversionis insularum Indie et omnium gentium nationum. Ad Ferdinandum et Helysabeth &c., reges nostros hyspanos. (2a)

✠

In Summa Angelica sub dicto expositio

Sacra Scriptura exponitur quattuor modis. Primo secundum, hystoriam, hystoria est rei geste narratio, ab hystrion, quod est videre, vel cognoscere; quia apud veteres nemo scribebat hystoriam nisi interfuisset. Secundo, allegorice, a leon quod est aliud, et gore quod est dicere, vel locutio; et est quando per unum factum datur intelligi aliud, quod est credendum. Tertio, tropologice, a tropos quod est conversio et logos quod est sermo; et est quando per unum factum datur intelligi fatiendum. Quarto, anagogice, ab ana quod est sursum et goge quod est ductio; et est quando per unum factum datur intelligi desiderandum, scilicet gloria.

Item Iohannes Gerson et in Decretis

Littera gesta docet:
quid credas allegoria;
moralis quid agas;
quo tendas anagogia.

Item in Rationali divini offitiorum

Quadruplex sensus Sacre Scripture aperte insinuatur in hac dictione Ierusalem. Hystorice enim significat, civitatem illam terrestrem ad quam peregrini petunt. Allegorice, significat Ecclesiam militantem. Tropologice, significat quamlibet fidelem animam. Anagogice, significat celestem Ierusalem, sive patriam, vel regnum celorum.

His prelibatis, oremus.

Deus, qui corda hominum sine strepitu verborum doces et sine labore quique linguas balbutientium facis disertas, et qui presto ades in omni tempore o[p]portuno, (2b) intuere mentis nostre conceptum, et propitius esto desiderio nostro. Nos enim quoniam non cognovimus litteraturam, introibimus in potentiam tuam. Quia beatus est homo quem tu erudieris, Domine, et de lege tua docueris eum. Fac ergo, quesumus, ut eo, quo de te et de loco sancto tuo

100

ere begins the book, or handbook, of sources, statements, opinions and prophecies on the subject of the recovery of God's Holy City and Mount Zion, and on the discovery and evangelization of the islands of the Indies and of all other peoples and nations. To Ferdinand and Elizabeth [Isabella], etc., our hispanic rulers.[1]

✠

From the *Summa* of the Angelic Doctor [Thomas Aquinas], on Exposition[2]

The Holy Scripture is expounded by four methods. The first, is as history, which is a narration of things that happened, from 'hystrion', a word meaning 'to see or to recognize'; among the ancients no one wrote history unless he had been present. The second is allegory, from 'leon' a word meaning 'differently', and 'gore' a word meaning 'speak' or 'expression'; and this is where the given material is to be understood as standing for something else, which is a doctrine to be believed. The third is tropology, from the word 'tropos' which means 'conversion' and the word 'logos' which means 'statement'; and this is where the given material is to be understood as teaching us how we should act. The fourth is anagoge, from 'ana' which means 'upward' and 'goge' which means 'leading'; and this is where the given material is to be understood as describing what is to be desired, namely the heavenly glory.

From Jean Gerson and the *In Decretis*[3]

The literal teaching tells facts;
The allegory tells what you should believe;
The moral interpretation tells how you should act;
The anagogy tells where you are going.

From *In Rationali divini offitii*

The fourfold interpretation of Holy Scripture is clearly implicit in the word Jerusalem. In a historical sense, it is the earthly city to which pilgrims travel. Allegorically, it indicates the Church in the world. Tropologically, Jerusalem is the soul of every believer. Anagogically, the word means the Heavenly Jerusalem, the celestial fatherland and kingdom.

After gathering these things, let us pray.

God, who teaches the hearts of men effortlessly and without the clamor of words, and who art a present help in every time of need, give understanding. For we are not learned in literature, but we take up this task in thy power. For blessed is the man who learns from thee, Lord, whom thou teaches from thy law. We therefore pray thee to cause us to under-

conscripti sunt spiritu, sermones ac libros et prophetias intelligamus. Amen.

✠

Notandum quod in Sacra Scriptura aliquando ponitur tempus pro tempore, sicut preteritum pro futuro &c.

Nota

"Omnia quecumque audivi a Patre meo, nota feci vobis." Unde beatus Augustinus in quodam sermone, qui legitur a quibusdam in festo sancti Thome apostoli: "Dominus noster Yhesus Christus quod facturus est fecisse se dicit, qui ea, que futura sunt fecit. Sicut enim dicit per prophetam: 'foderunt manus meas et pedes'," nec ait: "fossuri sunt." Velut, preterita dicens, et ea tamen futura predicens. Ita et hoc loco ait omnia se nota fecisse discipulis, que se novit esse facturum in illa plenitudine scientie &c., que requirantur, si placet.

Augustinus in quodam sermone

Psalmo 21

Unde et beatus Isydorus libro I, De summo bono, capitulo 25

Est et illa de temporibus figura, per quam quedam, que futura sunt, quasi iam gesta narrantur; ut est illud: "foderunt manus meas et pedes meos, dinumeraverunt omnia ossa mea," et "diviserunt sibi vestimenta mea;" et his similia. Sed cur que adhuc fatienda erant, iam facta narrantur? Quia que nobis adhuc futura sunt, apud Dei eternitatem iam facta sunt. Et cetera, que secuntur atque precedunt, per totum. (3a)

Isydorus
Psalmo 21

In Glosa Nicolai de Lyra super Danielem super capitulo 8

 Notandum ad evidentiam sequentis littere quod in Sacra Scriptura aliquando est duplex sensus litteralis, quia ea, que sunt facta in Veteri Testamento, sunt figure eorum, que fiunt in Novo, dicente Apostolo, primo Corintiis, decimo capitulo: "omnia in figura contingebant illis." Ideo, quando in Veteri Testamento predicitur aliquid esse impletum in aliqua persona Veteris Testamenti, verius tamen et perfectius in aliqua Novi Testamenti. Tunc est ibi duplex sensus literalis: unus minus principalis, et alius principalior, de illo scilicet, in quo perfectius vide impletur verbum predictum. Verbi gratia, I Paralippemenon XXII dicitur: "ego ero ei in patrem, et ipse erit mihi in filium." Quod est verbum Domini loquentis de Salamone, qui fuit filius Dei per adoptionem in principio regni sui, propter

Corintiis 10

I Paralipomenon 22

stand the things that are written by the Spirit in words and books and prophecies concerning thee and thy holy place. Amen.

It should be noted that in the Holy Scriptures the verbs in the past tense are sometimes used for the future, and so with the other tenses &c.[4]

Note

"All things, whatsoever I have heard of my Father, I have made known to you." (John 15:15).[5] / Concerning this text which is the lesson for the day of Thomas the Apostle, the comment is made by St. Augustine, "Our Lord Jesus Christ said that he had already accomplished that which he was going to do, and he did things which were spoken of as future. In the same way, he declared through the prophet, 'They pierced my hands and my feet,' rather than 'They will pierce.' Thus, he spoke in the past tense as he predicted future things. Likewise, in this text he said that he had revealed all things to his disciples, which in the fullness of his knowledge he knew he was going to do,' etc. (These things should be looked for, if you will.)

Comment by Augustine

Psalms 21

From the *De summo bono* of Isidore of Seville, Book I, Chapter 25[6]

There is a style of using tenses wherein future things are narrated as if they had already taken place. For example, "They pierced my hands and my feet," and "They have numbered all my bones, and "They parted my garments amongst them," (Psalm 22:17–19) and things similar to this. But why should future events be described as having already happened? It is because things that are still future to us, have already happened according to God's viewpoint in eternity. Also the things that follow, and that come before, through the whole section.

Isidore
Psalms 21

From the comments of Nicolas of Lyra on Daniel, Chapter 8[7]

The following passages demonstrate the fact that there is sometimes in the Holy Scripture a twofold literal meaning, for events that happened / in the Old Testament are figurative descriptions of things that will take place in the New Testament. Thus, the Apostle Paul says in the tenth chapter of First Corinthians (verse 11), "Now all these things happened to them in figure." That is, when in the Old Testament it is said that something is fulfilled in some Old Testament person, it is more truly and perfectly fulfilled somewhere in the New Testament. In these cases there is a twofold literal meaning, and the one is more important than the other when it fulfills more perfectly the thing that was predicted. For example, in Paralipomenon 22 (I Chronicles 22:10) it is said, "And he shall be a son to me: and I will be a father to him." This is the word of the Lord to Solomon, who was a son of God by adoption at the beginning

I Corinthians 10

I Chronicles 22

II Regum 12

quod "amabilis Domino" dictus est, ut patet secundo Regum, capitulo duodecimo, et sic verbum illud impletum est ad litteram in Salamone. Perfectius autem impletum est in Christo, qui est filius Dei per naturam, cuius figura fuit Salomon. Et ideo, illa auctoritas ad litteram intelligitur de Salamone et de Christo, de Salamone minus principaliter, et de Christo principalius. Propter quod Apostolus (3b) ad Hebreos I a[l]legat predictam auctoritatem tamquam de Christo dictam ad litteram. Sic est in proposito quia sub similitudine arietis et [h]irei tractat Daniel de pugna regni Grecorum et Medorum. Principalis eius intentio est tractare de pugna Antichristi vel membrorum eius, et christianorum. Et ideo est ibi duplex sensus literalis ut patet ex predictis &c. (4a)

ad Hebreos I

Carta del Almyrante al Rey y á la Rreyna

Christianísimos & muy altos prínçipes.

La rasón que tengo de la restituçión de la Casa Santa á la Santa Yglesia militante es la syguiente.

Muy altos Rreyes: De muy pequeña hedad entré en la mar navegando é lo he continuado fasta oy. La mesma arte ynclina á quien le prosigue a desear de saber los secretos d'este mundo. Ya pasan de XL años que yo voy en este uso. Todo lo que fasta oy se navega todo lo he andado. Trauto y conversaçión he tenido con gente sabia, heclesiásticos é seglares, Latinos y Griegos, Judíos y Moros y con otros muchos de otras setas. Á este mi deseo fallé á Nuestro Señor muy propicio, y ove d'él para ello espírito de ynteligençia: en la marinería me fiso abondoso, de astrología me dió lo que abastava, y así de geometría y arismética, y engenio en el ánima, y manos para debusar espera, y en ella las çibdades, rŷos y montañas, yslas y puertos, todo en su propio sytio.

En este tiempo he yo visto y puesto estudio en ver de todas escrituras: cosmografía, ystorias, corónicas, y fylosofía, y de otras artes, á que me abrió Nuestro Señor el entendimiento con mano palpable á que era hasedero navegar de aquí á las Yndias, y me abrió la voluntad para la hexecuçión d'ello. Y con este fuego vine á Vuestras Altezas. Todos aquellos que supieron de mi ynpresa con rixa le negaron burlando. Todas las çiencias, de que dise ariba, non me aprovecharon, ni las abtoridades d'ellas. En sólo Vuestras Altezas quedó la fee, y costançia. ?Quién dubda que esta lunbre non fuese del Espírito Santo, asý como de mi? El qual con rrayos de claridad maravillosos consoló con su santa y sacra Escritura, á vos muy alta y clara, con quarenta y quatro libros del Viejo Testamento, y quatro Hevangelios, con veynte y tres Hepístolas de aquellos bienaventurados apóstoles, abibándome que yo prosyguiese y de contino, sin çesar un momento, me abíban con gran priesa.

of his rule, and because of this he is called "beloved by the Lord" in
Second Kings 12 (II Samuel 12:25), and the statement is literally fulfilled
in Solomon. However, it is more perfectly fulfilled in Christ, who is by
his nature the Son of God, and Solomon is a type of Christ. Therefore,
this text refers literally to both Solomon and Christ, but more importantly
to Christ, and to Solomon in a lesser sense. Thus, in chapter 1 of the
letter to the Hebrews [verse 5], the Apostle claims that this text is a
literal prophecy concerning Christ. The same is true of the statement
in which Daniel speaks figuratively of the war between the kings of the
Greeks and the Medes in the similitude of a ram and a goat. His principal
intention is to deal with the struggle between the Antichrist (or his supporters) and Christians. We have here another example of a twofold literal
meaning, as appeared in the preceding, etc. /

From Hebrews I (margin, left)

II Kings 12 (margin, right)

Letter from the Admiral to the King and Queen[8]

Most Christian and noble rulers:

The following is a statement of my proposal for the restoration of the
House of God to the Holy Church Militant.

Most eminent rulers: At a very early age I began to navigate upon
the seas, which I have continued to this day. Mine is a calling that inclines
those who pursue it to desire to understand the world's secrets. Such
has been my interest for more than forty years, and I have sailed all
that can be sailed in our day. I have had business and conversation with
learned men among both laity and clergy, Latins and Greeks, Jews and
Moslems, and many others of different religions. I prayed to the most
merciful Lord concerning my desire, and he gave me the spirit and the
intelligence for it. He gave me abundant skill in the mariner's arts, an
adequate understanding of the stars, and of geometry and arithmetic. He
gave me the mental capacity and the manual skill to draft spherical maps,
and to draw the cities, rivers, mountains, islands and ports, all in their
proper places.

During this time, I have searched out and studied all kinds of texts:
geographies, histories, chronologies, philosophies and other subjects. With
a hand that could be felt, the Lord opened my mind to the fact that
it would be possible to sail from here to the Indies, and he opened my
will to desire to accomplish the project. This was the fire that burned
within me when I came to visit Your Highnesses. All who found out
about my project denounced it with laughter and ridiculed me. All the
sciences which I mentioned above were of no use to me. Quotations of
learned opinions were no help. Only Your Majesties had faith and perse-
verance. Who can doubt that this fire / was not merely mine, but also
of the Holy Spirit who encouraged me with a radiance of marvelous illumination from his sacred Holy Scriptures, by a most clear and powerful
testimony from the forty-four books of the Old Testament, from the four
Gospels, from the twenty-three Epistles of the blessed Apostles—urging
me to press forward? Continually, without a moment's hesitation, the
Scriptures urge me to press forward with great haste.[9]

Milagro ebidentísimo quiso faser Nuestro Señor en esto del viaje de las Yndias por me consolar á mí y á otros en estótro de la Casa Santa. Siete años pasé aqui en su real corte, disputando el caso con tantas (4b) personas de tanta abtoridad y sabios en todas artes, y en fin concluyeron que todo hera vano, y se desistieron con esto d'ello. Después, paró en lo que Jhesu Christo nuestro redentor diso, y de antes avía dicho por boca de sus santos profetas. Y así se deve decreher que parerá est'otro; y en fe d'ello, si lo dicho no abasta, doy el sacro Evangelio, en que dixo que todo pasaría, mas no su palabra maravillosa, y con esto diso que todo hera nesçesario que se acabase quanto por él y por los profetas estava escrito.

Yo dise que diría la rasón, que tengo, de la restitución de la Casa Santa á la Santa Yglesia. Digo que yo deso todo mi navegar desde hedad nueva y las pláticas que yo aya tenido con tanta gente en tantas tierras y de tantas setas, y dexo las tantas artes y escrituras de que yo dyxe ariba; solamente me tengo á la santa y sacra Escritura, y á algunas abtoridades proféticas de algunas presonas santas, que por revelaçión divina han dicho algo d'esto.

Pudiera ser que Vuestras Altezas y todos los otros que me conosçen, y á quien esta escritura fuere amostrada, que en secreto ó públicamente me reprehenderán de reprehensión de diversas maneras: de non doto en letras, de lego marinero, de honbre mundanal &c.

Respondo aquello, que dixo san Mateus "O Señor, que quisistes tener secreto tantas cosas á los sabios y rebelástelas á los ynoçentes!" Y el mesmo San Mateos: "yendo Nuestro Señor en Jherusalem cantaban los mochachos: !osana fijo de David! Los scribas, por le tentar, le preguntaron sy oŷa lo que desían; y él les respondió que sŷ, disiendo: "?no sabéys vos, que de la boca de los niños é ynoçentes se pronuiisçia la verdad?" Ô más largo de los apóstole, que dixieron cosas tan fundadas en espeçial San Juan: "yn prinçipio erat verbum et verbum erat apud Deum, &c." Palabras tan altas de personas que nunca deprehendieron letras.

Digo que el Espíritu Santo obra en Christianos, Judíos, Moros y en todos otros de toda seta, y no solamente en los sabios, más en los ynorantes; que en mi tiempo yo he visto aldeano que da cuenta del çielo y estrellas y del curso d'ellas mejor que otros, que gastaron dineros en ello; y digo que no solamente el Espíritu Santo rebela las cosas de porvenir á las (5a) criaturas racionales, mas nos las amuestra por señales del çielo, del ayre, y de las bestias, quando le aplaz, como fué del boy que fabló en Rroma al tiempo de Julio Çésar, y en otras muchas maneras que serían prolixas para desir y muy notas para todo el mundo.

La Sacra Escritura testifica en el Testamento Viejo por boca de los profetas, y en el Nuebo por nuestro redentor Jhesu Christo, qu'este mundo a de aver fin: los señales de quando esto aya de

Senacain VII tragetide Medee in choro audax nimium: Vernán los tardos años del mundo

The Lord purposed that there should be something clearly miraculous in this matter of the voyage to the Indies, so as to encourage me and others in the other matter of the Household of God.[10] I spent seven years here in your royal court discussing this subject with the leading persons in all the learned arts, and their conclusion was that all was in vain. That was the end, and they gave it up. But afterwards it all turned out just as our redeemer Jesus Christ had said, and as he had spoken earlier by the mouth of his holy prophets. This is the way we really should believe that the other matter will turn out. If what I have said is not already sufficient to recommend such belief, I submit the gospel texts in which he said that all things would pass away, but not his marvelous Word, and he also said that all things must be fulfilled that were said by him and written by the prophets.

I said that I would present my case for the restitution of the House of God to the Holy Church. Now I lay aside all of my lifetime experience as a navigator, and my discussions with many people of many lands and cultures. And I lay aside all the sciences and books that I indicated above. I hold only to the sacred Holy Scriptures, and to the interpretations of prophecy by certain devout persons who have spoken on this subject by divine illumination. /

Possibly Your Highnesses and all those who know me and who see this book will privately or even publicly reproach me by various kinds of criticism: that I am unlearned in literature, a layman, a mariner, a common worldly man, etc.

I respond to this in the words of Matthew (11:25), "O Lord . . . because thou hast hid these things from the wise and prudent and hast revealed them to little ones."[11] Again, according to Matthew (21:15–16), when the Lord was entering Jerusalem, the children sang "Hosanna to the son of David," and the scribes tested him by asking if he heard what they were saying; and he answered "yes," and said, "Do you not know that the truth is heard from the mouth of children and the simple?" Or in more general terms, the apostles spoke the most solid realities, as especially St. John (1:1), "[in] the beginning was the Word: and the Word was with God," etc., and these exalted statements were made by persons who had never studied literature.

I believe that the Holy Spirit works among Christians, Jews and Moslems, and among all men of every faith, not merely among the learned, but also among the uneducated.[12] In my own experience, I have met a simple villager who could explain the sky and stars and their movements better than those who paid their money to learn these things. I also believe that the Holy Spirit reveals future events not only in rational beings, but also discloses them to us in signs in the sky, in the atmosphere and in animals, whenever it pleases him, as was the case with the ox that spoke in Rome in the days of Julius Caesar, and in many other ways too numerous to recount, that are well known throughout the world.

The Holy Scriptures testify in the Old Testament by the mouth of / the prophets, and in the New Testament by our Savior Jesus Christ, that this world must come to an end. The signs concerning the time when

Seneca, 7, Tragedy of Media in the chorus, 'audax nimium': In the latter years of the world . . .

ser diso Mateo y Marco y Lucas; los profetas abondosamente tanbién lo avían predicado.

Santo Agostin diz que la fin d,este mundo ha de ser en el sétimo millenar de los años de la criaçión d'él; los sacros teólogos le siguen en espeçial el cardenal Pedro de Ayliaco en el verbo XI y en otros lugares, como diré abaso.

De la criaçión del mundo ó de Audán fasta el avenimiento de Nuestro Señor Jhesu Christo son çinco mill é tresientos y quarenta é tres años y tresientos y diez é ocho días, por la cuenta del rey don Alonso, la qual se tiene por la más çierta. Pedro de Ayliaco, Elucidario astronomice concordie cum theolgica et hystorica veritate, sobre el verbo X. Con los quales poniendo mill y quingentos y uno ynperfeto son por todos seys mill ochoçientos quarenta y çinco ynperfetos.

Segund esta cuenta no falta salvo çiento é çinquenta y çinco años para conplimiento de siete mill, en los quales dise ariba por las abtoridades dichas que avrá de feneçer el mundo.

Nuestro Redentor diso que antes de la consumaçión d'este mundo se abrá de conplir todo lo qu'estava escrito por los profetas.

Los profetas, escriviendo, fablavan de diversas maneras el de porvenir por pasado y el pasado por venir, y asymismo del presente; y disieron muchas cosas por semejança, otras propincas á la verdad y otras por entero á la letra; y uno más que otro, y uno por mejor manera, y otro no tanto. Ysaŷs es aquéli que más alaba san Gerónimo y santo Agostín y los otros dotores, á todos, apruevan y tienen en grande reverençia: de Ysaŷa disen que no solamente propheta, más hevangelista. Este puso toda su diligençia á escrevir lo venidero, y llamar toda la gente á nuestra santa fee católica. (5b)

Muchos santos dotores y sacros teólogos escryvieron sobre todas las profeçías, y los otros libros de la sacra Escritura; mucho nos alunbraron de lo que teníamos ynnoto, bien que en ello en muchas cosas discordan; algunas ovo de que no le fué alargado la ynteligençia.

Torno á replicar mi protestaçión de no ser dicho presunçioso sin çiençia, y me allego de contino al desir de San Mateus, que diso: "O Señor, que quisyste tener secreto tantas cosas á los sabios y rebelástelas á los ynoçentes;" y con esto pago y con la espiriençia que d'ello se a visto.

Grandísyma parte de las profeçías y sacra Es[cri]ptura está ya acabado; ellas lo diseñ y la Santa Yglesia á alta boz sin çesar lo está disiendo, y no es menester otro testimonio. De una diré, porque

this must happen are given by Matthew, Mark and Luke. The prophets also predicted it repeatedly.

Saint Augustine says that the end of this world will take place in the seventh millennium after the age of the creation of the world. The theologians of the Church follow this view, in particular, Cardinal Petrus Aliacus [Pierre d'Ailly] in Statement XI (of the *Vigintiloquium*), and in other references that I will cite below.

From the creation of the world, or from Adam, until the advent of our Lord Jesus Christ there were five thousand, three hundred and forty-three years, and three hundred and eighteen days, according to the calculation by King Alfonso, which is considered to be the most exact. Following Petrus Aliacus [Pierre d'Ailly], in the tenth heading of his *Explanation of the Agreement of Astronomy with Biblical and Historical Records,* if we add to these years an additional one thousand, five hundred and one years of waiting, this makes a total of six thousand, eight hundred, forty-five years of waiting for the completion of the age.

According to this calculation, only one hundred and fifty years are lacking for the completion of the seven thousand years which would be the end of the world according to the learned opinions that I have cited above.[13]

Our Savior said that before the consummation of this world, first must be fulfilled all the things that were written by the prophets.

The prophets expressed themselves in various manners in their writings. Sometimes they referred to the future as already past, and to the past as still to come, and similarly with the present. Also, they announced many things figuratively and others by things closely approaching the actual, and yet others in an entirely literal manner. One prophet says more, another says less, and yet another says it in a better manner. Isaiah is the one that is appreciated and esteemed / more than all the others by Jerome, Augustine and the other theologians. They say that Isaiah is not merely a prophet, but is a gospel writer as well. He is the one who concentrated every effort upon describing future events and upon calling all peoples to the holy catholic faith.

Many revered teachers and theologians have written about the prophecies and the various books of the Holy Scriptures. Although they disagree with each other frequently, they have enlightened us greatly concerning things that we did not previously understand. There were some things that they did not comprehend themselves.

At this point I must repeat that I do not wish to be taken for someone speaking presumptuously out of ignorance. Happily, I can add without hesitation the words from Matthew [11:25], "O Lord . . . because thou hast hid these things from the wise and prudent and hast revealed them to little ones." This I offer on my own behalf, together with the results that one has discovered by personal experience.

By far the greatest portion of the prophecies of the Holy Scriptures has already been fulfilled. The Scriptures themselves testify to this, and the clear voice of the Holy Church unceasingly bears the same testimony, so that no other witness is needed. But I will speak of a particular proph-

haz á mi caso, y la qual me descansa y fas contento quantas vezes yo pienso en ella.

Yo soy pecador grabísimo: la piadad y misiricordia de Nuestro Señor sienpre que yo he llamado por ellas, me han cobierto todo; consolación suabísima he fallado en hechar todo mi cuydado á contenplar su maravilloso conspeto.

Ya dise que para la hesecuçión de la ynpresa de las Yndias no me aprovechó rasón ni matemática, ni mapamundos; llenamente se cunplió lo que diso Ysaŷas. Y esto es lo que deseo de escrevir aquí por le redusir á Vuestras Altezas á memoria, y porque se alegren del otro, que yo le diré de Jherusalem por las mesmas autoridades, de la qual ynpresa, si fee ay tengan por muy çierto la vitoria.

Acuérdense Vuestras Altezas de los Hevangelios y de tantas promesasi que Nuestro Redentor nos fiso, y quán esprimentado está todo: San Pedro, quando saltó en la mar andovo sobríella en quanto la fee fué firme. Quien toviere tanta fee, como un grano de paniso, le obedeçerán las montañas; quien toviere fee, demande, que todo se le dará. Pusad y abriros han. No deve nadie de temer á tomar qualquiera ynpresa en nonbre de Nuestro Salvador, seyendo justa y con sana yntinçión para su santo serviçio: á Santa Catalina socorrió después que vido la prueva d'ella. Acuérdense Vuestras Altezas que con pocos dineros tomaron la ynpresa d'este reyno de Granada. La determinaçión de toda cosa la desó Nuestro Señor á cada uno en su albedrío, bien que á muchos amonesta. Ninguna (6a) cosa le falta, que sea en el poder de la gente para dársela. !Ô qué Señor tam bueno, que dessea que faga la gente, con que le sea él á cargo! De día y de noche y todos momentos le debrían las gentes dar gratias devotíssimas.

Yo dise arriba que quedava mucho por complir de las prophetías, y digo que son cosas grandes en el mundo, y digo que la señal es que Nuestro Señor da priessa en ello: el predicar del Evangelio en tantas tierras de tan poco tiempo acá me lo diçe.

El abad Johachín, calabrés, diso que había de salir de España quien havía de redificar la Casa del monte Sión.

El cardenal Pedro de Ayliaco mucho escrive del fin de la seta de Mahoma, y del avenimiento del Antechristo en un tratado que hiso De concordia astronomie, veritatis et narrationis historice, en el qual recita el dicho de muchos astrónomos sobre las diez reboluciones de Saturno, y en espeçial en el fin del dicho libro en los nueve postreros capítulos. (6b)

Psalmo 2

Ego autem constitutus sum rex ab eo super Syon montem sanctum eius, predicans prceptum eius. Dominus dixit ad me: "filius meus

ecy, because it applies particularly to my experience, and it refreshes me and makes me rejoice every moment when I think of it.

I am only a most unworthy sinner, but ever since I have cried out for grace and mercy from the Lord, they have covered me completely. I have found the most delightful comfort in making it my whole aim in life to enjoy his marvelous presence.

Already I pointed out that for the execution of the journey to the Indies / I was not aided by intelligence, by mathematics or by maps. It was simply the fulfillment of what Isaiah had prophesied, and this is what I desire to write in this book, so that the record may remind Your Highnesses, and so that you may rejoice in the other things that I am going to tell you about our Jerusalem upon the basis of the same authority. If you have faith, you may be certain that there will be success also in that other project.

Let Your Highnesses take note of the Gospels, and of the many promises that our Savior made to us, and of the way in which experience has proved them all. Saint Peter stepped out upon the water, and to the extent that his faith remained firm, he walked upon it. Whoever finds so much faith as a grain of mustard seed will be obeyed by the mountains. Knock and it must be opened unto you. No one should be afraid to undertake any project in the name of our Savior, if it is a just cause and if he has the pure intention of his holy service. He aided St. Catherine after he had tested her. Let Your Highnesses remember how short were the funds with which you undertook the project for the Kingdom of Granada. The working out of all things is left to the freedom of each individual by the Lord, even though he gives directions to many. He is in need of nothing that is in the power of man to give him. Oh what a gracious Lord, who desires people to do things for which he makes himself responsible! Day and night, moment by moment, the people should give him their devoted gratitude.

I said above that much of the prophecies remained to be fulfiled, and I believe that these are great events for the world. I believe that there is evidence that our Lord is hastening these things. This evidence is the fact that the Gospel must now be proclaimed to so many lands in such a short time. /

The Abbot Joachim [of Fiore], a Calabrian, said that the restorer of the House of Mt. Zion would come out of Spain.[14]

Cardinal Petrus Aliacus [Pierre d'Ailly] wrote much concerning the end of the sect of Mohammed and the coming of the Antichrist in his treatise on the *Accord of Astronomical Truth and History*. There he reports the opinions of many astronomers on the ten revolutions of Saturn, especially at the end of the book, in the last nine chapters.

Psalm 2

[L 2:6–8, AV Psalm 2:6–8][15]

But I am appointed king by him over Sion his holy mountain, preaching his commandment. The Lord hath said to me: Thou art my son; this

es tu; ego hodie genui te. Postula a me, et dabo tibi gentes, hereditatem tuam et possessionem tuam teriminos terre." &c.

Psalmo 5

Introibo in domum tuam; adorabo ad templum sanctum tuum in
timore tuo &c.

Psalmo 8

Domine, Dominus noster, quam admirabile est nomen tuum in universa terra. &c.

Psalmo 9

Increpasti gentes, et periit impius: nomen eorum delesti in eternum
et in seculum seculi &c. Psallite Domino, qui habitat in Syon;
annuntiate inter gentes studia eius, &c. Miserere mei, Domine; vide
humilitatem meam de inimicis meis. Qui exaltas me de portis mortis,
ut annuntiem omnes laudationes tuas in portis filie Syon. Exultabo
in salutari tuo; infixe sunt gentes in interitu, quem fecerunt &c.
Convertantur peccatores in infernum, omnes gentes, que obliviscun-
tur Deum &c. Exsurge, Domine, non confortetur homo; iudicentur
gentes in conspectu tuo. Constitue, Domine, legislatorem super eos,
sciant gentes quoniam homines sunt &c. Dominus regnabit in eternum et in seculum seculi: peribitis gentes de terra illius &c. (7a)

Psalmo 17

Constitues me in caput gentium. Populus, quem non cognovi, servivit mihi; et in auditu auris obedivit mihi &c. Propterea confitebor
tibi in populis, Domine, et nomini tuo psalmum dicam &c.

Psalmo 18

Celi enarrant gloriam Dei, et opera manuum eius annuntiat firmamentum. Dies diei eructat verbum, et nox nocti indicat scientiam.
Non sunt loquele neque sermones, quorum non audiantur voces

day have I begotten thee. Ask of me, and I will give thee the Gentiles for thy inheritance, and the uttermost parts of the earth for thy possession. &c.

Psalm 5

[L 5:8b, AV Psalm 5:7b]

I will come into thy house; I will worship towards thy holy temple, in thy fear. &c.

Psalm 8

[L 8:2a, AV Psalm 8:1a]

O Lord, our Lord: how admirable is thy name in the whole earth! &c.

Psalm 9

[L 9:6, 12, 14–16a, 18, 20–21, 37; AV Psalm 9:5, 11, 13–15a, 17, 19–20, 10:16]

Thou hast rebuked the Gentiles, and the wicked one hath perished; / thou hast blotted out their name for ever and ever. &c. Sing ye to the Lord, who dwelleth in Sion: declare his ways among the Gentiles. &c. Have mercy on me, O Lord: see my humiliation which I suffer from my enemies. Thou that liftest me up from the gates of death, that I may declare all thy praises in the gates of the daughter of Sion. I will rejoice in thy salvation: the Gentiles have stuck fast in the destruction which they prepared. &c. The wicked shall be turned into hell, all the nations that forget God. &c. Arise, O Lord, let not man be strengthened: let the Gentiles be judged in thy sight. Appoint, O Lord, a lawgiver over them: that the Gentiles may know themselves to be but men. &c. The Lord shall reign to eternity, yea, for ever and ever: ye Gentiles shall perish from his land. &c.

✠

Psalm 17

[L 44b–45, 50; AV Psalm 18:43b–44, 49]

Thou wilt make me head of the Gentiles. A people which I knew not hath served me: at the hearing of the ear they have obeyed me. &c. Therefore will I give glory to thee, O Lord, among the nations: and I will sing a psalm to thy name. &c.

Psalm 18

[L 18:2–5, AV Psalm 19:1–4]

The heavens are telling of the glory of God; the firmament proclaims his handiwork. One day speaks to another and night to night shares its knowledge. Without speech or language or sound of any voice, their voice

eorum: in omnem terram exivit sonus eorum et in fines orbis terre verba eorum.

Psalmo 19

Exaudiat te Dominus in die tribulationis; protegat te nomen Dei Iacob. Mittat tibi auxilium de sancto et de Syon tueatur te &c.

Psalmo 21

Reminiscentur et convertentur ad Dominum universi fines terre, et adorabunt in conspectu eius universe familie gentium. Quoniam Domini est regnum, et ipse dominabitur gentium &c.

Psalmo 23

Domini est terra et plenitudo eius orbis terrarum et qui habitant in eo &c.

Psalmo 25

Domine, dilexi decorem domus tue et locum habitationis tue &c. (7b)

Psalmo 26

Unam petii a Domino, hanc requiram, ut inhabitem in domo Domini omnibus diebus vite mee; ut videam voluntatem Domini et visitem templum eius &c.

Psalmo 28

Et in templo eius omnes dicent gloriam (') &c. Et sedebit Dominus rex in eternum &c.

Psalmo 32

Misericoria Domini plena est terra &c. Timeat Dominum omnis terra; ab eo autem commoveantur omnes inhabitantes orbem &c.

goes out through all the earth, their words reach to the end of the world.
/

Psalm 19

[L 19:2–3, AV Psalm 20:1–2]

May the Lord hear thee in the day of tribulation: may the name of the God of Jacob protect thee. May he send thee help from the sanctuary: and defend thee out of Sion. &c.

Psalm 21

[L 21:28–29, AV Psalm 22:27–28]

All the ends of the earth shall remember, and shall be converted to the Lord: And all the kindreds of the Gentiles shall adore in his sight. For the kingdom is the Lord's; and he shall have dominion over the nations. &c.

Psalm 23

[L 23:1, AV Psalm 24:1]

The earth is the Lord's and the fullness thereof: the world and all they that dwell therein. &c.

Psalm 25

[L 25:8, AV Psalm 26:81]

I have loved, O Lord, the beauty of thy house: and the place where thy glory dwelleth. &c.

Psalm 26

[L 26:4, AV Psalm 27:4]

One thing I have asked of the Lord, this will I seek after: that I may dwell in the house of the Lord all the days of my life. That I may see the delight of the Lord: and may visit his temple. &c.

Psalm 28

[L 28:b, 10b; AV Psalm 29:9b, 10b]

And in his temple all shall speak his glory. &c. And the Lord shall sit king forever. &c. /

Psalm 32

[L 32:5b, 8; AV Psalm 33:5b, 8]

The earth is full of the mercy of the Lord. &c. Let all the earth fear the Lord: and let all the inhabitants of the world be in awe of him. &c.

Psalmo 42

Emitte lucem tuam et veritatem tuam; ipsa me deduxerunt et adduxerunt in montem sanctum tuum et in tabernacula tua &c.

Psalmo 45

Vacate, et videte quoniam ego sum Deus: exaltabor in gentibus, et exaltabor in terra. (8a)

Psalmo 46

Omnes gentes, plaudite manibus; iubilate Deo in voce exultationis. Quoniam Dominus excelsus, terribilis; rex magnus super omnem terram. Subiecit populos nobis et gentes sub pedibus nostris &c. Regnavit Deus super gentes &c.

✠

Psalmo 47

Magnus Dominus et laudabilis nimis in civitate Dei nostri, in monte sancto eius. Fundatur exultatione universe terre mons Syon, latera aquilonis, civitas regis magni &c. Sicut audivimus, sic vidimus in civitate Domini virtutum, in civitate Dei nostri &c. Secundum nomen tuum, Deus, sic et laus tua in fines te[r]re; iustitia plena est dextera tua. Letetur mons Syon &c. Circumdate Syon et complectimini eam &c. per totum.

Psalmo 49

Deus, Deorum dominus, locutus est et vocavit terram. A solis ortu usque ad occasum; ex Syon speties decoris eius.

Psalmo 50

Benigne fac in bona voluntate tua Syon et edificentur muri Ierusalem &c.

Psalmo 56

Nota Confitebor tibi in populis, Domine et psalmum dicam tibi in gentibus, quoniam magnificata est usque ad celos misericordia tua, et

Psalm 42

[L 42:3, AV Psalm 43:3]

Send forth thy light and thy truth: they have conducted me, and brought me unto thy holy hill, and into thy tabernacles. &c.

Psalm 45

[L 45:11, AV Psalm 46:10]

Be still and see that I am God. I will be exalted among the nations, and I will be exalted in the earth.

Psalm 46

[L 46:2–4, 9a; AV Psalm 47:1–3, 8a]

 O clap your hands, all ye nations: shout unto God with the voice of joy, for the Lord is high, terrible: a great king over all the earth. He hath subdued the people under us: and the nations under our feet. &c. God shall reign over the nations. &c.

✠

Psalm 47

[L 47:2–3, 9a, 11–12a, 13; AV Psalm 48:1–2, 8a, 10–11a, 12]

 Great is the Lord, and exceedingly; to be praised in the city of our God, in his holy mountain. With the joy of the whole earth is mount Sion founded, on the sides of the north, the city of the great king. &c. As we have heard, so have we seen, in the city of the Lord of hosts, in the city of our God. &c. According to thy name, O God, so also is thy praise unto the ends of the earth: thy right hand is full of justice. Let mount Sion rejoice &c. Surround Sion, / and encompass her. &c. to end.

Psalm 49

[L 49:1–2, AV Psalm 50:1–2a]

The God of gods, the Lord hath spoken: and he hath called the earth. From the rising of the sun, to the going down thereof: out of Sion the loveliness of his beauty.

Psalm 50

[L 50:20, AV Psalm 51:18]

Deal favorably, O Lord, in thy good will with Sion; that the walls of Jerusalem may be built up. &c.

Psalm 56

[L 56:10–12, AV Psalm 57:9–11]

Note   I will give praise to thee, O Lord, among the people: I will sing a psalm to thee among the nations. For thy mercy is magnified even to the heavens:

usque ad nubes veritas tua. Exaltare super celos, Deus, et super omnem terram gloria tua.

Psalmo 58

Intende ad visitandas omnes gentes &c. Ad nihilum deduces omnes gentes &c. Et scient quia Deus dominabitur Iacob et finium terre.

Psalmo 64

Nota Te decet hymnus, Deus, in Syon; et tibi reddetur votum in Ierusa lem. Exaudi orationem meam; ad te omnis caro veniet &c. Beatus, quem elegistii et assumpsisti; inhabitabit in atriis tuis. Replebimur in bonis domus tue; sanctum est templum tuum, mirabile in equi-tate. Exaudi nos, Deus salutaris noster, spes omnium finium terre et in mari longe &c.

Ex libro
Psalmo 65

Iubilate Deo omnis terra, psalmum dicite nomini eius; date gloriam laudi eius &c. "Omnis terra adoret te, et psallat tibi; psalmum dicat nomini tuo &c." Oculi eius super gentes respitiunt &c. Benedicite, gentes, Deum nostrumi et auditam facite vocem laudis eius. Introibo in domum tuam in holocaustis; reddam tibi vota mea, que distinxe-runt labia mea, et locutum est os meum in tribulatione mea &c.

Psalmo 66

Confiteantur tibi populi, Deus; confiteantur tibi populi omnes. Le-tentur et exultent gentes, quoniam iudicas populos in equitate et gentes in terra dirigis &c.

Psalmo 67

A templo tuo in Ierusalem tibi offerent reges munera.

and thy truth unto the clouds. Be thou exalted, O God, above the heavens: and thy glory above all the earth.

Psalm 58

[L 58:6b, 9b, 14b; AV Psalm 59:5b, 8b, 13b]

Attend to visit the nations. &c. Thou shalt bring all the nations to nothing. &c. And they shall know that God will rule Jacob and all the ends of the earth.

Psalm 64

[L 64:2–3, 5–6; AV Psalm 65:1–2,–5]

Note A hymn, O God, becometh thee in Sion: and a vow shall be paid to thee in Jerusalem. O hear my prayer: all flesh shall come to thee. &c. Blessed is he whom thou hast chosen and taken to thee: he shall dwell in thy courts. We shall be filled with the good things of thy house: holy is thy temple, wonderful in justice. / Hear us, O God our Saviour, who art the hope of all the ends of the earth, and in the sea afar off. &c.

✠

From the Book
Psalm 65

[L 65:1b–2, 4, 7b, 8, 13–14; AV Psalm 66:1–2, 4, 7b, 8, 13–14]

Shout with joy to God, all the earth: sing ye a psalm to his name: give glory to his praise. &c. Let all the earth adore thee and sing to thee: let it sing a psalm to thy name, &c. His eyes behold the nations. &c. O bless our God, ye Gentiles: and make the voice of his praise to be heard. I will go into thy house with burnt offerings: I will pay thee my vows, which my lips have uttered, and my mouth hath spoken, when I was in trouble. &c.

Psalm 66

[L 66:4–5, AV Psalm 67:3–4]

Let people confess to thee, O God: let all people give praise to thee. Let the nations be glad and rejoice: for thou judgest the people with justice, and direct the nations upon earth. &c.

Psalm 67

[L 67:30, AV Psalm 68:29]

From thy temple in Jerusalem, kings shall offer presents to thee.

Psalmo 68

Quoniam zelus domus tue comedit me; et opprobria exprobrantium tibi ceciderunt super me &c. Quoniam Deus salvam fatiet Syon et edificabuntur civitates Iude &c.

Psalmo 71

Reges Tharsis et insule munera offerent; reges Arabum et Sabba dona adducent; et adorabunt cum omnes reges; omnes gentes servient ei &c. Sit nomen eius benedictum in secula &c. Omnes gentes servient ei &c. Et replebitur maiestate eius omnis terra &c.

Psalmo 73

Redemisti virgam hereditatis tue: mons Syon in quo habitasti in eo &c. Incederunt igni sanctuarium tuum; in terra polluerunt tabernaculum nominis tui &c. Deus autem rex noster ante secula, operatus est salutem in medio terre. (9a)

Psalmorum
Psalmo 75

Notus in Iudea Deus: in Israel magnum nomen eius. Et factus est in pace locus eius, et habitatio eius in Syon &c.

Psalmo 78

Deus, venerunt gentes in hereditatem tuam, polluerunt templum sanctum tuum, posuerunt Ierusalem in pomorum custodiam &c.

Psalmo 81

Surge, Deus, iudica terram; quoniam tu hereditabis in omnibus gentibus.

Psalmo 83

Quam dilecta tabernacula tua, Domine virtutum! Concupiscit et deficit anima mea in atria Domini &c. Etenim benedictionem dabit legislator, ibunt de virtute in virtutem; videbitur Deus deorum in Syon.

Psalm 68

[L 68:10, 36a, AV Psalm 69:9, 35a]

For the zeal of thy house hath eaten me up: and the reproaches of them that reproached thee are fallen upon me. &c. For God will save Sion: / and the cities of Juda shall be built up. &c.

Psalm 71

[L 71:10–11, 17a, 17d, 19b; AV Psalm 72:10–11, 17a, 17d, 19b]

The kings of Tharsis and the islands shall offer presents: the kings of the Arabians and of Saba shall bring gifts. And all kings of the earth shall adore him: all nations shall serve him. &c. Let his name be blessed for evermore. &c. All nations shall magnify him. &c. And the whole earth shall be filled with his majesty. &c.

Psalm 73

[L 73:2b, 7, 12; AV Psalm 74:2b, 7, 1]

The scepter of thy inheritance which thou hast redeemed: Mount Sion in which thou hast dwelt. &c. They have set fire to thy sanctuary: they have defiled the dwelling place of thy name on the earth. &c. But God is our king before ages: he hath wrought salvation in the midst of the earth.

Of the Psalms
Psalm 75

[L 75:2–3, AV Psalm 76:1–2]

In Judaea, God is known: his name is great in Israel. And his place is in peace: and his abode in Sion. &c.

Psalm 78

[L 78:1, AV Psalm 79]

O God, the heathens are come into thy inheritance: they have defiled thy holy temple: they have made Jerusalem as a place to keep fruit. &c.

Psalm 81

[L 81:8, AV Psalm 82:8]

Arise, O God, judge thou the earth: for thou shalt inherit / among all the nations.

Psalm 83

[L 83:2–3a, 8; AV Psalm 84:1–2a, 7]

How lovely are thy tabernacles, O Lord of hosts. My soul longeth and fainteth for the courts of the Lord. &c. For the lawgiver shall give a blessing; they shall go from virtue to virtue: the God of gods shall be seen in Sion.

Psalmo 85

Non est similis tui in diis, Domine; et non est secundum opera tua. Omnes gentes, quascumque fecisti, venient et adorabunt coram te, Domine; et glorificabunt nomen tuum. Quoniam magnus es, et fatie[n]s mirabilia: tu es Deus solus &c.

Psalmo 86

Fundamenta eius in montibus sanctis; diligit Dominus portas Syon super omnia tabernacula Iacob. Gloriosa dicta sunt de te, civitas Dei &c.

Psalmo 88

Misericordias Domini in eternum cantabo &c. Confitebuntur celi mirabilia tua; etenim veritatem tuam in ecclesia sanctorum &c. Tunc locutus es in visione sanctis tuis &c. Inveni David servum meum &c. per totum. (9b)

Psalmo 91

Bonum est confiteri Domino et psallere nomini tuoi Altissime &c. Plantati in domo Domini, in atriis domus Dei nostri fiorebunt. Adhuc multiplicabuntur in senecta uberi et bene patientes erunt, ut annuntient &c.

Psalmo 92

Dominus regnavit, Decorem indutus est; indutus est Dominus forti-tudinemi et precinxit se &c. Testimonia tua credibilia facta sunt nimis: domum tuam decet sanctitudo, Domine, in longitudinem die-rum.

Psalmo 95

Cantate Domino canticum novum; cantate Domino, omnis terra &c. Annuntiate inter gentes gloriam eius, in omnibus populis mira-

Psalm 85

[L 85:8–10, AV Psalm 86:8–10]

There is none among the gods like unto thee, O Lord: and there is none according to thy works. All the nations thou hast made shall come and adore before thee, O Lord: and they shall glorify thy name. For thou art great and dost wonderful things: thou art God alone. &c.

Psalm 86

[L 86:1b–3, AV Psalm 87:1–3]

The foundations thereof are in the holy mountains: The Lord loveth the gates of Sion above all the tabernacles of Jacob. Glorious things are said of thee: O city of God. &c.

Psalm 88

[L 88:2a, 6, 20a, 21a; AV 89:1a, 5, 19a, 20a]

The mercies of the Lord I will sing for ever. &c. The heavens shall confess thy wonders, O Lord: and thy truth in the church of the saints. &c. Then thou spokest in a vision to thy saints. &c. I have found David my servant. &c, to end. /

Psalm 91

[L 91:2, 14–16a; AV 92:1, 13–15a]

It is good to give praise to the Lord: and to sing to thy name, O most High. &c. They that are planted in the house of the Lord shall flourish in the courts of the house of our God. They shall still increase in a fruitful old age: and shall be well treated, that they may shew. &c.

Psalm 92

[L 92:1b, 5; AV Psalm 93:1a, 5]

The Lord hath reigned, he is clothed with beauty: the Lord is clothed with strength, and hath girded himself. &c. Thy testimonies are become exceedingly credible. Holiness becometh thy house, O Lord, unto length of days.

Psalm 95

95:1b, 3–5, 7–10a; AV Psalm 96:1, 3–5, 7–10a]

Sing ye to the Lord a new canticle: sing to the Lord, all the earth. &c. Declare his glory among the Gentiles: his wonders among all people.

bilia eius. Quoniam magnus Dominus, et laudabilis nimis; terribilis est super omnes deos. Quoniam omnes dii gentium demonia; Dominus autem celos fecit &c. Afferte Domino patrie gentium, afferte Domino gloriam et honorem; afferte Domino gloriam nomini eius. Tollite hostias et introite in atria eius, adorate Dominum in atrio sancto eius. Commoveatur a fatie eius universa terra; dicite in gentibus quia Dominus regnavit &c. per totem.

Psalmo 96

Dominus regnavit. Exultet terra; letentur insule multe &c. A[n] nuntiaverunt celi iustitiam eius; et viderunt omnes populi gloriam eius. Confundantur omnes qui adorant sculptilia et qui gloriantur in simulacris suis. Adorate eum, omnes angeli eius. Audivit et letata est Syon &c. per totum.

Psalmo 97

Notum fecit Dominus salutare suum; in conspectu gentium revelavit iustitiam suam &c. (10a)

Psalmo 98

Dominus regnavit. Irascantur populi; qui sedet super cherubyn, moveatur terra. Dominus in Syon magnus et excelsus super omnes populos &c. Exaltate Dominum Deum nostrum et adorate in monte sancto eius; quoniam sanctus Dominus Deus noster &c.

Psalmo 99

Iubilate Domino omnis terra &c.

Psalmo 101

Tu exsurgens misereberis Syon, quia tempus miserendi eius, quia venit tempus &c. Et timebunt gentes nomen tuum, Domine, et omnes reges terre gloriam tuam. Quia edificavit Dominus Syon et videbitur in gloria sua &c. Ut annuntient in Syon nomen Domini et laudem eius in Ierusalem &c. per totum.

For the Lord is great, and exceedingly to be praised: he is to be feared above all gods. For all the gods of the Gentiles are devils: but the Lord made the heavens. Bring ye to the Lord, O ye kindreds of the Gentiles, bring ye to the Lord glory and honor: bring to the Lord glory unto his name. Bring up sacrifices, and come into his courts: adore ye the Lord in his holy court. Let all the earth be moved at his presence. Say ye among the Gentiles: The Lord hath reigned. &c, to end.

Psalm 96

[L 96:1b, 6–8a; AV Psalm 97:1, 6–8a]

The Lord hath reigned, let the earth rejoice: let many islands be glad. &c. / The heavens declared his justice: and all people saw his glory. Let them be all confounded that adore graven things, and that glory in their idols. Adore him, all you his angels: Sion heard, and was glad. &c, to end.

Psalm 97

[L 97:2, AV Psalm 98:2]

The Lord hath made known his salvation: he hath revealed his justice in the sight of the Gentiles. &c.

Psalm 98

[L 98:1b–2, 9; AV Psalm 99:1–2, 9]

The Lord hath reigned, let the people be angry: he that sitteth on the cherubims, let the earth be moved. The Lord is great in Sion, and high above all people. &c. Exalt ye the Lord our God, and adore at his holy mountain: for the Lord our God is holy. &c.

Psalm 99

[L 99:2a, AV Psalm 100:1]

Sing joyfully to God, all the earth. &c.

Psalm 101

[L 101:14, 16–17, 22; AV Psalm 102:13, 15–16, 21]

Thou shalt arise and have mercy on Sion: for it is time to have mercy on it, for the time is come. &c. And the Gentiles shall fear thy name, O Lord, and all the kings of the earth thy glory. For the Lord hath built up Sion: and he shall be seen in his glory. &c. That they may declare the name of the Lord in Sion; and his praise in Jerusalem. &c, to end. /

Psalmo 104

Confitemini Domino et invocate nomen eius; annuntiate inter gentes opera eius &c. Ipse Dominus Deus noster; in universa terra iuditia eius.

Psalmo 105

Confitemini Domino, quoniam bonus; quoniam in seculum misericordia eius &c. Salvos fac nos, Domine Deus noster, et congrega nos de nationibus, ut confiteamur nomini sancto tuo et gloriemur in laude tua &c.

Psalmo 107

Confitebor tibi in populis, Domine; et psallam tibi in nationibus. Quia magna [est] super celos misericordia tua et usque ad nubes veritas tua. Exaltare super celos, Deus, et super omnem terram gloria tua. Ut liberentur dilecti tui. salvum fac dextera tua, et exaudi me. Deus locutus est in sancto suo &c. (10b)

Psalmo 112

Sit nomen Domini benedictum; ex hoc nunc et usque in seculum. A solis ortu usque ad occasum, laudabile nomen Domini. Excelsus super omnes gentes Dominus &c.

Psalmo 113

Non nobis, Domine, non nobis, sed nomini tuo da gloriam. Super misericordia tua et veritate tua; ne quando dicant gentes: "ubi est Deus eorum?" Deus autem noster in celo; omnia, quecumque voluit, fecit. Simulacra gentium argentum et aurum, opera manuum hominum. Os habent et non loquentur; oculos habent et non videbunt &c.

Psalmo 115

Dirupisti vincula mea: tibi sacrificabo hostiam laudis et nomen Domini invocabo. Vota mea Domino reddam in conspectu omnis populi eius in atriis domus Dominii in Inedio tui, Ierusalem.

Psalm 104

[L 104:1b, 7; AV Psalm 105:1, 7]

Give glory to the Lord, and call upon his name: declare his deeds among the Gentiles., &c. He is the Lord our God: his judgments are in all the earth.

Psalm 105

[L 105:1b, 47; AV Psalm 106:1, 47]

Give glory to the Lord, for he is good: for his mercy endureth for ever. &c. Save us, O Lord, our God, and gather us from among the nations: That we may give thanks to thy holy name, and may glory in thy praise. &c.

Psalm 107

[L 107:4–8a, AV Psalm 108:3–7a]

I will praise thee, O Lord, among the people: and I will sing unto thee among the nations. For thy mercy is great above the heavens: and thy truth even unto the clouds. Be thou exalted, O God, above the heavens, and thy glory over all the earth: that thy beloved may be delivered. Save with thy right hand and hear me. God hath spoken in His holiness. &c.

Psalm 112

[L 112:2–4a, AV Psalm 113:2–4a]

Blessed be the name of the Lord: from henceforth now and for ever. From the rising of the sun unto the going down of the same, the name of the Lord is worthy of praise. The Lord is high above all nations. &c.

Psalm 113

[L 13:1–5, AV 115:1–5]

Not to us, O Lord, not to us: but to thy name give glory. For thy mercy, and for thy truth's sake: lest the Gentiles should say: Where is / their God? But our God is in heaven: he hath done all things whatsoever he would. The idols of the Gentiles are silver and gold, the works of the hands of men. They have mouths and speak not: they have eyes and see not. &c.

Psalm 115

[L 115:15c–19, AV Psalm 116:16c–19a]

Thou hast broken my bonds. I will sacrifice to thee the sacrifice of praise: and I will call upon the name of the Lord. I will pay my vows to the Lord in the sight of all his people: in the courts of the house of the Lord, in the midst of thee, O Jerusalem.

Psalmo 116

Laudate Dominum, omnes gentes; laudate eum, omnes populi. Quoniam confirmata est super nos misericordia eius; et veritas Domini manet in eternum.

Psalmo 121

Letatus sum in his que dicta sunt mihi: "in domum Domini ibimus." Stantes erant pedes nostri in atriis tuis, Hierusalem &c.

Psalmo 125

In convertendo Dominus captivitatem Syon; facti sumus sicut consolati. Tunc repletum est gaudio os nostrum; et lingua nostra exultatione. Tunc dicent inter gentes: "magnificavit Dominus facere cum eis &c." (11a)

Psalmo 127

Beati omnes, qui timent Dominum, qui ambulant in viis eius &c. Benedicat tibi Dominus ex Syon; et videas bona Ierusalem omnibus diebus vite tue. Et videas filios filiorum tuorum, pacem super Israel.

Psalmo 128

Dominus iustus concidet cervices peccatorum. Confundantur et convertantur retrorsum omnes, qui oderunt Syon &c.

Psalmo 131

Memento, Domine, David, et omnis mansuetudinis eius &c. Ecce audivimus eum in Effrata, invenimus eum in campis silve. Introibimus in tabernaculum eius, adorabimus in loco, ubi steterunt pedes eius &c. Et filii eorum usque in seculum sedebunt super sedem tuam. Quoniam elegit Dominus Syon; elegit eam in habitationem sibi &c.

Psalmo 133

Ecce, nunç benedicite Dominum, omnes servi Domini; qui statis in domo Dominii in atriis domus Dei nostri. In noctibus extollite

Psalm 116

[L 116:1a–2, AV Psalm 117:1–2a]

O praise the Lord, all ye nations: praise him, all ye people. For his mercy is confirmed upon us: and the truth of the Lord remaineth for ever.

Psalm 121

[L 121:1b–2, AV Psalm 122:1–2]

I rejoiced at the things that were said to me: We shall go into the house of the Lord. Our feet were standing in thy courts, O Jerusalem. &c.

Psalm 125

[L 125:1b–2, AV Psalm 126:1–2]

When the Lord brought back the captivity of Sion, we became like men comforted. Then was our mouth filled with gladness: and our tongue with joy. Then shall they say among the Gentiles: The Lord hath done great things for them.

Psalm 127

[L 127:1b, 5–6; AV Psalm 128:1, 5–6]

Blessed are all they that fear the Lord: that walk in his ways. &c. / May the Lord bless thee out of Sion: and mayest thou see the good things of Jerusalem all the days of thy life. And mayest thou see thy children's children, peace upon Israel.

Psalm 128

[L 128:4–5, AV 129:4–5]

The Lord who is just will cut the necks of sinners. Let them all be confounded and turn back that hate Sion.

Psalm 131

[L 131:1b, 6–7, 12b–13; AV Psalm 132:1, 6–7, 12b–13]

O Lord, remember David: and all his meekness. &c. Behold we have heard of it in Ephrata: we have found it in the fields of the wood. We will go into his tabernacle: we will adore in the place where his feet stood. &c. Their children also for evermore shall sit upon thy throne. For the Lord hath chosen Sion: he hath chosen it for his dwelling. &c.

Psalm 133

[L 133:1b–3, AV 134:1–3]

Behold now bless ye the Lord: all ye servants of the Lord: Who stand in the house of the Lord, in the courts of the house of our God. In the

manus vestras in sancta, et benedicite Dominum. Benedicat tibi Dominus ex Syon qui fecit celum et terram.

Psalmo 134

Laudate nomen Domini, laudate, servi, Dominum, qui statis in domo Domini, in atriis domus Dei nostri &c. Benedictus Dominus ex Syon, qui habitat in Ierusalem &c.

Psalmo 135

Confitemini Domino, quoniam bonus &c. Confitemini Deo deorum &c. Confitemini Domino dominorum &c. per totum. (11b)

Psalmo 137

In conspectu angelorum psallam tibi; adorabo ad templum sanctum tuum, et confitebor nomini tuo &c. Confiteantur tibi, Domine, omnes reges terre; quia audierunt omnia verba oris tui &c.

Psalmo 144

Confiteantur tibi, Domine, omnia opera tua, et sancti tui benedicant tibi. Gloriam regni tui dicent et potentiam tuam loquentur. Ut notam fatiant filiis hominum potentiam tuam et gloriam magnificentie regni tui. Regnum tuum regnum omnium seculorum; et dominatio tua in omni generatione et generatione &c.

Psalmo 145

Lauda, anima mea, Dominum, laudabo Dominum in vita mea; psallam Deo meo, quam diu fuero &c. Regnabit Dominus in secula, Deus tuus, Syon in generatione et generatione.

Psalmo 147

Lauda, Ierusalem, Dominum; lauda Deum tuum, Syon &c. per totum.

nights lift up your hands to the holy places: and bless ye the Lord. May the Lord out of Sion bless thee, he that made heaven and earth.

Psalm 134

[L 134:1b–2, 21; AV Psalm 135:1b–2, 21]

Praise ye the name of the Lord: O you his servants, praise the Lord: You that stand in the house of the Lord: in the courts of the house of our God. &c. Blessed be the Lord out of Sion, who dwelleth in Jerusalem. &c. /

Psalm 135

[L 135, 1b, 2a, 3a; AV Psalm 136:1a, 2a, 3a]

Praise the Lord, for he is good. &c. Praise ye the God of gods. &c. Praise ye the Lord of lords. &c, to end.

Psalm 137

[L 137:1b–2a, 4; AV Psalm 138:1b–2a, 4]

I will sing praise to thee in the sight of the angels: I will worship towards thy holy temple, and I will give glory to thy name. &c. May all the kings of the earth give glory to thee: for they have heard all the words of thy mouth. &c.

Psalm 144

[L 144:10–13a, AV Psalm 145:10–13]

Let all thy works, O Lord, praise thee: and let thy saints bless thee. They shall speak of the glory of thy kingdom: and shall tell of thy power: To make thy might known? to the sons of men: and the glory of the magnificence of thy kingdom. Thy kingdom is a kingdom of all ages: and thy dominion endureth throughout all generations. &c.

Psalm 145

[L 145:2a, 10; AV Psalm 146:1b–2, 10a]

Praise the Lord, O my soul: in my life I will praise the Lord: I will sing to my God as long as I shall be. &c. The Lord shall reign for ever: thy God, O Sion, unto generation and generation.

Psalm 147

[L 147:12, AV Psalm 147:12]

Praise the Lord, O Jerusalem: praise thy God, O Sion. &c, to end. /

Psalmo 148

Laudate Dominum de celis &c. Reges terre, et omnes populi; principes et omnes iudices terre; iuvenes et virgines, senes cum iunioribus laudent nomen Domini; quia exaltatum est nomen eius solius &c.

Psalmo 149

Cantate Domino canticum novum &c. Et filie Syon exultent in rege suo &c.

Psalmo 150

Omnis spiritus laudet Dominum. Amen. (12a)

Oratio Salomonis. Ecclesiastici 36

Miserere, Domine, plebi tue, super quam invocatum est nomen tuum; et Israel, quem coequasti primogenito tuo. Miserere civitati sanctificationis tue, Ierusalem, civitati requiei tue. Reple Syon inenarrabilibus virtutibus tuis, et gloria tua populum tuum. Da testimonium, qui ab initio creature tue sunt, et suscita precationes, quas locuti sunt in nomine tuo prophete priores. Da mercedem, Domine, sustinentibus te, ut prophete tui fideles inveniantur. Et exaudi orationem servorum tuorum, secundum benedictionem Aaron de populo tuo, et dirige nos in viam iustitie, ut sciant omnes, qui habitant terram, quia tu es Deus conspector seculorum.

> Haré semejante á este mi siervo
> al sabio varón sagaz y prudente,
> que funda y ordena por modo exelente.

Isydorus, libro 7. Ethymologiarum, capitulo 8

Prophetie genera sunt septem. Primum genus extasis, quod est mentis excessus, sicut vidit Petrus vas illud summissum de celo, in stupore mentis, cum variis animalibus. Secundum genus visio, sicut apud Isayam dicentem: "Vidi Dominum sedentem super solium excelsum." Tertium genus sompnium, sicut Iacob subnixam in celo scalam dormiens vidit. Quartum genus per nubem, sicut ad Moysem

Psalm 148

[L 148:1b, 11–13; AV Psalm 148:1b, 11–13a]

Praise ye the Lord from the heavens. &c. Kings of the earth and all
people: princes and all judges of the earth: Young men and maidens.
Let the old with the younger, praise the name of the Lord: for his name
alone is exalted. &c.

Psalm 149

[L 149:1b, 2b; AV Psalm 149:1b, 2b]

Sing ye to the Lord a new canticle. &c. And let the children of Sion
be joyful in their king. &c.

Psalm 150

[L 150:5b, AV Psalm 150:6a]

Let every spirit praise the Lord. Amen.

✠

The Prayer of Solomon, Ecclesiasticus 36

[L 36:14–19]

Have mercy on thy people, upon whom thy name is invoked: and upon
Israel, whom thou hast raised up to be thy firstborn. Have mercy on
Jerusalem, the city which thou has sanctified, the city of thy rest. Fill
Sion with thy unspeakable words, and thy people with thy glory. Give
testimony to them that are thy creatures from the beginning: and raise
up the prophecies which the former prophets spoke in thy name. Reward
them that patiently wait for thee, that thy prophets may be found faithful:
and hear the prayers of thy servants. According to the blessing of Aaron
over thy people. And direct us into the way of justice: and let all know
that dwell upon the earth, that thou art God, the beholder of all ages. /

> This is the way I shall make my servant to be
> A knowing man wise and prudent,
> Who founds and arranges in an excellent manner.[16]

✠

Isidore [of Seville], *Etymologies*, Book 7, Chapter 8[17]

There are seven different kinds of prophecies. The first kind is the ecstatic
state, which is beyond and outside of the ordinary mind, as was the mind
of Peter when he saw high in the heavens that vessel filled with various
animals [Acts 14:10–11]. The second kind is the vision, which was the
state of Isaiah when he said, "I saw the Lord sitting upon a throne high
and elevated" [Isaiah 6:6]. The third kind is the dream, as Jacob saw
in his sleep a ladder leaning upwards into heaven [Genesis 28:12]. The
fourth kind is through a cloud, as when the Lord spoke to Moses and

et ad Iob post plagam loquitur Deus. Quintum genus vox de celo, sicut ad Abraam sonuit dicens: "Ne iniitias manum tuam super puerum." Et apud Saulum in via: "Saule, Saule, quid me persequeris?" Sextum genus accepta parabola, sicut apud Salomonem in Proverbiis, et apud Balaam, eum evocaretur a Balach. Septimum genus repletio Sancti Spiritus, sicut pene apud omnes prophetas.

Sequitur

Alii tria genera visionum dixerunt. Unum secundum oculos corporis &c. Alterum secundum spiritum, quo imaginamur ea que per corpus sentimus &c. Tertium autem genus visionis est quod neque corporeis sensibus, neque ulla parte anime qua corporalium rerum imagines capiuntur, sed per intuitum mentis quo intellecta conspicitur veritas &c., ut ibidem. (13a)

✠

Rabí Samuel, &c.

En una epistola, ó carta trasladada de arávigo en rromançe, la qual embió el rrabí Samuel de Israel, natural de la çibdad de Fis, á maestre Ysaach, rrabbí de la synagoga de Marrucos &c., los quales después fueron buenos y fieles christianos.

Capítulo 16

Señor mỹo maestro. Como nos entre nos, et yo entre my leo, et nos leemos que so et que somos fijos de Jacob patriarcha, mucho he pavor que sea complido en nos aquello, que es dicho por la boca de Ysaías en el capítulo XXX: "Matar te ha Dios, o Israel, et llamará sus siervos por otro nombre." Temor he, señor, que aquellos siervos son los gentiles, á los quales deve ser puesto aquel nombre, segund que diçe Moysén: "Serán los gentiles á la cabeça, et el pueblo incrédulo á la cola;" segund que nos somos, ya son más de mill años. Aun de los gentiles diçe Hieremias en el capítulo VI: "Fenchir se ha la tierra de Dios, et sobrará asỹ como la agua del mar." Et d'ellos diçe Salomón en el 3 libro de los Rreyes en el capítulo XLVIII en la su oratión assỹ: "Señor Dios, quando veniere el avenediso, et el de tierra agena á la sancta Casa tuya, et llamare aỹ el tu sancto nombre muy bendito, oyr lo has, Señor mỹo, porque todas las cosas aprendan temer el tu nombre, assỹ como el tu pueblo de Ysrael." ?Pues, señor mỹo, en qué nos gloriamos, et porqué menospretiamos los gentiles, pues que Salomón los façe partiçipan-

Ysaías 30

Moysén

Hiermías

III Regum
capitulo 48

to Job after his sufferings. The fifth kind is the voice from heaven, as the voice that spoke to Abraham saying, "Lay not thy hand upon the boy" [Genesis 22:11–12]; and the voice that said to Saul upon the road, "Saul, Saul, why persecutest thou me?" [Acts 9:4]. The sixth kind is received in the form of a parable, as was the case with Solomon in the Book of Proverbs, and with Balaam when he was commissioned by Balach. The seventh kind of prophecy is the filling with the Holy Spirit, as was the case with nearly all the prophets.

Continuation

[From the same chapter of the *Etymologies*]

Some have said that there are three kinds of prophetic vision. One kind is a vision with the physical eyes of the body, &c. Another is a vision of the spirit, in which an image is formed of things that can be sensed by the body, &c. Still a third kind of vision does not involve the physical senses or any part of the mind in which images of material things are formed, but as an intuition of the mind in which truth appears and is / understood. &c. in the same place.

✠

Rabbi Samuel &c.[18]

From an epistle, or letter translated from Arabic into Latin, which Rabbi Samuel of Israel, born in the city of Fez, sent to the teacher Isaac, Rabbi of the synagogue of Morocco, &c, who later became good and faithful Christians.

Chapter 16

My dear teacher. Among ourselves we have always read that we are the sons of the patriarch Jacob, and I believed it. But I fear greatly that there has come to pass upon us that which was prophesied by the mouth of Isaiah in the thirtieth chapter: that God would destroy Israel, and call his servants by another name. I fear, sir, that those servants are the Gentiles, upon whom that name has been placed, just as Moses said that the Gentiles would be at the head and the unbelieving people at the tail. This is just where we have been now for more than a thousand years. Jeremiah also speaks of the Gentiles when he says in chapter six that God's land must be covered, and remain so as the water of the sea. Solomon also speaks of them in the third book of the Kings, in chapter 48, when he prays [III Kings 8:41–43, paraphrased], "Lord God, when the stranger shall come from a foreign land to thy holy House, and shall there call upon thy holy and most blessed name, then hear him, my Lord, for they shall all learn to fear thy name, just as the people of Israel." Therefore, Sir, why should we be proud, / and why do we despise the Gentiles, when Solomon makes them to be participants in the fear of

Isaiah 30

Moses

Jeremiah

III Kings 48

tes del temor del Señor, et de la Casa sancta suya et por ventura Dios nos desechó á nos de aquella su sancta Casa, assŷ como nos dixo? Et aun d'estos gentiles dise Moysén en el IV libro de la Ley: "Esto dise el Señor: fenchir se ha toda la tierra de la gloria del Señor." Et d'ellos dise David en el psalmo XXI: "Ante ti vernán et convertir se han al Señor todos los fines de la tierra i esso mismo diçe Isaias en el capitulo 55: "O Casa sancta, vino la tu lumbre, et la gloria del Señor sobre ti es nasçida; andarán las gentes en la tu lumbre." Señor mŷo, ?quién son (13b) los que venieron á la Casa del Señor, sy non las gentes estrañas, que erravan al Señor, adorando los dolos? Et non solamente las gentes, mas aun los príncipes d'ellos, et de los quales dixo que andarian en la lumbre de la sancta Casa, nos andamos errados d'ella ya son más de mill año[s]. Otrosŷ diçe este mesmo Isaías en el capitulo LXV: "Cata que la gente, que non sabías, llamarási et las nationes, que e non cognosçieron vernán á ti;" segund que de fecho paresçe, son ya más dé mill años, ca el Christo, que fué embiado, seguía la Ley, que nos fué dada, vino a las gentes, que ley non supieroni et advenieron et él les dió ley nueva, et pura, et sancta; et por esto diçe Isaŷas en el capítulo XLII: "Concordaron las gentes et los rreyes d'ellas, et aiuntáronse en la Casa del Señor," et non tiene assŷ este passo la nuestra transladitión. Et aun señor mŷo, temo que [de] aquellos fué dicho lo que se lee en este mesmo capítulo, que diçe: "Adiuntadvos, et venid todos los de los gentiles, que fuestes salvos por Dios." Et d'ellos diçe otra ves Isaías en el capítulo LXIIII: "Buscaron á my, los que preguntavan por my, et falláro[n]me los que me buscavan." Et más diçe Hieremías en el capítulo III: "Aiuntarse an todas las gentes en el nombre del Señor en la Casa sancta, et non andarán más en la maldad de sus corazones." Et diçe más Hieremías en el capítulo XVI: "Ahé Dios, Señor mŷo, et Dios mŷo, á ti vernán todos desde de los postrimeros fines de la tierra, et dirán: non heredaron los nuestros padres, sy non mentira et maldad." Et aun d'estos mesmos gentiles diçe Sophonías propheta en el capitulo III: "Otorgado es que las gentes, que fablen en el nombre del Señor et que lo sirvan en ombro uno, et que lo sirva todo omen en su lugar, et todas las yslas de la tierra." Esso mismo dixo Zacharías propheta en el capítulo II: "Allégrate, Casa de Syón que yo verné á ti et moraré en medio de ti. En aquel día se allegarán á Dios las gentes en su muchedumbre." (14a)

Marginal notes:

Moysén, Numeri, capitulo 14

Psalmo 21

Isaie 55

Isaye 65 capítulo

Isaie capítulo 42

Ibidem

Isaye capítulo 64

Hieremie capítulo III

idem capítulo 16

Sophonías capítulo 3

Zacharías capítulo 2

✠

Diçe aun este mesmo propheta en el capítulo 8: "Esto dise el Señor de las huestes: vernán gentes muchas de muchos lugares, et dirá el varón á su veçino: vamos, et busquemos al Señor en bien." Et, my señor, estas prophetías complidas son et cómplense oy á los nuestros ojos; ca, señor, claramente vees como todos los pueblos

Zacharías 8

the Lord and in the Lord's holy House? Is it not possible that God has rejected us from that holy House, just as was prophesied? And Moses says about these Gentiles in the Fourth Book of the Law, "Thus saith the Lord: The whole earth will be filled with the glory of the Lord." And David says of them in Psalm 21, "They shall come before thee, and all the ends of the earth shall be converted to the Lord." Isaiah says the same in chapter 55, "O holy House, thy light has come, and the glory of the Lord has risen upon thee; the Gentiles shall walk in thy light." Dear Sir, who are those that have come to the House of the Lord, if not the foreign Gentiles who had strayed to the Lord while they were worshipping idols? And not only the Gentiles, but even their princes will walk in the light of the holy House, according to his prophecy, while we have been wandering far from it already for more than a thousand years. Furthermore Isaiah says in chapter 65 "The people that thou knewest not shalt thou call, and the Gentiles who did not know thee shall come to thee." This is exactly what appears to have been happening for more than a thousand years already; because the Messiah who was sent and who fulfilled the law that was given to us, came to the Gentiles who did not know the law, and they approached and he gave them a new law that is pure and holy. And for this reason Isaiah says, in chapter 42, "The Gentiles agreed together, and their kings, and they assembled in the House of the Lord," and this passage does not read the same in our version. Furthermore, dear sir, I fear that the passage in the same chapter refers to them, saying, "Assemble yourselves, and come, and draw near together, all of the Gentiles who have been saved by God." [Isaiah 45:20]. And Isaiah speaks again / of them in chapter 64: "They sought me who inquired about me, and they who sought me found me." And furthermore Jeremiah says in chapter 3, "All the Gentiles shall assemble together in the name of the Lord in the holy House, and they shall no more walk in the evil of their hearts." And furthermore Jeremiah says in chapter 16 [Jeremiah 16:19], "O God, my Lord and my God, to thee shall all come from the uttermost ends of the earth, and they shall say, 'Our fathers inherited nothing but lies and evil'." Furthermore, Zephaniah speaks of the same Gentiles in chapter 3, "It has been determined that the Gentiles who speak in the name of the Lord and who serve him with one shoulder in his place, and who serve him each man in his place, and all the islands of the earth." [Zephaniah 3:9 and context, paraphrased] The prophet Zachariah says the same in the second chapter, "Rejoice, O House of Zion, for I will come to thee, and will dwell in the midst of thee. And many nations shall be joined to God in one day."

✠

Furthermore, the same prophet [Zachariah] says in chapter 8, "Thus saith the Lord of hosts: many nations shall come from many places, and a man shall say to his neighbor: Come, and let us seek the Lord for our good." Furthermore, dear sir, these prophecies have been fulfilled, and they are being fulfilled today before our eyes. For, sir, you see clearly

Margin notes:
Moses, Numbers 14

Psalms 21

Isaiah 55

Isaiah 65

Isaiah 42

The same

Isaiah 64

Jeremiah 3

The same, Chapter 16

Zephaniah 3

Zachariah 2

Zachariah 8

et todas las lenguas leen los libros de la ley et de los prophetas, et el Psalterio et desechados ya los ŷdolos, en que ni[n]guno d'ellos cree por la doctrina de Moysén y de Aarón que creieron aquel Justo, del qual dice el propheta Abacuch en el capítulo 3: "Saliste, Señor, en salud del tu pueblo con el tu Christo." Abacuch 3

Idem rabí Samuel, capítulo 17

Temo, mi señor, que Dios vençedor vivificó et dió vida á estas gentes por la su fe, et él nos mató á nos con la incredulidat et dureza, segund qu'él dise por la boca de Isaías en el capítulo LXV; onde dise assŷ: "Esto dise el Señor: ?porqué vos llamé, et non me rrespondistes? Los mys siervos comerán et vos fambrearedes; catad, que los mys siervos veverán et vos peresceredes de sed; los mys siervos se alegrarán en alegría de coraçon, et vos seredes confundidos en amargura de vuestro coraçón. Et matar te ha Dios, o Israel, et llamará sus siervos por otro nombre. En el qual nombre bendiçirá aquel Dios, que es bendicho sobre la tierra. Amen. Et nos veemos las rredemptiones d'este nombre bendicho de Dios sobre la fas de la tierra, et veemos que á nos derramó en captiverio por todo el mundo, et por las quatro partes d'él, ya son más de mill años. Et claramente paresçe en nos el rrostro de la ira de Dios, non para castigari mas para destruir. Et aqueste es el matamiento, con el qual amenasó Dios que nos mataría. Et aquestas gentes, las quales Dios llama syervos suyos, rreçebieron ya lo que Dios prometió en la Ley, ante de la muerte del nuestro primero nombre, segund la orden de las palabras, que son dichas por Isaías. Et la fambre et Isaie la sed, que nos padesçemos, non es de pan, mas es de las orationes, quc es sequedad de las nuestras ánimas, et fambre (14b) de la palabra de Dios, segund que dixo el propheta Amos en el capitulo VI: "Et tu, señor mŷo, sabes esta cosa más larga et claramente que yo." Amos capítulo 6

Ysaie 65

Idem rabí Samuel, capitulo 18

Pavor he yo, señor mío maestro, que aquestas gentes han et ovieron mill años de vida después que fué muerto Israel. Las quales gentes non havían cosa de bien antes que creyesen en Dios, et en su Christo, et ellas nos fiçieron ser aquellas bestias, de las quales diçe el propheta Abacuch que non han cabdillo. Et aquestas gentes, después que fueron alimpiadas por la fe, han sus ayunos, et sus fiestasi et sus cerimonias de la ley nueva, et aun más todas aquellas cosas, que son contenidas en la Ley vieja, quanto pertenesçe á limpiesa. Et vees, señor, como en todo lenguaje, et en todo rincón, et en todo lugar, et en Oriente, et en Occidente las gentes confiessan el nombre del Señor. Et non creyeron en él por Moysén ny por alguno de los prophetas, como quier que sean studiosos en la Ley, et en los libros de los prophetas, mas Dios los llamó por los discipu- Abacuch, I capítulo Nota

how all peoples of all languages are reading the books of the law and of the prophets and the Psalms, and they have already destroyed the idols in which none of them believes as a result of the doctrine of Moses and of Aaron, and they have believed in that Righteous One of whom the prophet Habakkuk speaks in chapter 3, / "Thou wentest forth for the salvation of thy people with thy Christ." [Habakkuk 3:13.]   Habakkuk 3

The same Rabbi Samuel, Chapter 17

Dear sir, I fear that the mighty God has quickened and given life to these Gentiles by faith in him, and that he has killed us with unbelief and hardness, according to what he spoke by the mouth of Isaiah in chapter 65, where he said thus: "Why have I called you, and you have not answered me? My servants shall eat, and you shall be hungry. Behold, my servants shall drink, and you shall perish of thirst. My servants shall rejoice with joyfulness of heart, and you shall be confounded in the bitterness of your hearts. And God shall slay thee, O Israel, and shall call his servants by another name, in which name he that is blessed upon the earth shall bless God. Amen." [Isaiah 5:12–16 paraphrased.] And we see the redemptions of that name that is blessed of God upon the face of the earth, and we see that he has scattered us in captivity throughout the whole world, into the four corners of it, for more than a thousand years already. And clearly the face of the anger of God appears to be against us, not for chastisement, but for destruction. And this is the same slaughter with which God warned that he would destroy us. And these Gentiles, whom God calls his servants, have already received that which God promised in the Law, before the death of our first name, following the order of the words which were spoken by Isaiah. And the hunger and the thirst that we suffer is not for bread, but it is for prayer for which our spirits are thirsty, and hunger for the word of God, just as was spoken by the prophet Amos in chapter 6. And you, dear sir, understand this matter / much more deeply and clearly than I do.   Isaiah 65   Isaiah   Amos 6

The same Rabbi Samuel, Chapter 18

I am afraid, my dear teacher, that those Gentiles have life, and have had it for a thousand years after the death of Israel. Those Gentiles did not have anything good before they believed in God and in his Christ, and they have made us to be like those animals without a ruler which are described by the prophet Habakkuk [1:14]. And those Gentiles, after they have been cleansed by faith, have their fasts and feasts and ceremonies of the new law, and even more they have all those things which are contained in the old law and which pertain to purifying. And you see, sir, how in every language, in every corner and in every place, both in the east and in the west, the Gentiles confess the name of the Lord. And they do not believe in God because of Moses or because of any one of the prophets, however much they study the law and the books of the prophets, but God has called them to be disciples of the Righteous   Habakkuk 1   Note

los del Justoi el qual salió con Dios en salud d'ellos, segund que
Abacuch 3 capítulo dise Dios por la boca del propheta Abacuch. Aquestos discípulos
de aqueste Justo fueron fijos nuestros et de los fijos de Ysrael,
los quales en otro nombre son llamados apóstolos. Et mucho me
temo, señor, que aquestos son aquellos, los quales dise Dios por
Psalmo 18 la boca de David en el psalmo XVIII: "En toda la tierra salió el
sonido d'ellos, et en los postrimeros fines de la tierra fueron espasi-
das sus palabras." Et porque el propheta demuestra que d'estos
fabló et non de nos, por tanto diçe más adelante que non será lengua
ny palabra que non oya las voçes d'ellos. Enpero, esto non se puede
complir en nuestra lengua hebraica. Ca ni[n]gunas gentes non obe-
desçieron á nuestros padres Moysén Aarón et á los otros, antes
los mataron et dessecharon de sŷ. Enpero, las gentes saben oy á
Moysén et á los prophetas, et cognoscen á Dios, et façen ley nueva,
segu[n]d que los apóstolos los enseñaron &c. (15a)

Divi Augustini

Soliloquia, capitulo XXVI: Recordare misericordie tue a[n]tique,
qua nos a principio &c. Requirantur. (15b)

Divi Augustini

Prius quam me   Soliloquia, capitulo XXVI: Prius quam me formares in utero, no-   Augustini
formares, novisti me   visti me, et ante quam exirem de vulva, quidquid tibi placuit preor-   Soliloquia 26
dinasti [de] me. Que et qualia sint in libro tuo scripta de me, in
secreto consistorii tui &c.

Prevalebit Dominus adversus eos, et exterminabit omnes deos   Augustini De
gentium terre. Et adorabunt eum, unusquisque de loco suo, omnes   divinatione
insule gentium, aut non credebant ista sibi futura, qui in templis   demonum
gentium colebantur. De divinatione demonum.

Iterum repetit in eodem libro: "prevalebit," inquid, "Dominus,   Idem
adversus eos, et exterminabit omne[s] deos gentium terre, et adorabunt eum, unusquisque de loco suo, omnes insule gentium." Neque
enim sole insule, sed ita omnes gentes, ut etiam omnes insule gentium, quando quidem alibi non insulas nominat, sed universum
Universum ordem   orbem terrarum, dicens: "Commemorabuntur et convertentur ad   Psalmo 21
et omnes insulas   Dominum universi fines terre, et adorabunt in conspectu eius uni-
convertentur ad   verse patrie gentium. Quoniam Domini est regnum, et ipse domina-
Dominum   bitur gentium."

Iterum in eodem: "Dominus dixit ad me: filius meus es tu, ego   Psalmo 2
hodie genuite; postula a mei et dabo tibi gentes hereditatem tuam,
et possessionem tuam terminos terre." His atque huiusmodi profeti-
cis documentis predictum ostenditur (16b) quod videmus impleri

One, the One who went forth with God for their salvation, according to what God said by the mouth of the prophet Habakkuk [3:13]. Those disciples of that Righteous One were our children, sons of Israel, who are known by another name as apostles. And, sir, I fear greatly that they were the ones intended, when God said by the mouth of David in Psalm 18 that their voice went out into the whole world, and that their words were spread to the uttermost ends of the earth. And because the prophet was indicating that he was speaking of them and not of us, he therefore said a little further on, that there would be no language nor speech in which / their voices would not be heard. Now, this cannot be fulfilled in our Hebrew language. For no gentiles obeyed our fathers Moses, Aaron and the others, but would rather have killed them and rejected them. However, the Gentiles today know Moses and the prophets, and they know God, and they obey the new law as they have been taught by the apostles. &c.

Habakkuk 3

Psalms 18

Saint Augustine

Soliloquies, Chapter 26:[19] Remember thy mercies of old, which were to us at the beginning &c. Search these things out.

Saint Augustine

Soliloquies, Chapter 26:[20] Before thou didst form me in the womb, thou knewest me, and before I went forth from the womb, thou didst preordain concerning me whatever was pleasing to thee. In thy book were written concerning me the things, and the kind of things, according to thy secret counsel, &c.

Before thou didst form me in the womb, thou knewest me . . .

Augustine, Soliloquies 26

The Lord shall win the victory against them, and destroy all the gods of the nations of the earth. All the inhabitants of the islands of the Gentiles shall worship before him, everyone in his own place. But the gods who were worshipped in the temples of the nations did not believe that this was to happen to them. *On the Divination of Demons.*

Augustine, On the Divination of Demons

He writes again in the same book: The Lord shall win the victory against them and destroy all the gods of the nations of the earth. All the inhabitants of the islands of the Gentiles shall worship before him, everyone from his own place. This does not refer only to the islands, but also to all the nations, which are referred to as all the islands of the Gentile, just as in another place he does not say the islands, but / speaks of the whole earth, saying [L Psalm 21:28f, AV Psalm 21:28]: "All the ends of the earth shall remember, and shall be converted to the Lord: and all the kindreds of the Gentiles shall adore in his sight. For the kingdom is the Lord's; and he shall have dominion over the nations."

The same

Psalms 21

All the ends of the earth and all the islands shall be converted to the Lord

Again in the same [Psalm 2:7–8]: "The Lord hath said to me: Thou art my son; this day have I begotten thee. Ask of me, and I will give thee the Gentiles for thy inheritance, and the utmost parts of the earth for thy possession." By these and other similar prophetic writings predictions are given of the things we know will be fulfilled in the future

Psalms 2

per Christum futurum fuisse, ut Deus Israeli; quem unum verum Deum inte[l]ligimus non in una ipsa gente que appellata est Israel, sed in omnibus gentibus coleretur et omnes falsos deos gentium et a templis eorum et a cordibus cultorum suorum demoliretur. Deus Ysrael non in ipsa

Iuditium Iterum repetit in eodem: "Audite me qui s[c]itis iuditium, populus meus, in quorum corde lex mea: opprobria hominum nolite metuere, et detractione eorum ne superemini; ne[c] quod vos spernunt magni duxeritis. Sicut enim vestimentum, ita per tempus absumentur, et sicut lana a tinea comedentur: iustitia autem mea in eternum manet." Augustini ut supra Isaye 51

In libro confessionum 9

At ille iu[s]sit Esayam profetam, credo, quod pre ceteris evangelii vocationisque gentium sit prenuntiator apercior.

In eodem, libro 12

Tu loquere in corde meo veraciter, solus enim loqueris; et dimi[t]tam eos foris sufflantes in pulverem et excitantes terram in oculos suos. Et intrem in cubile meum et cantem tibi amatoria gemens inenarrabiles gemitus in peregrinatione mea et recordans Iherusalem, patriam meam, Ierusalem matrem meam, teque super eam regnatorem, illustratorem, patrem, tutorem, maritum, castas et fortes delitias, et solidum gaudium, et omnia (16b) bona. Ineffabilia, simul omnia, quia unum summum et Verum bonum; et non avertar, donec in eius pacem, matris carissime, ubi sunt primitie spiritus mei, unde mihi ista certa sunt, co[l]ligas totum quod sum a dispersione et deformitate haci et conformes atque confirmes in eternum, Deus meus, misericordia mea.

In eodem, XIII

Item Augustinus ex Psalmo 18 Item debentur eis tamquam volatilibus propter benedi[c]tiones eorum que multiplicantur super omnem terram, quoniam in omnem terram exiit sonus eorum. Pascuntur autem his escis qui letantur eis, nec illi letantur eis quorum Deus venter est. Neque enim et in illis, qui prebent ista, ea, que dant, fructus est, sed quo animo dant.

De doctrina cristiana, libro II

Sed quo[d]libet vocentur ab [h]ominibusi sunt tamen sidera, que Deus instituit et ordinavit ut voluit; et est certus motus illorum, Augustinus

through Christ, so that the God of Israel; whom we know as the one true God will be worshipped not only in the single nation known as Israel, but he will be worshipped in all the nations, and all the false gods of the gentile nations will be destroyed both in their own temples and in the hearts of their worshippers.

God of Israel not (worshipped) in a single (nation)

A variation of   He writes again in the same book [Isaiah 51:7–8]: "Hearken to me, you that know what is just, my people who have my law in your heart: fear ye not the reproach of men and do not be afraid of their blasphemies. For just as a garment they shall be consumed in time, and as wool is consumed by the moth: but my righteousness shall remain in eternity."

Augustine's judgement above Isaiah 51

In Book 9 of the *Confessions*

[St. Augustine, Chapter 5]

Then he [Ambrose] directed me to the prophet Isaiah, I believe, because he predicts more clearly than the others concerning the gospel and the calling of the Gentiles.

In Book 12 of the same

[Chapter 16]

Speak thou the truth within my heart, for thou alone speakest so; and I will send them away snorting upon the dust and raising up dirt / into their own eyes. Myself, I will enter my room, and there sing to thee songs of love, sighing ineffable sighs in my pilgrimage, and remembering Jerusalem my fatherland, Jerusalem my mother, remembering thee ruling over her, the Light-giver, the Father, the Protector, the Spouse, the chaste and mighty delight, the wholesome joy, and all ineffable good things all at once, as the one supreme and true good. I will not be turned away until thou gatherest into the peace of that dearest mother Jerusalem (where are already the first fruits of my spirit and thus these things are assured to me) all that I am, from the scattered fragments and from this deformity, and do thou then reform me and reaffirm me in eternity, O God, my mercy.

In Book 13 of the same

[Chapter 25]

Same Augustine   They have as much right to them as the birds, for the sake of their thanks-
as from Psalms 18   givings that are multiplied across the whole earth, as throughout the whole earth the sound goes forth. And those who rejoice at this are nourished also by these fruits, but those whose God is their belly will not rejoice in them. For the fruit is not there because of those who give, or what they give, but because of the spirit in which they give.

On Christian Doctrine, Book 2

[Saint Augustine, Chapter 22]

Whatever they are called by men, they are still the stars that God has   Augustine
fashioned and arranged as he pleased. Their movement is reliable, by

quo tempora distingu[u]ntur atque variantur. Quem motum notare, cum quisquis nascitur, quomodo se habeat, facile est per eorum inventas cumscriptasque regulas, quos sancta Scriptura condempnat dicens: "Si enim tantum potuerunt scire, [ut] possent extimare seculum, quomodo eius dominum non facilius invenerunt?" (17a)

In eodem, libro III

Facile est, inquami hoc inte[l]ligere de illa domo Israel, de qua dicit Apostolus: "Videte Israel secundum carnem," quia hec omnnia carnalis populus Israel et fecit et passus est. Alia etiam, que secuntur, eidem intelliguntur populo convenire. Sed cum ceperit dicere: "Et sanctificabo nomen meum sanctum, illud magnum, quod pollutum est inter nationes, quod polluistis in medio earum; et scient gentes, quia ego Dominus," iam intemptus debet esse qui legit, quemadmodum speties excedatur et adiungatur genus. Sequitur enim et dicit: "Et dum sanctificabor in vobis ante oculos eorum, et accipiam vos de gentibus, et congregabo vos ex omnibus terris, et inducam vos in terram vestram, et aspergam vos aqua munda, et mundabimini ab omnibus simulacris vestris, et mundabo vos. Et dabo vobis cor novum, et spiritum novum dabo in vos, et auferam cor lapideum de carne vestra, et dabo vobis cor carneum, et spiritum meum dabo in vos et faciam, ut in iusticiis meis ambuletis, et iudicia mea custodiatis, et faciatis. Et habitabitis in terra, quam dedi patribus vestris, et eritis michi in populum, et ego ero vobis in Deum. Et mundabo vos ex omnibus inmundiciis vestris." Hoc de novo Testamento esse prophetatum, ad quod pertinet non solum illa una gens in reliqui[i]s suis, de guibus (17b) alibi scriptum est: "Si fuerit numerus filiorum Israel sicut arena maris, reliquie salve fient," verum etiam cetere gentes, que promisse sunt patribus eorum, qui etiam nostri sunt, non ambigit quisquis intuetur et lavacrum regenerationis hic esse promissum, quod nunc videmus omnibus gentibus redditum. Et illud quod ait Apostolus, cum Novi Testamenti gratiam coinmendareti ut in comparatione veteris emineret: "Epistola nostra vos estis, scripta, non atramento, sed in tabulis cordis carnalibus," hinc esse respicit et perspicit ductum ubi iste propheta dixit: "Et dabo vobis cor novum, et spiritum novum dabo in vos, et auferam cor lapideum de carne vestra, et dabo vobis cor carneum." Cor quippe carneum, unde ait Apostolus, "tabulis cordis carnalibus," a corde lapideo voluit vitam sentientem discerni, et per vitam sentientem significavit intelligentem. Sic fit Israel spiritualis, non unius

Marginal notes:

ex Ecechiele 36

ex dictis Apostolus ad Roman 9

II Corintiis III

Ezechielis 36

II Corintiis III

Augustini De doctrina cristiana

Ysaye

which the seasons change and are identified. When anyone is born, it is easy to note the arrangement of this movement, through the use of the rules discovered and written by those who are accused by the Holy Scriptures, saying, "If they could know so much that they would be able to measure the world, why were they not able first to discover its Lord?" [Wisdom 13:9]. /

In Book 3 of the same

[Chapter 34, pp. 38b–49]

It seems clear to me that this applies to the house of Israel concerning whom the Apostle says, "Behold Israel according to the flesh" [I Corinthians 10:18], because the people of Israel according to the flesh both did and experienced all these things. And other things that follow also can

From Ezekiel 36 be applied to the same people. But when the text begins to say, "And I will sanctify my great and holy name, which was profaned in the midst of them, which you polluted in the midst of them; and the heathen shall know that I am the Lord" [Ezekiel 36:23], the careful reader should already discover how the species has been overreached and the genus has been included. The text continues, and says [Ezekiel 36:23–29]: "And then I shall be sanctified among you before their eyes. For I will gather you from among the Gentiles, and assemble you from all lands, and I will lead you into your own land. And I will sprinkle you with pure water, and you shall be cleansed from all your idols, and I will make you clean. And I will give you a new heart, and I will give a new spirit within you. I will take away the stony heart from your flesh, and I will give you a heart of flesh. I will put my Spirit within you, and I will make you to walk in my judgments, and you shall keep my commandments, and do them. And you shall dwell in the land that I gave to your fathers; and you shall be my people, and I will be your God. And I

Sayeth the Apostle will cleanse you from all your uncleannesses." This is prophesied of the *Isaiah*
in Romans 9 New Testament, to which belongs not merely that one nation in its surviving remnant, of whom it is written elsewhere [Isaiah 10:22], "If the number of the children of Israel be as the sand of the sea, yet a remnant of them shall be saved. But also the other nations, which were promised to their patriarchs who were also our patriarchs. No one who studies this can doubt that here is promised that fountain of regeneration that we now see / made available to all nations of Gentiles. And that which the Apostle said, as he was commending the grace of the New Testament, and its superiority in comparison with the Old [II Corinthians 3:2, 3]:

II Corinthians 3 "You are our epistle . . . written not with ink, but . . . in fleshy tables of the heart," obviously refers to and points clearly at what the prophet

Ezekiel 36 said [Ezekiel 36:26]: "A new heart also will I give you, and a new spirit will I put within you; and I will take away the stony heart out of your

II Corinthians 3 flesh, and I will give you an heart of flesh." Now the heart of flesh, of which the Apostle says "the fleshy tables of the heart," he intended to distinguish sentient life from the stony heart, and by sentient he meant intelligent life. The spiritual Israel is thus not made up of only one nation,

Augustine, On Christian Doctrine

gentis, sed omnium, que promisse sunt patribus eorum in semine, quod est Christus. Hi[c] ergo Israel spiritualis ab illo Israel carnali, qui est unius gentis, novitate gratie, non nobilitate patrie, et mente, non gente, distinguitur. Sed altitudo prophetica dum de illo vel ad illum loquitur, latenter transit adhuc, et cum iam de isto, vel ad istum loquitur (18a) adhuc de illo vel ad illum loqui videtur; non intellectum Scripturaum nobis quasi hostiliter invidens, sed exer-

Ezechielis 36 cens medicinaliter cor nostrum. Unde et illud quod ait: "et inducam vos in terram vestram;" et paulo posti tamquam id ipsum repetens: "et habitabitis in terra vestra, qua[m] dedi patribus vestris," non carnaliter sicut carnalis Israel, sed spiritualiter et spiritualis debemus accipere. Ecclesia quippe sine macula et ruga ex omnibus gentibus congregata, atque in eternuin regnatura cuin Christo, ipsa est beatorum terra viventium, ipsa est intelligenda patribus data; quando eis certa et immutabili Dei volumptate promissa est, quoniam ipsa promissionis vel predestinationis firmitate iam data est, que danda suo tempore a patribus credita est, sicut de ipsa gratia, que sanctis datur, scribens ad Thimotheum Apostolus ait,

II Thimoteo I "Non secundum opera nostra, sed secundum suum propositum et gratiam, que data est nobis in Christo Ihesu ante secula eterna, manifestata autem nunc per adventum Salvatoris nostri." Datam dixit gratiam, quando non erant adhuc quibus daretur; quoniam in dispositione ac predestinatione Dei iam factum erat quod suo tempore futurum erat, quo esse dixit manifestatam. Quamvis hec possint intelligiet de terra futuri seculi, quando erit celum novum, (18b) et terra nova, in qua iniusti habitare non poterunt. Et ideo recte dicitur piis, quod ipsa sit terra eorum, que ulla ex parte non erit impiorum; quia et ipsa similiter data est, quando danda firmata est.

In libro I, de concessu evangelistarum.
capitulo 29, 28, 29, 30, 31, 32, 33, 34, 35, 36, 37, 38.

Augustini in libro
De concessu
evangelistarum In omnibus capitulis predictis multa dixit de Iudeis et de eis, que ventura sunt: de quibus non scripsi propter prolixitatem. Aliquid tamen reducam hic ad memoriam.

In capitulo 29: Neque enim temporibus cristianis, sed ante tanto prerdictum est, quod per cristianos impletur. Ipsi Iudei qui remanserunt inimici nominus Christi, de quorum etiam futura perfidia in illis propheticis literis tacitum non est, ipsi habent et legunt prophetam dicentem: "Domine Deus meus et refugium meum in die malo-

Marginal notes (right):
India est in extremo terre, in oriente, et Hispania cum Ethiopia in occidente. Inter medium est mare Occeanum. Iam Indi veniunt et evertunt ydola.

Hyeremie 16

but of all those nations who were promised to the patriarchs in the prophesied seed, who is Christ. Therefore, this spiritual Israel is to be distinguished from the Israel of the flesh which is a single nation, by the newness of the grace rather than by nobility of patrimony, by knowledge rather than by race. But the mountaintop panorama of prophecy, passes imperceptibly from the one vista to the other, speaking now of the Israel of the flesh and next of the spiritual Israel, without indicating the transition. This is not a hostile intent to withhold from us the understanding of the Scriptures, but a wise provision of medicinal exercise for our hearts.

Ezekiel 36 Therefore we should also interpret the statement, "And I will bring you into your own land," and again a little later, almost a repetition, "And ye shall dwell in the land that I gave to your fathers," not as applying in a physical way to Israel according to the flesh, but in a spiritual way to the spiritual Israel. For the Church, without spot or wrinkle, gathered from all the nations, intended to reign with Christ in eternity, is herself the land of those who are blessed and who live. The Church should be understood as the gift to the patriarchs, when it was promised to them by the sure and immutable revealed will of God. For by the certainty / of the promise or predestination this gift has already been given, which was believed by the patriarchs yet to be given in its own time. In the same way the Apostle wrote to Timothy of the same grace given to the II Timothy 1 saints [II Timothy 1:9, 10], "Not according to our works, but according to his own purpose and grace, which was given us in Christ Jesus before the world began but now made manifest by the appearing of our Savior." He refers to grace as already given at a time when those to whom it was to be given did not yet even exist, because in the providence and predestination of God things are already completed which are to take place in their own time, which he declares to be revealed. This may refer also, in some way, to the end of an age yet to come, when there will be a new heaven and a new earth, which the unrighteous shall not be able to inhabit. Thus it is rightly said to the pious, that this land itself is theirs, of which no part is for the unbelievers; because it is just as if it were actually given, when promised that it shall be given.

Book 1 of *Harmony of the Gospels*, Chapter 29

[St. Augustine; also chapters 28, 29, 30, 31, 32, 33, 34, 35, 36, 37, 38]

Augustine, Harmony of the Gospels In all of the chapters mentioned above, many things are written about the Jews and about those who are still to come. I have not written all of these things for the sake of brevity. However, I have given a sample here for a reminder.

India is in the farthest lands in the east, Spain and Ethiopia in the west, between them is the Ocean Sea. In India, they venerate and raise up idols.

From Chapter 29: The things that are accomplished by Christians belong not only to the Christian times, but were predicted very long ago. The very Jews who have continued to be enemies to the name of Christ, whose future faithlessness was predicted in the prophetic writings, both have and listen to the prophet who says [Jeremiah 16:19]: "O Lord my God, and my refuge in the day of evil, the Gentiles shall come unto

Jeremiah 16

rum, ad te gentes venient ab extremo terrei et dicent: vere mendatia coluerunt patres nostri simulacra, et non est illis utilitas." Ecce nunc fit, hec sunt gentes ab extremo terre veniunt ad Christum ista dicentes, et simulacra frangentes. Et hoc etiam magnum est, quod Deus prestitit E[c]clesie sue ubique di[f]fuse, ut gens Iudea merito debe[l]lata et dispersa per terras, (19a) ne a nobis hec composita putarenturi codices prophetarum nostrorum ubique portaret et inimica fidei nostre testis fieret veritatis nostre. Quomodo ergo discipuli Christi docuerunt quod a Christo non didicerunt, sicut stulti desipiendo iactitant, ut deorum gentilium et simulacrorum superstitio deleretur? Numquid et illas prophetias que nunc leguntur in codicibus inimicorum Christii possunt dici finxisse discipuli Christi? Quis enim hoc evertit, nisi Deus Israel? Ipsi enim populo dictum est per divinas voces factas ad Moysem: "Audi, Israel, Dominus Deus tuus Deus unus est. Non facies tibi idolum, neque cuiusquam similitudinem, neque in celo sursum, neque in terra deorsum." Ut autem etiam evertat ista, ubi potestatem acceperit, sic ei precipitur: "Non adorabis deos illorum, sed neque servies eis: non facies secundum opera ipsorum, sed deponendo depones et confringendo confringes simulacra eorum."

Deuteronomii 6

Levitici 26

Exodi 26

Augustini ut supra In capitulo 30: Quis autem dicat Christum atque christianos non pertinere ad Israel, cum Israel nepos fuerit Habrae, cui primo et deinde Ysach filio eius et deinde ipsi Israel nepoti eius dictum est quod iam commemoravi: "In semine tuo benedicentur omnes gentes." Quod fieri iam videmus in Christo. Cum inde exorta sit illa virgo, de qua propheta populi Israel et Dei Israel cecinit dicens: "Ecce virgo concipiet et pariet filium et vocabitur nomen eius Emanuel." Interpretratur (19b) enim Emanuel, 'nobiscum Deus.' Deus Israel ergo, qui prohibuit alios deos coli, qui prohibuit idola fabricari, qui precepit everti, qui per prophetam dixit gentes ab extremo terre dicturas: "Vere mendatia coluerunt patres nostri, simulacra, in quibus non est utilitas," ipse per Christi nomen et christianorum fidem istarum omnium superstitionum eversionem iu[s]sit, promisit, ex[h]ibuit. Frustra ergo miseri, quia blasfemare Christum etiarn a diis suis, hoc est a demonibus nomen Christi metuentibus prohibiti sunt, volunt ab eo doctrinam istam facere alienam, qua christiani contra ydola disputant easque omnes falsas religiones ubi potuerint eradicant.

Genesis 26

Isaye 7

Hyeremie 16

Augustini libro De concessu evangelistarum In capitulo 31: Iam subditos Christi nomini? Sicut longe ante promisit, dicens per prophetam: et adorabunt eum omnes reges terre, omnes gentes servient illi.

Psalmo 71

thee from the ends of the earth, and shall say, / Surely our fathers have worshipped mendacious idols, and there is no profit in them." See, now that is being done, these are the Gentiles who come from the ends of the earth to Christ, saying these things, and destroying their idols. And this also is great, which God has granted to his Church everywhere throughout the world, that the Jewish nation, deservedly overthrown and dispersed through all lands, lest people should think these things were composed by us, carry everywhere the books of our prophets, and thus the enemies of our faith have been made to be witnesses of its truth. How therefore can the disciples of Christ have taught what they did not learn from Christ, as the foolish foolishly insist, as they have overthrown the superstition of the heathen gods and images? Can it be said that these prophecies which now are read in the books of the enemies of Christ, could have been fabricated by the disciples of Christ? Who then has overthrown the heathen gods, except the God of Israel? For to this people was it said by those divine voices that spoke to Moses [Deuteronomy 6:4], "Hear, O Israel; the Lord thy God is one God." [Leviticus 26:1] "Thou shalt not make unto thee any graven image, or any likeness of anything that is in heaven above or that is in the earth beneath." And, so that they would destroy these, wherever they had the power to do so, this commandment was given [Exodus 23:24]: "Thou shalt not bow down to their gods, nor serve them; thou shalt not do after their works, but thou shall utterly overthrow them, and completely destroy their images."

Deuteronomy 6

Leviticus 26

Exodus 26

Augustine continued From Chapter 30: But who is to say that Christ and Christians have nothing to do with Israel, when Israel was the grandson of Abraham, to whom first, as later to his son Isaac, and later to his grandson Israel himself, it was said, which I have already mentioned, "In thy seed shall all nations be blessed." Which we see already fulfilled in Christ. For it was of this line / the Virgin came, of whom a prophet of the people of Israel and of the God of Israel sang, saying [Isaiah 7:14, Matthew 1:23], "Behold a virgin shall conceive and bear a son; and his name shall be called Emanuel." For translated, Emanuel means "God with us." The God of Israel, therefore, who prohibited the worship of other gods, who prohibited that idols be made, who commanded to destroy them, who by the prophet said the gentile nations from the uttermost part of the earth would say, "Surely, our fathers worshipped false idols, in which is no benefit;" this same God by the name of Christ and by the faith of Christians, has commanded, promised and accomplished the overthrow of all these superstitions. In vain, therefore, these miserable men, knowing they have been prohibited from blaspheming the name of Christ, even by their own gods, that is, by demons who fear the name of Christ, want to make this doctrine something foreign to Him, in which Christians dispute against idols, and destroy all false religions wherever they are able.

Genesis 26

Isaiah 7

Jeremiah 16

Augustine, Harmony of the Gospels From Chapter 31: Now made subject to the name of Christ? Just as long before he promised, saying by the prophet [Psalm 72:14], "Yea, all kings of the earth shall worship him: all nations shall serve him."

Psalms 71

Idem   In capitulo 34: "Non sunt loquele neque sermones, quorum non   Psalmo 18
audiantur voces eorum. In omnem terram exivit sonus eorum, et
in fines orbis terre verba eorum."

Isaye 54   In capitulo 36: Dixit enim Dominus: "Dilata locum tabernaculi tui,   Idem
et aulas tuas confige; non est quod parcas; po[r]rige longius funicu-
los et palos validos constitue. Etiam atque etiam in dexteram atque
in sinistram partem extende; semen enim tuum hereditabit gentes;
et civitates, que (20a) deserte erant, inhabitabis. Non est quod me-
tuas prevalebis enim; nec erubescas, quod detestabilis fueris; confusionem enim in perpetuum oblivisceris, ignomin[i]e viduitatis tue
non eris memor. Quoniam ego sum Dominus, qui facio te, Dominus
nomen ei, et qui eruit te, ipse Deus Israel universe terre vocabitur."

In libro 2, capitulo *77*, de conce[s]su evangelistarum

Idem Augustini   Quod ergo Matheus ait: "Et predicabitur hoc evangelium regni in   Mathei 24
universo orbe in testimonium omnibus gentibus, et tunc veniet con-
sumatio." Et Marcus eodem ordine ita commemorat: "In omnes gen-   Marci 13
tes primum oportet predicari evangelium." Non dixit: "Et tunc
veniet consumatio," sed hoc significat quod ait, "primum," id est
et "in omnes gentes primum oportet predicari evangelium." Significat utique, "primum," ante quam veniat consumatio. Item quod
Matheus ait: "Cum ergo videritisi abhominationem desolationis, que   Mathei 24
dicta [est] a Daniele propheta, stantem in loco sancto, qui legit
inte[l]ligat," hoc Marcus dixit ita: "Cum autem videritis abhominationem desolationis stantem, ubi non debet, qui legit inte[l]ligat."
In qua mutatione verbi exposuit tamquam sententiam; ideo quippe
ubi "non debet," quia in loco sancto non debet. Lucas autem non
ait: "Cum autem videritis abhominationem desolationis, stantem in
loco sancto," aut "ubi non debet," sed ait: (20b) "Cum autem; vide-   Luce 21
ritis circumdari ab exercitu Iherusalem, tunc scitote quia a[p]
propinquavit desolatio eius." Tunc erit ergo abhominatio desolationis in loco sancto. Qu[o]d Matheus autem ait: "Tunc qui in Iudea
sunt, fugiant ad montes; et qui in tecto, non descendat tollere aliquid
de domo sua; et, qui in agro, non revertatur tollere tunicam suam,"
totidem pene verbis hec etiam Marcus commemorat. Lucas autem:
"Tunc qui in Iudea sunt," inquid, "fugiant in montes." Hec sicut
illi duo; cetera vero aliter. Sequitur enim, et dixit: "Et, qui in medio
eius, discedant; et qui in regionibus, non intrent in eam. Quia dies
ultionis hi sunt, ut impleantur omnia que scripta sunt."

Idem Augustini   In libro 3, capitulo 25: Post illam quippe exprob[r]ationem, secutus
ait idem Marcus: "Et dixit eis: euntes in mundum universum, predi-

The same From Chapter 34 [Psalm 19]: "There are no speech nor words, where   Psalms 18
their voices are not heard. Their sound has gone out into all the earth,
and their words to the end of the world."

Isaiah 54 From Chapter 36 [Isaiah 54:2–5]: For the Lord said: "Enlarge the place   The same
of thy tent, and stake out thy courts; there is no reason to hold back;
lengthen the cords, and place strong stakes. Again and again, extend on
the right and on the left. / For thy seed shall inherit the nations, and
thou shall dwell in the cities that were deserted. There is nothing to fear.
Thou shalt prevail. Do not be ashamed, because thou wast detestable.
For thou shalt forget thy confusion for ever, and not remember thy widow-
hood. For I am the Lord who made thee. The Lord is his name, who
also brought thee out, he the God of Israel; shall be called the God of
the whole earth."

Book 2, Chapter 77, *Harmony of the Gospels*

Augustine That which Matthew states [24:14], "And this gospel of the kingdom   Matthew 24
continued shall be preached in all the world for a witness unto all nations, and
then shall the end come." And Mark in the same connection reports that
[Mark 13:10]: "And the gospel must first be published among all nations."   Mark 13
He did not say, "and then shall the end come;" but he indicates the same
when he uses the word 'first' as, "And the gospel must first be published
among all nations." In both places it means 'first' before the end comes.
Likewise when Matthew says [Matthew 24:15]: "When ye therefore shall   Matthew 24
see the abomination of desolation, spoken of by Daniel the prophet, standing in the holy place, whoso readeth, let him understand;" Mark says
thus [Mark 13:14]: "But when ye shall see the abomination of desolation,
spoken of by Daniel the prophet, standing where it ought not, let him
that readeth understand." In this change the words express the same
meaning, for indeed "where it ought not," is that it ought not be in the
holy place. Luke however does not say, "When you see the abomination
of desolation, standing in the holy place," or "where it ought to be." But
he says [Luke 21:20]: "When you shall see Jerusalem compassed with   Luke 21
an army, then know that the desolation thereof is nigh." At that time
therefore will the abomination of desolation be in the holy place. Moreover, what Matthew says [Matthew 24:16–18]: "Then let / them which
be in Judea flee into the mountains; and let him which is on the housetop
not come down to take anything out of his house; neither let him which
is in the field return back to take his clothes;" is reported by Mark in
almost the same words. But Luke [Luke 21:21]: has, "Then let them
which are in Judea flee to the mountains." He agrees with the other
two, but the rest is different. For he then says, "And let them which
are in the midst of it depart out; and let not them that are in the countries
enter thereinto: for these be the days of vengeance, that all things which
are written may be fulfilled."

Augustine From Book 3, Chapter 25: After this warning, Mark at once continues
continued [16:15–16]: "And he said unto them, Go ye into all the world, and preach

Marci 16 cate evangelium omni creature. Qui crediderit et baptizatus fuerit, salvus erit; qui vero non crediderit, condempnabitur." Hoc ergo predicaturi, quoniam qui non crediderit condempnabitur. (21a)

✠

In evangelio secundum Marcum, capitulo 16 [15]

Euntes in mundum universum, predicate evangelium omni creature, &c. ut supra.   Marci 16

Mathei 24, capitulo [14]

Et predicabitur hoc evangelium regni in universo orbe, in tes ti- monium omnibus gentibus &c. Glosa: "Et predicabitur evangelium regni," idest evangelium Christi, quod introducit ad regnum celeste &c. "In universo mundo," quod enim ante destructionem civitatis per Tytum et Vespasianum in tribus partibus orbis, scilicet Asia, Africa et Europa, predicatum sit evangelium Christi, patet sic: vi- vente enim Petro, fides predicata est in Italia &c. Que requirantur, si placet.   Mathei 24 Nicolai de Lyra

Sequitur in eadem Glosa

"In testimonium omnibus gentibus," quasi dicat: ad hoc predicanda est fides in universo orbe, ut testimonium Christi audiretur in omni gente; secundum quod dictum fuit apostolis Actuum primo: "Eritis mihi testes in Ierusalem, et Iudea, et Samaria, et usque ad ultimum terre."   Actuum I

Item sequitur

 Considerandum autem, quod alia est predicatio evangelii futura in omnibus gentibus quantum ad efficatiam, sic quod omnes gentes recipient fidem Christi; et hoc erit in consumatione seculi.   Nicolae de Lyra

Nota

Quonian oritur questio, quo inodo predicatum fuerit evangelium Christi per totum orbem, vel quo modo manet adhuc predicandum, requiratur el Tostado super Matheum, capitulo XXIV, questione XLVI, per totum &c. (21b)   El Tostado

Mark 16 the gospel to every creature. He that believeth and is baptized shall be saved; but he that believeth not shall be damned." Therefore, they were to preach that whoever would not believe should be condemned.

✠

In the Gospel according to Mark, Chapter 16[21]

Go ye into the whole world and preach the gospel to every creature, &c. as above. [v. 15]   Mark 16

Matthew, Chapter 24

And this gospel of the kingdom shall be preached in the whole world, for a testimony to all nations &c. Gloss [Nicholas of Lyra]. "And the gospel of the kingdom shall be preached." This refers to the gospel of Christ, which gives admittance into the heavenly kingdom &c. "In the whole world." It is clear that before the destruction of the city by Titus and Vespasian the gospel had been preached in the three parts of the world, that is, Asia, / Africa and Europe, since while Peter was still living the faith was preached in Italy. &c. These things should be studied further, if you will.   Matthew 24   Nicolas of Lyra

In the same Commentary

[Nicholas of Lyra]

"For a testimony to all nations." This is the same as saying that the faith is to be preached in the whole world in order that the testimony of Christ might be heard in every nation, according to what was said to the apostles in the first chapter of the Acts [Acts 1:8b]: "you shall be witnesses unto me in Jerusalem, and in all Judea and Samaria, and even to the uttermost part of the earth."   Acts I

Continuation in the same

 It must be taken into consideration, however, that there is another preaching of the gospel that is yet to take place, with such effectiveness that all the Gentiles will accept the faith of Christ; and this shall take place at the end of the age.   Nicolas of Lyra

Note

Since the question has been raised, as to how the gospel of Christ will be preached throughout the whole world, or to what extent this preaching remains yet to be accomplished, this subject is treated by Alfonso Tostato[22] in chapter 24 of his book on Matthew, the whole of question 46 &c.   El Tostato

✠

Mathei, capitulo 28

Data est mihi omnis potestas in celo et in terra. Euntes ergo docete omnes gentes, baptizantes eos in nomine Patris, et Filii, et Spiritus Sancti, docentes eos servare omnia quecumque mandavi vobis.

Psalmo 71

"Et dominabitur a mari usque ad mare, et a flumine usque ad terminos orbis terrarum." Glosa: Idest super totam terram mari circumdatam. Licet enim Occeanus sit unum mare, tamen secundum diversas sui partes varie nominatur: utpote mare Orientale a parte orientis, et eodem modo a parte austri et aquilonis. In omnibus enim istis terris aliqui receperunt fidem Christi per predicationem apostolorum, aliorumque discipulorum, secundum quod dictum fuit supra psalmo XVIII, exponendo illud: "In omnem terram exivit sonus eorum" &c. "Et a flumine," scilicet paradisi terrestris, "usque ad terminos orbis terrarum," idest usque terminos orbis constituti circa terram per circuitum. Et isti termini protenduntur usque ad ultimum celum, et tantum protenditur potestas Christi. Propter quod dicit Matheus ultimo: "Data est michi omnis potestas in celo et in terra" &c. ut supra. (22a)

✠

Item Augustinus in libro de divinatione demonum

Iste ergo Deus, quem nemo, ut dixi, illorum ausus est negare verum Deum, illos falsos esse deos et omnino deserendos, eorumque templa et simulacra et sacra evertenda per suos vates, hoc est prophetas, aperta denuntiatione predixit, aperta potestate precepit, aperta veritate complevit &c. Sequitur.

Attende diligenter
Quod autem, ipsum essent culture gentes, externiinatis diis falsis, quos antea colebant a prophetis eius esse predictum paulo ante commemoravi, et nunc repeto: "Prevalebit," inquit, "Deus adversus eos,   Sophonie et exterminabit omnes deos gentium terre, et adorabunt eum, unusquisque de loco suo, omnes insule gentium." Neque sole insule sed ita omnes gentes, ut etiam omnes insule gentium, quandoquidem alibi non insulas nominat, sed universum orbem terrarumi dicens: "Commemorabuntur et convertentur ad Dominum universi fines

✠

Matthew, Chapter 28

[18–20]

All power is given to me in heaven and in earth. Going therefore, teach all nations: baptizing them in the name of the Father and of the Son / and of the Holy Ghost, teaching them to observe all things whatsoever I have commanded you.

Psalm 71

[L 71:8, AV Psalm 72]

And he shall rule from sea to sea: and from the river to the ends of the earth. Gloss [Nicholas of Lyra]. That is, upon the whole earth encircled by the sea. The ocean can be called a single sea, although it is called by various names according to its different parts. Thus it is called the Eastern Ocean in the eastern part, and in the same way with the southern and northern part. Moreover, in all of those lands some people have received faith in Christ by the preaching of the apostles and other disciples, just as is above written in Psalm 18 [Psalm 19] explaining it: "Their sound hath gone forth into all the earth" &c. And "from the river," that is from the earthly paradise, "unto the ends of the earth," that is, to the ends of the globe which are formed by a circle around the earth. And these "ends" extend to the highest heaven, and so great is the extent of the power of Christ. Because of this, Matthew said in the last chapter, as quoted above: "All power is given to me in heaven and in earth." &c as above.

✠

Saint Augustine, *On the Divination of Demons*

This God, whom none of them (the false gods), as I said, dared to deny to be the true God, is the one who foretold by his oracles, that all these others were false gods, that they would be completely abandoned and that their temples, their idols and their altars would be overthrown. He had foretold it openly in his word, he commanded it openly by his power, he accomplished it openly in reality &c. and what follows. /

The prophets had predicted that one day the Gentiles, after having exterminated the false gods that they had before worshipped, would give their worship to God. Just as I cited before, now I repeat: "The Lord Zephaniah
shall prevail against them, and he shall exterminate all the gods of the nations of the earth, and they shall worship him, each one in his place,
Well said all the islands of the Gentiles." [Zephaniah 2:11] Not merely the islands, but all the Gentile nations that are similarly spread out as all the islands of the Gentiles, since in another place he does not call them islands, but the whole globe of the earth, when he says: "All the ends of the earth

terre; et adorabunt in conspectu eius universe patrie gentium. Quoniam Domini est regnum, et ipse dominabitur gentium." Et cetera, que sunt notatione digna. Sequitur.

Nota   Hiis atque huiusmodi propheticis documentis predictum ostenditur, quod videmus impleri per Christum, futurum fuisse ut Deum Israel, quem unum Deum verum intelligunt, non in una ipsa gente que a[p]pellata est Israel, sed in omnibus gentibus coleretur, et omnes falsos deos gentium et a templis eorum et a cordibus cultorum suorum demoliretur &c.

Necesse est ergo ut impleantur omnia hec, &c. que secuntur usque in finem.

✠

Hec Augustinus ut supra. Ubi per totum ipsum libellum singula clarius declarantur, que ego dimitto requirenda causa brevitatis. (22b–23b) (24a)

Petrus de Aliaco cardinalis
In libro de legibus et sectis, capitulo 4

Quinto, ponit doctor iste quod de destructione legis Machumeti certitudinaliter locuntur astronomi; nam secundum quod Albumazar dixit, lex illa non potest durare ultra sexcentos nonaginta tres annos, sed tantum ipsa durabit, nisi propter aliquam causam incidentem abrevietur tempus, secundum quod prius tactum est, que abreviatio potest fier maior, vel minor ex causis diversis. Et, ut iste doctor dicit, tunc quando hec scripsit, iam erat annus Arabum sexcentesimus sexagesimus quintus, a tempore Machometi, et ideo concludebat quod cito destrueretur, et quod istud erat magnum solatium christianis, unde laudandus erat Deus, qui philosophis dedit talem lucem sapientie, per quam lex veritatis confirmatur et roboratur, et per quam percipi[m]us inimicos fidei destrui debere. Et pro concordia [h]uius sententie inducit Scripturam a Apocalipsi, que dixit quod numerus bestie est sexcentum LXIII, qui numerus est minor predicto per XXX annos. Sed in multis locis subticet aliquod de numero completo; nam hic est mos Scripture, ut dicit Beda, et hoc forsan voluit Deus quod non exprimeretur totaliter, sed aliqualiter o[c]cultaretur, sicut et cetera que (24b) in Apocalipsi scribuntur: quia forte ante illud tempus ultimum, quod huic sectei secundum eius causam principalem, determinat Albumazar, continget quod Saraceni destruentur, aut per Tartaros, aut per christianos, sicut iam tunc maxima pars Sarracenorum destructa erat per Tartaros, et caput regni, quod fuit Baldach; et Caliph, qui fuit sicut

Marginal notes:

Albumazar

Apocalypsis 13

Nota de consumatione legis Machometi

shall remember and shall turn to the Lord; and all the families of the Gentiles shall worship before him. For the kingdom is the Lord's, and he shall rule the nations." And what follows deserves also to be noted. He continues.

Note   These quotations, and others like them taken from the prophets, demonstrate sufficiently this prediction that we see accomplished by Christ, that one day the God of Israel, whom we recognize as the only true God, will be worshipped not merely by a single nation called the people of Israel, but among all the Gentile nations, and that he will destroy all the false gods from their temples and from the heart of their Gentile worshippers.

It is therefore necessary that all these things should be fulfilled. &c. The things that follow until the end.

✠

Augustine wrote what is quoted above. Throughout the whole of that little book, other things are pointed out even more clearly, but I omit them for the sake of brevity.[23]/

Cardinal Pierre d'Ailly[24]
From the *Book of Laws and Sects*, Chapter 4

Fifthly, this learned writer records the things that astronomers say with certainty concerning the overthrow of the Mohammedan power. For according to what Albumazar said, that government cannot continue for more than six hundred ninety-three years, but it would last for that long, unless because of some coincidental cause the time should be shortened, and accordingly he first mentioned that the shortening could be either greater or less, depending on different causes. And, as this learned writer says, then, when he wrote these things, it was already the Arabian year 665 from the time of Mohammed, and therefore he concluded that it would be overthrown soon, and that this would be a great encouragement to Christians, for which God should be praised who had given such light of knowledge to philosophers, by which knowledge the light of truth is confirmed and strengthened, and by which we perceive that the enemies of the faith are to be destroyed. And for the confirmation of this statement he cited the Scriptures in the Apocalypse (chapter 13), which says that the number of the beast is 663, [25]which number is thirty less than the prediction. But in many places some part of the complete number is concealed; for this is the manner of the Scriptures, as Beda says, and perhaps God purposed that this should not be expressed completely, but should be hidden in some way, as the other things that are written in the Apocalypse: that perhaps before the final time of that sect, which Albumazar fixed according to its principal cause, it happens that the Saracens should be overthrown either by the Tartars or by Christians, as already then the larger part of the Saracens had been overthrown by the Tartars, and the ruler, who was Baldach, and Caliph, who was as their pope. But

Albumazar (margin)

Apocalypse 13 (margin)

Note the consumation of Mohammed power (margin)

papa eorum. Sed his non obstantibus, licet iam postea tempus magnum lapsum sit, tamen experientia docet quod nondum secta illa perditionis destructa est: sed proh dolor! sepe et multum contra christianos invalescit, unde patet quod in hac opinione fragilis est et exigua, seu invalida certitudo.

Sexto, dicit iste doctor quod quia credimus quod post legem Macometi nulla secta veniet, nisi lex Anticristi, et astronomi similiter in hoc concordant quod erit aliquis potens, qui legem fedam et magicam constituet post Machumetum, que omnes alias suspendit; ideo multum e[s]set utile E[c]clesie Dei considerare de tempore istius legis; an cito veniet post destructionem legis Machometi, an multum longe. Et et[h]icus philosophus dicit in sua Cosmographia, quod gens que fuit clausa inter portas Caspias irruet in mundum et obviabit Anticristo et eum vocabit (25a) Deum deorum. Iam vero, ut dicit: Tartari qui fuerunt intra portas illas inde exierunt? Nam porte ille fracte sunt, sicut retulerunt aliqui christiani, qui per medium earum transierunt. Hoc ergo inducit quasi signum proximi adventus Anticristi; unde, concludendo, dicit: scio quod si E[c]clesia vellet revolvere textum sacrum et prophetias sacras Sibile et Merlini, Aquile et Ioachim, et multorum aliorum, insuper istorias, et libros philosophorum, atque iuberet considerari vias astronomie, inveniretur su[f]ficiens suspicio, vel magis certitudo de tempore Anticristi. Sed his videtur obviare dictum Christi: "Non est vestrum nosse tempora, vel momenta, que Pater posuit in sua potestate" et illud: "De die autem illa et hora nemo scit &c." Quid autem super his dicendum sit, non est presentis operis diffinire; sed de hac materia tractavi in quodam sermone de adventu Domini, super verbo: "Scitote quoniam prope est regnum Dei."

[marginal note:] Ethycus phylosophus

[marginal note:] Actuum I
Mathei 24

In Vigintiloquium, in verbo XI

Augustinus, secundo De civitate Dei, ubi ait quod sexti mi[l]lenarii annorum mundi posteriora spatia suo tempore volvebantur, ubi incidenter notandum est, quod Augustinus ibidem non assertive, ut quidam crediderunt, sed solum recitative (25b) ponit illam opinionem, que dicebat, quod primevam creationem ideo distinxit Deus per sex dies, ut significaret quod omnia, que per totam durationem seculi huius facere disposuerat, in sex annorum millenariis adimpleret. Hanc siquidem opinionem in pluribus locis et spetialiter, ut supra dictum est in fine libri De civitate Dei assertive repellit. Aliam quoque in titulo salmi sexti, illorum videlicet, qui adventum Domini ad iuditium post septem milia annorum ab Adam futurum credide-

these things notwithstanding, it is clear that already / a long time has elapsed afterward, since experience shows that the sect of perdition has not yet been overthrown; but, sad to say, often and greatly it has grown strong against Christians, whence it is clear that the reliability of that opinion is weak and thin, if not invalid.

Sixthly, this learned writer says that since we believe that after the rule of Mohammed no sect will come except the rule of the Antichrist, and the astronomers likewise agree in this that there will be some powerful person who will establish an abominable and magical government after Mohammed, which will replace all the others; therefore it would be very useful to the Church of God, to pay careful attention to the period of that government; whether it will come suddenly after the overthrow of the government of Mohammed, or a very long while after. And the moral philosopher says in his Cosmography, that the race that had been closed in behind the Caspian doors will break out into the world, and will meet with the Antichrist, and will call him the god of gods. Indeed, as he says: the Tartars who had been behind those doors, from where did they come out? For those doors were broken down, as was reported by certain Christians who passed right through them. Therefore he considers this to be a sign of the approaching advent of the Antichrist; from which he concludes by saying: I know that if the Church would study carefully the sacred text and the sacred prophecies of Sybil and Merlin, of Aquila and Joachim, and many others, along with the histories, and the books of the philosophers, and would order to be considered the ways of astronomy, there would be found a general idea or even a certainty concerning the time of the Antichrist. But these things appear to be contradicted by the saying of Christ: "It is not for you to know the times or the seasons that the Father has placed in his power;" and that one: "but of the day and the hour no man knows" etc. What then about these things is to be said, it is not for the present work to conclude; but I have dealt with this material in a sermon on / "The Coming of the Lord," on the text: "know that the kingdom of God is near."

Moral philosopher — marginal note to the paragraph above.

Acts I — marginal note.
Matthew 24 — marginal note.

From the *Twenty Discussions*, Section XI

Augustine, in the second part of the City of God [Book 22, Chapter 30], where he says that the days of the sixth and last age (or millennium) of the world were passing in his time. Here, incidentally, it should be noted that Augustine does not present that opinion declaratively, as some have believed, but only by way of quotation, he reported the opinion which held that God had divided the primeval creation in six days so as to signify that all things which he purposed to make throughout the whole duration of this world, he would fulfil in six periods of a thousand years. Since indeed he rejects that opinion declaratively in many places, and especially, as noted above, at the end of the book The City of God. Likewise, another opinion in the introduction of Psalm 6, the opinion of those who believe the second advent of the Lord in judgment will take place after seven thousand years from Adam, since seven thousand

runt, ut septem milia annorum tamquam septem dies transeant, deinde illud tempus tamquam dies octava adveniat. De talibus autem coniecturis quid catholice tenendum sit, dudum satis probabiliter, explicavi in quodam sermone de adventu Domini super verbo: Mathei 24 "Scitote quoniam prope est regnum Dei." Sed his omissis ad propositum redeamus.

In Elucidario astronomice concordie cum teologia in verbo X

A Creatione Ade usque ad Christum, secundum Alphonsum, sunt annos quinque milia tercentum quadraginta tribus, et dies CCCVIII.

In libro de concordia astronomice veritatis et narrationes istorie, 57

Post predi[c]tas decem revolutiones Saturni secute sunt (26a) alie decemi et complete anno Christi 1189 vel circiter. Circa quod tempus Innocentius tertius, multis bonis operibus gloriosus, digne cathedram Petri tenebat; cuius tempore a Franchis et Venetis capta est Constantinopolis, similiter innumerabilis Sarracinorum multitudo, contra Ispanos veniens, ad patriam suam confusa redit. His diebus Livonia pro magna parte conversa est ad fidem. Anno vero pontificatus sui 17 Rome celebratum est consilium generale pro residuo Terre Sancte, ubi etiam pro statu Universalis E[c]clesie multa utilia statuta fuerunt, ubi etiam abbatis Ioachim libellum, quem contra magistrum Petrum Lumbardi composuiti dampnavit; insuper etiam Almaricum cum sua heretica doctrina; non tamen doctrina dicti abbatis Ioachin dampnata est, qui in Calabria fioruit, pluresque libros utiles scripsit. Quia regibus et principibus requirentibus ab ipso de peregrinatione, quam faciebant in Terram Sanctam, predixit quod parum proficerenti eo quod nondum tempus proficiendi advenisset. Hoc tempore imperabat Federicus primus, qui largus, strenuus et facundus in omnibus fuit gloriosus.

In libro de concordia astronomice veritatis et narrationis historie, capitulo 61

Sed quia de adventu Antechristi locuti sumus, (26b) sciendum est quod Methodius martir, de quo in libro illustr[i]um virorum meminit Geronimus, de principio et consumatione seculi inulta scripsit, que divina relatione accepi[s]se dicitur; inter que aliqua commemorat, que erunt preambula Antichristi. Quorum primuni est illa dissentio, de qua in secunda ad Thessalonicenses epistola dicit Apostolus: "Nisi venerit dissentio primum &c. Sed de hac iam aliquid breviter tetigimus. Secundum preambulum est, quod pos[t]quam

years would pass just as seven days, whence that time would arrive as the eighth day. However, what should be universally held of such conjectures, I explained fitly enough a short while ago in a sermon on "The

Matthew 24 Coming of the Lord," upon the text, "Know that the kingdom of God is near." But, setting those things aside, let us return to the subject.

From the *Display of the Harmony of Astronomy and Theology,* Subject 10

From the creation of Adam to Christ, according to [King] Alfonso [X], there are 5343 years and 308 days. /

From *Book of Harmony of True Astronomy and Record of History,* Chapter 57

Following the aforementioned ten revolutions of Saturn there followed ten more revolutions, which were completed in A.D. 1189 or thereabouts. At about that time Innocent III, famed for his many good deeds, was the worthy occupant of the see of Peter. In his time Constantinople was taken by the French and the Venetians, at the same time as an innumerable multitude of Saracens, coming against Spain, returned to their homeland in disarray. In those days Livonia was in large part converted to the Christian faith,. In the 17th year of his pontificate there was celebrated in Rome a general council for the unfinished business relating to the Holy Land; also many profitable things were decreed for the condition of the universal church; also the book of the Abbot Joachim (which he wrote against Master Peter Lombard), was condemned; moreover also Almaricus with its heretical teaching was condemned; however the teaching of said Abbot Joachim was not condemned, who flourished in Southeast Italy (Calabria), and who wrote many useful books. Indeed, when kings and princes consulted him concerning the journey that they made into the Holy Land, he predicted that they would make but small progress, since the right time for success had not yet arrived. In this time, Frederick I was reigning, and he was profuse, active and persuasive in all things and was famous.

From *Book of Harmony of True Astronomy and Record of History,* Chapter 61

But since we have spoken about the coming of the Antichrist, it should be mentioned that the martyr Methodius, of whom Jerome writes in the book of famous men, wrote many things about the beginning and the consummation of the world, / which he is said to have received by divine guidance. Among these he records some precursory events which were to take place prior to the Antichrist. Of these the first is that apostasy of which the Apostle Paul speaks in the Second Letter to the Thessalonians: "Unless there come a revolt first" etc. [II Thessalonians 2:3, Douay]. But we have already dealt with this briefly. The second precursory event

absorta fuerint plurima regna, que adversus regnum Romanorum confiixerant, consurgent pro illis adversus Romanum imperium filii Israel, filii Agar, de quibus Daniel predixit; et hoc erit in septimo millenario annorum mundi eo quod a[p]propinquabit consumatio seculi, et non erit longitudo amplius temporis. Hic tamen attende, quod, sicut dicit Ystoria scolastica, Methodius per 200 annos ab Adam ciliades, idest etates seculi per annorum millenaria annotavit. Tertium preambulum est, quod terram promissionis propter peccata inhabitantium in ea obtinebunt filii Ysmael, idest Sarraceni, que deberet esse terra christianorum. (27a) Et hec evenient propter iniquitates varias, specialiter propter peccata sodomie; multaque mala enumerat, que super diversis regnis et regionibus ventura predixit. Et adhuc applicat illud Apostoli: "Nisi venerit dissentio primum &c.," dicens quod dissentio est disciplina vel correptio, qua corripie[n]tur universi habitatores terre, de qua diffuse prosequitur. Quartum preambulum est, quod predicto tempore dissentionis, idest discipline et correptionis, minuetur spiritus perfectorum, et multi abnegabunt veram fidem, etiam sine aliqua vi, tormentis aut flagellis, et associabuntur transgressoribus, sicut de his predixit Apostolus. Et hec omnia fient, ut per tribulationes probentur et manifestentur electi. Quintum preambulum est, quod post tribulationem, que fiet a filiis Ysmael, ipsi iocundantes in victoriis eorum, gloriantesque, quia desolaverunt Persidam et Romaniam, Ciciliam quoque et Syriam, Capadociam et Ysauriam, Africam quoque, vel Ciciliam, et eos, qui inhabitant proxime Romam et insulas, et blasfemantes dicent: nequaquam habebunt christiani ereptionem de manibus nostris. Tunc subito ex[s]urget super eos tribulatio et exiliet rex Grecorum sive Romanorum in furore magno a mari Ethiopie super habitantes terram promissionis, et erit rex Romanorum imponens (27b) iugum super eos septies tantum, quantum erat iugum eorum super terram. Sextum preambulum erit, quod postquam indignatio et furor regis Romanorum exarserit super eos, qui abnegaverunt Christum, erit pax et tranquillitas magna super terram, qualis nondum est facta, sed neque est similis ulla eo quod novissima est in fine seculorum. Et hec est illa, quam Apostolus exposuit; quia, cum dixerint: pax et securitas, tunc eis superveniet subito interitus, de qua Christus loquitur in evangelio. Septimum preambulum erit, quod post illam pacem, tunc reserabuntur porte aquilonis, et egredientur virtutes gentium illarum, quas conclusit Alexanderi et concutietur omnis terra a conspectu carum, et variis crudelitatibus corrumpetur et contaminabitur ab eis. Post ebdomadam vero temporis, quando comprehenderint civitatem Ioppem, mittet Dominus unum ex principibus militie sue, et percutiet eos in uno momento temporis. Octavum preambulum erit, quod postea

is that, after many kingdoms will have been overthrown, which contended against the kingdom of the Romans, there will rise up for them against the Roman dominion the sons of Israel, the sons of Hagar concerning whom Daniel predicted. And this will be in the seventh thousand-year period of the world, in which the end of the age will approach, and there will no more remain a very long time. But consider at this point that, as the Scholastic History says, Methodius figured the chiliads, that is the ages of the world by thousands of years, up to 200 years from the time of Adam. The third precursory event is that, through the sins of its inhabitants, the Promised Land will be possessed by the sons of Ishmael, that is the Saracens, although the land should belong to Christians. And these things will happen because of various iniquities, especially because of sins of sodomy; also he enumerates many evils which he predicted would come upon various kingdoms and regions. This is the application of that saying of the Apostle Paul: "Unless there comes a revolt first," etc., indicating that the revolt is in teaching or an apostasy in which all the inhabitants of the earth will be swept along as it spreads ever more widely. The fourth precursory event is that in the predicted time of the revolt, that is the false teaching and the falling away, the spirits of the saints will grow faint, and many will renounce the true faith, even without suffering any kind of force, tortures or punishments, and they will be united with the transgressors, as the Apostle has predicted concerning them. And all these things will take place / in order that the elect may be tested and revealed. The fifth precursory event will take place after the tribulation which will be caused by the sons of Ishmael when they rejoice in their victories and boast that they have conquered Farsistan, Romania, Cicilia, as well as Capadocia, Isauria, also Africa or Sicily, and those who dwell nearest Rome and the islands; they will boast and say that it is impossible for the Christians ever to recover these lands from them. Then, suddenly, tribulation shall overtake them, and the king of the Greeks or Romans shall spring forth in great fury from the sea of Ethiopia upon the inhabitants of the Promised Land, and the king of the Romans shall press a yoke upon them seven times as great as was their yoke upon the earth. The sixth precursory event shall take place after the indignation and rage of the king of the Romans have been kindled upon those who rejected Christ. There will be peace and great tranquillity upon the earth, such as has never yet existed, and there will never be any like it since this is the last, at the end of the ages. This is that peace concerning which the Apostle explained "For when they shall say, Peace and security; then shall sudden destruction come upon them," [I Thessalonians 5:3, Douay], concerning which Christ also spoke in the Gospel. The seventh precursory event shall be, that after that peace, then shall be unlocked the gates of the north, and there shall come forth the forces of those peoples whom Alexander shut up inside them, and the whole earth shall be shattered before them, and by various barbarous cruelties shall be wasted and defiled by them. But after a week [heptad] of time, when they shall have attacked the city of Joppa, the Lord will send one of the princes of his host and shall conquer them in a moment

descendet rex Romanorum, et morabitur in Hierusalem septimana temporis et dimidia, quod est 10 anni et dimidius, et tunc apparebit filius perditionis. (28a–28b) (29a)

✠

Isaie 11

In die illa, radix Iesse, qui stat in signum populorum, ipsum gentes deprecabuntur, et erit sepulchrum eius gloriosum. Et erit in die illa: adiitiet Dominus secundo manum suam ad possidendum residuum populi sui, quod relinquetur ab Assyriis et ab Egypto et a Phetros et ab Ethiopia, et ab Ennam et a Sennaar, et ab Emath, et ab insulis maris. Et levabit Dominus signum in nationes et congregabit profugos Israel.

Isaie 14

Et quid respondebitur nuntiis gentis? "Quia Dominus fundavit Syon et in ipso sperabunt pauperes populi eius."

Isaie 19

In die illa erit altare Domini in medio terre Egipti, et titulus Domini iuxta terminum eius. Et erit in signum et [in] testimonium Domino exercituum in terra Egypt &c.

Isaie 25

Et fatiet Dominus exercituum in monte hoc convivium pinguium, convivium vindemie &c. Et precipitabit in monte isto fatiem vinculi colligati super omnes populos et telam, quam orditus est super omnes nationes &c.

Et dicent in die illa &c. "Et exultabimus, et letabimur in salutari eius. Quia requiescet manus Domini in monte isto &c." per totum. (29b)

of time. The eighth precursory event shall be that after the king of the Romans shall come and shall remain in Jerusalem for a week and a half of time, that is ten / years and one half, and then shall appear the Son of Perdition.

Isaiah 11[26]

In that day, the root of Jesse, who standeth for an ensign of the people, him the Gentiles shall beseech: and his sepulchre shall be glorious. And it shall come to pass in that day, that the Lord shall set his hand the second time to possess the remnant of his people, which shall be left from the Assyrians, and from Egypt, and from Phetros, and from Ethiopia, and from Elam, and from Sennaar, and from Emath, and from the islands of the sea. And he shall set up a standard unto the nations: and shall assemble the fugitives of Israel.

Isaiah 14

[14:32]

And what shall be answered to the messengers of the nations? That the Lord hath founded Sion, and the poor of his people shall hope in him.

Isaiah 19

[19:19–20a]

In that day, there shall be an altar of the Lord in the midst of the land of Egypt, and a monument of the Lord at the borders thereof. It shall be for a sign and for a testimony to the Lord of hosts, in the land of Egypt. &c.

Isaiah 25

[25:6a, 7, 9a, 9c — 10a]

And the Lord of hosts shall make unto all people, in this mountain, a feast of fat things: a feast of wine, &c. And he shall destroy in this mountain the face of the bond with which all people were tied and the web that he began / over all nations. &c.

And they shall say in that day &c. We shall rejoice and be joyful in his salvation. For the hand of the Lord shall rest in this mountain. &c. to end.

domus patris eius, vasorum diversa genera, omne vas parvulum, a vasis craterarum usque ad omne vas musicorum. In die illa, dicit Dominus exercituum: auferetur paxillus, qui fixus fuerat in loco fideli; et frangetur et cadet, et peribit quod pependerat in eo, quare Dominus locutus est &c.

Isaie 55

Omnes sitientes, venite ad aquas; et qui non habetis argentum, properate, edite, et comedite &c. Inclinate aurem vestram et venite ad me; audite, et vivet anima vestra, et feriam vobiscum pactum sempiternum, misericordias David fideles. Ecce testem populis dedi eum, ducem ac preceptorem gentibus. Ecce gentem, quam nescie- bas, vocabis, et gentes, que non cognoverunt te, ad te current prop- ter Dominum Deum tuum et sanctum Israel, qui glorificavit te &c. Et erit Dominus nominatus in signum eternum, quod non auferetur. (30b)

✠ *De Preterito*

Ysaias, capitulo 24

Hi levabunt vocem suam atque laudabunt; cum glorificatus fuerit Dominus, hinnient de mari. Propter hoc in doctrinis glorificate Do- minum; in insulis maris nomen Domini Dei Israel. A finibus terre laudes vidimus, gloriam iusti. Secretum mihi, secretum mihi.

Ysaias, capitulo 41

Aliter taceant   Taceant ad me insule, et gentes mutent fortitudinem; accedant et tunc loquantur, simul ad iudicium propinquamus. Quis suscitavit ab oriente iustum, vocavit eum, ut sequeretur se? Dabit in con- spectu eius gentes, et reges obtinebit; dabit quasi pulverem gladio eius, sicut stipulam vento raptam arcui eius. Persequetur eos, transi- bit in pace, semita in pedibus eius non apparebit. Quis hoc operatus est, et fecit, vocans generationes ab exordio? Ego Dominus, primus et novissimus ego sum. Viderunt insule, et timuerunt, extrema terre obstupuerunt, a[p]propinquaverunt, et accesserunt.

upon him all the glory of his father's house, diverse kinds of vessels, every little vessel; from the vessels of cups even to every instrument of music. In that day, saith the Lord of hosts, shall the peg be broken and shall fall: and that which hung thereon shall perish, because the Lord hath spoken it. &c.

Isaiah 55

[55:1a, 3–5, 13b]

All you that thirst, come to the waters: and you that have no money, make haste, and eat. &c. Incline your ear and come to me. Hear and your soul shall live. And I / will make an everlasting covenant with you, the faithful; mercies of David. Behold I have given him for a witness to the people, for a leader and a master to the Gentiles. Behold thou shalt call a nation which thou knewest not: and the nations that knew not thee shall run to thee, because of the Lord thy God, and for the Holy One of Israel; for he hath glorified thee. &c. And the Lord shall be named for an everlasting sign that shall not be taken away.

✠ Concerning What Has Already Taken Place [27]

Isaiah, Chapter 24

[24:14–16a]

These shall lift up their voice and shall give praise: when the Lord shall be glorified, they shall make a joyful noise from the sea. Therefore glorify ye the Lord in instruction: the name of the Lord God of Israel in the islands of the sea. From the ends of the earth we have heard praises, the glory of the just one. And I said: My secret to myself, my secret to myself.

Isaiah, Chapter 41

[41:1–5]

Keep silent Let the islands keep silence before me, and the nations take new strength. Let them come near, and then speak: let us come near to judgment together. Who hath raised up the just one from the east, hath called him to follow him? He shall give the nations in his sight, and he shall rule over kings: he shall give them as the dust to his sword, as stubble driven by the wind, to his bow. Ye shall pursue them, he shall pass in peace: no path shall appear after his feet. Who hath wrought and done these things, calling the generations from the beginning? I, the Lord, am the first and the last. The islands saw it, and feared: the ends of the earth were astonished: they drew near, and came. /

Ysaias, capitulo 42

Ecce servus meus, suscipiam eum; electus meus complacuit sibi in illo anima mea; dedi spiritum meum super eum iudicium gentibiis proferet. Non clamabit, nec accipiet personam, nec audietur (31a) vox eius foris. Calamum quassatum non conteret, et lignum fumigans non extinguet; in veritatem educet iuditium. Non erit tristis, neque turbulentus, donec ponat in terra iuditium; et legem eius insule expectabunt. Ego, Dominus, vocavi te in iustitia et a[p]prehendi manum tuam et servavi te. Et dedi te in fedus populi, in lucem gentium; ut aperires oculos cecorum, et educeres de conclusione vinctum, de domo carceris sedentes in tenebris. Ego Dominus, hoc est nomen meum; gloriam meam alteri non dabo, et laudem meam scul[p]tilibus. Que prima fuerunt, ecce venerunt; nova quoque ego annuntio; antequam oriantur, audita vobis faciam. Cantate Domino canticum novum, laus eius ab extremis terre; qui descenditis in mare, et plenitudo eius; insule, et habitatores earum. Levetur desertum, et civitates eius; in domibus habitabit Cedar; laudate, habitatores Petre, de vertice montium clamabunt. Ponent Domino gloriam et laudem eius in insulis nuntiabunt. Dominus sicut fortis egredietur, sicut vir preliator suscitabit zelum; vociferabit et clamabit, super inimicos suos confortabitur. Tacui semper, silui, patiens fui; sicut parturiens loquar, dissipabo et a[b]sorbebo simul. Desertos faciam montes, et colles, et omne germen eorum exsi[c]cabo; ponam flumina in insulas, et stagna arefaciam. Et ducam cecos in viam quam nesciunt; et in semitis, quas ignoraverunt, ambulare eos faciam; ponam tenebras coram eis in lucem, et prava in recta; hec verba feci eis, et non dereliqui eos. (31b)

Idem ibidem

Ysaias, capitulo 43

Et nunc hec dicit Dominus creans te Iacob, et formans te Israel. Noli timere, quia redemi te et vocavi te nomine tuo: meus es tu. Cum transieris per aquas, tecum ero, et flumina non operient te; cum ambulaveris in igne, non combureris, et flamma non ardebit in te; quia ego Dominus Deus tuus, sanctus Israel, salvator tuus, dedi propitiationem tuam, Egyptum, Ethiopiam et Saba pro te. Ex quo honorabilis factus es in oculis meis, et gloriosus; ego dilexi te et dabo homines pro te et populos pro anima tua. Noli timere, quia ego tecum sum; ab oriente adducam semen tuum, et ab occidente congregabo te. Dicam aquiloni: "da" et austro: "noli pr[o]hi-

Isaiah, Chapter 42

[42:1–4, 6–16]

Behold my servant: I will uphold him. My elect: my soul lighteth in him. I have given my spirit upon him: he shall bring forth judgment to the Gentiles. He shall not cry, nor have respect to person: neither shall his voice be heard abroad. The bruised reed he shall not break, and smoking flax he shall not quench: he shall bring forth judgment unto truth. He shall not be sad nor troublesome, till he set judgment in the earth: and the islands shall wait for his law. I, the Lord, have called thee in justice, and taken thee by the hand, and preserved thee. And I have given thee for a covenant of the people, for a light of the Gentiles: That thou mightest open the eyes of the blind, and bring forth the prisoner out of prison, them that sit in darkness out of the prison house. I, the Lord: this is my name. I will not give my glory to another, nor my praise to graven things. The things that were first, behold they are come: and new things do I declare. Before they spring forth, I will make you hear them. Sing ye to the Lord a new song: his praise is from the ends of the earth. You that go down to the sea, and all that are therein: ye islands, and ye inhabitants of them. Let the desert and the cities thereof be exalted: Cedar shall dwell in houses. Ye inhabitants of Petra, give praise: they shall cry from the top of the mountains. They shall give glory to the Lord, and shall declare his praise in the islands. The Lord shall go forth as a mighty man: as a man of war shall he stir up zeal. He shall shout and cry: he shall prevail against his enemies. I have always held my peace. I have kept silence, I have been patient. I will speak now as a woman in labor: I will destroy, and swallow up at once. I will lay waste the mountains and hills, and will make all their grass to wither: and I will turn rivers into islands and will dry up the standing pools. And I will lead the blind into the way which they know not: and in / the paths which they were ignorant of I will make them walk: I will make darkness light before them, and crooked things straight. These things have I done to them, and have not forsaken them.

Same place as before

Isaiah, Chapter 43

[43:1–7a]

And now thus saith the Lord that created thee, O Jacob, and formed thee, O Israel: Fear not, for I have redeemed thee, and called thee by thy name. Thou art mine. When thou shalt pass through the waters, I will be with thee: and the rivers shall not cover thee. When thou shalt walk in the fire, thou shalt not be burned: and the flames shall not burn in thee. For I am the Lord thy God, the Holy One of Israel, thy Saviour: I have given Egypt for thy atonement, Ethiopia and Saba for thee. Since thou becamest honorable in my eyes, thou art glorious. I have loved thee: and I will give men for thee, and people for thy life. Fear not, for I am with thee. I will bring thy seed from the east, and gather thee from the west. I will say to the north: Give up. And to the south: Keep not

bere, affer filios meos de longinquo et filias meas ab extremis terre. Et omnes, qui invocant nomen meum" &c.

Ysaias, capitulo 44

Et nunc audi, Iacob serve meus, et Israel, quem elegi. Hec dicit Dominus, faciens et formans te ab utero auxiliator tuus: Noli timere, serve meus Iacob, et rectissime, quem elegi. E[f]fundam enim aquas super sitientem et fluenta super aridam: e[f]fundam spiritum meum super semen tuum et benedictionem meam super stirpem tuam &c.

Ibidem   Laudate, celi, quoniam misericordiam fecit Dominus; iubilate, extrema terre, (32a) resonate, montes, laudationem, saltus, et omne lignum eius; quoniam redimit Dominus Iacobi et Israel gloriabitur &c. Convertens sapientes retrorsum; et scientiam corum stultam facie[n]s. Suscitans verbum servi sui et consilium nuntiorum suorum complens. Qui dico Iherusalem: "habitaberis," et civitatibus Iude: "edificabimi[ni]," et deserta eius suscitabo. Qui dico profundo: "desolare, et flumina tua arefaciam." Qui dico Ciro: "pastor   Nota meus es et omnem voluntatem meam complebis." Qui dico Iherusalem: "edificaberis," et templo: "fundaberis."

Ysaias, capitulo 45

Hec dicit Doininus Christo meo Ciro: Cuius a[p]prehendi dexteram, ut subiiciam ante faciem eius gentes et dorsa regum vertam et aperiam coram eo ianuas, et porte non claudentur. Ego ante te ibo; et gloriosos terre humiliabo; portas ereas conteram, et vectes ferreos confringam. Et dabo tibi thesauros absconditos et archana secretorum; ut scias, quia ego Dominus, qui voco nomen tuum, Deus Israel. Propter servum meum Iacobi et Israel electum meum, et vocavi te nomine tuo; a[s]similavi te, et non cognovisti me. Ego Dominus, et non est amplius; extra me non est Deus; accinxi te, et non cognovisti me; et sciant hi, qui ab ortu solis, et qui ab o[c]-cidente, quoniam absque me non est Deus &c. (32b)

Ysaias, capitulo 46

Consilium meum stabit et omnis voluntas mea fiat. Vocans ab oriente iustum et de terra longinqua virum voluntatis mee; et locutus sum et a[d]ducam illud; creavi et faciam illud. Audite me duro corde,

back: bring my sons from afar, and my daughters from the ends of the earth. And every one that calleth upon my name. &c.

Isaiah, Chapter 44

[1–3, 23, 25b–28]

And now hear, O Jacob, my servant, and Israel whom I have chosen. Thus saith the Lord that made and formed thee, thy helper from the womb: Fear not, O my servant Jacob, and thou most righteous whom I have chosen. For I will pour out waters upon the thirsty ground and streams upon the dry land: I will pour out my spirit upon thy seed and my blessing upon thy stock. &c.

The same   Give praise, O ye heavens, for the Lord hath shown mercy: shout / with joy, ye ends of the earth. Ye mountains, resound with praise, thou, O forest, and every tree therein: for the Lord hath redeemed Jacob, and Israel shall be glorified. &c. [I am the Lord] That turn the wise backward, and that make their knowledge foolish: That raise up the word of my servant and perform the counsel of my messengers, who say to Jerusalem: Thou shalt be inhabited; and to the cities of Juda: You shall be built, and I will raise up the wastes thereof. Who say to the deep: Be thou desolate, and I will dry up thy rivers. Who say to Cyrus: Thou Note art my shepherd, and thou shalt perform all my pleasure. Who say to Jerusalem: Thou shalt be built. And to the temple: Thy foundations shall be laid.

Isaiah, Chapter 45

[45:1–6a]

Thus saith the Lord to my anointed Cyrus, whose right hand I have taken hold of, to subdue nations before his face, and to turn the backs of kings, and to open the doors before him: and the gates shall not be shut. I will go before thee and will humble the great ones of the earth. I will break in pieces the gates of brass and will burst the bars of iron. And I will give thee hidden treasures and the concealed riches of secret places: that thou mayest know that I am the Lord who call thee by thy name, the God of Israel. For the sake of my servant Jacob and Israel my elect, I have even called thee by thy name. I have made a likeness of thee: and thou hast not known me. I am the Lord, and there is none else: there is no God besides me. I girded thee: and thou hast not known me: That they may know who are from the rising of the sun, and they who are from the west, that there is no God besides me &c.

Isaiah, Chapter 46

[46:10b–13]

My counsel shall stand, and all my will shall be done. Who calls a bird from the east [Columbus text: "who call a just man from the east"], and from a far country the man of my own will. And / I have spoken and

qui longe estis a iustitia. Prope feci iustitiam meam, et non elongabitur, et salus me[a] non morabitur. Dabo in Syon salutem, et in Israel gloriam meam.

Ysaias, capitulo 49

Audite, insule, et a[t]tendite, populi, de longe: Dominus ab utero vocavit me de ventre matris mee recordatus est nominis mei. Et posuit os meum quasi gladium acutum; in umbra manus sue protexit me et posuit me sicut sagi[c]tam electam; in faretra sua abs[c]ondit me. Et dixit michi: Servus meus es tu, Israel, quia in te glorificabor. Et ego dixi &c. Et glorificatus sum in oculis Domini, et Deus meus factus est fortitudo mea. Et dixit: Parum est ut sis michi servus ad suscitandas tribus Iacobi et feccs Israel convertendas. Dedit cnim te in lucem gentium, ut sis salus mea usque ad extremum terre &c.

Ysaias, capitulo 51

Audite me, qui sequimini quod iustum est, et queritis (33a) Dominum: a[t]tendite ad petram, unde excisi estis, et ad cavernam laci, de qua precisi estis. A[t]tendite ad Abraam patrem vestrum et ad Sarram que peperit vos; quia unum vocavi eum, et benedixi ei et multiplicavi eum. Consolabitur ergo Dominus Syon et cons[ol]abitur omnes ruinas eius; et ponet desertum eius quasi delitias, et solitudinem eius quasi [h]ortum Domini. Gaudium et letitia invenietur in ea, gratiarum actio et vox laudis. A[t]tendite ad me, populus meus, et tribus mea me audite, quia lex a me exiet, et iuditium meum in lucem populorum requiescit. Prope est iustus meus egressus est salvator meus, et brachia mea populos iudicabunt; me insule expectabunt et brachium meum sustinebunt. Levate in celum oculos vestros et videte sub terra deorsum; quia celi sicut fumus liquescent, et terra sicut vestimentum atteretur, et [h]abitatores eius sicut hec interibunt. Salus autem mea in sempiternum erit, et iustitia non deficiet. Audite me qui s[c]itis iustum, populus meus lex mea in corde eorum; nolite timere obprobrium hominum et blasfemias eorum ne metuatis. Sicut enim vestimentum sic comedet eos vermis, et sicut lanam sic devorabit eos tinea; salus autem mea in sempiternum erit, et iustitia mea (33b) in generationes generationum. Consurge, consurge, induere fortitudinem, brachium Domini; consurge sicut in diebus antiquis, in generationibus seculorum. Numquid non tu percu[s]sisti superbum, vulnerasti draconem? Numquid non tu persi[c]casti mare, aquam abissi vehementis; qui posuisti profundum maris viam, ut transirent liberati? Et nunc qui redempti sunt

will bring it to pass: I have created, and I will do it. Hear me, O ye hardhearted, who are far from justice. I have brought my justice near: it shall not be afar off, and my salvation shall not tarry. I will give salvation in Sion and my glory in Israel.

Isaiah, Chapter 49

[49:1–4a, 5b–6]

Give ear, ye islands, and hearken, ye people from afar. The Lord hath called me from the womb: from the bowels of my mother he hath been mindful of my name. And he hath made my mouth like a sharp sword. In the shadow of his hand he hath protected me and hath made me as a chosen arrow. In his quiver he hath hidden me. And he said to me: Thou art my servant Israel, for in thee will I glory. And I said, &c. And I am glorified in the eyes of the Lord: and my God is made my strength. And he said: It is a small thing that thou shouldst be my servant, to raise up the tribes of Jacob and to convert the dregs of Israel. Behold, I have given thee to be the light of the Gentiles, that thou mayest be my salvation even to the farthest part of the earth. &c.

Isaiah, Chapter 51

[51:1–13a, 16–18, 22b–23a]

Give ear to me, you that follow that which is just, and you that seek the Lord. Look unto the rock whence you are hewn and to the hole of the pit from which you are dug out. Look unto Abraham your father and to Sara that bore you: for I called him alone, and blessed him, and multiplied him. The Lord therefore will comfort Sion: and will comfort all the ruins thereof. And he will make her desert as a place of pleasure and her wilderness as the garden of the Lord. Joy and gladness shall be found therein, thanksgiving and the voice of praise. Hearken unto me, / O my people, and give ear to me, O my tribes: for a law shall go forth from me, and my judgment shall rest to be a light of the nations. My just one is near at hand, my saviour is gone forth, and my arms shall judge the people. The islands shall look for me and shall patiently wait for my arm. Lift up your eyes to heaven, and look down to the earth beneath: for the heavens shall vanish like smoke, and the earth shall be worn away like a garment, and the inhabitants thereof shall perish in like manner. But my salvation shall be for ever: and my justice shall not fail. Hearken to me, you that know what is just, my people who have my law in your heart: fear ye not the reproach of men and be not afraid of their blasphemies. For the worm shall eat them up as a garment and the moth shall consume them as wool: but my salvation shall be for ever, and my justice from generation to generation. Arise, arise, put on strength, O thou arm of the Lord: arise as in the days of old, in the ancient generations. Hast not thou struck the proud one, and wounded the dragon? Hast not thou dried up the sea, the water of the mighty deep: who madest the depth of the sea a way, that the

a Domino revertentur et venient in Syon laudantes, et letitia sempiterna super capita eorum; gaudium et letitiam tenebunt, fugiet dolor et gemitus. Ego, ego ipse consolabor vos. Quis tu ut timeas ab homine mortali et a filii[s] hominis, qui quasi fenum ita arescet? Et oblitus es Domini factoris tuii qui tetendit celos et fundavit terram &c.

Posui verba mea in ore tuo et in umbra manus mee protexi te, ut plantes celos et fundes terram et dicas ad Syon: Populus meus es tu. Elevare, elevare, consurge Iherusalem que bibisti de manu Domini calicem ire eius; usque ad fundum calicis soporis bibisti et potasti usque ad feces. Non est qui sustentet eam ex omnibus filiis quos genuit; et non est qui a[p]prehendat manum eius ex omnibus filiis quos enutrivit &c.

Eccc tuli de manLi tua calicem soporis, fundum calicis indigiiationis mee, non adiicies ut (34a) bibas illum ultra. Et ponam illum in manu eorum qui te humiliaverunt &c.

Ysaias, capitulo 52

Consurge, consurge, induere fortitudine tua, Syon; induere vestimentis glorie tue, Iherusalem, civitas sancta; quia non adiiciet ultra ut pertranseat per te incircuncisus et immundus. Excutere de pulvere, consurge, sede, Iherusalem; solve vincula colli tui, captiva filia Syon. Quia hec dicit Dominus: Gratis venundati estis, et sine argento redimemini &c. Quam pulcri super montes pedes a[n]-nuntia[n]tis et predica[n]tis pacem; a[n]nuntia[n]tis bonum, predica[n]tis salutem, dicentis Syon: Regnabit Deus tuus! Vox speculatorum tuorum: levaverunt vocem, simul laudabunt; quia oculo ad oculum videbunt, cum converterit Dominus Syon. Gaudete, et laudate simul, deserta Iherusalem; quia consolatus est Dominus po-

Nota pulum suum, redemit Iherusalem. Paravit Dominus brachium sanctum suum in oculis omnium gentium; et videbunt omnes fines terre salutare Dei nostri. Recedite, recedite, exite inde, pollutum nolite tangere; exite de medio eius, mundamini qui fertis vasa Domini. Qui non in tumultu exibitis, nec in fuga properabitis; precedet enim vos Dominus, et congregabit vos Deus Israel. Ecce intelliget (34b) servus meus, exaltabitur et elevabitur, et sublimis erit valde. Sic opstupuerunt super te multi, sic inglorius erit inter viros aspectus eius, et forma eius inter filios hominum. Iste asperget gentes multas. Super ipsum continebunt reges os suum; quia quibus non est narratum de eo, viderunt; et qui non audierunt, contemplati sunt.

Ysaias, capitulo 57

Et omnes eos auferet ventus, tollet aura. Qui autem fiduciam habet mei, hereditabit terram, et possidebit montem sanctum meum.

delivered might pass over? And now they that are redeemed by the Lord shall return and shall come into Sion singing praises: and joy everlasting shall be upon their heads. They shall obtain joy and gladness:. sorrow and mourning shall flee away. I, I myself, will comfort you. Who art thou, that thou shouldst be afraid of a mortal man and of the son of man who shall wither away like grass? And thou hast forgotten the Lord thy maker, who stretched out the heavens and founded the earth, &c. I have put my words in thy mouth and have protected thee in the shadow of my hand, that thou mightest plant the heavens and found the earth and mightest say to Sion: Thou art my people. / Arise, arise, stand up, O Jerusalem, which hast drunk even to the bottom of the cup of dead sleep, and thou hast drunk even to the dregs. There is none that can uphold her among all the children that she hath brought forth: and there is none that taketh her by the hand among all the children that she hath brought up. &c. Behold I have taken out of thy hand the cup of dead sleep, the dregs of the cup of my indignation. Thou shalt not drink it again any more. And I will put it in the hand of them that have oppressed thee. &c.

Isaiah, Chapter 52

[52:1–3, 7–15]

Arise, arise, put on thy strength, O Sion, put on the garments of thy glory, O Jerusalem, the city of the Holy One: for henceforth the uncircumcised and unclean shall no more pass through thee. Shake thyself from the dust, arise, sit up, O Jerusalem: loose the bonds from off thy neck, O captive daughter of Sion. For thus saith the Lord: You were sold gratis, and you shall be redeemed without money. &c. How beautiful upon the mountains are the feet of him that bringeth good tidings and that preacheth peace, of him that sheweth forth good, that preacheth salvation, that saith to Sion: Thy God shall reign! Rejoice and give praise together, O ye deserts of Jerusalem, for the Lord hath comforted his

Note people: he hath redeemed Jerusalem. The Lord hath prepared his holy arm in the sight of all the Gentiles: and all the ends of the earth shall see the salvation of our God. Depart, depart, go ye out from thence: touch no unclean thing. Go out of the midst of her. Be ye clean, you that carry the vessels of the Lord. For you shall not go out in a tumult: neither / shall you make haste by flight. For the Lord will go before you: and the God of Israel will gather you together. Behold my servant shall understand: he shall be exalted and extolled, and shall be exceeding high. As many have been astonished at thee, so shall his visage be inglorious among men and his form among the sons of men. He shall sprinkle many nations: kings shall shut their mouth at him. For whom it was not told of him have seen: and they that heard not have beheld.

Isaiah, Chapter 57

[57:13b]

But the wind shall carry them all off, a breeze shall take them away. But he that putteth his trust in me shall inherit the land and shall possess my holy mount.

Ysaias, capitulo 59

Insulis vicem re[d]det. Et timebunt, qui ab occidente, nomen Domini, et qui ab ortu solis, gloriam eius; cum venerit quasi fiuvius violentus, quem spiritus Domini cogit. Et venerit Syon redemptor &c.

Ysaias, capitulo 60

Surge, illuminare, Iherusalem; quia venit lumen tuum, et gloria Domini super te orta est. Quia ecce tenebre operie[n]t terrami et caligo populos; super te autem orietur Dominus et gloria eius in te videbitur. Et ambulabunt gentes in lumine tuo, et reges in splendore ortus tui. Leva in circuitu oculos tuos, et vide: omnes isti congregati sunt, venerunt tibi; filii tui de longe venient, (35a) et filie tue de latere surgent. Tunc videbis et afflues, et mirabitur et dilatabitur cor tuum, quando conversa fuerit ad te fortitudo maris, fortitudo gentium venerit tibi. Inundatio camellorum operiet te, dromedarii Madiam et Epha: omnes de Sabba venient, aurum et thus deferentes et laudem Domino a[n]nuntiantes. Omne pecus Cedar congregabitur tibi, arietes Nabaiot ministrabunt tibi: offerentur super placabili altari meo, et domum maiestatis mee glorificabo. Qui sunt isti, qui ut nubes volant, et quasi columbe ad fenestras suas? Me enim insule expectanti et naves maris in principio, ut a[d]ducam filios tuos de longe; argentum eorum et aurum cum eis, nomini Domini Dei tui, et sancto Israel, quia glorificavit te. Et edificabunt filii peregrinorum muros tuos, et reges eorum ministrabunt tibi; in indignatione enim mea percu[s]si te, et in reconciliatione tua misertus sum tui. Et aperientur porte tue iugiter, die ac nocte non cl[a]udentur, ut afferatur ad te fortitudo gentium, et reges eorum a[d]ducantur. Gens enim et regnum, quod non servierit tibi, peribit; et gente[s] solitudine vastabuntur. Gloria Libani ad te veniet, abies et buxus, et pinus simul, ad ornandum locum sanctificationis mee; et locum pedum meorum glorificabo. Et venient ad te curvi filii eorum qui humiliaverunt te, et (35b) adorabunt vestigia pedum tuorum omnes qui detrahebant tibi, et vocabunt te civitatem Domini, Syon Sancti Israel. Pro eo quod fuisti derelicta, et odio habita, et non erat qui per te transiret, ponam te in superbiam seculorum, gaudium in generatione et generationem; et suges lac gentium, et mamilla regum lactaberis; et scies quia ego Dominus salvans te, et redempto[r] tuus

Aqui es colocuti

Isaiah, Chapter 59

[9:18b–20a]

He will repay the like to the islands. And they from the west shall fear the name of the Lord: and they from the rising of the sun, his glory: when he shall come as a violent stream which the spirit of the Lord driveth on: And there shall come a redeemer to Sion. &c.

Isaiah, Chapter 60

[60:1–22]

Arise, be enlightened, O Jerusalem: for thy light is come, and the glory of the Lord is risen upon thee. For, behold, darkness shall cover the earth and a mist the people: but the Lord shall arise upon thee, and his glory shall be seen upon thee. And the Gentiles shall walk in thy light, and kings in the brightness of thy rising. Lift up thy eyes round about and see: all these are gathered together, they are come to thee. Thy sons shall come from afar and thy daughters shall rise up at thy side. Then shalt thou see / and abound, and thy heart shall wonder and be enlarged: when the multitude of the sea shall be converted to thee, the strength of the Gentiles shall come to thee. The multitude of camels shall cover thee, the dromedaries of Madian and Epha. All they from Saba shall come, bringing gold and frankincense and shewing forth praise to the Lord. All the flocks of Cedar shall be gathered together unto thee: the rams of Nabaioth shall minister to thee. They shall be offered upon my acceptable altar: and I will glorify the house of my majesty. Who are these that fly as clouds, and as doves to their windows? For, the islands wait for me, and the ships of the sea in the beginning: that I may bring thy sons from afar, their silver and their gold with them, to the name of the Lord thy God and to the Holy One of Israel, because he hath glorified thee. And the children of strangers shall build up thy walls, and their kings shall minister to thee: for in my wrath have I struck thee and in my reconciliation have I had mercy upon thee. And thy gates shall be open continually: they shall not be shut day nor night, that the strength of the Gentiles may be brought to thee, and their kings may be brought. For the nation and the kingdom that will not serve thee shall perish: and the Gentiles shall be wasted with desolation. The glory of Libanus shall come to thee, the fir tree and the box tree and the pine tree together, to beautify the place of my sanctuary: and I will glorify the place of my feet. And the children of them that afflict thee shall come bowing down to thee: and all that slandered thee shall worship the steps of thy feet and shall call thee the City of the Lord, the Sion of the Holy One of Israel. Because thou wast forsaken and hated, and there was none that passed through thee, I will make thee to be an everlasting glory, a joy unto generation and generation. And thou shalt suck the milk of the Gentiles: and thou shalt be nursed with the breasts of kings. And thou shalt know that I am the Lord thy Saviour and thy Redeemer, the Mighty One of Jacob. / For brass I will bring gold, and

Water is discussed

fortis Iacob. Pro ere afferam aurum, et pro ferro afferam argentum et pro lignis es et pro lapidibus ferrum; et ponam visitationem tuam pacem et prepositos tuos iustitiam. Non audietur ultra iniquitas in terra tua, vastitas et cont[r]icio in terminis tuis, et o[c]cupabit salus muros tuos, et portas tuas laudatio. Non erit tibi amplius sol ad lucendum per diem, nec splendor lune illuminabit te; sed erit tibi Dominus in lucem sempiterna[m], et Deus tuus in gloriam tuam. Non occidct ultra sol tuus, et luna tua non minuetur; quia Dominus erit tibi in lucem sempiternam, et complebuntur dies lu[c]tus tui. Populus autem tuus omnes iusti, in perpetuum [h]ereditabunt terra[m], germen plantationis mee, opus manus mee ad glorificandum. Minimus erit in mille, et parvulus in gentem fortissimam. Ego Dominus in tempore eius subito faciam istud. (36b)

Ysaias, capitulo 62

Propter Syon non tacebo et propter Iherusalem non quiescam, donec egrediatur ut splendor iustus eius, et salvator eius ut lampas accendatur. Et videbunt iustum tuum, et cuncti reges inclitum tuum; et vocabitur tibi nomen novum, quod os Domini nominavit. Et eris corona glorie in manu Domini, et diadema regni in manu Dei tui. Non vocaberis ultra Derelicta, et terra tua non vocabitur amplius desolata; sed vocaberis: voluntas mea in ea, et terra tua inhabitata; quia co[m]placuit Domino in te; et terra tua inhabitabitur. Habitabit enim iuvenis cum virgine, et habitabunt in te filii tui. Et gaudebit sponsus super sponsami et gaudebit super te Deus tuus. super muros tuos, Iherusalem, constitui custodes, tota die et tota nocte in perpetuum non tacebunt. Qui remi[ni]scimini Domini, ne taceatis, et ne detis silentium ei, donec stabiliat et donec ponat Iherusalem in terra. Iuravit Dominus in dextera sua et brachio fortitudinis sue: Si dedero triticum tuum ultra cibum inimicis tuis, et si biberint filii alieni vinum tuum in quo laborasti. Quia qui congregabunt illud, ecce [e]dent, et laudabunt Dominum; et qui comportant illud, bibent in atriis sanctis meis. Transite, transite per portas, preparate viam populo. Planum facite iter et eligite lapides et elevate signum ad populos. Ecce Dominus (36b) auditum fecit in extremis terre, dicite filie Syon: ecce salvator tuus venit: ecce merces eius cum eo, et opus eius corain illo. Et vocabunt eos populus sanctus, redempti a Domino. Tu autem vocaberis: quesita civitas, et non derelicta.

Ysaias, capitulo 63

Quis est iste qui venit de Edom, tinctis vestibus de Rosra? Iste formosus in stola sua, gradiens in multitudine fortitudinis sue &c.

for iron I will bring silver, and for wood brass, and for stones iron: and I will make thy visitation peace, and thy overseers justice. Iniquity shall no more be heard in thy land and, wasting nor destruction in thy borders: and salvation shall possess thy walls, and praise thy gates. Thou shalt no more have the sun for thy light by day, neither shall the brightness of the moon enlighten thee: but the Lord shall be unto thee for an everlasting light, and thy God for thy glory. Thy sun shall go down no more and thy moon shall not decrease. For the Lord shall be unto thee for an everlasting light: and the days of thy mourning shall be ended. And thy people shall be all just: they shall inherit the land for ever, the branch of my panting, the work of my hand, to glorify me. The least shall become a thousand, and a little one a most strong nation: I, the Lord, will suddenly do this thing in its time.

Isaiah, Chapter 62

[62:1–12]

For Sion's sake, I will not hold my peace, and for the sake of Jerusalem I will not rest till her just one come forth as brightness and her saviour be lighted as a lamp. And the Gentiles shall see thy just one, and all kings thy glorious one: and thou shalt be called by a new name which the mouth of the Lord shall name. And thou shalt be a crown of glory in the hand of the Lord and a royal diadem in the hand of thy God. Thou shalt no more be called 'Forsaken' and thy land shall no more be called 'Desolate': but thou shalt be called 'My pleasure in her,' and thy land 'Inhabited'. Because the Lord hath been well pleased with thee: and thy land shall be inhabited. For the young man shall dwell with the virgin: and thy children shall dwell in thee. And the bridegroom shall rejoice over the bride: and thy God shall rejoice over thee. Upon thy walls, Jerusalem, I have appointed / watchmen, all the day and all the night: they shall never hold their peace. You that are mindful of the Lord, hold not your peace. And give him no silence till he establish, and till he make Jerusalem a praise in the earth. The Lord hath sworn by his right hand and by the arm of his strength: Surely I will no more give thy corn to be meat for thy enemies: and the sons of the strangers shall not drink thy wine, for which thou hast labored. For they that gather it shall eat it and shall praise the Lord: and they that bring it together shall drink it in my holy courts. Go through, go through the gates, prepare the way for the people, make the road plain, pick out the stones, and lift up the standard to the people. Behold the Lord hath made it to be heard in the ends of the earth. Tell the daughter of Sion: Behold thy Saviour cometh. Behold his reward is with him and his work before him. And they shall call them: The Holy People, The Redeemed of the Lord. But thou shalt be called: A city, sought after and not forsaken.

Isaiah, Chapter 63

[63:1a]

Who is this that cometh from Edom, with dyed garments from Bosra, this beautiful one in his robe, walking in the greatness of his strength? &c.

Ysaias, capitulo 65

Quesierunt me qui ante non inte[r]rogabant, invenerunt qui non quesierunt me. Dixi: ecce ego, ecc[e] ego a[d] gentem que nesciebat me, et que non invocabat nomen meum. Expandi manus meas tota die ad populum incredulum, qui graditur in via non bona post cogitationes suas. Populus qui ad iracundiam provocat me ante faciem meam semper; qui immola[n]t in [h]ortis et sacrificant super late[re]s; qui habitant in sepulcris et in delubris idolorum dormiunt; qui coinedunt carnem sui[l]lam et ius prophanum in vasis eorum. Recede a me! Non a[p]propinques mihi, quia immundus es &c.

Quia oblivioni tradite sunt angustie priores (37a) et quia abscondite sunt ab oculis nostris. Ecce enim creo celos novos et terram novam; et non erunt in memoria priora et non ascendent super cor. Sed gaudebitis et exultabitis usque in sempiternum in his que ego creo, quia ecce ego creo Iherusalem exultationem et populum eius gaudium. Et exultabo in Iherusalem et gaudebo in populo meo; et non audietur in ea ultra vox fletus et vox clamoris. Non erit ibi amplius infans dierum et senex qui non impleat dies suos. Quoniam puer centum annorum morietur, et peccator centum annorum maledictus erit. Et edificabunt domos et habitabunt et plantabunt vineas et comedent fructus earum. Non edificabunt, et alius habitabit, non plantabunt, et alius comedet: secundum enim dies ligni erunt dies populi mei, et opera manuum eorum inveterabunt. Electi mei non laborabunt frustra neque generabunt in conturbatione; quia semen benedictorum est, et nepotes cum eis. Eritque antequam clament, ego exaudiam &c.

Ysaias, capitulo 66

Ego autem opera eorum et cogitationes eorum venio, ut congregem cum omnibus gentibus et linguis; et venient et videbunt gloriam meam. Et ponam (37b) in eis signum et mittam ex eis, qui salvati fuerint, ad gentes in mare, in Africam, in Lydiam, tenentes sagittam; in Italiam, et Greciam, ad insulas longe, ad eos, qui non audierunt de me et viderunt gloriam meam. Et annuntiabunt gloriam meam gentibus, et adducent omnes fratres vestros de cunctis gentibus donum Domino, in equis, et in quadrigis, et in lecticis, et in mulis, et in carrucis, ad montem sanctum meum lherusalem, dicit Dominusi quomodo si inferant filii Israel munus in vase mundo domum Domini. Et assumam ex eis in sacerdotes, et levitas, dicit Dominus. Quasi sicut celi novi, et terra novai que ego facio stare coram me, dicit Dominus Deus sic stabit semen vestrumi et nomen vestrum. Et erit mensis ex mense, sabbatum ex sabbato veniet omnis caro,

Isaiah, Chapter 65

[65:1–5a, 16b–24a]

They have sought me that before asked not for me: they have found me that sought me not. I said: Behold me, Behold me, to a nation that did not know me and that did not call upon my name. I have spread forth my hands all the day to an unbelieving people, who walk in a way that is not good, after their own thoughts. A people that continually provoke me to anger before my face: that immolate in gardens and sacrifice upon / bricks. That dwell in sepulchers and sleep in the temple of idols: that eat swine's flesh, and profane broth is in their vessels. That say: Depart from me. Come not near me, because thou art unclean. &c.

Because the former distresses are forgotten and because they are hid from my eyes. For behold I create new heavens and a new earth: and the former things shall not be in remembrance, and they shall not come upon the heart. But you shall be glad and rejoice for ever in these things which I create: for behold I create Jerusalem, a rejoicing, and the people thereof, joy. And I will rejoice in Jerusalem and joy in my people: and the voice of weeping shall no more be heard in her, nor the voice of crying. There shall no more be an infant of days there, nor an old man that shall not fill up his days: for the child shall die a hundred years old, and the sinner being a hundred years old shall be accursed. And they shall build houses and inhabit them: and they shall plant vineyards and eat the fruit of them. They shall not build and another inhabit: they shall not plant and another eat. For as the days of a tree, so shall be the days of my people: and the work of their hands shall be of long continuance. My elect shall not labor in vain, nor bring forth in trouble; for they are the seed of the blessed of the Lord, and their posterity with them. And it shall come to pass that before they call, I will hear. &c.

Isaiah, Chapter 66

[66:18–24]

But I know their works and their thoughts: I come that I may gather them together with all nations and tongues: and they shall come and shall see my glory. And I will set a sign among them, and I will send of them that shall be saved, to the Gentiles into the sea, into Africa and Lydia, them that draw the bow: into Italy and Greece, to the islands afar off, to them that / have not heard of me and have not seen my glory. And they shall declare my glory to the Gentiles: And they shall bring all your brethren of all nations for a gift to the Lord, upon horses and in chariots and in litters and on mules and in coaches, to my holy mountain Jerusalem, saith the Lord, as if the children of Israel should bring an offering in a clean vessel into the house of the Lord. And I will take of them to be priests and Levites, saith the Lord. For as the new heavens and the new earth, which I will make to stand before me, saith the Lord: so shall your seed stand, and your name. And there shall be month after month and sabbath after sabbath: and all flesh shall come

ut adoret coram facie mea, dicit Dominus. Et egredientur e[t] videbunt cadavera virorum qui prevaricati sunt in me; vermis eorum non morietur, et ignis eorum non extinguetur; et erunt usque ad satietatem visionis omni carni.

Hieremias, capitulo 2

Transite ad insulas Cethin et videte et in Cedar mittite et considerate vehementer et videte si factum est huiuscemodi. Si mutavit gens deos suos, et certe ipsi non sunt dii. (38a)

Hieremias, capitulo 3

Convertimini, filii, revertentes, dicit Dominus; quia ego vir vester; et assumam vos unum de civitate, et duos de cognatione, et introducam vos in Syon et dabo vobis pastores iuxta cor meum, et pascent vos scientia et doctrina. Cumque multiplicati fuerit[is], et creveritis in terra in diebus illis, ait Dominus: non dicet ultra: archa testamenti Domini, neque ascendit super cor, neque recordabuntur illius, nec visitabitur, nec fiet ultra. In tempore illo vocabunt Iherusalem solium Domini; et congregabuntur ad eam omnes gentes in nomine Domini in Iherusalem, et non ambulabunt post pravitatem cordis sui pessimi. In diebus illis ibit domus Iuda ad domum Israel &c.

Hieremias, capitulo 4

Annuntiate in Iuda, et in Iherusalem auditum facite; loquimini et canite tuba in terra; clamate fortiter, et dicite: congreg[a]mini et ingrediamur civitates munitas. Levate signum in Syon &c.

Ecce auditum est in Iherusalem: custodes venire de terra longinqua, et dare super civitates Iude vocem suam &c.

Hieremias, capitulo 10

Argentum involutum de Tarsis affertur, et aurum de (38b) Ophyr; opus artificis, et manus erarii; hiacintus et purpura indumentum eorum.

Hieremias, capitulo 16

Propterea ecce dies venient, dicit Dominus, et non dicetur ultra: vivit Dominus, qui eduxit filios Israel de terra Egypti; sed: vivit Dominus, qui eduxit filios Israel de terra aquilonis, et de universis terris &c.

Ad te gentes venient ab extremis terre.

to adore before my face, saith the Lord. And they shall go out and see the carcasses of the men that have transgressed against me. Their worm shall not die and their fire shall not be quenched: and they shall be a loathsome sight to all flesh.

Jeremiah, Chapter 2

[2:10–11a]

Pass over to the isles of Cethim and see, and send into Cedar and consider diligently: and see if there hath been done nothing like this. If a nation hath changed their gods, and indeed they are not gods.

Jeremiah, Chapter 3

[3:14–18a]

Return, O ye revolting children, saith the Lord: for I am your husband: and I will take you, one of a city, and two of a kindred, and will bring you into Sion. And I will give you pastors according to my own heart: and they shall feed you with knowledge and doctrine. And when you shall be multiplied and increase in the land in those days, saith the Lord, they shall say no more: The ark of the covenant of the Lord. Neither shall it come upon the heart, neither / shall they remember it, neither shall it be visited, neither shall that be done any more. At that time Jerusalem shall be called the Throne of the Lord: and all the nations shall be gathered together to it, in the name of the Lord, to Jerusalem, and they shall not walk after the perversity of their most wicked heart. In those days the house of Juda shall go to the house of Israel. &c.

Jeremiah, Chapter 4

[4:5–6a,16b]

Declare ye in Juda, and make it heard in Jerusalem: speak, and sound with the trumpet in the land. Cry aloud, and say: Assemble yourselves, and let us go into strong cities. Set up the standard in Sion. &c.

Behold it is heard in Jerusalem that guards are coming from a far country and give out their voice against the cities of Juda. &c.

Jeremiah, Chapter 10

[10:9a]

Silver spread into places is brought from Tharsis, and gold from Ophir, the work of the artificer and of the hand of the coppersmith: violet and purple is their clothing.

Jeremiah, Chapter 16

[16:14–15a,9b]

Therefore, behold the days come, saith the Lord, when it shall be said no more: The Lord liveth, that brought forth the children of Israel out of the land of the north and out of all the lands. &c.

To thee the Gentiles shall come from the ends of the earth. /

Hieremias, capitulo 23

Non formidabunt ultra, et non pavebunt; et nullus queretur ex numero, dicit Dominus. ecce dies veniunt, dicit Dominus: et suscitabo David germen iustum; et regnabit rex et sapiens erit; et faciet iudicium et iustitiam in terra. In diebus illis salvabitur Iuda, et Israel habitabit confidenter; et hoc est nomen quod vocabunt eum, Dominus iustus noster. Propter hoc ecce dies veniunt, dicit Dominus, et non dicent ultra: vivit Dominus, qui eduxit filios Israel de terra Egypti; sed: vivit Dominus, qui eduxit et adduxit semen domus Israel de terra aquilonis, et de cunctis terris, ad quas eieceram eos illuc; et habitabunt in terram suam &c.

Numquid nunc celum et terram ego impleo, dicit Dominus? (39a)

Hieremias, capitulo 30

Et erit in die illa, ait Dominus exercit[u]um: co[n]teram iugum eius de collo tuo, et vincula eius dirumpam, et non dominabuntur ei amplius alieni; sed servient Domino Deo suo, et David regi suo, quem suscitabo eis. Tu ergo ne timeas, serve meus Iacob, ait Dominus, neque paveasi Israel; quia ecce ego salvabo te de terra longinqua, et semen tuum de terra captivitatis eorum &c.

Hieremias, capitulo 31

Surgite, et ascendamus in Syon ad Dominum Deum nostrum. Quia hec dicit Dominus: exultate in leticia Iacob, et hi[n]nite contra caput gentium; personate et canite, et dicite: salva, Domine, populum tuum, reliquias Israel. Ecce ego a[d]duam eos de terra aquilonis, et congregabo eos ab extremis terre &c.

In fletu venient, et in misericordia reducam eos, et educam eos per torrentes aquarum in via recta &c. Audite verbum Domini, gentes, et annuntiate in insulis que procul sunt, et dicite: qui dispersit Israel, congregabit eum; et custodiet eum sicut pastor gregem suum. Redemit enim Dominus Iacob, et liberavit eum de inanu potentioris. et venient et laudabunt in monte Syon &c.

Hieremias, capitulo 33

Ecce dies venient, dicit Dominus: et suscitabo (39b) verbum bonum, quod locutus sum ad domum Israel, et ad domum Iuda. In diebus illis et in tempore illo germinare faciam David germen

Jeremiah, Chapter 23

[23:4b–8,24b]

They shall fear no more and they shall not be dismayed. And none shall be wanting of their number, saith the Lord. Behold the days come, saith the Lord, and I will raise up to David a just branch. And a king shall reign, and shall be wise, and shall execute judgment and justice in the earth. In those days shall Juda be saved and Israel shall dwell confidently: and this is the name that they shall call him: The Lord, Our Just One. Therefore, behold the days come, saith the Lord, and they shall say no more: The Lord liveth, who brought up the children of Israel, out of the land of Egypt: But, The Lord liveth, who hath brought out and brought hither the seed of the house of Israel, from the land of the north and out of all the lands to which I had cast them forth: and they shall dwell in their own land. &c.

Do not I fill heaven and earth, saith the Lord?

Jeremiah, Chapter 30

[30:8–10a]

And it shall come to pass in that day, saith the Lord of hosts, that I will break his yoke from off thy neck and will burst his bands: and strangers shall no more rule over him. But they shall serve the Lord their God and David their king, whom I will raise up to them. Therefore, fear thou not, my servant Jacob, saith the Lord, neither be dismayed, O Israel: for behold, I will save thee from a country afar off, and thy seed from the land of their captivity &c.

Jeremiah, Chapter 31

[31:6b–8a,9a,10–12a]

Arise, and let us go up to Sion to the Lord our God. For thus saith the Lord: Rejoice ye in the joy of Jacob and neigh before the head of the Gentiles. Shout ye and sing, and say: Save, O Lord, thy people, the remnant of Israel. Behold I will bring them from the north country / and will gather them from the ends of the earth.

They shall come with weeping: and I will bring them back in mercy. And I will bring them through the torrents of waters in a right way. &c. Hear the Word of the Lord, O ye nations, and declare it in the islands that are afar off, and say: He that scattered Israel will gather him: and he will keep him as the shepherd doth his flock. For the Lord hath redeemed Jacob and delivered him out of the hand of one that was mightier than he. And they shall come and give praise in mount Sion. &c.

Jeremiah, Chapter 33

[33:14–16, 19–23, 2b–2b]

Behold the days come, saith the Lord, that I will perform the good word that I have spoken to the house of Juda. In those days and in that time I will make the bud of justice to spring forth unto David: and he shall

iustitie; et faciet iudic[i]um et iustitiam in terra. In diebus illis salvabitur Iuda, et Israel habitabit confidenter; et hoc est nomen, quod vocabunt eum, Dominus iustus noster &c.

Et factum est verbum Domini ad Ieremiam, dicens: hec dixit Dominus: si irritum potest fieri pactum meum cum die, et pactum meum cum nocte, ut non sit dies et nox in tempore suo; et pactum meum irritum esse poterit cum David, servo meo, ut non sit ex eo filius qui regnet in trono eius, et levite et sacerdotes ministri mei. Sicut enumerari non po[s]sunt stelle celi, et metiri arene maris; sic multiplicabo semen David servi mei, et levitas ministros meos. et factum est verbum Domini ad Ieremiam &c. Si pactum meum inter diem et noctem, et leges celo et terre non posui; equidem et semen Iacob et David servi mei proiciam, ut non assumam de semine eius principes seminis Habraam, Ysac et Iacob; reducam (40a) enim conversionem eorum, et miserebor eis.

Barut, capitulo 4

Adduxit enim super illos gentem de longinquo, gentem improbam et alterius lingue; qui non sunt reveriti senem, neque puerorum miserti sunt &c.

Emisi enim vos cum luctu et ploratu; reducet autem vos mihi Dominus cum gaudio et iocunditate in sempiternum. Sicut enim viderunt vicine Syon captivitatem vestram a Deo, sic videbunt et in celeritate salutem vestram in Deo, que superveniet vobis cum honore magno, et splendore eterno &c.

Circumspice, Iherusalem, ad orientem, et vide iocunditatem a Deo tibi venientem. Ecce enim veniunt filii tui, quos dimisisti dispersos, veniunt co[l]lecti ab oriente usque ad occidentem, in verbo sancti gaudentes in honorem Dei.

Barut, capitulo 5

Exue te, Iherusalem, stola luctus, et vexationis tue; indue te decore et honore, que a Deo tibi est, sempiterna gloria. Circumdabit te Deus diployde iustitie et imponet mitram capiti tuo honoris eterni. Deus enim ostendet splendorem suum in te, qui sub celo est. Nominabitur enim tibi (40b) nomen tuum a Deo in sempiternum: pax iusticie, et honor pietatis. Exurge, Israel, et sta in excelso; et circumspice ad orientem et vide collectos filios tuos ab oriente sole usque ad occidentem, in verbo sancti gaudentes Dei memoria. Exierunt enim abs te pedibus ducti ab inimicis; adducet autem illos

do judgment and justice in the earth. In those days shall Juda be saved and Jerusalem [Columbus: "and Israel"] shall dwell securely. And this is the name that they shall call him, The Lord our just one. &c.

And the word of the Lord came to Jeremiah, saying thus saith the Lord: If my covenant with the day can be made void, and my covenant with the night, that there should not be day and night in their season: Also my covenant with David my servant may be made void, that he should not have a son to reign upon his throne, and with the Levites and priests, my ministers. As the stars of heaven cannot be numbered, nor the sand of the sea be measured: so will I multiply the seed of David my servant and the Levites my ministers. And the word of the Lord came to Jeremiah. &c. If I have not set my covenant between day and night, and laws to heaven and earth: Surely I will also cast off the seed of Jacob and of David my servant, so as not to take any of his seed to be rulers of the seed of Abraham, Isaac and Jacob. For I will / bring them back from their captivity and will have mercy on them.

Baruch, Chapter 4

[15–16a, 23–24, 36–37]

For he hath brought a nation upon them from afar, a wicked nation and of a strange tongue: Who have neither reverenced the ancient nor pitied children. &c.

For I sent you forth in mourning and weeping: but the Lord will bring you back to me with joy and gladness for ever. For as the neighbors of Sion have now seen your captivity from God, so shall they also shortly see your salvation from God, which shall come upon you with great honor and everlasting glory. &c.

Look about thee, O Jerusalem, towards the east, and behold the joy that cometh to thee from God. For behold thy children come whom thou sentest away scattered: They come gathered together from the east even to the west, at the word of the Holy One, rejoicing for the honor of God.

Baruch, Chapter 5

[5:1–9]

Put off, O Jerusalem, the garment of thy mourning and affliction: and put on the beauty and honor of that everlasting glory which thou hast from God. God will clothe thee with the double garment of justice and will set a crown on thy head of everlasting honor. For God will shew his brightness in thee to every one under heaven. For thy name shall be named to thee by God for ever: the peace of justice and honor of piety. Arise, O Jerusalem [Columbus: "Israel"], and stand on high, and look about towards the east, and behold thy children gathered together from the rising to the setting sun, by the word of the Holy One, rejoicing in the remembrance of God. For they went out from thee on foot, led by the enemies: / but the Lord will bring them to thee, exalted with

Dominus ad te portatos in honorem sicut filios regni. Constituit enim Deus humiliare omnem montem excelsum et rupes perennes et convalles replere in equalitatem terre; ut ambulet Israel diligenter in honorem Dei. Obumbraverunt autem silve et omne lignum suavitatis, Israel mandato Dei. Adducet enim Deus Israel cum iocunditate in lumine maiestatis sue, cum misericordia, et iusticia, que est ex ipso.

Ezechiel, capitulo 3

Non enim ad populum profundi sermonis et ignote lingue tu mitteris, ad domum Israel. Neque ad populos multos profundi sermonis et ignote lingue, quorum non possis audire sermones; et si ad illos mi[t]teris, ipsi audirent te.

Ezechiel, capitulo 27

Insule multe negociatio manus tue &c. Venditores Saba, et Rema, ipsi nego[t]iatores (41a) tui; cum universis primis aromatibus, et lapide precioso, et auro, quod proposuerunt in mercato tuo &c.

Universi habitatores insularum obstupuerunt super te; et reges earum omnes tempestate percussi mutaverunt vultus.

Ezechiel, capitulo 28

Idcirco ecce ego a[d]ducam super te alienos, robustissimos gentium &c.

Quando congregavero domum Israel de populis, in quibus dispersi sunt, sanctificabor in eis coram gentibus &c.

Ezechiel, capitulo 32

Omnes hi incircuncisi, interfectique gladio.

Ezechiel, capitulo 34

Ego autem Dominus ero eis in Deum; et servus meus David princeps in medio eorum &c.

Ezechiel, capitulo 35

Letante universa terra, in solitudine te redigam &c.

honor as children of the kingdom. For God hath appointed to bring down every high mountain and the everlasting rocks and to fill up the valleys, to make them even with the ground: that Israel may walk diligently to the honor of God. Moreover the woods and every sweet-smelling tree have overshadowed Israel by the commandment of God. For God will bring Israel with joy in the light of his majesty, with mercy and justice that cometh from him.

Ezekiel, Chapter 3

[3:5–6]

For thou art not sent to a people of a profound speech and of an unknown tongue, but to the house of Israel: Nor to many nations of a strange speech and of an unknown tongue, whose words thou canst not understand: and if thou wert sent to them, they would hearken to thee.

Ezekiel, Chapter 27

[27:15b, 22, 35]

Many islands were the traffic of thy hand. &c. The sellers of Saba and Reema, they were thy merchants: with all the best spices and precious stones and gold, which they set forth in thy market. &c.

All the inhabitants of the islands are astonished at thee: and all their kings being struck with the storm have changed their countenance.

Ezekiel, Chapter 28

[28:7a,25b]

Therefore behold, I will bring upon thee strangers, the strongest of the nations. &c.

When I shall have gathered together the house of Israel out of the people among whom they are scattered, I will be sanctified in them before the Gentiles. &c. /

Ezekiel, Chapter 32

[32:25b]

All these are uncircumcised and slain by the sword.

Ezekiel, Chapter 34

[34:24a]

And I the Lord will be their God: and my servant David the prince in the midst of them. &c.

Ezekiel 35

[35:14b]

When the whole earth shall rejoice I will make thee a wilderness.

Ezechiel, capitulo 36

Cum sanctificatus fuero in vobis coram eis. Tollam quippe vos de gentibus, et congregabo vos de universis terris, et a[d]ducam vos in terram vestram, (41b) et e[f]fundam super vos aquam mundam, et mundabimini ab omnibus inquinamentis vestrisi et ab universis ydolis vestris mundabo vos. Et dabo vobis cor novum et spiritum novum ponam in medio vestri et auferam cor lapideum de carne vestra et dabo vobis cor carneum. Et spiritum meum ponam in medio vestri; et faciam ut in preceptis meis ambuletis et iudicia mea custodiatis et operemini. Et habita[bi]tis in terra, quam dedi patribus vestris et eritis mihi in populumi et ego ero vobis in Deum. Et salvabo vos ex universis inquinamentis vestris &c.

Non propter vos ego faciam, ait Dominus Deusi notum sit vobis &c.

In die, qua mundavero vos ex omnibus iniquitatibus vestris, et habitari fecero urbes et [in]stauravero ruinosa et terra deserta fuerit exculta, que quondam erat desolata in oculis omnis viatoris, dicent: terra illa inculta, facta est ut [h]ortus voluptatis &c.

Multiplicabo eos sicut gregem hominum, ut gregem sanctum, ut gregem Iherusalem in solemnitatibus eius: sic erunt civitates deserte plene gregibus hominum &c.

Ezechiel, capitulo 37

Ecce ego assumam filios Israel de medio nationum (42a) ad quas abierunt et congregabo eos undique et a[d]ducam eos ad humum suam. Et faciam eos gentem unam in terra in montibus Israel; et rex unus erit omnibus imperans, et non erunt ultra due gentes nec dividentur amplius in duo regna &c.

Et erunt mihi populus, et ego ero eis Deus. Et servus meus David rex super eos, et pastor unus erit omnium eorum; in iudiciis meis ambulabunt et mandata mea custodient, et facient ea. Et habitabunt super terram, quam dedi servo meo Iacob, in qua habitaverunt patres vestri; et habitabunt super eam ipsi, et filii eorum, et filii filiorum eorum, usque in sempiternum; et David servus meus princeps corum in perpetuum. Et percuciam illis fedus pacis, pactum sempiternum erit eis; et fundabo eos, et multiplicabo, et dabo sanctificationem meam in medio eorum in perpetuum. Et erit tabernaculum meum in eis; et ero eis Deus, et ipsi erunt mihi populus. Et scient gentes quia ego Dominus sanctificator Israel, cum fuerit sanctificatio mea in medio eorum in perpetuum.

Ezekiel 36

[36:23b–29a, 32a, 33b–35a, 37b–38a]

When I shall be sanctified in you before their eyes. For I will take you from among the Gentiles and will gather you together out of all the countries and will bring you into your own land. And I will pour upon you clean water and you shall be cleansed from all your filthiness: and I will cleanse you from all your idols. And I will give you a new heart and put a new spirit within you: and I will take away the stony heart out of your flesh and will give you a heart of flesh. And I will put my spirit in the midst of you: and I will cause you to walk in my commandments and to keep my judgments and do them. And you shall dwell in the land which I gave to your fathers: and you shall be my people and I will be your God. And I will save you from all your uncleannesses. &c.

Is it not for your sakes that I will do this, saith the Lord God, be it known to you. &c.

In the day that I shall cleanse you from all your iniquities / and shall cause the cities to be inhabited and shall repair the ruinous places, and the desolate land shall be tilled, which before was waste in the sight of all that passed by. They shall say: This land that was untilled is become as a garden of pleasure. &c.

I will multiply them as a flock of men, as a holy flock, as the flock of Jerusalem in her solemn feasts: so shall the waste cities be full of flocks of men. &c.

Ezekiel 37

[37:21b–22, 23b–28]

Behold, I will take the children of Israel from the midst of the nations whither they are gone, and I will gather them on every side and will bring them to their own land. And I will make them one nation in the land on the mountains of Israel, and one king shall be over them all. And they shall no more be two nations: neither shall they be divided any more into two kingdoms. &c.

And they shall be my people, and I will be their God. And my servant David shall be king over them: and they shall have one shepherd. They shall walk in my judgments and shall keep my commandments and shall do them. And they shall dwell in the land which I gave to my servant Jacob, wherein your fathers dwelt: and they shall dwell in it, they and their children and their children's children, forever. And David my servant shall be their prince for ever. And I will make a covenant of peace with them: it shall be an everlasting covenant with them. And I will establish them and will multiply them and will set my sanctuary in the midst of them for ever. And my tabernacle shall be with them: and I will be their God, and they shall be my people. And the nations shall know that I am the Lord, the sanctifier of Israel, when my sanctuary shall be in the midst of them / for ever.

Ezechiel, capitulo 38

ln novissimo annorum venies ad terram, que reversa est alio, et congregata est de populis multis ad montes Israel &c.

Ezechiel, capitulo 39

Nunc reducam captivitatem Iacobi et miserebor omnis (42b) domus Israel &c.

Et reduxero eos de populis et congregavero de terris inimicorum suorum et sanctificatus fuero in eis in oculis gentium plurimarum &c.

Daniel, capitulo 8

Ecce autem [h]ircus caprarum veniebat ab occidente super faciem tocius terrei et tangebat terram &c.

Intellige, fili hominis, quoniam in tempore finis complebitur visio &c.

Daniel, capitulo 11

De adventu Antichristi

Et convertat faciem suain ad insulas et capiet multas et cessare faciet principem opprobrii sui &c.

Daniel, capitulo 12

Capitulum istum est de consumacione seculi

In tempore autem illo consurget Michael princeps magnus, qui stat pro filiis populi tui &c.

Osee, capitulo 1

Et erit numerus filiorum Israel quasi arena maris, que sine mensura est, et non numerabitur. Et erit: in loco ubi dicetur eis: non populus meus vos, dicetur eis: filii Dei viventis &c.

Osee, capitulo 3

(43a) Dies multos exspectabis me; non fornicaberis, et non eris cum viro; sed et ego exspectabo te. Quia dies multos sedebunt filii Israel sine rege et sine principe et sine sacrificio et sine altari et sine ephot

Ezekiel, Chapter 38

[38:8b]

At the end of years thou shalt come to the land that is returned from the sword [Columbus: "returned from another"], and is gathered out of many nations, to the mountains of Israel. &c.

Ezekiel, Chapter 39

[39:25b, 27]

But now, I will end the captivity of my people and have mercy upon them, etc.

And I shall have brought them back from among the nations and shall have gathered them together out of the lands of their enemies and shall be sanctified in them in the sight of many nations. &c.

Daniel, Chapter 8

[8:5b, 17b]

And behold a he-goat came from the west on the face of the whole earth, and he touched [not] the ground. &c.

Understand, O son of man, for in the time of the end the vision shall be fulfilled. &c.

Daniel, Chapter 11

[11:18a]

Advent of Antichrist   And he shall turn his face to the islands and shall take many: and he shall cause the prince of his reproach to cease. &c.

Daniel, Chapter 12

[12:1a]

This chapter is the consumation of the age   But at that time shall Michael rise up, the great prince, who standeth / for the children of thy people. &c.

Hosea, Chapter 1

[1:10]

And the number of the children of Israel shall be as the sand of the sea that is without measure and shall not be numbered. And it shall be in the place where it shall be said to them: You are not my people: it shall be said to them: Ye are the sons of the living God. &c.

Hosea, Chapter 3

[3:3b–5]

Thou shalt wait for me many days. Thou shalt not play the harlot and thou shalt be no man's: and I also will wait for thee. For the children of Israel shall sit many days without king and without prince and without sacrifice and without altar and without ephod and without theraphim.

et sine theraphim. Et post hec revertentur filii Israel et querent Dominum Deum suum et David regem suum; et pavebunt ad Dominum et ad bonum eius in novissimo dierum.

Iohel, capitulo 2

Cantate tuba in Syon ululate in monte sancto meo &c.

Similis ei non fuit a principio, et post eum non erit usque in annos generationis et generationis &c.

Fatiem eius contra mare Orientale, et extremum eius usque ad mare novissimum; et ascendet fetor eius, et ascendet putredo eius, quia superbe egit. Noli timere, terra, exulta et letare; quoniam magnificavit Dominus, ut faceret. Nolite time[re], animalia regionis; quia germinaverunt speciosa deserti, quia lignum attulit fructum suum, ficus et vinea dederunt virtutem suam. (43b) Et, filie Syon, exultate et letamini in Domino Deo vestro; quia dedit vobis doctorem iustitie et descendere faciet ad vos imbrem matutinum et serotinum sicut in principio. Et implebun[tur] arec frumento, et redundabunt torcularia vino et oleo. Et reddam vobis annos, quos comedit locusta, brucus, et rubigo, et eruca; fortitudo mea magna quam misi in vos. Et comedetis vescentes et saturabimini et laudabitis nomen Domini Dei vestri, qui fecit mirabilia vobiscum; et non confundetur populus meus in sempiternum. Et scietis quia in medio Israel ego sum; ego Dominus Deus vester, et non est amplius; et non confundetur populus meus in eternum.

Iohel, capitulo 2

Et erit post hec: effundam spiritum meum super omnem carnem; et prophetabunt filii vestri, et filie vestre; senes vestri somnia somniabunt. Sed et super servos meos et ancillas in diebus illis effundam spiritum meum. Et dabo prodigia in celo et in terra, sanguinem et igneni et vaporem fumi. Sol convertetur in tenebras et luna in sanguinem, ante quam veniat dies Domini mag[n]us (44a) et horribilis. Et omnis qui invocaverit nomen Domini, salvus erit; quia in monte Syon et in Iherusalem erit salvatio, sicut dixit Dominus, et in residuis, quos Dominus vocaverit. Quia ecce in diebus illis, et in tempore illo, cum convertero captivitatem Iuda et Iherusalem; congregabo omnes gentes, et deducam eas in vallem Iosaphat; et disceptabo cum eis ibi super populo meo et [h]ereditate mea Israel, quos disperserunt in nationibus, et terram meam diviserunt. Et super populum meum miserunt sortem; et posuerunt puerum in prostibulo et puellam vendiderunt pro vino, ut biberent. Verum quid michi et vobis, Tyrus et Sydoni et omnis terminus Palestinorum?

Capitulo 3

And after this the children of Israel shall return and shall seek the Lord their God and David their king: and they shall fear the Lord and his goodness in the last days.

Joel, Chapter 2

[2:1a2b, 20b–27]

Blow ye the trumpet in Sion, sound an alarm in my holy mountain. &c.

The like to it hath not been from the beginning, nor shall be after it even to the years of generation and generation. &c.

With his face towards the east sea and his hinder part towards the utmost sea: and his stench shall ascend and his rottenness shall go up, because he hath done proudly. Fear not, O land, be glad and rejoice: for the Lord hath done great things. Fear not, ye beasts of the fields: for the beautiful places of the wilderness are sprung, for the tree hath brought forth its fruit: the fig tree and the vine have yielded their strength. / And you, O children of Sion, rejoice and be joyful in the Lord your God: because he hath given you a teacher of justice, and he will make the morning and the evening rain to come down to you as in the beginning. And the floors shall be filled with wheat, and the presses shall overflow with wine and oil. And I will restore to you the years which the locust and the bruchus and the mildew, and the palmerworm have eaten: my great host which I sent upon you. And you shall eat in plenty and shall be filled: and you shall praise the name of the Lord your God who hath done wonders with you: and my people shall not be confounded for ever.

Joel, Chapter 2

[2:28–32, 3:1–1]

And it shall come to pass after this, that I will pour out my spirit upon all flesh: and your sons and your daughters shall prophesy: your old men shall dream dreams [Columbus omitted: "and your young men shall see visions"]. Moreover upon my servants and handmaids in those days I will pour forth my spirit. And I will shew wonders in heaven: and on earth, blood and fire and vapor of smoke. The sun shall be turned into darkness and the moon into blood: before the great and dreadful day of the Lord doth come. And it shall come to pass that everyone that shall call upon the name of the Lord shall be saved: for in mount Sion, Chapter 3 and in Jerusalem shall be salvation, as the Lord hath said, and in the residue whom the Lord shall call. For behold in those days and in that time when I shall bring back the captivity of Juda and Jerusalem: I will gather together all nations and will bring them down into the valley of Josaphat: and I will plead with them there for my people and for my inheritance Israel, whom they have scattered among the nations and have parted my land. And they have cast lots upon my people: and / the boy they have put in the stews, and the girl they have sold for wine, that they might drink. But what have you to do with me, O Tyre and Sidon and all the coast of the Philistines? Will you revenge yourselves

Numquid ulcionem vos reddetis michi? Et ulciscimini vos contra me, cito velociter reddam vicissitudinem vobis super caput vestrum. Argentum enim meum et aurum tulistis; et desiderab[il]ia mea et pulche[r]rima intulistis in delubra vestra. Et filios Iuda et filios Iherusalem vendidistis filiis Grecorum, ut longe faceretis eos de finibus suis. Ecce ego suscitabo eos de loco in quo vendidistis eos; et convertam retributionem vestram in caput vestrum. Et vendam filios vestros et filias vestras in manibus filiorum Iuda, et venundabunt (44b) eos Sabeis, genti longinque, et quia Dominus locutus est. Clamate hoc in gentibus, sanctificate bellum, suscitate robustos; ascendant, accedant omnes viri bellatores. Concidite aratra vestra in gladios et ligones vestros in lanceas. Infirmus dicat: "quia ego fortis sum." Erumpite, et venite, omnes gentes, de circuitui et congregamini; ibi o[c]cumbere faciet Dominus robustos tuos. Consurgant et ascendant gentes in vallem Iosaphat; quia ibi sedebo ut iudicem omnes gentes in circuitu. Mittite falces, quoniam maturavit messis; venite, et descendite, quia plenum est torcular, exub[e]rant torcularia; quia multiplicata est malicia eorum. Populi, populi, in valle concisionis; iuxta est dies Domini in valle concisionis. Sol et luna obtenebrati sunt, et stelle retraxerunt splendorem suum. Et Dominus de Syon rugiet et de Iherusalem dabit vocem suam; et movebuntur celi et terra; et Dominus spes populi sui et fortitudo filiorum Israel. Et scietis quia ego Dominus Deus vester, habitans in Syon in monte sancto meo; et erit Iherusalem sancta, et alieni non transibunt per eam amplius. Et erit in die illa: stillabunt montes dulcedinem, et colles fluent lacte; et per omnes rivos Iuda ibunt aque; (45a) et fons de domo Domini egredietur, et irrigabit torrentem spinarum. Egyptus in desolatione erit et Idumea in desertum perditionis; pro eo quod inique egerint in filios Iudai et e[f]funderint sanguinem innocentem in terra sua. Et Iudea in eternum habitabitur, et Iherusalem in generatione et generationem. Et mundabo sanguinem eorum, quos non mundaveram; et Dominus commorabitur in Syon &c.

Amos, capitulo 9

Vide glossa — In die illa suscitabo tabernaculum David, quod cecidit; et r[e]edificabo aperturas murorum eius, et ea que corruerant instaurabo; et r[e]edificabo eum sicut in diebus antiquis. Ut possideant reliquias Idumee, et omnes nationes, eo quod invocatum sit nomen meum super eos; dicit Dominus faciens hec. Ecce dies venient, dicit Dominus; et comprehendet arator messorem, et calcator uve mittentem semen; et stillabunt montes dulcedinem, et omnes colles culti erunt. Et convertam captivitatem populi mei Israel; et edificabunt civitates desertas, et inhabitabunt; et plantabunt vineas, et bibent vinum

on me? And if Juda will revenge yourselves on me, I will very soon return you a recompense upon your own head. For you have taken away my silver and my gold: and my desirable and most beautiful things you have carried into your temples. And the children of Juda and the children of Jerusalem you have sold to the children of the Greeks, that you might remove them far off from their own country. Behold, I will raise them up out of the place wherein you have sold them: and I will return your recompense upon your own heads. And I will sell your sons and your daughters by the hands of the children of Juda: and they shall sell them to the Sabeans, a nation far off, for the Lord hath spoken it. Proclaim ye this among the nations: prepare war, rouse up the strong: let them come, let all the men of war come up. Cut your ploughshares into swords and your spades into spears. Let the weak say: I am strong. Break forth and come, all ye nations, from round about, and gather yourselves together: there will the Lord cause all thy strong ones to fall down. Let them arise and let the nations come up into the valley of Josaphat: for there I will sit to judge all nations round about. Put ye in the sickles, for the harvest is ripe: come and go down, for the press is full, the vats run over: for their wickedness is multiplied. Nations, nations in the valley of destruction: for the day of the Lord is near in the valley of destruction. The sun and the moon are darkened: and the stars have withdrawn their shining. And the Lord shall roar out of Sion and utter his voice from Jerusalem: and the heavens and the earth shall be moved: and the Lord shall be the hope of his people and the strength of the children of Israel. And you shall know that I am the Lord you God, / dwelling in Sion my holy mountain: and Jerusalem shall be holy and strangers shall pass through it no more. And it shall come to pass in that day, that the mountains shall drop down sweetness, and the hills shall flow with milk: and waters shall flow through all the rivers of Juda: and a fountain shall come forth of the house of the Lord, and shall water the torrent of thorns. Egypt shall be a desolation and Edom a wilderness destroyed: because they have done unjustly against the children of Juda and have shed innocent blood in their land. And Judea shall be inhabited forever, and Jerusalem to generation and generation. And I will cleanse their blood which I had not cleansed: and the Lord will dwell in Sion.

Amos, Chapter 9

[9:11–15]

See gloss In that day I will raise up the tabernacle of David, that is fallen: and I will close up the breaches of the walls thereof and repair what was fallen: and I will rebuild it as it was in the days of old. That they may possess the remnant of Edom and all nations, because my name is invoked upon them: saith the Lord that doth these things. Behold the days come, saith the Lord, when the ploughman shall overtake the reaper and the threader of grapes him that soweth seed: and the mountains shall drop sweetness, and every hill shall be tilled. And I will bring back the captivity of my people Israel: and they shall build the abandoned cities and inhabit

earum; et facient [h]ortos, et comedent fructus eorum. Et plantabo eos super humum suam; et non evellam eos ultra de terra sua, quam dedi eis, dicit Dominus Deus tuus. (45b)

Abdies, capitulo 1

Quomodo enim bibisti super montem sanctum meum, bibent omnes gentes iugiter; et bibent, et absorbebunt, et erunt quasi non sint. Et in monte Syon erit salvatio, et erit Sanctus; et possidebit domus Iacob eos qui possederant. Et erit domus Iacob ignis, et domus Iosep[h] fla[m]ma, et domus Esau stipula: et succendentur in eis, et devorabunt eos; et non erunt reliquie domus Esau, quia Dominus locutus est. Et hereditabunt hi, qui ad austrum sunt, montem Esau et qui in campestribus Philistinii; et possidebunt regionem Efraim. Et regionem Samarie; et Beniamin possidebit Galad. Et transmigratio exercitus huius filiorum Israel, omnia loca Cananeorum usque ad Sareptam; et transmigratio Iherusalem, que in Bosforo est, possidebit civitates austri. Et ascendent salvatores montem Syon iudicare montem Esau; et erit Domino regnum.

Micheas, capitulo 4

Et erit in novissimo dierum: erit mons, mons domus Domini preparatus in vertice montium et sublimis super colles; et fluent ad eum populi. Et properabunt gentes multe et dicent: venite, ascendamus ad montem Domini, et ad domum (46a) Dei Iacob; et docebit nos de viis suis, et ibimus in semitis eius; quia de Syon egredietur lex, et verbumn Domini de Iherusalem. Et iudicabit inter populos multos, et corripiet gentes fortes usque in longinquim: et concidet gladios suos in vomeres, et [h]astas suas in ligones; non sumet gens adversum gentem gladium; et non dicent ultra: bellige[r]ate. Et sedebit vir subtus vineam suam, et subtus ficum suam, et non erit quid deterreat; quia os Domini exercituum locutum est. Quia omnes populi ambulabunt unusquisque in nomine Dei sui; nos autem ambulabimus in nomine Dei nostri in eternum et ultra. In die illa, dicit Dominus, congregabo claudicantem; et eam, quam eieceram, co[l]ligam, et [quam] affixeram consolabo. Et ponam claudicantem in reliquias, et eam, que laboraverat, in gentem robustam; et regnabit Dominus super eos in montem Syon ex hoc nunc et usque in eternum. Et tu, turris gregis, nebulosa filia Syon usque ad te veniet; et veniat potestas prima, regnum filie Iherusalem. Numquid rex

them: and they shall plant vineyards and drink the wine of them: and shall make gardens and eat the fruits of them. And I will plant them upon their own land: and I will no more pluck them out of their land which I have given them, saith the Lord thy God. /

Obadiah, Chapter 1

[1:16–21]

For as you have drunk upon my holy mountain, so all nations shall drink continually: and they shall drink and sup up, and they shall be as though they were not. And in mount Sion shall be salvation, and it shall be holy: and the house of Jacob shall possess those that possessed them. And the House of Jacob shall be a fire and the house of Joseph a flame and the house of Esau stubble: and they shall be kindled in them and shall devour them: and there shall be no remains of the house of Esau, for the Lord hath spoken it. And they that are toward the south shall inherit the mount of Esau, and they that are in the plains, the Philistines: and they shall possess the country of Ephraim and the country of Samaria: and Benjamin shall possess Galaad. And the captivity of this host of the children of Israel, all the places of the Canaanites even to Sarepta: and the captivity of Jerusalem that is in Bosphorus shall possess the cities of the south. And saviors shall come up into mount Sion to judge the mount of Esau: and the kingdom shall be for the Lord.

Micah, Chapter 4

[4:1–8, 9b–13, 5:1]

And it shall come to pass in the last days that the mountain of the house of the Lord shall be prepared in the top of mountains and high above the hills: and people shall flow to it. And many nations shall come in haste and say: Come, let us go up to the mountain of the Lord and to the house of the God of Jacob: and he will teach us of his ways and we will walk in his paths. For the law shall go forth out of Sion, and the word of the Lord out of Jerusalem. And he shall judge among many people and rebuke strong nations afar off: and they shall beat their swords into ploughshares and their spears into spades. Nation shall not take sword against nation: neither shall they learn war any more. / And every man shall sit under his vine and under his fig tree, and there shall be none to make them afraid: for the mouth of the Lord of hosts hath spoken. For all people will walk every one in the name of his god: but we will walk in the name of the Lord our God for ever and ever. In that day, saith the Lord, I will gather up her that halteth: and her that I had cast out, I will gather up: and her whom I had afflicted. And I will make her that halted, a remnant, and her that hath been afflicted, a mighty nation. And the Lord will reign over them in mount Sion, from this time now and for ever. And thou, O cloudy tower of the flock of the daughter of Sion, unto thee shall it come: yea, the first power shall come, the kingdom to the daughter of Jerusalem. Hast thou no king in thee, or

non est tibi, aut consiliarius tuus periit, quia comprehendit te dolor sicut parturientem? Dole, et satage, filia Syon quasi parturiens; quia nunc egredieris de civitate, et habitabis in regione, et venies usque ad Babilonem; ibi liberaberis, (46b) ibi redimet te Dominus de manu inimicorum tuorum. Et nunc congregate sunt super te gentes multe que dicunt: lapidetur, et aspiciat in Syon oculus noster. Ipsi autem non cognoverunt cogitationes Domini, et non intellexerunt consilium eius; quia congregavit eos quasi fenum aree. Surge, e[t] tritura, filia Syon; quia cornu tuum ponam ferreum, et ungulas tuas ponam ercas; et conminues populos multos, et interficies Domino rapinas eorum, et fortitudinem eorum Domino universe terre. Nunc vastaberis, filia latronis; obsidionem posuerunt super nos, in virga percucient maxillam iudicis Israel.

Micheas, capitulo 5

Et tu Bethlem Eph[r]ata, parvulus es in mi[l]libus Iuda; ex te mihi egredietur qui sit dominator in Israel &c.

Micheas, capitulo 6

Numquid dabo primogenitum meum pro scelere meo, et fructum ventris pro peccato anime mee? Indicabo tibi, O homo, quid sit bonum, et quid Dominus requirat a te. (47a)

Sophonias, capitulo 2

Horribilis Dominus super eos, et a[t]tenuabit omnes deos terre; et adorabunt eum viri de loco suo, omnes insule gentium. Sed et vos, Ethiopes, interfecti gladio meo eritis &c.

Sophonias, capitulo 3

Ve provocatrix et redempta, civitas columba! Non audivit vocem, et suscepi disciplinam; in Domino non est confisa, ad Deum suum non a[p]propinquavit. Principes eius in medio eius quasi leones rugientes; iudices eius lupi vespere, non relinquebant in mane. Prophete eius vesani, viri infideles; sacerdotes eius polluerunt sanctum, iniuste egerunt contra legem. Dominus iustus in medio eius

is thy counsellor perished, because sorrow hath taken thee as a woman in labor? Be in pain and labor, O daughter of Sion, as a woman that bringeth forth: for now shalt thou go out of the city and shalt dwell in the country and shalt come even to Babylon. There thou shalt be delivered: there the Lord will redeem thee out of the hand of thy enemies. And now many nations are gathered together against thee, and they say: Let her be stoned and let our eye look upon Sion. But they have not known the thoughts of the Lord and have not understood his counsel: because he hath gathered them together as the hay of the floor. Arise and tread, O daughter of Sion: for I will make thy horn iron and thy hoofs I will make brass: and thou shalt beat in pieces many peoples and shalt immolate the spoils of them to the Lord, and their strength to the Lord of the whole earth. Now shalt thou be laid waste, O daughter of the robber. They have laid siege against us: with a rod shall they strike the cheek of the judge of Israel.

Micah, Chapter 5

[5:2a]

And thou, Bethlehem Ephrata, art a little one among the thousands of Juda: out of thee / shall he come forth unto me that is to be the ruler in Israel. &c.

Micah, Chapter 6

[6:7b–8a]

Shall I give my firstborn for my wickedness, the fruit of my body for the sin of my soul? I will shew thee, O man, what is good and what the Lord requireth of thee.

Zephaniah, Chapter 2

[2:1–20]

The Lord shall be terrible upon them and shall consume all the gods of the earth: and they shall adore him, every man from his own place, all the islands of the Gentiles. You, Ethiopians, also shall be slain with my sword. &c.

Zephaniah, Chapter 3

[3:1–20]

Woe to the provoking and redeemed city, the dove. She hath not harkened to the voice, neither hath she received discipline: she hath not trusted in the Lord, she drew not near to her God. Her princes are in the midst of her as roaring lions, her judges are evening wolves: they left nothing for the morning. Her prophets are senseless men without faith, her priests have polluted the sanctuary: they have acted unjustly against the law. The just Lord is in the midst thereof, he will not do iniquity: in the

non faciet iniquitatem; mane, mane iudicium suum dabit in luce, et non abscondetur; nescivit autem iniq[u]us confusionem. Disperdidi gentes, et dissi pati sunt anguli eorum; desertas feci vias eorum, dum non est qui transeat; desolate sunt civitates eorum, non remanente viro, neque ullo habitatore. Dixi: a[t]tamen timebis mei suscipiens disciplinam! Et non peribit habitaculum eius, propter omnia in quibus visitavi eam. Verumtamen diluculo surgentes corruperunt omnes cogitationes suas. Quapropter expecta me, dicit Dominus, in die resu[r]rexionis mee in futurum; quia iudicium meum ut congregem gentes, (47b) et co[l]ligam regna; et e[f]fundam super eos indignationem meam, omnem iram furoris mei; in igne enim zeli mei devorabitur omnis terra. Quia tunc re[d]dam populis labium electum, ut invocent omnes nomen Domini, et serviant ei [h]umero uno. Ultra flumina Ethiopie, inde su[p]plices mei, filii dispersorum meorum deferent munus mihi. In die illa non confunderis super cunctis adinventionibus tuis, quibus prevaricata es in me; quia tunc auferam de medio tui magnilo quos superbie tue, et non adicies exaltari amplius in monte sancto meo. Et derelinquam in medio tui populum pauperem et egenum; et sperabunt in nomine Domini. Reliquie Israel non facient iniquitatem, nec loquentur mendacium, et non invenietur in ore eorum lingua dolosa; quoniam ipsi pascentur, et accubabunt, et non erit qui exte[r]reat. Lauda, filia Syon iubilai Israel; letare, et exulta in omni corde, filia Iherusalem. Abstulit Dominus iudicium tuum, avertit inimicos tuos; rex Israel Dominus in medio tui, non timebis malum ultra. In die illa dicetur Iherusalem: noli timere: Sion non di[s]solvantur manus tue. Dominus Deus tuus in medio tui fortis, ipse salvabit; gaudebit super te in leticia, silebit in dilectione tua, et exultabit super te in laude. Nugas, que a lege (48a) recesserant, congregabo, quia ex te erant; ut non ultra habeas super eis opprobrium. Ecce ego interficiam omnes qui afflixerunt te in tcmpore illo; et salvabo claudicantem; et eam, que eiecta fuerat, congregabo; et ponam eos in laudem et in nomen in omni terra confusionis eorum: in tempore illo quo a[d]ducam vos, et in tempore quo congregabo vos; dabo enim vos in nomen et in laudem omnibus populis terre, cum co[n]vertero captivitatem vestram coram oculis vestris, dicit Dominus.

Zac[h]arias, capitulo 1

Et dixit ad me angelus, qui loquebatur in me: clama dicens: hec dicit Dominus exercituum: zelatus sum Iherusalem et Syon zelo magno. Et ira magna ego irascor super gentes opLilentas; quia ego iratus sum parum, ipsi vero adiverunt in malum. Propterea hec dicit Dominus: revertar ad Iherusalem in misericordiis; et domus mea

morning, in the morning, he will bring his judgment to light and it shall not be hid: but the wicked men hath not known shame. I have destroyed the nations, and their towers are beaten down: I have made their ways desert so that there is none that passeth by. Their cities are desolate: there is not a man remaining nor any inhabitant. I said: Surely thou wilt fear me, thou wilt receive correction: and her dwelling shall not perish for all things wherein I have visited her. But they rose / early and corrupted all their thoughts. Wherefore respect me, saith the Lord, in the day of my resurrection that is to come for my judgment is to assemble the Gentiles and to gather the kingdoms and to pour upon them my indignation, all my fierce anger: for with the fire of my jealousy shall all the earth be devoured. Because then I will restore to the people a chosen speech, [so] that [they may] call upon the name of the Lord and may serve him with one shoulder. From beyond the rivers of Ethiopia shall my suppliants, the children of my dispersed people, bring me an offering. In that day thou shalt not be ashamed for all thy doings wherein thou hast transgressed against me: for then I will take away out of the midst of thee thy proud boasters and thou shalt no more be lifted up because of my holy mountain. And I will leave in the midst of thee a poor and needy people: and they shall hope in the name of the Lord. The remnant of Israel shall not do iniquity nor speak lies, nor shall a deceitful tongue be found in their mouth: for they shall feed and shall lie down, and there shall be none to make them afraid. Give praise, O daughter of Sion shout, O Israel: be glad, and rejoice with all thy heart, O daughter of Jerusalem. The Lord hath taken away thy judgments, he hath turned away thy enemies. The king of Israel the Lord is in the midst of thee: thou shalt fear evil no more. In that day it shall be said to Jerusalem: Fear not. To Sion: Let not thy hands be weakened. The Lord thy God in the midst of thee is mighty: he will save, he will rejoice over thee, with gladness, he will be silent in his love, he will be joyful over thee in praise. The triflers that were departed from the law, I will gather together, because they were of thee: that thou mayest no more suffer reproach for them. Behold I will cut off all that have afflicted thee at that time: and I will save her that halteth and will gather her that was cast out: and I will get them praise and a name / in all the land where they had been put to confusion. At that time, when I will bring you: and at the time that I will gather you: for I will give you a name, and a name of distinction among all the peoples of the earth. They will praise you when I return your fortunes before your very eyes, saith the Lord.

Zachariah, Chapter 1

[1:14–17]

And the angel that spoke in me said to me: Cry thou, saying: Thus saith the Lord of hosts I am zealous for Jerusalem and Sion with a great zeal. And I am angry with a great anger with the wealthy nations: for I was angry a little, but they helped forward the evil. Therefore thus saith the Lord: I will return to Jerusalem in mercies. My house shall be built

edificabitur in ea, ait Dominus exercituum: et perpendiculum extendetur super Ihierusalem. Ad[h]uc clama, dicens: hec dicit Dominus
exercituum: ad[h]uc affluent civitates mee bonis: et consolabitur
adhuc Iherusalem &c.

Zacharias, capitulo 2

Et levavi oculos meos, et vidi: et ecce vir, (48b) et in manu eius
funiculus mensorum. et dixi: quo tu vadis? Et dixit ad me: ut metiar
Iherusalem et Iudeam, quanta sit longitudo eius, et quanta latitudo
eius. Et ecce angelus, qui loquebatur in me, egrediebatur, et alius
angelus egrediebatur in occursum eius. Et dixit ad eum: cur[re],
loquere ad puerum istum, dicens: absque muro habitabitur Iherusalem pre multitudine hominum et iumentorum in medio eius. Et ego
ero ei, ait Dominus, murus ignis in circuitu; et in gloria ero in
medio eius. O, O, O! Fugite de terra aquilonis, dicit Dominus,
quoniam in quatuor ventos celi dispersi vos, dicit Dominus. O Syon,
fuge, que habitas apud filiam Babilonis. Quia hec dicit Dominus
exercituum: post gloriam misit me ad gentes, que expoliaverunt
vos: qui enim tetigerit vos, tangit pupillam oculi mei. Quia ecce
ego levo manum meam super eos, et erunt prede [h]is, qui serviebant sibi; et cognoscetis quia Dominus exercituum misit. Lauda
et letare, filia Syon; quia ecce ego venio, et habitabo in medio tui,
ait Dominus. et a[p]plicabuntur gentes multe ad Dominum in die
illa, et erunt mihi in populum, et habitabo in medio tui; et scies
quia Dominus exercituum misit me ad te. Et posidebit domus Iuda
parte[m] suam in terra sanctificata, (49a) et eliget adhuc Ihierusalem. Sileat omnis caro a facie Domini, quia consu[r]rexit de habitaculo sancto suo.

Zacharias, capitulo 8

Et factum est verbum Domini exercituum, dicens: hec dicit Dominus exercituum: zelatus sum Syon zelo magno, et indignatione
magna zelatus sum eam. Hec dicit Dominus exercituum: reversus
sum ad Syon et habitabo in medio Iherusalem; et vocabitur Iherusalem civitas veritatis, et mons Domini exercituum, mons sanctificatus. Hec dicit Dominus exercituum: ad[h]uc habitabunt senes et
anus in plateis Iherusalem et viri baculus in manu eius pre multitudine dierum. Et platee civitatis complebuntur infantibus et puellis
ludentibus in plateis eius. Hec dicit Dominus exercituum: si videbitur di[f]ficile in oculis reliquiarum populi [h]uius in diebus illis,
numquid in oculis meis di[f]ficile erit? Dicit Dominus exercituum.
Hec dicit Dominus exercituum: ecce ego salvabo populum meum
de terra orientis, et de terra o[c]casus solis. Et a[d]ducam eos,

in it, saith the Lord of hosts: and the building line shall be stretched forth upon Jerusalem. Cry yet, saying: Thus saith the Lord of hosts: My cities shall yet flow with good things: and the Lord will yet comfort Sion and will yet choose Jerusalem. &c.

Zachariah, Chapter 2

[2:1–13]

And I lifted up my eyes and saw: and behold a man with a measuring line in his hand. And I said: Whither goest thou? And he said to me: To measure Jerusalem and to see how great is the breadth thereof and how great the length thereof. And behold the angel that spoke in me went forth: and another angel went out to meet him. And he said to him: Run, speak to this young man, saying: Jerusalem shall be inhabited without walls, by reason of the multitude of men and of the beasts in the midst thereof. And I will be to it, saith the Lord, a wall of fire round about: and I will be in glory in the midst thereof. O, O, O! Flee ye out of the land / of the north, saith the Lord: for I have scattered you into the four winds of heaven, saith the Lord. O Sion, flee, thou that dwellest with the daughter of Babylon. For thus saith the Lord of hosts: After the glory, he hath sent me to the nations, that have robbed you: for he that toucheth you toucheth the apple of my eye. For behold I lift up my hand upon them, and they shall be a prey to those that served them: and you shall know that the Lord of hosts sent me. Sing praise and rejoice, O daughter of Sion: for behold I come and I will dwell in the midst of thee: saith the Lord. And many nations shall be joined to the Lord in that day: and they shall be my people: and I will dwell in the midst of thee. And thou shalt know that the Lord of hosts hath sent me to thee. And the Lord shall possess Juda his portion in the sanctified land: and he shall yet choose Jerusalem. Let all flesh be silent at the presence of the Lord: for he is risen up out of his holy habitation.

Zachariah, Chapter 8

[8:1–23]

And the word of the Lord of hosts came to me, saying: Thus saith the Lord of hosts: I have been jealous for Sion with a great jealousy, and with a great indignation have I been jealous for her. Thus saith the Lord of hosts: I am returned to Sion: and I will dwell in the midst of Jerusalem. And Jerusalem shall be called: The City of Truth and the Mountain of the Lord of Hosts, The Sanctified Mountain. Thus saith the Lord of hosts: There shall yet old men and old women dwell in the streets of Jerusalem, and every man with his staff in his hand through multitude of days. And the streets of the city shall be full of boys and girls, playing in the streets thereof. Thus saith the Lord of hosts: If it seem hard in the eyes of the remnant of this people in those days, shall it be hard in my eyes, saith the Lord of hosts? Thus saith / the Lord of hosts: Behold I will save my people from the land of the east and from the land of the going

et habitabunt in medio Iherusalein; et erunt mihi in populum, et ego ero eis in Deum, in veritate et in iustitia. Hec dicit Dominus exercituum: confortentur manus vestre, qui auditis in his diebus sermones istos per os prophetarum, (49b) in die quo fundata est domus Domini exercituumi ut templum edificaretur. Siquidem ante dies illos merces hominum non erat, nec merces iumentorum erat; neque introeunti, neque exeunti erat pax pre tribulatione; et dimisi omnes homines, unumquemque contra proximum suum. Nunc autem non iuxta dies priores ego faciam reliquiis populi [h]uius, dicit Dominus exercituum, sed semen pacis erit; vinea dabit fructum suum, et terra dabit germen suum, et celi dabunt rorem suum; et possidere faciam reliquias populi [h]uius universa hec. Et erit: sicut eratis maledi[c]tio in gentibus, domus Iuda, et domus Israel; sic salvabo vos, et eritis benedictio; nolite timere, confortentur manus vestre. Quia hec dicit Dominus exercituum: sicut cogitavi ut affligerem vos, cum ad iracundiam provocassent patres vestri me, dicit Dominus, et non sum misertus; sic conversus cogitavi in diebus istis ut benefaciem domui Iuda et Iherusalem; nolite tiniere. Hec sunt ergo verba que facitis: loquimini veritatem unusquisque cum proximo suo; veritatem et iudicium pacis iudicate in portis vestris. Et unusquisque malum contra amicum suum ne cogitetis in cordibus vestris; et iuramentum mendax ne diligatis; omnia enim hec sunt que odi, dicit Dominus. Et (50a) factum est verbum Domini exercituum ad me, dicens: hec dicit Dominus exercituum: ieiunium quarti, et ieiunium quinti, et ieiunium septimi, et ieiunium decimi erit domui Iude in gaudium et letitiam et in solemni[ta]tes preclaras; veritatem tamen et pacem diligit. Hec dicit Dominus exercituum: usquequo venient populi et habitent in civitatibus multis, et vadant habitatores, unus ad alt[er]um, dicentes: eamus, et deprecemur faciem Domini, et queramus Dominum exercituum: vadam etiam ego. Et venient populi multi et gentes robuste ad querendum Dominum exercituum in Iherusalem, et deprecandam faciem Domini. Hec dicit Dominus exercituum: in diebus illis, in quibus a[p]prehendent decem homines ex omnibus linguis gentium, et a[p]prehendent fimbriam viri iudei, dicentes: ibimus vobiscum.

Zacharias, capitulo 9

Onus verbi Domini in terra Hadrach et Damasci, requiei eius; quia Dominus est oculus hominis et omnium tribuum Israel. Emath quoque in termiis eius, et Tyrus et Sydon; assunipserunt quippe sibi sapientiam valde. Et edificavit Tyrus munitionem suam et coacervavit argentum quasi humum et aurum ut lutum platearum. Ecce Dominus possidebit eam, et percucient in mari fortitudinem eius, et ergo igni devorabitur. Videbit Ascaloni et timebit; (50b) et Gaza,

down of the sun. And I will bring them: and they shall dwell in the midst of Jerusalem: and they shall be my people. And I will be their God in truth and in justice. Thus saith the Lord of hosts: Let your hands be strengthened, you that hear in these days these words by the mouth of the prophets, in the day that the house of the Lord of hosts was founded, that the temple might be built. For before those days there was no hire for men, neither was there hire for beasts, neither was there peace to him that came in nor to him that went out, because of the tribulation: and I let all men go every one against his neighbor. But now I will not deal with the remnant of this people according to the former days, saith the Lord of hosts. But there shall be the seed of peace: the vine shall yield her fruit and the earth shall give her increase and the heavens shall give their dew. And I will cause the remnant of this people to possess all these things. And it shall come to pass that as you were a curse among the Gentiles, O house of Juda and house of Israel, so will I save you: and you shall be a blessing. Fear not: let your hands be strengthened. For thus saith the Lord of hosts: As I purposed to afflict you, when your fathers had provoked me to wrath, saith the Lord, and I had no mercy: so turning again I have thought in these days to do good to the house of Juda and Jerusalem. Fear not. These then are the things which you shall do: Speak ye truth every one to his neighbor: judge ye truth and judgment of peace in your gates: And let none of you imagine evil in your hearts against his friend: and love not a false oath. For all these are the things that I hate, saith the Lord. And the word of the Lord of hosts came to me, saying: Thus / saith the Lord of hosts: The fast of the fourth month and the fast of the fifth and the fast of the seventh and the fast of the tenth shall be to the house of Juda joy and gladness and great solemnities: only love ye truth and peace. Thus saith the Lord of hosts: Until people come and dwell in many cities, and the inhabitants go one to another, saying: Let us go and entreat the face of the Lord and let us seek the Lord of hosts: I also will go. And many peoples and strong nations shall come to see the Lord of hosts in Jerusalem and to entreat the face of the Lord. Thus saith the Lord of hosts: In those days wherein ten men of all languages of the Gentiles shall take hold and shall hold fast the skirt of one that is a Jew, saying: We will go with you, for we have heard that God is with you.

Zachariah 9

[9:1–17]

The burden of the word of the Lord in the land of Hadrach and of Damascus, the rest thereof: for the eye of man and of all the tribes of Israel is the Lord's. Emath also in the borders thereof and Tyre and Sidon: for they have taken to themselves to be exceeding wise. And Tyre hath built herself a strong hold and heaped together silver as earth, and gold as the mire of the streets. Behold the Lord shall possess her and shall strike her strength in the sea: and she shall be devoured with fire. Ascalon shall see and shall fear: and Gaza, and shall be very sorrowful: and

et dolebit nimis; et Accaron quoniam confusa est spes eius; et peribit rex de Gaza, et Ascalon non habitabitur. Et sedebit separator in Azoto, et disperdam superbiam Filistinorum. Et aufferam sanguinem eius et de medio dentium eius, et relinquetur etiam ipse Deo nostro, et erit quasi dux in Iudai et Acoron quasi Iebuseus. Et circumdabo domum meam ex iis qui militant mihi euntes et reventes, et non transibit super eos ultra exactor; quia nunc vidi in oculis meis. Exulta satis, filia Syon iubila, filia Iherusalem. Ecce rex tuus veniet tibi iustus et salvator ipse, pauper et ascendens super asinam et super pullum filium asine. Et disperdam quadrigam ex Efraim et equum de Iherusalem, et dissipabitur arcus belli, et loquetur pacem gentibus. Et potestas eius a mari usque ad mare et a fluminibus usque ad fines terre. Tu quoque in sanguine testamenti tui emisisti vinctos tuos de lacu, in quo non est aqua. Convertimini ad munitionemi vincti spei, hodie quoque a[n]nuntians duplicia re[d]dam tibi. Quoniam extendi mihi Iudam quasi archum, implevi Efraym; et suscitabo filios tuos, Syoni super filios tuos, Grecia, et ponam te quasi (51a) gladium. Et Dominus Deus super eos videbitur; et exibit ut fulgur iaculum eius; et Dominus Deus in tuba canet, et vade[t] in turbine austri. Dominus exercituum proteget eos; et devorabunt, et subiicient lapidibus funde; et bibentes inebriabunt[ur] quasi a vino et replebuntur ut fiale et quasi cornua altaris. Et salvabit eos Dominus Deus eorum in die illa, ut gregem populi sui; quia lapides sancti elevabuntur super terram eius. Quid enim bonum eius est, et quid pulcrum eius, nisi frumentum electorum, et vinum germinans virgines?

Zacharias, capitulo 11

Si bonum est in oculis vestris, afferte mercedem meam; et si non quiescite. Et appenderunt mercedem meam triginta argenteos. Et dixit Dominus ad me: proice illud ad statuarium, decorum precium, quo a[p]preciatus sum ab eis. Et tuli triginta argenteos, et proieci illos in domo Domini ad statuarium &c.

Zacharias, capitulo 13

In die illa erit fons patens domui David et habitantibus Iherusalem in ablutionem peccatoris et menstruate. Et erit in die illa, dicit Dominus (51b) exercituum: disperdam nomina idolorum de terra, et non memorabuntur ultra; et pseudoprophetas et spiritum immundum auferam de terra. Et erit, cum prophetaverit quispiam ultra,

Accaron, because her hope is confounded. And the king shall perish from Gaza: and Ascalon shall not be inhabited. And the divider shall sit in Azotus: and I will destroy the pride of the Philistines. And I will take away his blood out of his mouth and his abominations from between his teeth: and even he shall be left to our God. And he shall be as a governor in Juda, and Accaron as a / Jebusite. And I will encompass my house with them that serve me in war, going and returning: and the oppressor shall no more pass through them. For now I have seen with my eyes. Rejoice greatly, O daughter of Sion, shout for joy, O daughter of Jerusalem: Behold thy King will come to thee, the just and saviour. He is poor and riding upon an ass and upon a colt, the foal of an ass. And I will destroy the chariots out of Ephraim and the horse out of Jerusalem: and the bow for war shall be broken. And he shall speak peace to the Gentiles: and his power shall be from sea to sea, and from the rivers even to the end of the earth. Thou also, by the blood of thy testament, hast sent forth thy prisoners out of the pit wherein is no water. Return to the strong hold, ye prisoners of hope: I will render thee double, as I declare today. Because I have bent Juda for me as a bow, I have filled Ephraim: and I will raise up thy sons, O Sion, above thy sons, O Greece: and I will make thee as the sword of the mighty. And the Lord God shall be seen over them and his dart shall go forth as lightning: and the Lord God will sound the trumpet and go in the whirlwind of the south. The Lord of hosts will protect them: and they shall devour and subdue with the stones of the sling. And drinking they shall be inebriated as it were with wine: and they shall be filled as bowls and as the horns of the altar. And the Lord their God will save them in that day, as the flock of his people: for holy stones shall be lifted up over his land. For what is the good thing of him and what is his beautiful thing, but the corn of the elect and the wine springing forth virgins.

Zachariah, Chapter 11

[11:12b–13]

If it be good in your eyes, bring hither my wages: and if not, be quiet. And they weighed for my wages thirty pieces of silver. And / the Lord said to me: Cast it to the statuary, a handsome price, that I was prized at by them. And I took the thirty pieces of silver and I cast them into the house of the Lord, to the statuary. &c.

Zachariah, Chapter 13

[13:1–9]

In that day there shall be a fountain open to the house of David and to the inhabitants of Jerusalem: for the washing of the sinner and of the unclean woman. And it shall come to pass in that day, saith the Lord of hosts, that I will destroy the names of idols out of the earth, and they shall be remembered no more: and I will take away the false prophets and the unclean spirit out of the earth. And it shall come to pass that

dicent ei pater eius et mater eius qui genuerunt eum: non vives, quia mendatium locutus es in nomine Domini; et configent eum pater eius et mater eius, genitores eius, cum prophetaverit. Et erit: in die illa confundentur prophete, unusquisque ex visione sua cum prophetaverit; nec operientur pallio saccino ut mentiantur; sed dicet: non sum propheta, homo agricola ego sum; quoniam Adam exemplum meum ab adolescentia mea. Et dicetur ei: quid sunt plage iste in medio manuum tuarum? Et dicet: his plagatus sum in domo eorum qui diligebant me. Framea, suscitare super pastorem meum et super virum co[h]erentem mihi, dicit Dominus exercituum: percute pastorem, et dispergentur oves; et convertam manum meam ad parvulos. Et erunt in omni terra, dicit Dominus; partes due in ea dispergentur et deficient; et terciam partem per ignem, et uram eos sicut uritur argentum, et probabo eos sicut probatur aurum. Ipse vocabit nomen meum, et ego exaudiam eum. Et dicam: populus meus es; et ipse dicet: Dominus Deus meus &c. (52a)

Zacharias, capitulo 14

Ecce dies Domini veniunt, dicit Dominus, et dividentur spolia tua in medio tui. Et congregabo omnes gentes ad Iherusalem et prelium, et capietur civitas, et vastabuntur domus, et mulieres violabuntur; et egredietur media pars civitatis in captivitatem, et reliquum populi non auferetur ex urbe. Et egredietur Dominus et preliabitur contra gentes illas, sicut preliatus est in dic certaminis. Et stabunt pedes eius in die illa super montem Olivarum, qui est contra Iherusalem ad orientem; et scindetur mons Olivarum ex media parte sui ad orientem et ad occidentem, prerupto. Grandi valde; et separabitur medium montis ad aquilonem et medium eius ad meridiem. Et fugietis ad vallem montium eorum, quoniam coniungetur vallis montium usque ad proximum; et fugietis sicut fugistis a facie terremotus in diebus Osie regis Iuda; et veniet Dominus Deus meus, omnesque sancti cum eo. Et erit in die illa: non erit lux, sed frigus et gelu. Et erit dies una, que nota est Domino, non dies, neque nox; et in tempore vesperi erit lux. Et erit in die illa: exibunt aque vive de Iherusalem; medium earum ad marc orientale, et medium carum ad mare novissimum; in estate et yeme erunt. Et erit Doininus rex super omnem terram (52b) in die illa erit Dominus unus, et erit nomen eius unum. Et revertetur omnis terra usque ad desertum de colle Reinmon ad austrum Iherusalem; et exaltabitur, et habitabit in loco suo, a porta Beniamin usque ad locum porte prioris, et

when any man shall prophesy any more, his father and his mother that brought him into the world shall say to him: Thou shalt not live, because thou hast spoken a lie in the name of the Lord. And his father and his mother, his parents, shall thrust him through when he shall prophesy. And it shall come to pass in that day that the prophets shall be confounded, every one by his own vision, when he shall prophesy: neither shall they be clad with a garment of sackcloth, to deceive. But he shall say: I am no prophet. I am a husbandman: for Adam is my example from my youth. And they shall say to him: What are these wounds in the midst of the hands? And he shall say: With these I was wounded in the house of them that loved me. Awake, O sword, against my shepherd and against the man that cleaveth to me, saith the Lord of hosts. Strike the shepherd, and the sheep shall be scattered. And I will turn my hand to the little ones. And they shall be in all the earth, saith the Lord: two parts in it shall be scattered and shall perish, but the third part shall be left therein. And I will bring the third part through the fire and will refine them as silver is refined: and I will try them as gold is tried. They shall call on my name, and I will hear them. I will say: Thou art my people. And they shall say: The Lord is my God. /

Zachariah, Chapter 14

[1:1–21]

Behold the days of the Lord shall come: and thy spoils shall be divided in the midst of thee. And I will gather all nations to Jerusalem to battle: and the city shall be taken, and the houses shall be rifled, and the women shall be defiled: and half of the city shall go forth into captivity. And the rest of the people shall not be taken away out of the city. Then the Lord shall go forth and shall fight against those nations, as when he fought in the day of battle. And his feet shall stand in that day upon the mount of Olives, which is over against Jerusalem toward the east: and the mount of Olives shall be divided in the midst thereof to the east and to the west with a very great opening: and half of the mountain shall be separated to the north, and half thereof to the south. And you shall flee to the valley of those mountains, for the valley of the mountains shall be joined even to the next: and you shall flee as you fled from the face of the earthquake in the days of Ozias king of Juda: and the Lord my God shall come, and all the saints with him. And it shall come to pass in that day, that there shall be no light, but cold and frost. And there shall be one day, which is known to the Lord, not day, not night: and in the time of the evening there shall be light. And it shall come to pass in that day that living waters shall go out from Jerusalem: half of them to the east sea and half of them to the last sea: they shall be in summer and in winter. And the Lord shall be king over all the earth. In that day there shall be one Lord, and his name shall be one. And all the land shall return even to the desert, from the hill to Remmon to the south of Jerusalem: and she shall be exalted and shall dwell in her own place, from the gate of Benjamin even to the place of the former

usque ad portam angulorum; et a turre Ananehel usque ad torcularia regis. Et habitabunt in ea, et anathema non erit amplius; sed sedebit Iherusalem secura. Et hec erit plaga, qua percutiet Dominus omnes gentes que pugnaverunt adversus Iherusalem; tabescet caro un[i]uscuiusque stantis super pedes suos, et oculi eius contabescent in foraminibus suis, et lingua eorum contabescet in ore suo. In die illa erit tumultus Domini magnus in eis; et apprehendet vir manum proximi sui. Sed et Iudas pugnabit adversus Iherusalem; et congregabuntur divitie omnium gentium in circuitu, aurum, et argentum, et vestes multe satis. Et sic erit ruina equi, et muli, et camelli, et asini, et oninium iumentorum, que fuerint in castris illi[s], sicut ruina hec. Et omnes qui reliqui fuerint de universis gentibus, que venerunt contra Iherusalemi ascendent ab anno in annum, ut adorent regem, Dominum exercituum, et celebrent festivitatem tabernaculorum. Et erit: qui non ascenderit (53a) de familiis terre ad Iherusalem ut adoret regem, Dominum exercituum, non erit super eos imber. Quod et si familia Egipti non ascenderit et non venerit, nec super eos erit, sed erit ruina, qua percutiet Dominus omnes gentes, que non ascenderint ad celebrandam festivitatem tabernaculorum. Hoc erit peccatum Egypti, et hoc peccatum omnium gentium, que non ascenderint ad celebrandam festivitatem tabernaculorum. In die illa erit quod super frenum equi est, sanctum Domino; et erunt lebetes in domo Domini quasi phiale coram altari. Et erit omnis lebes in Iherusalem et in Iuda sanctificatus Domino exercituum; et venient omnes immolantes, et sument ex eis, et coquent in eis; et non erit mercator ultra in domo Domini exercituum in die illo &c.

> Es temperancia tiento y manera,
> que todos contino devemos tener
> en nunca temptar dezir ni hazer
> cosa, que deva no ser hazedera.
> és ésta la larga y estrecha carrera,
> adó de contino virtud es hallada,
> sin ser cometida, ni ser salteada
> del vicio, ni d'él quedalle dentera. (53b)

Quare fremuerunt gentes &c. dicunt Hebrei moderni, quod David fecit hunc psalmum, laudando Deum de victoria habita de Philisteis, qui ascenderunt. (54b)

gate, and even to the gate of the corners: and from the tower of Hananeel even to the king's winepresses. And people shall dwell in it, and / there shall be no more an anathema: but Jerusalem shall sit secure. And this shall be the plague wherewith the Lord shall strike all nations that have fought against Jerusalem: the flesh of every one shall consume away while they stand upon their feet, and their eyes shall consume away in their holes, and their tongue shall consume away in their mouth. In that day there shall be a great tumult from the Lord among them: and a man shall take the hand of his neighbor, and his hand shall be clasped upon his neighbor's hand. And even Juda shall fight against Jerusalem: and the riches of all nations round about shall be gathered together, gold and silver and garments in great abundance. And the destruction of the horse and of the mule and of the camel and of the ass and of all the beasts that shall be in those tents shall be like this destruction. And also they that shall be left of all nations that came against Jerusalem shall go up from year to year to adore the King, the Lord of hosts, and to keep the feast of tabernacles. And it shall come to pass that he that shall not go up of the families of the land to Jerusalem to adore the King, the Lord of hosts, there shall be no rain upon them. And if the family of Egypt go not up nor come: neither shall it be upon them. But there shall be destruction wherewith the Lord will strike all nations that will not go up to keep the feast of tabernacles. This shall be the sin of Egypt, and this the sin of all nations that will not go up to keep the feast of tabernacles. In that day that which is upon the bridle of the horse shall be holy to the Lord: and the cauldrons in the house of the Lord shall be as the phials before the altar. And every caldron in Jerusalem and Juda shall be sanctified to the Lord of hosts: and all that sacrifice shall come, and take of them and shall seethe in them: and the merchants shall be no more in the house of the Lord of hosts in that day. &c. /

Temperance is the intention and style,
that always all of us should maintain
in never attempting to say or to do
anything, which should not be carried to completion.
This is the long and narrow road,
where at any time virtue is to be found,
without the commission or the surprise encounter
of evil, or its inner presence.

Why have the Gentiles raged? &c. [Psalm 2:1]. The modern Hebrews say that David composed this psalm in praise to God for the victory they obtained over the Philistines, as they returned. [From the *Glossa ordinaria* of Nicholas of Lyra].[28]

✚ *De Presenti et Futuro*

Ysaias, capitulo 2

Cura prophete est de vocatione gentium et de adventu Christi.

Jeremias in suo prologo.

Et erit in novissimis diebus preparatus mons domus Domini in vertice montium, et elevabitur super colles, et fluent ad eum omnes gentes. Et ibunt populi multi, et dicent: venite, ascendamus ad montem Domini, ad domum Dei Iacobi et docebit nos vias suas, et ambulabimus in semitis eius; quia de Sion exibit lex, et verbum Domini de Iherusalem.

Ysaias, capitulo 5

Et elevabit signum in nationibus procul, et sibilabit ad eum de finibus terre; et ecce festinus velociter veniet.

Ysaias, capitulo 6

Et dixit: donec desolentur civitates absque habitatore, et domus sine homine, et terra relinquetur deserta. Et longe faciet Dominus homines, et multiplicabitur que derelicta fuerat in medio terre. Et ad[h]uc in ea decimatio, et convertetur, et erit in ostensionem sicut terebintus, et sicut quercus, que expandit ramos suos; semen sanctum erit id quod steterit in ea.

Ysaias, capitulo 8

Congregamini, populi, et vincemini, et audite, universe procul terre.

Ysaias, capitulo 12

Notas facite in populis adinventiones eius; mementote (55a) quoniam excelsum est nomen eius. Cantate Domino quoniam magnifice fecit; a[n]nuntiate hoc in universa terra. Exulta, et lauda, habitatio Sion; quia magnus in medio tui sanctus Israel.

Ysaias, capitulo 18

Ve terre, cymbalo alarum, que est trans flumen Ethiopie! Qui mittit in mare legatos, et in vasis papyri super aquas: ite angeli veloces

✠ *On the Present and the Future*

Isaiah, Chapter 2

The prophet is calling attention to the nations and the advent of Christ

Jeremiah in his prologue

[2:2–3]

And in the last days the mountain of the house of the Lord shall be prepared on the top of mountains, and it shall be exalted above the hills: and all nations shall flow unto it. And many people shall go and say: Come, and let us go up to the house of the God of Jacob: and he will teach us his ways, and we will walk in his paths. For the law shall come forth from Sion: and the word of the Lord from Jerusalem.

Isaiah, Chapter 5

[5:26]

And he will lift up a sign to the nations afar off, and will whistle to them from the ends of the earth: and behold they shall come with speed swiftly. /

Isaiah, Chapter 6

[6:11b–13]

And he said: Until the cities be wasted without inhabitant, and the houses without man, and the land shall be left desolate. And the Lord shall remove men far away: and she shall be multiplied that was left in the midst of the earth. And there shall be still a tithing therein: and she shall turn, and shall be made a show as a turpentine tree, and as an oak that spreadeth its branches. That which shall stand there shall be a holy seed.

Isaiah, Chapter 8

[8:9a]

Gather yourselves together, O ye people: and be overcome, and give ear, all ye lands afar off.

Isaiah, Chapter 12

[12:4b–6]

Make his works known among the people: remember that his name is high. Sing ye to the Lord, for he hath done great things: shew this forth in all the earth. Rejoice, and praise, O thou habitation of Sion: for great is he that is in the midst of thee, the Holy One of Israel.

Isaiah, Chapter 18

[18:1–7]

Woe to the land, the winged cymbal, which is beyond the rivers of Ethiopia. That sendeth ambassadors by the sea, and in vessels of bulrushes

ad gentem convulsam, et dilaceratam; ad populum terribilem, post quem non est alius; ad gentem ex[s]pectantem et conculcatam, cuius dirupuerunt flumina terram eius, ad montem nominis Domini exercituum, montem Syon. Omnes habitatores orbis, qui moramini in terra, cum elevatum fuerit signum in montibus, videbitis, et clangorem tube audietis; quia hec dicit Dominus ad me: ego quiescam, et considerabo in loco meo, sicut meridiana lux clara est, et sicut nubes roris in die messis. Ante messem enim totus effloruit, et immatura perfectio germinavit, et precidentur ramusculi eius falcibus; et que derelicta fuerint, abscindentur, excutientur. Et relinquentur simul avibus montium et bestiis terre; et estate perpetua erunt super eum volucres, et omnes bestie terre super illum hyemabunt. In tempore illo, deferetur munus Domino exercituum a populo divulso et dilacerato; a populo terribili, post quem non fuit alius; a gente ex[s]pectante, et conculcata, cuius diripuerunt flumina terram eius; ad locum nominis Domini exercituum, montem Syon. (55b)

Ysaias, capitulo 26

In die illa cantabitur canticum istud in terra Iuda: urbs fortitudinis nostre salvator, ponetur in ea murus et antemurale. aperite portas, et ingredietur gens iusta, custodiens veritatem. vetus error abiit; servabis pacem; pacem, quia in te speravimus.

Ysaias, capitulo 33

Audite, qui longe estis, que fecerim, et cognoscite, vicini, fortitudinem meam. Conte[r]riti sunt in Syon peccatores, possedit timor ipocritas. Regem in decore videbunt oculi eius, cernent terram de longe. Respice Syon, civitatem solempnitatis nostre: oculi tui videbunt in Iherusalem habitationem opulentam, tabernaculum quod nequaquam transferri poterit; nec auferentur clavi eius in sempiternum &c. (56a)

I Paralipomenon, capitulo 17

Nunc itaque sic loqueris ad servum meum David: hec dicit Dominus exercituum: ego tuli te, cum in pascuis sequereris gregem, ut esses dux populi mei Israel; et fui tecum quocumque perrexisti; et interfeci omnes inimicos tuos coram te, fecique tibi nomen quasi unius magnorum, qui celebrantur in terra. Et dedi locum populo meo Israel; plantabitur, et habitabit in eo, et ultra non co[m]-

upon the waters. Go, ye swift angels, to a nation rent and torn in pieces: to a terrible people, after which there is no other: to a nation expecting and trodden under foot, whose land the rivers have spoiled. All ye inhabitants of the world, who dwell on the / earth, when the sign shall be lifted up on the mountains, you shall see, and you shall hear the sound of the trumpet. For thus saith the Lord to me: I will take my rest, and consider in my place, as the noon light is clear, and as a cloud of dew in the day of harvest. For before the harvest it was all flourishing, and it shall bud without perfect ripeness, and the sprigs thereof shall be cut off with pruning hooks: and what is left shall be cut away and shaken out. And they shall be left together to the birds of the mountains and the beasts of the earth: and the fowls shall be upon them all the summer, and all the beasts of the earth shall winter upon them. At that time shall a present be brought to the Lord of hosts, from a people rent and torn in pieces: from a terrible people, after which there hath been no other: from a nation expecting, expecting, and trodden under foot, whose land the rivers have spoiled, to the place of the name of the Lord of hosts, to mount Sion.

Isaiah, Chapter 26

[26:1–3]

In that day shall this canticle be sung in the land O Juda. [Sion], that city of our strength: a saviour, a wall and a bulwark shall be set therein. Open ye the gates: and let the just nation, that keepeth the truth, enter in. The old error is passed away, thou wilt keep peace: peace, because we have hoped in thee.

Isaiah, Chapter 33

[33:13–14a, 7, 20]

Hear, you that are far off, what I have done: and you that are near, know my strength. The sinners in Sion are afraid, trembling hath seized upon the hypocrites. His eyes shall see the king in his beauty: they shall see the land far off. Look upon Sion, the city of our solemnity: thy eyes shall see Jerusalem, a rich habitation, a tabernacle / that cannot be removed. Neither shall the nails thereof be taken away for ever. &c.

I Chronicles, Chapter 17

[I Chronicles 17:7–15]

Now therefore thus shalt thou say to my servant David: Thus saith the Lord of hosts: I took thee from the pastures, from following the flock, that thou shouldst be ruler of my people Israel. And I have been with thee withersoever thou hast gone: and have slain all thy enemies before thee, and have made thee a name like that of one of the great ones that are renowned in the earth. And I have given a place to my people Israel. They shall be planted, and shall dwell therein, and shall be moved no

movebitur; nec filii iniquitatis atterent eos, sicut a principio, ex diebus, quibus dedi iudices populo meo Israel, et humiliavi universo[s] inimicos tuos. A[n]nuntio ergo tibi, quod edificaturus sit tibi Dominus domum. Cumque impleveris dies tuos, ut vadas ad patres tuos, suscitabo semen tuum post te, quod erit de filiis tuis; et stabiliam regnum eius. Ipse edificabit mihi domum, et firmabo solium eius usque in eternum. Ego ero ei in patrem, et ipse erit mihi in filium; et misericordiam meam non auferam ab eo, sicut abstuli ab eo, qui ante te fuit. Et statuam eum in domo mea, et in regno meo usque in sempiternum; et tronus eius erit firmissimus in perpetuum. Iuxta omnia verba hec et iuxta universam visionem istam, sic locutus est Natam ad David &c. (56b)

I Paralipomenon, capitulo 23

Requiem dedit Dominus Deus Israel populo suo, et habitationem Iherusalem usque in eternum. Nec erit officii levitarum, ut ultra portent tabernaculum, et omnia vasa eius ad ministrandum &c.

I Paralipomenon, capitulo 28

Convocavit igitur David onines principes Israel &c.

Cogitavi ut edificarem domum, in qua requiescet archa federis Domini &c.

Salamon filius tuus edificavit domum meam, et atria mea; ipsum enim mihi in filium, et ego ero ei in patrem. Et firmabo regnum eius usque in eternum, si perseveraverit facere precepta mea, et iudicia, sicut et [h]odie &c.

Si quesieris eum, invenies; si autem dereliqueris eum, proiciet te in eternum &c.

I Paralipomenon, capitulo 29

Tria milia talenta auri de auro Ophir &c. Scio, Deus meus, quod probes corda et simplicitatem diligas &c.

II Paralipomenon, capitulo 6

Nunc ergo, Domine Deus Israel, imples servo tuo patri meo (57a) David quecumque locutus es, dicens: non deficiet ex te vir coram mei qui sedeat super tronum Israel; ita tamen si custodierint filii tui vias meas, et ambulaverint in lege mea, sicut et tu ambulasti coram me &c.

more: neither shall the children of iniquity waste them, as at the beginning. Since the days that I gave judges to my people Israel, and have humbled all thy enemies. And I declare to thee, that the Lord will build thee a house. And when thou shalt have ended thy days to go to thy fathers, I will raise up thy seed after thee, which shall be of thy sons: and I will establish his kingdom. He shall build me a house: and I will establish his throne for ever. I will be to him a father, and he shall be to me a son: and I will not take my mercy away from him, as I took it from him that was before thee. But I will settle him in my house, and in my kingdom for ever: and his throne shall be most firm for ever. According to all these words, and according to all this vision, so did Nathan speak to David. &c.

I Chronicles, Chapter 23

[I Chronicles 23:25b–26]

The Lord, the God of Israel, hath given rest to his people, and a habitation in Jerusalem for ever. And it shall not be the office of the Levites / to carry any more the tabernacle, and all the vessels for the service thereof. &c.

I Chronicles, Chapter 28

[I Chronicles 28:1a, 2b,6–7, 9b]

And David assembled all the chief men of Israel, &c.

I had a thought to have built a house, in which the ark of the covenant of the Lord might rest. &c.

Solomon thy son shall build my house and my courts. For I have chosen him to be my son: and I will be a father to him. And I will establish his kingdom for ever, if he continue to keep my commandments, and my judgments, as at this day. &c.

If thou seek him, thou shalt find him: but if thou forsake him, he will cast thee off for ever.

I Chronicles, Chapter 29

[I Chronicles 29:4a,17a]

Three thousand talents of gold of the gold of Ophir. &c. I know, my God, that thou provest hearts and lovest simplicity. &c.

II Chronicles, Chapter 6

[II Chronicles 6:16]

Now then, O Lord God of Israel, fulfill to thy servant David my father, whatsoever thou hast promised him, saying: There shall not fail thee a man in my sight, to sit upon the throne of Israel; yet so that thy children take heed to their ways, and walk in my law, as thou hast walked before me. &c.

2 Paralipomenon, capitulo 7

Apparuit autem ei Dominus nocte, et ait: audivi orationem tuam, et elegi locum istum mihi in domum sacrificii &c.

Tu quoque si ambulaveris coram me, sicut ambulavit David pater tuus, et feceris iuxta omnia, que precepi tibi, et iustitias meas iudiciaque servaveris, suscitabo tronum regni tui, sicut pollicitus sum David patri tuo, dicens: non auferetur de stirpe tua vir, qui non sit princeps in Israel. Si autem adversi fueritis, et reliqueritis iustitias meas, et precepta mea, que proposui vobis, et abeuntes serviertis diis alienis, et adoraveritis eos, evellam vos de terra mea, quam dedi vobis; et domum hanc, qua[m] edificavi nomini meo, proiciam a facie mea, et tradam eam in parabolam, et in exemplum cunctis populis. Et domus ista erit in proverbium universis transeuntibus, et dicent stupentes: quare fecit Dominus sic terre huic et domui (57b) huic? Respondebuntque: quia dereliquerunt Dominum Deum patrum suorum, qui eduxit eos de terra Egipti, et a[p]prehenderunt deos alienos, et adoraverunt eos, et coluerunt; iccirco venerunt super eos universa hec mala.

I Paralipomenon, capitulo 8

Omnia quecumque voluit, fecit rex Salamon atque disposuit, edificavit in Iherusalem, et in Libano, et in universa terra &c.

Tunc abiit Salomon in Asiongaber, et in Hailath ad oram maris Rubrii que est in terra Edom. Misit ergo ei Hiram per manus servorum suorum naves, & nautas gnaros maris, et abierunt cum servis Salomonis in Ophiri tuleruntque inde quadri[n]genta quinquaginta talenta auri, et a[t]tulerunt ad regem Salomonem. (58a)

Item: I Paralipomenon, capitulo 16

In illo die fecit David principem ad confitendum Domino Asaphi et fratres eius. Confitemini Do1nino, et invocate nomen eius; notas facite in populis adinventiones eius &c.

Cantate Domino omnis terra; annuntiate ex die in diem salutare eius. Narrate in gentibus gloriam eius; et in cunctis populis mirabilia eius. Quia magnus Dominus, et laudabilis nimis; et horribilis super omnes deos. Omnes etenim dii populorum ydola; Dominus autem celos fecit. Confessio et magnificentia coram eo; fortitudo et gaudium in loco eius. Afferte Domino, familie populorum, afferte Domino gloriam et imperium. Date gloriam Domino nomini eius; levate sacrificium, et venite in conspectu eius; et adorate Dominum in

II Chronicles, Chapter 7

[II Chronicles 7:12, 17–22]

And the Lord appeared to him by night, and said: I have heard thy prayer, and / I have chosen this place to myself for a house of sacrifice. &c.

And as for thee, if thou walk before me, as David thy father walked, and do according to all that I have commanded thee, and keep my laws and my judgments: I will raise up the throne of thy kingdom, as I promised to David thy father, saying: There shall not fail thee a man of thy stock to be ruler in Israel. But if you turn away, and forsake my justices, and my commandments, which I have set before you, and shall go and serve strange gods, and adore them, I will pluck you up by the root out of my land which I have given you: and this house which I have sanctified to my name, I will cast away from before my face, and will make it a byword, and an example among all nations. And this house shall be for a proverb to all that pass by. And they shall be astonished and say: Why hath the Lord done thus to this land, and to this house? And they shall answer: Because they forsook the Lord, the God of their fathers, who brought them out of the land of Egypt, and laid hold on strange gods, and adored them, and worshipped them: therefore all these evils are come upon them.

II Chronicles, Chapter 8

[II Chronicles 8:b]

All that Solomon had a mind, and designed, he built in Jerusalem, and in Libanus, and in all the land &c.

Then Solomon went to Asiongaber, and to Ailath, on the coast of the Red Sea, which is in the land of Edom. And Hiram sent him ships by the hands of his servants, and skillful mariners. And they went with Solomon's servants to Ophir: and they took thence four hundred and fifty talents of gold, and brought it to king Solomon. /

Item: I Chronicles, Chapter 16

[I Chronicles 16:7–8, 23–36][29]

In that day David made Asaph the chief to give praise to the Lord with his brethren. Praise ye the Lord, and call upon his name: make known his doings among the nations. &.

Sing ye to the Lord, all the earth: shew forth from day to day his salvation. Declare his glory among the Gentiles: his wonders among all people. For the Lord is great and exceedingly to be praised: and he is to be feared above all gods. For all the gods of the nations are idols: but the Lord made the heavens. Praise and magnificence are before him: strength and joy in his place. Bring ye to the Lord, O ye families of the nations: bring ye to the Lord glory and empire. Give to the Lord glory to his name; bring up sacrifice, and come ye in his sight: and adore

decore sancto. Commoveatur a fatie eius omnis terra; ipse enim fundavit orbem immobilem. Letentur celi, et exultet terra; et dicant in nationibus: Dominus regnavit. Tonet mare, et plenitudo eius; exultent agri, et omnia, que in eis sunt. Tunc laudabunt ligna saltus coram Domino; quia venit iudicare terram. Confitemini Domino, quoniam bonus, quoniam in eternum misericordia eius. Et dicite: salva nos, Deus salvator noster, et congrega nos, et erue., de genti-bus, ut confiteamur nomini sancto tuo, et exultemus in carminibus tuis. Benedictus Dominus Deus Israel ab eterno usque in eternum; et dicat omnis populus: amen, et hymnum Deo.

Dopo el peccato delli primi parentii cadendo l'homo de male en pegio, perdete la simigliança de Dio, et como dice el psalmista, prese similitudine de bestia. (58b)

Memorare

Memorare con grand tiento,
ó hombre, qualquier que seas,
tener siempre en pensamiento
á Dios y su ma[n]damiento,
sy con él reynar deseas.

Novissima

Para mientes que proveas,
pues nescessario es morir,
qu'en el tiempo del partyr
el camino llano veas.

Novíssima proveyeron
siempre los sanctos varones,
del mundo se suspendieron,
á Christo siempre sirvieron,
sufriendo tribulationes,
dexando las afectiones
carnales de vanidad.
déveste con humildad
refrenar de tus passiones. (59a) (59b)

Seneca in VII, Tragetide
Medee in choro: "audax nimium"

Venient annis
secula seris, quibus Oceanus
vincula rerum laxet, & ingens
pateat te[l]lus Tiphisque novos
detegat orbes, nec sit terris
ultima Tille.

the Lord in holy becomingness. Let all the earth be moved at his presence: for he hath founded the world immoveable. Let the heavens rejoice, and the earth be glad: and let them say among the nations: The Lord hath reigned. Let the sea roar, and the fullness thereof: let the fields rejoice, and all things that are in them. Then shall the trees of the wood give praise before the Lord: because he is come to judge the earth. Give ye glory to the Lord, for he is good: for his mercy endureth for ever. And say ye: Save us, O God our saviour; and gather us together; and deliver us from the nations: that we may give glory to thy holy name, and may rejoice in singing thy praises. Blessed be the Lord the God of Israel from eternity to eternity. And let all the people say, Amen, and a hymn to God.

After the sin of the first parents, man fell from bad to worse and lost the likeness of God, and as the Psalmist says, / he took on the likeness of a beast.[30]

Remember	Remember with careful attention,[31] O man, whoever you are, Always to keep your thoughts upon God and his commandment, If you wish to rule with Him.
Preparing	Prepare for the future now, Since death is inevitable, That at the time of your parting You will see the straight road ahead.

Preparing for the last days
Always the saintly men
Separated themselves from the world,
And always served Christ,
Suffering tribulations,
Sacrificing their own desires
Of the flesh, and the pride of life.
Clothed with humility
To restrain their passions. /

Seneca, Book 7, Tragedy of Medea,[32]
From the Chorus, "audax nimium"

The time will come
In a number of years, when Oceanus
Will unfasten the bounds, and a huge
Land will stretch out, and Typhis the pilot
Will discover new worlds, so
The remotest land will no longer be Thule.

Vernán los tardos años del mundo ciertos tiempos en los quales el mar Ocçéano afloxerá los atamentos de las cosas, y se abrirá una grande tierra, y um nuebo marinero como aquél que fué guya de Jasón que obe nombre Tiphi, descobrirá nuebo mundo, y estonçes non será la ysla Tille la postrera de las tierras.

✠

El año de 1494, estando yo en la ysla Saona, que es al cabo oriental de la ysla Española, obo eclipsis de la luna á 14 de setiembre, y se falló que había diferençia de ali al cabo de San Viçente en Portugal çinco oras y más de media.

Juebes 29 de febrero de 1504, estando yo en las Yndias en la ysla de Janahica en el poerto que se diz de Santa Gloria, que es casi en el medio de la ysla, de la parte septentrional, obo eclipsis de la luna, y porque el comienço fué primero que el sol se pusiese, non pude notar salvo el término de quando la luna acabó de bolver en su claridad, y esto fué muy certificado dos oras y media pasadas de la noche çinco ampolletas muy çiertas.

La diferençia del medio de la ysla de Janahica en las Yndias con la ysla de Cális en España es siete oras y quynze minutos; de manera que en Cális se puso el sol primero que en Janahica con siete oras y quinze minutos de ora. Vide almanach.

En el poerto de Santa Gloria en Janahica se alça el polo diez et ocho grados, estando las Guardas en el braço. (60a)

✠

Luce, capitulo 1

Ecce enim ex hoc beatam me dicent omnes generationes. Glosa: Idest Iudei et gentiles. Ex omnibus generationibus aliqui sunt conversi ad fidem, qui confitentur istam virginem beatam. Hoc etiam patet in Saracenis; unde in Alcorano Machometi dicitur: de Maria virgine dixerunt angeli: O Maria, Deus annuntiat tibi verbum ex ipso, et erit nomen eius Iesus, filius Marie. Et alibi, in eodem libro, dixerunt angeli: O Maria, Deus utique elegit te, purificavit te, et elegit te claram super mulieres seculorum &c.

Nota in Alcorano

Mathei 8

Dico autem vobis, quod multi ab oriente et occidente venient, et recumbent cum Abraam et Isaac et Iacob in regno celorum. Glosa:

In the latter years of the world will come certain times in which the Ocean Sea will relax the bonds of things, and a great land will open up, and a new mariner like the one who was the guide of Jason, whose name was Typhis, will discover a new world, and then will the island of Thule no longer be the farthest land.

✠

In the year 1494, when I was in the island Saona, which is at the eastern end of the island Hispaniola, there was an eclipse of the moon on the 14th of September, and it was found that there was a difference from there to the Cape of St. Vincent in Portugal of five hours and more than one half.

Thursday, the 29th of February of 1504, when I was in the Indies in the island of Jamaica, in the port which is called Santa Gloria, which is almost in the center of the island, in the northern part, there was an eclipse of the moon, and because the beginning occurred before the sun set, I was able to note only the precise time when the moon fully returned to its brightness, and this was very accurately measured as two hours and one half elapsed / of the night [after sunset], that is five very exact glasses.

The difference from the center of this island of Jamaica in the Indies from the island of Calis in Spain is seven hours and fifteen minutes; this means that in Calis the sun sets before in Jamaica by seven hours and fifteen minutes of an hour (see the almanac).

In the port of Santa Gloria in Jamaica the pole [star] rises to eighteen degrees, when the Guards are in the arm.

✠

Luke, Chapter 1

[1:48b][33]

"Behold from henceforth all generations shall call me blessed."
Commentary: [*Glossa ordinaria* of Nicholas of Lyra] That is, Jews and Gentiles. From all generations some are converted to the faith, who confess that this Virgin is blessed. This appears even among the Saracens, where it is said by Mohammed in the Koran: The angels said of the   Note in Koran
Virgin Mary, "O Mary, God announces to thee the Word from Himself, and his name shall be Jesus, the son of Mary." And in another place, in the same book, the angels said, "O Mary, God has especially chosen thee, purified thee, and designated thee to be famous above the women of the ages," etc.

Matthew 8

[8:11]

"And I say to you that many shall come from the east and the west, and shall sit down with Abraham and Isaac and Jacob in the kingdom of heaven." Commentary: [*Glossa ordinaria* of Nicholas of Lyra] Because

Quia multitudo gentilium in diversis partibus orbis existentium per predicationem apostolorum conversa est ad fidem.

Mathei 2

Ecce magi ab oriente venerunt Hierosolimam, dicentes: ubi est qui natus est rex Iudeorum? Vidimus enim stellam eius in oriente, et venimus adorare eum. Glosa: Per hoc figurabatur quod fides Christi erat a gentibus devote recipienda &c. Quia magi, qui gentiles erant, ipsum Christum devote quesierunt, et inventum adoraverunt &c.

Unde et in hymno canitur: sic magi ab ortu solis per stelle inditium porantes tipum gentium primi offerunt munera. (60b)

✠

Iohannis 10

Ego sum pastor bonus; et cognosco oves meas, et cognoscunt me mee &c. Et alias oves habeo, que non sunt ex hoc ovili; et illas oportet me adducere, et vocem meam audient, et fiet unum ovile, et unus pastor.

Glosa: Nicolay &c.

Et ne crederetur quod solum pro Iudeis deberet mori, propter hoc quod dicitur Mathei 15: "Non sum missus nisi ad oves, que perierunt, domus Israel;" ideo hoc removet, dicens: "et alias oves habeo, que non sunt ex hoc ovili," idest de synagoga Iudeorum, sed de populo gentili. "Et illas oportet me adducere," quod factum est per predicationem apostolorum, ut habetur Actuum XIII, Christo principaliter operante in eorum predicatione, secundum quod dicitur Marci ultimo: "Illi autem profecti predicaverunt ubique, Domino cooperante" &c. "Et vocem meam audient:" quia, Iudeis repellentibus fidem Christi, gentiles eam devote receperunt ad predicationem apostolorum, secundum quod habetur Actuum XIII, ubi dicitur quod Paulus et Barnabas dixerunt Iudeis: "Vobis oportebat primum loqui verbum Dei; sed quoniam repellitis illud, et indignos vos iudicatis vite eterne, ecce convertimur ad gentes; sic enim nobis precepit Dominus;" et sequitur: "Audientes ergo gentes gavise sunt, et glori-

a multitude of the Gentiles existing in the various parts of the earth is converted to the faith by the preaching of the apostles. /

Matthew 2

[2:1b–2]

"Behold, there came wise men from the east to Jerusalem, saying, Where is he that is born king of the Jews? For we have seen his star in the east, and are come to adore him. &c."

Commentary: [*Glossa ordinaria* of Nicholas of Lyra] By this it was represented that the Christian faith was to be received devoutly "by the nations etc., because the magi, who were Gentiles, searched devoutly for the same Christ, and when they had found him, they worshipped, &c.

For this reason, it is also sung in the hymn: "Thus the magi from the East, by the disclosure of the star, bearing the type of the Gentiles, the first offered gifts."

John 10

[10:14,16]

I am the good shepherd: and I know mine, and mine know me &c. And other sheep I have that are not of this fold: them also I must bring. And they shall hear my voice: and there shall be one fold and one shepherd.

Commentary of Nicholas &c.

[Nicholas of Lyra, *Glossa ordinaria*]

And lest it should be thought that he was to die for the Jews only, because of what is said in Matthew 15: "I was not sent except to the perishing sheep of the house of Israel;" he thus removes this impression by saying: "and other sheep I have, who are not of this sheep fold," that is, not of the synagogue of the Jews, but of the Gentile people. "And it is necessary that I should gather them;" which has been accomplished by the preaching of the apostles, as is found in Acts 13, where Christ is the principal worker in their preaching, according to what is said in the last chapter of Mark: "however they went about preaching everywhere, the Lord working with them" etc. "And they shall hear my voice;" because, when the Jews rejected the Christian faith, the Gentiles received it devoutly at the / preaching of the apostles, according to what is found in Acts 13, where it is said that Paul and Barnabas said to the Jews: "It is necessary for you to hear first the word of God; but since you reject it, and judge yourselves as unworthy of eternal life, behold we turn to the Gentiles; for thus the Lord instructed us;" and there follows: "therefore the Gentiles rejoiced as they heard, and they glorified the word of

ficabant verbum Domini." "Et fiet unum ovile," idest una Ecclesia ex Iudeis et gentilibus collecta &c.

Gregorius

Quia vero non solum Iudeam, sed etiam gentilitatem redimere venerat, adiungit: et alias oves habeo, que non sunt ex hoc ovili.

Augustinus, De verbo Domini

Loquebatur enim primo de ovili de genere carnis Israel. Erant autem alii de genere fidei ipsius Israel, extra erant: adhuç in gentibus erant predestinati, nondum congregati. "Non ergo sunt de hoc ovili;" quia non sunt de genere carnis Israel; sed erunt de hoc ovili; nam sequitur: "et illos oportet me adducere." &c. (61a)

Chrisostomus

Ostendit utrosque dispersos, et pastores non habentes. Sequitur: "Et vocem meam audient," ac si dicant: quid miramini, si hii me sunt secuturi, et vocem meam audituri, quando alios videbitis me sequentes, et vocem meam audientes? Deinde et futuram eorum prenuntiat unionem, unde subdit: "Et fiet unum ovile, et unus pastor."

Item Gregorius in homeliis

Quasi ex duobus gregibus unum ovile efficitur; quia iudaicum et gentilem populum in sua fide coniungit.

✠

Augustinus, libro 18. De civitate Dei, capitulo 33

Hyeremias propheta de maioribus est, sicut Ysayas &c. De vocatione gentium, que fuerat futura, et eam nunc impletam cernimus, sic locutus est: "Dominus Deus meus et refugium meum in die malorum, ad te gentes venient ab extremo terre, et dicent: vere mendatia coluerunt patres nostri simulacra, non est in eis utilitas." Quia vero non erant eum agnituri Iudei, a quibus eum et occidi oportebat, sic idem propheta significat: "Grave cor per omnia, et homo est,

the Lord." "And there shall be one sheepfold," that is one Church gathered from among the Jews and the Gentiles. &c.

Gregory the Great[34]

To indicate that he had come to redeem not only the Jews but also the Gentile world, he adds: "and other sheep I have, that are not of this sheepfold."

Saint Augustine, *Of the Word of the Lord*

[Sermon 138]

For he speaks first of the sheepfold of the family of Israel according to the flesh. But there were others of the family of the same Israel according to faith, who were outside: all this while there were those predestinated among the Gentiles, who had not yet been gathered in. Therefore they are not now of this sheepfold; for they are not of the family of Israel according to the flesh; but they shall be of this sheepfold; for there follows: "and it is necessary for me to gather them" &c.

Chrysostom

[Saint John Chrysostom, Homily 60][35]

He shows that both are scattered, and do not have shepherds. There follows: "and they shall hear my voice," as if they should speak out: "Why are you surprised if these are to follow me and are to hear my voice, when you shall see the others following me and hearing my voice?" And next he foretells their future unification, when he adds: "and there shall be one sheepfold, and one shepherd." /

Item. Saint Gregory, in the *Homilies*[36]

So to speak, from two flocks one sheepfold is made; for he unites the Jewish and the Gentile people by faith in him.

✠

Saint Augustine, *On the City of God*, Book 18, Chapter 33

Jeremiah is among the major prophets, like Isaiah &c. Concerning the calling of the Gentiles, which was then to take place in the future, and now we see that it has already been fulfilled, he said this: [Jeremiah 16:19] "O Lord my God and my refuge in the day of troubles, to thee the Gentiles shall come from the ends of the earth and shall say: Surely our fathers have possessed lies, images which have no usefulness in them." And indeed that the Jews would not recognize him, by whom he would have to be killed, thus the same prophet indicates: [Jeremiah 17:9 translated otherwise than Vulgate] "The heart is heavy in all things; and he

et quis cognoscet eum?" Huiusmodi est et illud quod in libro 17 posui Testamentum Novum, cuius est mediator Christus. Ipse quippe Hieremias ait: "Ecce dies veniunti dicit Dominus, et consumabo super domum Iacob Testamentum Novum," &c. que ibi leguntur. Sophonie autem prophete, qui cum Hieremia prophetabat, hec predicta de Christo interim ponam: "Ex[s]pecta me, dicit Dominus, in die resurrectionis mee, in futurum; quia iuditium meum, ut congregem gentes, et colligam regna." Et iterum: "Horribilis," inquit, "Dominus super eos, et exterminabit omnes deos terre; et adorabit eum vir de loco suo, omnes insule gentium." Et Paulo post item inquit: "Pervertam in populis linguam, et progenies eius, (61b) ut invocent omnes nomen Domini, et serviant ei sub uno iugo; a finibus fluminum Ethyopie afferent hostias mihi. In illo die non confunderis ex omnibus adinventionibus tuis, quas impie egisti in me; quia tunc auferam abs te pravitates iniurie tue; et iam non adiities, ut magnificeris super montem sanctum meum. Et subrelinquam in te populum mansuetum et humilem. Et verebuntur a nomine Domini, qui reliqui fuerunt in Israel." Hee sunt reliquie, de quibus alibi prophetatur, quod Apostolus etiam commemorat: "Si fuerit numerus filiorum Israel sicut arena maris, reliquie salve fient." Hec quippe in Christum illius gentis reliquie crediderint.

Nota

 De convocatione et conversione omnium gentium quantum et quam clare et aperte locutus fuerit apostolus Paulus in omnibus epistolis suis, si scire placuerit, legantur et relegantur eedem epistule eius a principio usque ad finem, et ab eodem apostolo Paulo, predicatore gentium, evidentissime edocebitur, quomodo Dominus noster Yhesus Christus venit in mundum pro conversione et salute earum &c., ut in precedentibus prelibatum est &c.

Id ipsum dico de libro, qui intitulatur: Actus apostolorum, in quo similiter per totum tractatur de convocatione & conversione filiorum Israel, et omnium gentium &c.

Hoc annotavi in rei memoriam, et quia longum esset omnia in hoc presenti tractatu transcribere &c.

is a man, and who recognizes him?" To the same effect is what I have put in the 17th book, about the New Testament, of which Christ is the mediator. Indeed the same Jeremiah says, [Jeremiah 3:33 translated otherwise than Vulgate] "Behold, the day shall come, says the Lord, when I will consummate upon the house of Jacob a New Testament," and the other things that are read there. Also the prophet Zephaniah prophesied along with Jeremiah, and here I will reflect upon these things he predicted about Christ: [Zephaniah 3:8] "Expect me, saith the Lord, in the day of my resurrection that is to come; for my judgment is to assemble the Gentiles and to gather the kingdoms." And again: [Zephaniah 2:11] "The Lord shall be terrible upon them and shall exterminate all the gods of the earth; and they shall adore him, every man from his own place, all the islands of the Gentiles." And a little later he says again [Zephaniah 3:9–12 varies from Vulgate]: "I will change the language among the people, and his offspring, that all may call upon the name of the Lord, and may serve him under one yoke; / from the borders of the river of Ethiopia they shall bring offerings to me. In that day thou shalt not be ashamed for all thy invented doings wherein thou hast transgressed against me: for then I will take away from the midst of thee the unrighteous deeds of thy lawlessness; and thou shalt no more go on magnifying thyself upon my holy mountain: and I will leave in the midst of thee a meek and humble people; and they shall fear the name of the Lord who shall be left in Israel." These are the remnant people, of whom it is elsewhere prophesied, which the Apostle also reminds us: [Isaiah 10:22, Romans 9:27] "If the number of the children of Israel be as the sand of the sea, a remnant shall be saved." Indeed these are the remnants of that nation, who shall have believed in Christ.

Note[37]

 As to the calling and the conversion of all the nations, so much and so very clearly and openly the Apostle Paul has spoken in all his epistles, if you should wish to know about it, those epistles of his can be read and re-read from beginning to end, and by that same Apostle Paul, the preacher to the Gentiles, it will be most clearly proved, how our Lord Jesus Christ came into the world for their conversion and salvation &c., as in the foregoing selections it is examined &c.

The same thing I say about the book which is entitled "The Acts of the Apostles," in which likewise all throughout is dealt with the calling and the conversion of the children of Israel, and of all the Gentiles &c.

I wrote this down just as a reminder, because it would be too lengthy to transcribe all of it in this present treatise &c. /

✠

Sequitur (62a)

✠

Ex homelia beati Augustini
super evangelium secundum Matheum:

"Egressus Iesus, secessit in partes Tiri et Sidonis," &c. Mulier ista cananea erat ex gentibus &c. Tirus et Sidon non erant civitatespopuli Israel, sed gentium; quamvis vicine illi populo &c. que secuntur. Ex quibus oritur questio: unde nos ad ovile Christi de gentibus venimus, si non est missus nisi ad oves, que perieru[n]t domus Israel? &c. Sequitur post multa: ad gentes enim ipse non ivit, sed discipulos misit. Et illic impletum est quod propheta dixit: "Populus quem non cognovi, servivit mihi." Videte quam alta, quam evidensi qua expressa prophetia: "Populus quem non cognovii," id est, cui presentiam meam non exhibui, "servivit mihi." Quomodo? Sequitur: "Ob auditu auris obedivit mihi;" hoc est, non videndo, sed audiendo crediderunt. Ideo gentium maior est laus. Illi enim viderunt, et occiderunt; gentes audierunt, et crediderunt. Ad gentes aut vocandas et congregandas, ut impleretur quod modo cantavimus: "Congrega nos gentibus, ut confiteamur nomini tuo, et gloriemur in laude tua," ille Paulus apostolus missus est. Minimus ille factus magnus, non per se, sed per eum quem persequebatur, missus est ad generationes, ex latrone pastori ex lupo ovis. Missus est gentes ille apostolus minimus, et multum laboravit in gentibus, et per eum gentes crediderunt, sicut testes sunt eius epistole. Sequitur: Habes hoc et in evangelio sacratissime figuratum &c., ubi scilicet agitur de suscitatione filie archisinagogi, et curatione mulieris fiuxum sanguinis patientis. Quarum filia archisinagogi illa significabat populum Iudeorum, propter quem venerat Christus, qui dixit: "Non sum missus, nisi ad oves, que perierunt domus Israel." Illa vero mulier que fluxum sanguinis patiebatur, Ecclesiam figurabat ex gentibus, ad quam per presentiam corporis Christus non erat missus. Et reliqua per totum, que omnia multum faciunt ad propositum, et ideo, si placet, tota ipsa homelia conscribatur de verbo ad verbum. (62b)

✠

There follows

✠

From the Homily of Saint Augustine
on the Gospel according to Matthew

[Sermon No. 77]

"Jesus went out . . . withdrew into the land of Tyre and Sidon &c." [Matthew 5:21ff]

This Canaanite woman was from among the Gentiles &c. Tyre and Sidon were not cities of the people of Israel, but of the Gentiles, although close neighbors of the people of Israel &c. and the following. A question arises from these words: How have we, who are Gentiles, entered into the sheepfold of Christ, if he was not sent except to the sheep of the house of Israel who were perishing? &c. And the following, much later: Jesus Christ did not himself go to the Gentiles, but he sent his disciples to them. And in this way was fulfilled what the prophet said: [Psalm 17:45a, Vulgate] "A people which I knew not hath served me." You see how profound that prophecy is, how clear, how explicit. "A people which I knew not," that is, to whom I did not introduce myself, "has served me." How is that? The prophet continues. "at the hearing of the ear they have obeyed me." That is, it was not by seeing but by hearing that they came to believe. See the greater glory of the Gentiles. The Jews saw him and put him to death. The Gentiles heard and believed. Now it was for the calling and gathering of the Gentiles, to accomplish what we were singing about just a few moments ago, [Psalm 105:47b] "Gather us from among the Gentiles, that we may confess thy name and may glory in thy praise," that the apostle Paul was sent out. He, the least of the apostles, was made the greatest. Not because of himself, but by the grace of him whom he had persecuted, he was sent to the generations [Gentiles]. He was changed from a criminal to a pastor, from a wolf to a sheep. This least of the apostles was sent to the Gentiles, and he labored much among the Gentiles, and the Gentiles received the faith from him, as his letters testify. There follows later: You have in the Gospel a sacred example &c., where it deals with the raising of the daughter of the leader of the synagogue, and the healing of the / woman who suffered an issue of blood. Of which, this daughter of the chief of the synagogue represents the Jewish people, for whom Christ came, who said: "I was not sent except to the lost sheep of the house of Israel." On the other hand, that woman with an issue of blood represents the church of the Gentiles, to whom Christ was not sent in his physical presence. And so on through all of it, which is all very much to the point, and indeed, if you will, this whole sermon can be written out word for word.

Quare fremuerunt gentes &c.

Dicunt moderni Hebrey quod David fecit hunc psalmum, laudando
Deum de victoria habita de Philisteis, qui ascenderunt ad pugnan-
dum contra eum, quando audierunt eum fuisse inunctum publice
super totum Israeli ut habetur Regum 2, capitulo 9; et licet intellec-
tui ab ipsis tradito in multis consonet littera, tamen non videtur
tenenda, duabus de causis: prima, quia littera in pluribus discordat;
secunda, quia apostolus Paulus ad Hebreos primo per illud, quod
dicitur in hoc psalmo, probat Christum esse maiorem angelis, dicens: ad quem enim angelorum aliquando dixit: "Filius meus es
tu, ego hodie genui te?" Probatio enim valet ex sensu mistico, sed
tantum ex litterali, secundum quod dicit Augustinus contra Vincen-
tium Donatistam, et ideo secundum Apostolum, qui scivit Testamentum Gamalielis, et perfectius per illuminationem Spiritus Sancti
oportet dicere, quod iste psalmus inte[l]ligitur ad litteram de
Christo. Item Actus 4 Apostoli, post receptionem Spiritus Sancti,
hunc psalmum a[l]legaverunt, tamquam de Christo dictum, ut patet
in suo loco. Item rabi Salomon in pri[n]cipio hilius glose psalmi
dicit sic: "Magistri nostri exposuerunt hunc psalmum de rege Mes-
sia, per quem inte[l]ligitur Christus in lege & prophetis promissus;"
unde subdit: Sed ad intellectum psalmi planum, id est litteralem,
et propter responsionem ad hereticos exponitur de David." Ex hoc
dicto rabi Salomon 3 habemus: unum est quod doctores Hebreorum
antiqui intellexerunt hunc psalmum de Christo ad litteram. Secundum est, quod propter responsionem ad hereticos rabi Salomon et
alii posteriores doctores Hebreorum exposuerunt hunc psalmum de
David. Vocat autem hereticos conversos de iudaysmo ad fidem cat-
holicam, qui contra alios permanentes in perfidia arguebant de hoc
psalmo. Non potest autem argunientum fieri, nisi ex sensu litterali,
ut supra dictum est, et sic patet secundum homines litteratos de
iudaysmo conversos, quod psalmus iste intelligitur de Christo ad
litteram. Sic igitur duo predicta in verbo rabbi Salomonis inclusa
vera sunt. Sed tertium, quod ibi includitur, videtur omnino confic-
tum, scilicet quod psalmus iste ad litteram exponendus sit de David;
adtamen quia confitetur, quod antiqui doctores Hebreorum hunc
psalmum exposuerunt de Christo. (63a–66b) (67a)

Gozos del nascimiento de sant Juan Babtista

Gozos den más regozijo
este día que otros días,
que oy nasció el muy sancto hijo
de Ysabel y Zacharías.
Gozóse el verbo divino,

Why have the Gentiles raged &c.

[Psalm 2:1a; from the *Glossa ordinaria* of Nicholas of Lyra][38]

The modern Hebrews say that David composed this Psalm, praising God for the victory over the Philistines, who had come up to battle against him, when they had heard that he had been anointed publicly over all Israel, as is found in II Kings, chapter 9; and it can be said that the literal text agrees in many points with the interpretation that they have given, but for two reasons it does not appear to be tenable: first, because the literal text is in disagreement in more points; and secondly because the Apostle Paul in the first chapter to the Hebrews, by that which is said in this Psalm, proves that Christ is greater than the angels, saying: "to which of the angels did he ever say: Thou art my son, this day have I begotten thee?" For the proof does not stand on a mystical interpretation, but on the literal, just as Augustine says in writing against Vicentius the Donatist, and therefore according to the Apostle, who knew the Testament of Gamaliel, and more maturely [perfectly] by the illumination of the Holy Spirit it is fitting to say, that this Psalm should be interpreted in the literal sense as referring to Christ. Furthermore, in Acts 4, the apostles, after receiving the Holy Spirit, mentioned this Psalm as having been said concerning Christ, as appears in the text. Furthermore, Rabbi Solomon in the beginning / of his commentary on this Psalm says thus: Our teachers expounded this Psalm as referring to the reign of the Messiah, by whom they understood "Christ promised in the law and the prophets;" whereupon he adds: "but for the clear interpretation of the Psalm, that is the literal, and for the purpose of an answer to the heretics, it is interpreted as referring to David." From what is said by Rabbi Solomon we learn three things: the first is that the ancient teachers of the Hebrews understood this Psalm as referring to the Messiah in its literal meaning. The second is that, for the purpose of a response to the heretics Rabbi Solomon and other later Hebrew scholars interpreted the Psalm as referring to David. Now they called heretics those who were converted from Judaism to the Catholic faith, who made use of this Psalm in arguing against others who continued in unbelief. However, there can be no argument except on the basis of the literal interpretation, as was said above, and thus it is obvious according to the learned converts from Judaism that this Psalm is interpreted concerning Christ according to the literal sense. Thus, therefore, the two things mentioned above included in the words of Rabbi Solomon are true. But the third thing, which is included there, is obviously entirely fabricated, namely, that this Psalm should be interpreted as referring to David in its literal meaning; and that notwithstanding that he admits that the ancient Hebrew scholars expounded this Psalm as referring to the Christ [the Messiah].

Joy in the birth of Saint John the Baptist[39]

Joys more than usual cheer me
Today more than other days,
On this birthday of the holy son
Of Elizabeth and Zachariah.
God the Word rejoiced also, /

quando su primo saltava
en el vientre viejo digno,
que su madre visitava:
Y tu virgen qu'estarías
al parto de tal sobrino,
gozo sin tiento ny tino
rescibe con Zacharías. (67b)

✠ *De Futuro. In Novissimis.*

Hieremias, capitulo 25

Verbum, quod factum est ad Geremiam de omni populo, et reliqua totius ipsius capituli.

✠

Ex epistola legatorum genuensium ad reges Hyspanie
habita Barchinonie anno 1492

Abbas Ioachim Nec indigne, aut sine ratione assevero vobis, regibus amplissimis, maiora servari, quando quidem legimus predixisse Ioachinum abba-tem calabrum ex Hyspania futurum, qui arcem Syon sit reparatu-rus. (68a–76b, excised pages) (77a)

Qual sea la causa de tanto destierro,
por mill prolongado y más de quinie[n]tos,
los padres que fueron,
pastores, que fueron. Los tiempos passados. (77b)

✠

Tharsis in sacra Scriptura sepius reperitur et alibi &c.

Genesis 10 et I Paralipomenon 1

Tharsis interpretatur exploratio gaudii

De hoc nomine Tharsis notandum est quod

Nota. Tharis tria significat.

He sunt generationes filiorum Noe &c. Porro filii Gomer &c. Filii autem Iavan: Helysa et Tharsis, Cethin et Dodani.

Glosa: Et Tharsis a quo descenderunt Cilices. Unde et civitas metropolis eorum vocata est Tharsis. Unde natus fuit Paulus aposto-lus, ut habetur in Actibus apostolorum XXI. Sequitur in textu con-tinuatim: ab his divise sunt insule gentium in regionibus suis, unus-quisque secundum linguam suam et familias suas, in nationibus suis.

Nota: Ex predictis apparet: primo, quod Tharsis est nomen proprium viri; secundo, nomen civitatis in provincia Cilitie; tertio, nomen insule, ut etiam singilatim in subsequentibus patebit.

When his cousin leapt
In the aged and favored womb
Of her whom his mother visited;
And thou, Virgin, who wert present
At the birth of such a nephew;
The joyful news without listening or telling
Receive it with Zachariah!

✠ *Prophecies of the Future. The Last Days.* [40]

Jeremiah, Chapter 25

"The word that came to Jeremiah concerning all the people," and the remainder of this whole chapter.

✠

From the Letter of the Genoese Deputies to the Spanish Sovereigns Received in Barcelona in the Year 1492

Not undeservedly or without reason, I call earnestly to the attention of you, the most noble sovereigns, some very important things that are to

Abbot Joachim be observed, since indeed we did read that Joachim the Abbot of Southern Italy has foretold that he is to come from Spain who is to recover again the fortunes of Zion. [Ten pages missing at this point]

What could be the cause of such a long exile,[41]
Lengthened a thousand and over five hundred years
The fathers what were they? /
They were shepherds, long years ago.

✠

Tharsis is found frequently in the Holy Scriptures and elsewhere &c.[42]

Genesis 10 and I Chronicles

[10:1,3] and [I Chronicles 1:7]

The discovery of Tharsis joyfully explained These are the generations of the sons of Noah &c. And the sons of Gomer &c. And the sons of Javan: Elisa and Tharsis, Cethim and Dodanim.

Note that this is the name Tharsis Commentary: [*Glossa ordinaria* of Nicholas of Lyra] And Tharsis from whom the Cilicians are descended. Whence also their capital city is called Tharsis where the apostle Paul was born, as recorded in Acts of the Apostles, chapter 21. From there follow in the text continuously. From these

Note three signs of Tharsis the islands of the Gentiles were divided in their various regions, each one according to its own language, and by their various families in their various nations.[43]

Note: From the foregoing it can be seen: first, that Tharsis is the proper name of a man; secondly, the name of a city in the province of Cilicia; thirdly, the name of an island, as also will appear in each of the following quotations [note in hand of Columbus].

Libro II, Paralipomenon 20

Post hec iniit amicitias Iosaphat rex Iuda cum Ocozia rege Israel, cuius opera fuerunt impiissima. Et particeps fuit, ut faceret naves, que irent in Tharsis; feceruntque classem in Asyongaber. Prophethavit autem Heliezer filius Dodam de Maresa ad Iosaphath, dicens: quia habuisti fedus cum Ocozia, percussit Dominus opera tua, contriteque sunt naves, nec potuerunt ire in Tharsis.

Nota. Quod Tharsis est insula.

III Regum 10

Non erat argentum, nec alicuius pretii putabatur in diebus Salomonis, quia classis regis per mare cum classe Hyram semel per tres annos ibat in Tharsis, deferens inde aurum, et argentum, et dentes elephantorum, et simias, et pavos.

Tharsis insula

Hieremias 10

Argentum involutum de Tharsis affertur, et aurum de Ophyr; opus artificis, et manus erarii &c.

Tharsis insula

 Glosa: Argentum involutum in hebreo habetur argentum ductile. De Tharsis affertur, quia ibi invenitur argentum ductilius. (78a) Et aurum de Ophyr: tertio Regum, nono, nominatur locus iste Ophir, et ibi invenitur aurum valde bonum, ut ex sequenti textu & glosa datur intelligi &c.

III Regum 9

Classem quoque fecit rex Saloinon in Asiongaber, que est iuxta Haylam in littore maris Rubri, in terra Ydumee. Misitque Hyram in classe illa servos suos viros nauticos, et gnaros maris, cum servis Salomonis. Qui cum venissent in Ophyr, sumptum inde aurum quadringentorum viginti talentorum, detulerunt ad regem Salomonem.

Nota. Tharsis insula, que etiam dicitur Ophyr, in qua sunt minere auri, etc.

Glosa. "qui cum venissent in Ophyr:" nomen est provintie in India, in qua sunt montes habentes mineras auri, sed a leonibus et bestiis sevissimis habitantur; propter quod nullus ibi audet accedere, nisi navi stante prope littus ad refugium, et tunc naute explorantes horam, qua dicte bestie se elongant, subito exeunt, et terram effossam unguibus leonum in navem proiitiunt, et recedunt; que terra postea in fornacem proiicitur, et quod est ibi impuritatis consumitur, et amovetur virtute ignis, et remanet aurum purum.

II Chronicles, Chapter 20

[II Chronicles 20:35–37]

After these things Josaphat king of Juda made friendship with Ochozias king of Israel, whose works were very wicked. And he was partner with him in making ships, to go to Tharsis: and they made the ships in Asiongaber. And Eliezer the son of Dodau of Maresa prophesied to Josaphat, saying: Because thou hast made a league with Ochozias, the Lord hath destroyed thy works. And the ships are broken. And they could not go to Tharsis. /

Note that Tharsis is an island

III Kings 10

[AV I Kings 10:21b–22]

There was no silver, nor was any account made of it in the days of Solomon. For the king's navy, once in three years, went with the navy of Hiram by sea to Tharsis; and brought from thence gold, and silver, and elephants' teeth, and apes, and peacocks.

Island Tharsis

Jeremiah 10

[10:9a]

Silver spread into plates is brought from Tharsis, and gold from Ophir; the work of the artificer and the hand of the coppersmith &c.

Island Tharsis

Commentary: [*Glossa ordinaria* of Nicholas of Lyra] "Rolled silver" in the Hebrew means silver that can be beaten thin. "It is brought from Tharsis," because rolled silver is to be found there. "And gold from Ophir:" First Kings 9 calls this place Ophir, and the gold that is found there is exceedingly good, as from the text that follows, and the commentary, it is given to be understood &c.

III Kings 9

[AV I Kings 9:26–28]

And king Solomon made a fleet in Asiongaber, which is by Ailath, on the shore of the Red Sea, in the land of Edom. And Hiram sent his servants in the fleet, sailors that had knowledge of the sea, with the servants of Solomon. And they came to Ophir: and they brought from thence to king Solomon four hundred and twenty talents of gold.

Note the island of Tharsis, which they call Ophir, in which there is much gold, etc.

Commentary: [*Glossa ordinaria* of Nicholas of Lyra] "When they arrived in Ophir:" This is the name of a province in India, in which there are mountains containing mines of gold, but they are inhabited by lions and the most savage beasts; because of which no one dares approach there, unless the ship is holding close to the shore as a refuge and then the sailors ascertain the time when the said beasts are withdrawn, suddenly they come out / and they throw the ore dug up by the claws of the lions into the ship, and they withdraw; which ore is later cast into the furnace, and what is impurity is there consumed and removed by the power of the fire, and there remains the pure gold.

II Paralipomenon 9

Argentum enim in diebus illis pro nihilo reputabatur. Siquidem naves regis ibant in Tharsis cum servis Hyram, semel in annis tribus; et deferebant inde aurum, et argentum, et ebur, et simias, et pavos.

Tharsis insula

Iudith 2

Cumque pertransisset fines Assyriorum, venit ad magnos montes Ange, qui sunt a sinistro Cilitie &c. Predavitque omnes filios Tharsis, et filios Hysmael, qui erant contra fatiem deserti &c.

Tharsis civitas Cilitie

Psalmo 47

In spiritu vehementi conteres naves Tharsis. Glosa. Herodes enim audiens quod magi rediissent in terram suam per mare in navibus Tharsis, iratus eas su[c]cendit &c. (78b)

Tharsis civitas Cilitie

✠

Psalmo 71

Reges Tharsis, et insule munera offerent; reges Arabum, et Sabba dona adducent. Glosa: Hoc exponitur a quibusdam de regibus, qui venerant adorare Christum, qui erat de illis partibus. Potest etiam exponi de pluribus partibus, vel nationibus, que hic nominantur, quarum reges et principes fidem Christi acceperunt &c.

Tharsis civitas vel insula

Ione I

Et surrexit Ionas ut fugeret in Tharsis a fatie Domini, et descendit Ioppen, et invenit navem euntem in Tharsis; et dedit naulum eius, et descendit in eam ut iret cum eis in Tharsis a fatie Domini. Glosa. Tharsis civitas est Cilitie, de qua Paulus fuit oriundus. Actuum XXI: "Et descendit in Iopen," portus est in Iudea super mare Mediterraneum.

Tharsis civitas Cilitie

II Chronicles 9

[AV II Chronicles 9:20b–21]

For no account was made of silver in those days. For the king's ships went to Tharsis with the servants of Hiram, once in three years: and they brought thence gold and silver, and ivory, and apes, and peacocks.

Island Tharsis

Judith 2

[2:12a,13a]

And when he had passed through the borders of the Assyrians, he came to the great mountains of Ange, which are on the left of Cilicia &c. And [he] pillaged all the children of Tharsis, and the children of Ismahel, who were over against the face of the desert &c.

Tharsis a city in Cilicia

Psalm 47

[47:8]

With a vehement wind thou shalt break in pieces the ships of Tharsis.
    Commentary: [*Glossa ordinaria* of Nicholas of Lyra] For Herod hearing that the Magi had departed to their own country by sea in ships of Tarshish, was angry and burned them.

Tharsis a city in Cilicia

✠

Psalm 71

[71:10]

The kings of Tharsis and the islands shall offer presents: the kings of the Arabians and of Saba shall bring gifts.
    Commentary: [*Glossa ordinaria* of Nicholas of Lyra] This is expounded by some as a reference to those kings who / came to worship Christ, who were from those regions. It can also be expounded as a reference to the many regions or nations, which are named here, whose kings and princes embraced the Christian faith &c.

Tharsis a city and an island

Jonah 1

[1;3]

And Jonah rose up to flee into Tharsis from the face of the Lord: and he went down to Joppa, and found a ship going to Tharsis. And he paid the fare thereof and went down into it, to go with them to Tharsis from the face of the Lord.
    Commentary: [*Glossa ordinaria* of Nicholas of Lyra] Tharsis is a city of Cilicia, from which Paul came. Acts 21 [?] "And he went down to Joppa;" this is a seaport on the Mediterranean Sea.

Tharsis a city in Cilicia

Actuum 21 et 22

Ego homo sum quidem iudeus a Tharso Cilitie, non ignote civitatis
municeps.

Tharsis sive
Tharsum civitas
Cilitie

Alphonsi pal, in Vocabulario

Tharsum Perseus edificavit. In ea civitate Paulus fuit ortus. Tharsis
filius Iavan, a quo Cilices originem habuere; unde metropolis civitas
eorum dicitur Tharsis, que interpretatur exploratio gaudii. Scribitur
cum aspiratione, Tharsis. Hebreum est. Tharsis mare vel pelagus.

Tharsis in Ezechiel et Daniele: Ab Aquila interpretatur crisolitus,
a Symaco yacinthus. Ande quidam male putaverunt Tharsis Tharsum esse civitatem, nam et inter alios lapides, qui in ornatu summi
sacerdotis erant, eiusdem lapidis nomen inseritur.

Tharsis quoque quedam Indie regio nuncupatur, et ipsum mare,
quia colorem supradictorum lapidum imitatur. (79a) (79b)

Tharsum civitas
Cilitie.
Tharsis nomen
proprium viri.
Tharsis civitas
metropolis
Tharsis mare vel
pelagus
Tharsis lapis
crisolitus vel
iacinthus
Tharsis regio Indie
et ipsum mare etc.

✠

De insula Ophyr in qua habetur multum aurum &c. que insula
comprobatur esse Tharsis, ut in superioribus allegationibus.

III Regum 9

Auctoritates Perfectumque est templum. Classem quoque fecit rex Salomon in
Asyongaber, que est iuxta Haylam in littore maris Rubrii in terra
Idumea. Misitque Hyram in classe illa servos suos viros nauticos,
et gnaros maris, cum servis Salomonis. Qui cum venissent in Offir,
sumptum inde aurum quadrinentorum viginti talentorum, detulerunt ad regem Salomonem &c. In Glossa Nicolai dicitur quomodo
colligebatur aurum.

III Regum 10

Sed et classis Hyram, que portabat aurum de Ophyr, attulit ex
Ophyr ligna thina multa nimis, et gemmas pretiosas.

III Regum 22

Rex vero Iosaphat fecerat classes in mari, que navigarent in Ophyr
propter aurum &c.

Acts 21 and 22

[21:39, 22:3]

I am a Jew of Tarsus in Cilicia, a citizen of no mean city.

Tharsis when
Tharsis of Cilicia

Alfonso de Zamora, in the *Vocabularium*[44]

Perseus built Tharsum. Paul was raised in that city. Tharsis was the son of Javan, from whom the Cilicians derived their origin. Therefore their metropolitan city is called Tharsis, which can be translated as "the exploration of joy." It is written with the aspirant, Tharsis. This is in Hebrew. Tharsis is the sea, or the open sea.

Tharsis, city in
Cilicia

Tharsis as proper
name for residents

Tharsis in Ezekiel and Daniel. By Aquila this is translated as a topaz, by Symachus as a blue sapphire. Whence some have wrongly thought that Tharsis is the city of Tharsum, since also among the other stones, which were in the equipment of the high priest, the name of this stone is included. /

Tharsis as
metropolitian city

Tharsis as sea or
open sea

Tharsis is also the name by which a certain region of the Indies is called, and its sea, because it resembles the color of the above mentioned stones.

Tharsis as topaz
and sapphire

Tharsis a region in
India and its sea

Of the Island of Ophir in which there is much gold &c.
which island is demonstrated to be Tharsis,
as in the above evidences:

III Kings 9

[9:25b–28]

Authorities And the temple was finished. And king Solomon made a fleet in Asiongaber, which is by Ailath, on the shore of the Red Sea in the land of Edom. And Hiram sent his servants in the fleet, sailors that had knowledge of the sea, with the servants of Solomon. And they came to Ophir: and they brought from thence to king Solomon four hundred and twenty talents of gold &c. (In the Commentary of Nicholas of Lyra is described how the gold is collected.)

III Kings 10

[AV I Kings 10:11]

The navy also of Hiram, which brought gold from Ophir, brought from Ophir great plenty of thyine trees and precious stones.

III Kings 22

[AV 1 Kings 22:49a]

But king Josaphat made navies on the sea, to sail into Ophir for gold &c. /

Hieremie 10

Argentum involutum de Tharsis affertur, et aurum de Ophyr; opus artificis, et manus erarii &c.

David 1, Paralypomenon 29

Et super hec omnia, que obtuli in domum Dei mei, de peculio (80a) meo aurum et argentum do in templum Dei mei, exceptis his, que preparavi in edem sanctam, fiia milia talenta de auro Ophyr &c.

II Paralypomenon 8

Misit ergo ei Hyram per manus servorum suorum naves, et nautas gnaros maris, et abierunt cum servis Salomonis in Ophyr, tuleruntque inde quadringenta quinque talenta auri, et attulerunt ad regem Salomonem.

II Paralipomenon 9

Sed et servi Hyram cum servis Salomonis attulerunt aurum de Ophyr, et ligna thina, et gemmas pretiosissimas &c. (80b) (81a)

✠

De insula Cethyn, quam dicunt esse
Tharsis et Ophyr, scriptum est:

Isaye 23

Ululate naves maris; quia vastata est domus unde venire consueverant; de terra Cethyn revelatum est eis. Tacete qui habitatis in insula &c. In Cethyn consurgens transfreta &c.

Hieremie 2

Transite ad insulas Cethyn et videte; et in Cedar mittite, et considerate vehementer; et videte si factum est huiusmodi. Si mutavit gens deos suos, et certe ipsi non sunt dii.

Jeremiah 10

[10:9]

Silver spread into plates is brought from Tharsis, and gold from Ophir: the work of the artificer and of the hand of the coppersmith &c.

David I, Chronicles 29

[AV I Chronicles 29:3–4a]

Now over and above the things which I have offered into the house of my God I give, of my own proper goods, gold and silver for the temple of my God, besides what things I have prepared for the holy house. Three thousand talents of gold of the gold of Ophir &c.

II Chronicles 8

[AV II Chronicles 8:18]

And Hiram sent him ships by the hands of his servants, and skillful mariners. And they went with Solomon's servants to Ophir: and they took thence four hundred and fifty talent of gold, and brought to king Solomon.

II Chronicles 9

[AV II Chronicles 9:1C]

And the servants also of Yiram, with the servants of Solomon, brought gold from Ophir, and thyine trees, and most precious stones &c.

✠

Of the Island of Cethim which is said
to be Tarshish and Ophir, it is written:

Isaiah 23

[23:1b–2a, 12b]

Howl, ye ships of the sea, for the house is destroyed, from whence / they were wont to come: from the land of Cethim it is revealed to them. Be silent, you that dwell in the island &c. Arise and sail over to Cethim &c.

Jeremiah 2

[2:10–11a]

Pass over to the isles of Cethim and see, and send into Cedar and consider diligently: and see if there hath been done anything like this. If a nation hath changed their gods, and indeed they are not gods.

Genesis 10 et I Paralipomenon 1

Filii autem Iavam: Elysa ct Tharsis, Cethyn et Dodani. Ab his divise sunt insule gentium &c. (81b) (82a)

✠

Hec de insulis maris scripta sunt in sacra Scriptura:

Genesis 10

Ab his, scilicet Iavam, Helysa, et Tharsis, Cethy et Dodani, filiorum Gomer, filii Iapheth, filii Noe, divise sunt insule gentium in regionibus suis, unusquisque secundum linguam suam et familias suas in nationibus suis.

Hester 10

Rex vero Assuerus omnem terram, et cunctas maris insulas fecit tributarias.

Psalmo 71

Reges Tharsis, et insule munera offerent; reges Arabum, et Sabba dona adducent.

Psalmo 96

Dominus regnavit, exultet terra; letentur insule multe.

Ecclesiastici 47

Ad insulas longe divulgatum est nomen tuum, et dilectus es in pace tua.

Isaye II

Et erit in die illa: adiiciet Dominus secundo manum suam ad possidendum residuum populi sui, quod relinquetur ab Assiriis, et ab

Genesis 10 and I Chronicles 1

[10:4] and [I Chronicles 1:7]

And the sons of Javan: Elisa and Tharsis, Cethim and Dodanim. By these were divided the islands of the Gentiles &c.

These things are written concerning the islands
of the sea in the Holy Scriptures

Genesis 10

[10:5]

By these, that is by Javan, Elisa, and Tharsis, Cethim and Dodanim, of the sons of Gomer, of the son of Japeth, of the son of Noah, were divided the islands of the Gentiles in their lands: every one according to his tongue and their families in their nations.

Esther 10

[10:1]

And king Assuerus made all the land and all the islands of the sea tributary. /

Psalm 71

[71:10]

The kings of Tharsis and the islands shall offer presents: the kings of the Arabians and of Saba shall bring gifts.

Psalm 96

[96:1]

The Lord hath reigned, let the earth rejoice: let many islands be glad.

Ecclesiasticus 47

[47:17b]

Thy name went abroad to the islands far off: and thou wast beloved in thy peace.

Isaiah 11

[11:11]

And it shall come to pass in that day, that the Lord shall set his hand the second time to possess the remnant of his people, which shall be

Egypto, et a Phethros, et ab Ethiopia, et ab Elam, et a Senaar, et ab Emath, et ab insulis maris &c.

Isaye 24

In doctrinis glorificate Dominum; in insulis maris nomen Dei Israel &c. (82b)

Isaye 41

Taceant ad me insule, et gentes mutent fortitudinem &c. Viderunt insule, et timuerunt &c.

Isaye 42

 In veritate adducet iuditium. non erit tristis, neque turbulentus, donec ponat in terra iuditium; et legem eius insule ex[s]pectabunt.

Isaye 49

Audite, insule, et attendite, populi, de longe &c.

Isaye 51

Me insule ex[s]pectabunt, et brachium meum sustinebunt.

Isaye 60

Nota Me enim insule ex[s]pectant, et naves maris in principio, ut adducam filios tuos de longe.

Isaye 66

Nota Ponam in eis signum, et mittam ex eis qui salvati fuerint ad gentes in mare, in Affricam, in Lydiam, tenentes sagittam; in Italiam, et Gretiam, ad insulas longe, ad eos qui non audierunt de me, et non viderunt gloriam meam.

left from the Assyrians, and from Egypt, and from Phetros, and from Ethiopia, and from Elam, and from Sennaar, and from Emath, and from the islands of the sea &c.

Isaiah 24

[24:15]

Glorify ye the Lord in instruction: the name of the Lord God of Israel in the islands of the sea &c.

Isaiah 41

[41:1a,5a]

Let the islands keep silence before me, and the nations take new strength &c. The islands saw it, and feared &c. /

Isaiah 42

[42:3b–4]

 He shall bring forth judgment unto truth. He shall not be sad nor troublesome, till he set judgment in the earth: and the islands shall wait for his law.

Isaiah 49

[49:1a]

Give ear, ye islands, and hearken, ye people from afar &c.

Isaiah 51

[51:5b]

The islands shall look for me and shall patiently wait for my arm.

Isaiah 60

[60:9a]

Note For the islands wait for me, and the ships of the sea in the beginning: that I may bring thy sons from afar.

Isaiah 66

[66:19a]

Note And I will set a sign among them, and I will send of them that shall be saved, to the Gentiles into the sea, into Africa and Lydia, them that draw the bow: into Italy and Greece, to the islands afar off, to them that have not heard of me and have not seen my glory.

Hieremie 2

Transite ad insulas Cethyn et videte &c.

Hieremie 25

Et accepi calicem de manu Domini, et propinavi cunctis gentibus ad quas misit me Dominus; Ierusalem &c. Et regibus terre insularum qui sunt trans mare &c.

Hieremie 31

Audite verbum Domini, gentes, et annuntiate in insulis que procul sunt.

Hieremie 47

Depopulatus est enim Dominus Palestinos, reliquias insule Capadotie. (83a)

Ezechiel 26

Commovebuntur insule, et descendent de sedibus suis omnes principes maris.

Ezechiel 27

Preteriola de insulis Italie &c. Iacynthus et purpura de insulis Helisa &c. Insule multe negotiatio manus tue &c.

Danielis II

Et convertet fatiem suam ad insulas, et capiet multas.

I Machabeorum 6

Et de insulis maritimis. venerunt ad eum exercitus conductitii.

Jeremiah 2

[2:10a]

Pass over to the isles to Cethim and see &c.

Jeremiah 25

[25:17–18a,22b]

And I took the cup at the hand of the Lord, and I presented it to all the nations to drink of it, to which the Lord sent me: to wit, Jerusalem &c. And to the kings of the land of the islands / that are beyond the sea &c.

Jeremiah 31

[31:10a]

Hear the word of the Lord, O ye nations, and declare it in the islands that are afar off.

Jeremiah 47

[47:4b]

For the Lord hath wasted the Philistines, the remnant of the isle of Cappadocia.

Ezekiel 26

[26:15b,16a]

The islands shake, then all the princes of the sea shall come down from their thrones.

Ezekiel 27

[27:6b,7b,15b]

Things brought from the islands of Italy &c. Blue and purple from the islands of Elisa &c. Many islands were the traffic of thy hand &c.

Daniel 11

[11:18a]

And he shall turn his face to the islands and shall take many.

I Machabees 6

[6:29]

There came also to him from the islands of the sea hired troops. /

I Machabeorum 14

Et cum omni gloria sua accepit Ioppen in portum, et fecit introitum in insulis maris.

I Machabeorum 15

Et misit rex Anthiochus filius Demetrii epistolas ab insulis maris.

Apocalypsis 1

Fuit in insula, que appellatur Pathmos, propter verbum Dei.

Apocalypsis 6

Omnis mons, et insule de locis suis mote sunt.

Apocalypsis 16

Et omnis insula fugit, et montes non sunt inventi.

✠

Multa alia omittimus conscribenda de insulis maris, credentes hec pauca sufficere ad propositum nostrum.

Deo gratias. Amen.

I Machabees 14

[14:5]

And with all his glory he took Joppa for a haven and made an entrance to the isles of the sea.

I Machabees 15

[15:1a]

And King Antiochus the son of Demetrius sent letters from the isles of the sea.

Apocalypse 1

[Revelation 1:9b]

I was in the island which is called Patmos, for the word of God.

Apocalypse 6

[Revelation 6:14b]

Every mountain, and the islands, were moved out of their places.

Apocalypse 16

[Revelation 16:20]

And every sand fled away: and the mountains were not found.

✠

Many others we have omitted to write down concerning the islands of the sea, believing that these few suffice for our purpose.

Thanks be to God. Amen.

Don Asentio p. oooooo p.
Don Juan Martinez p. oooooo p.

Un monachado todos sanctos.
Cinco missas la Griega. Un monachado por el donado
I monachado de la cartuja por un frayle oooooo p.
Agendas oooooooooooooooooooooooooooo
Guadalupe ooooooooooooooo
Frayle de Anjago ooo p. (84a) (84b)

Ioel, capitulo 2	Psalterium, capitulo 4
Ioel, capitulo 3	Psalterium, capitulo 8
Amos, capitulo 9	Psalterium, capitulo 9
Abdia[s], capitulo 1	Psalterium, capitulo 10
Micheas, capitulo 4	Psalterium, capitulo 18
Micheas, capitulo 5	Psalterium, capitulo 19
Micheas, capitulo 6	Psalterium, capitulo 21
Naum, capitulo 1	Psalterium, capitulo 23
Abacuc, capitulo 1	Psalterium, capitulo 56
Sophonias, capitulo 2	Psalterium, capitulo 68
Sophonias, capitulo 3	Psalterium, capitulo 69
Zacharias, capitulo 1	Psalterium, capitulo 71
Zacharias, capitulo 2	Psalterium, capitulo 73
Zacharias, capitulo 3	Psalterium, capitulo 77
Zacharias, capitulo 6	Psalterium, capitulo 83
Zacharias, capitulo 8	Psalterium, capitulo 88
Zacharias, capitulo 9	Psalterium, capitulo 89
Zacharias, capitulo 11	Psalterium, capitulo 91
Zacharias, capitulo 13	Psalterium, capitulo 93
Zacharias, capitulo 14	Psalterium, capitulo 94
I Paralipomenon, capitulo 11	Psalterium, capitulo 96
Paralipomenon, capitulo 15	Psalterium, capitulo 105
Paralipomenon, capitulo 16	Psalterium, capitulo 109
Paralipomenon, capitulo 17	Psalterium, capitulo 110
Paralipomenon, capitulo 21	Psalterium, capitulo 111
Paralipomenon, capitulo 22	Psalterium, capitulo 112
Paralipomenon, capitulo 27	Psalterium, capitulo 113
Paralipomenon, capitulo 28	Psalterium, capitulo 114
Paralipomenon, capitulo 29	Psalterium, capitulo 115
II Paralipomenon, capitulo 1	Psalterium, capitulo 116
Paralipomenon, capitulo 2	Psalterium, capitulo 117
Paralipomenon, capitulo 5	Psalterium, capitulo 118
Paralipomenon, capitulo 6	Psalterium, capitulo 119
Paralipomenon, capitulo 7	Psalterium, capitulo 120
Paralipomenon, capitulo 8	Psalterium, capitulo 121
Paralipomenon, capitulo 9	Psalterium, capitulo 122
Paralipomenon, capitulo 16	Psalterium, capitulo 123
Paralipomenon, capitulo 18	Psalterium, capitulo 124
Paralipomenon, capitulo 20	Psalterium, capitulo 126
Paralipomenon, capitulo 21	Sapientia, capitulo 6
Esdre, capitulo 1	
Esdre, capitulo 3	
Esdre, capitulo 4	

Don Asentio, 6 pesetas
Don Juan Martinez, 6 pesetas

One monachado for All Saints [profession of monastic vows] /
Five masses for La Griega. One monachado for the lay brother
One monachado of the Carthusian for a monk, 6 pesetas
Agendas, 25 pesetas [notebook for memoranda]
Guadalupe, 15 pesetas
Brother De Anjago, 3 pesetas

Joel, Chapter 2   Psalms, Chapter 4
Joel, Chapter 3   Psalms, Chapter 8
Amos, Chapter 9   Psalms, Chapter 9
Obadiah, Chapter 1   Psalms, Chapter 10
Micah, Chapter 4   Psalms, Chapter 18
Micah, Chapter 5   Psalms, Chapter 19
Micah, Chapter 6   Psalms, Chapter 21
Nahum, Chapter 1   Psalms, Chapter 23
Habakkuk, Chapter 1   Psalms, Chapter 56
Zephaniah, Chapter 2   Psalms, Chapter 68
Zephaniah, Chapter 3   Psalms, Chapter 69
Zachariah, Chapter 1   Psalms, Chapter 71
Zachariah, Chapter 2   Psalms, Chapter 73
Zachariah, Chapter 3   Psalms, Chapter 77
Zachariah, Chapter 6   Psalms, Chapter 83
Zachariah, Chapter 8   Psalms, Chapter 88
Zachariah, Chapter 9   Psalms, Chapter 89
Zachariah, Chapter 11   Psalms, Chapter 91
Zachariah, Chapter 13   Psalms, Chapter 93
Zachariah, Chapter 14   Psalms, Chapter 94
I Chronicles, Chapter 11   Psalms, Chapter 96
I Chronicles, Chapter 15   Psalms, Chapter 105
I Chronicles, Chapter 16   Psalms, Chapter 109
I Chronicles, Chapter 17   Psalms, Chapter 110
I Chronicles, Chapter 21   Psalms, Chapter 111
I Chronicles, Chapter 22   Psalms, Chapter 112
I Chronicles, Chapter 27   Psalms, Chapter 113
I Chronicles, Chapter 28   Psalms, Chapter 114
I Chronicles, Chapter 29   Psalms, Chapter 115
II Chronicles, Chapter 1   Psalms, Chapter 116
II Chronicles, Chapter 2   Psalms, Chapter 117
II Chronicles, Chapter 5   Psalms, Chapter 118
II Chronicles, Chapter 6   Psalms, Chapter 119
II Chronicles, Chapter 7   Psalms, Chapter 120
II Chronicles, Chapter 8   Psalms, Chapter 121
II Chronicles, Chapter 9   Psalms, Chapter 122
II Chronicles, Chapter 16 Psalms, Chapter 123
II Chronicles, Chapter 18 Psalms, Chapter 124
II Chronicles, Chapter 20 Psalms, Chapter 126
II Chronicles, Chapter 21 Wisdom, Chapter 6
Ezra, Chapter 1
Ezra, Chapter 3
Ezra, Chapter 4

Non peccabis si el dolor
de los que mueren pensares,
y la fatiga y terror
que padesce el pecador
contigo bien contemplares;
y si bien considerares
la pacientia que terná
el justo quando verá
Que sale de tantos malos.

In eternum gozarán
los que lo bueno abraçaron,
y asimesmo llorarán
porque continuo arderán,
los que la malicia amaron;
y pues siempre se agradaron
del mundo y de sus cudicias,
de las eternas divitias
para siempre se privaron.

Tua con considerança.
deves muy mucho mirar
y en qué fin van á parar
los malos y su pujança
y la bienaventurança
que los justos alcançaron,
que á Dios y á César pagaron
su deuda en ygual balança.

Et tu deves resurtir
tu pensamiento en el cielo,
y de las cosas del suelo
con grand prudentia huyr;
y non quieras consentir
ser del vicio subjuzgado,
siempre seas avisado
á sabelle ressistir.

Memorare con grand tiento,
O hombre, qualquier que seas,
tener siempre en pensamiento
á Dios y su mandamiento,
si con él reynar deseas.
Para mientes que proveas,
pues nescessario es morir,
que en el tiempo del partir
el camino llano veas.

Novissima proveyeron
siempre los sanctos varones;
del mundo se suspendieron,
á Christo siempre sirvieron
sufriendo tribulationes,
dexando las affectiones
carnales de vanidad
déveste con humildad
refrenar de tus passiones.

You will not sin if you reflect[45]
On the pain of those who die,
And if the struggle and terror
That the sinner must suffer
You observe well within yourself,
And if you will consider well
The encouragement that will belong
To the justified when he shall see
That he is delivered from such ills.

In eternity some persons shall be happy
Because they have embraced righteousness.
And, likewise, others shall weep
And they shall continuously burn,
Because they have loved evil,
And because they always delighted
In the world and in its lusts.
Thus, from the eternal riches
They have forever separated themselves.

You should examine your own life
With the most careful consideration
Of the end to which will arrive
The wicked and all their gains,
And the blessedness
That the righteous will attain
Who to both God and Caesar have paid
Their debt in just measure.

And you should redirect
Your attention toward heaven,
And from the things of the earth
With much prudence flee,
And you should not permit yourself
To be subjugated by vice
Always be careful
To know how to resist it.

Remember with great skill,
O man, whoever you are,
To keep always in your thoughts
God and his commandment,
If you desire to rule with him.
Reflect how you can be ready,
Since it is necessary to die,
That at the time of departure
You will see the way clearly.

For the last things [death, judgment, heaven, hell]
The holy men were always prepared.
From the world they liberated themselves.
Christ they always served,
Suffering tribulations,
Abandoning the fondness
Of the flesh for vanity.
Divest yourselves, put on humility.
Hold in check your passions.

✠ *Notes*

1. In the hand of Father Gorricio to 2a.

2. St. Thomas Aquinas (c. 1225–74), Dominican scholastic philosopher and theologian known as "Doctor angelicus." Taught at University of Paris and Pontifical Curia in Rome. The *Summa theologica*, written after 1265, was intended as a summary of all known learning. Question I of Article 10 of Part I of the *Summa* contains most of this material. See chapter 2 of this study for an analysis of the fourfold interpretation of Scripture. Columbus notes this as his most prominent rule for the interpretation of prophecies relating to his chosen subjects: the holy city, Sion, the missionary evangelization of all nations, and the discovery of the islands of the Indies and the lands of all other nations.

3. John Gerson, chancellor, University of Paris (d. 1429). Succeeded Pierre d'Ailly as chancellor at Paris. Gerson was a renowned theologian and mystic who wrote more than one-hundred sermons and treatises. See *Opera omnia*.

4. A shift in focus in references to times; that is, the switching of past tenses and future tenses is the second important hermeneutical principle noted by Columbus for the interpretation of prophecy.

5. A slash / indicates that primary text begins on next page.

6. Isidore of Seville (c. 570–636) early Spanish archbishop and encyclopedist. Columbus likely used the 1483 Venice edition of Pietro Loslein de Langencen, *Etimologie e De Summo bono*.

7. End of Father Gorricio's hand, comments from Nicholas of Lyra in an unidentified hand. Nicolas of Lyra (c. 1265–1349), French Franciscan commentator, taught at Paris and produced commentaries on the whole Bible, first presenting the literal historical sense and then giving a moral or spiritual interpretation. These were frequently copied and printed with the Latin text of the Bible as *Glossa ordinaria super Scripturam sacram*, or "Standard Notes on the Bible." *Biblia Latina* [Cum postillis Nicolai de Lyra] (Venice, 1489). Although we have used *Glossa*, as does Columbus, this is more commonly called *Postillis*.

8. Believed to be in the hand of Christopher Columbus. This letter is the introduction or preface to the *Libro de las profecías*, explaining its purpose and contents. The letter is in Spanish while most of the quotations are in Latin. As Columbus writes about the "restoration of the House of God" and later, in the letter, the "house of Sion," his thoughts must be taken within the context of the foregoing hermeneutical principles. That is, he is speaking in both literal and figurative meanings. As noted, Jerusalem is not merely an earthly city but also, "allegorically, . . . the church in the world." Although Columbus called for a crusade, the literal regaining of the city of Jerusalem, his understanding of the prophesied "great events for the world" included a much more complete extending of the earthly kingdom of Christ.

9. Columbus's affirmation of his direct spiritual illumination from the Bible and the Holy Spirit is the most striking aspect of the *Libro de las profecías*. It is repeated many times here and in letters.

10. That is, a crusade to recapture Jerusalem and restore the ancient temple.

11. A favorite passage of Spiritual Franciscans and their successors who viewed themselves as the "little ones." See chap. 3.

12. The remarkable inclusiveness of this reference to Christians, Jews, Moslems, and "all people of every faith, not merely the learned, but also the uneducated" is not exceptional but is characteristic of Columbus. The intensity of his convictions and his sense of illumination were coupled with an unpretentious openness of personality and generous acceptance of people from all conditions.

13. One of Columbus's chief concerns was to trace the themes of biblical chronology, history, and prophecies of the last times. Such calculations appear elsewhere in his writings, most notably in the postilles to the books he owned.

14. These two passages are actually notes appended at the end of the letter. Columbus may have meant to incorporate them into the text later. The Abbot Joachim of Fiore was the most influential late medieval exegete of prophecy (see chap. 2). Joachim taught that before the end there would be a third age of the Holy Spirit, an age of restoration and renewal for the kingdom of Christ.

15. Father Gorricio's hand wrote the next fifteen pages.

16. Poem is added at bottom of f. 12a by an unidentified hand.

17. From *De Summo bono*.

18. Rabbi Samuel (of Fez) was a Jewish convert to Christianity in the late eleventh century at Toledo. He wrote a famous epistle in twenty-seven chapters to Rabbi Isaac, a Jew in Morocco, in which he systematically refuted Jewish objections to Christianity. The letter was translated into several languages (the original was in Arabic), including the Latin translation of 1329 by the Dominican Alfonso de Buen Hombre which was the one likely used by Columbus.

19. This single entry is on f. 15a. For the many quotations from St. Augustine, we refer the reader to *Sancti Aurelii Augustini hipponensis episcopi opera omnia*, ed. J. P. Migne (Parisiis, 1841–1902).

20. The next six pages are in an unidentified hand.

21. Here begins the hand of Father Gorricio for the next two pages.

22. Alfonso Tostado, a Spanish prelate born about 1400, became Bishop of Avila. He wrote numerous volumes on the lives of prominent biblical characters and a treatise on Matthew. The famous Spanish mystic died in 1455. See *Obras escogidas de filósofos con un discurso preliminar del excelentísimo é ilustrísimo Señor Don Adolfo de Castro*, ed. Adolfo de Castro y Rossi (Madrid, 1922).

23. The next three pages are blank in the manuscript.

24. The next six pages are by an unidentified hand, probably the same scribe as wrote ff. 15b–20b. Concerning Cardinal d'Ailly's *Imago mundi*, Columbus annotated these passages in the copy he owned.

25.   This number should be 666, not 663. Although 663 is the total of the numbers listed, the beast is to be identified by the number 666.

26.   Here begins the hand of Father Gorricio for the next two and a half pages.

27.   Here begins the hand of the young Ferdinand for the next twenty-eight pages.

28.   This is the only entry on f. 53b. Next page blank in manuscript.

29.   Next passage written by Father Gorricio.

30.   One of two notes written in Italian by Columbus. This one exhibits extraordinary knowledge of humanistic style.

31.   Written in an unidentified hand. Next page and a half blank in the manuscript.

32.   This page of notes written by Columbus himself.

33.   The next four and a half pages written by Father Gorricio.

34.   Pope Gregory I, the Great (c. 540–604). We are unable to find this reference in Gregory's writings.

35.   St. John Chrysostom, patriarch of Constantinople, church father and Doctor of the Church (c. 349–407). See *Opera omnia quae exstant* . . . , ed. D. Bernardi de Montfancon (Paris, 1728).

36.   *Sancti Gregorii magni Homiliae in Hiezechihelem prophetam*, ed. M. Adriaen (Turnholti, 1971).

37.   Note added at end of page by Columbus.

38.   Passage copied by an unidentified hand. Folios 63a–66b are missing from the manuscript.

39.   Poem written by an unidentified hand.

40.   This half page written by Father Gorricio. Next ten pages have been cut from the manuscript.

41.   Poem at bottom of f. 77a by an unidentified hand.

42.   Text written in Father Gorricio's hand to the end of the manuscript. He has confused Tarshish with Tarsus or has intentionally made them synonymous.

43.   Note in margin added in hand of Columbus.

44.   Alfonso de Zamora, Hebraist and rabbi (b. 1474) and professor of Hebrew at the University of Salamanca. Became a Christian in 1506. See F. Pérez Castro, *El manuscrito apologético de Alfonso de Zamora*.

45.   Poem added to margins surrounding lists of Scripture.

Bibliography

✤ Primary Sources, Collections, Bibliographies, and Textual Aids

Alvarez Seisdedos, F. *Cristóbal Colón: Libro de las profecías*, edited by F. Morales Padrón. Colección Tabula Americae, Spanish translation companion volume to facsimile edition. Madrid, 1984.

Arbolly Farando, D. *Contestación al discurso de D. Simon de la Rosa y Lopez, al ingresar en la Real Académia Sevillana de Bellas Letras, tretando de los libros y autógrafos de Cristóbal Colón, que existen en la Biblioteca Colombina.* Siviglia, 1891.

———. *Biblioteca Colombina, Catalogo de sus libros impresos de la santa metropolitana y patriarcal iglesia de Sevilla.* 7 vols. Seville, 1888–94.

Arriola, A. "Los libros de Colón. Examen de los que existen en la Biblioteca Colombina con anotaciónes marginales de don Cristóbal y D. Bartolomé Colón." *Boletín de la Real Sociedad Geográfica.* Madrid, 1889.

Bacon, Roger. *Opus maius.* Edited by J. Bridges. 2 vols. Oxford, 1897.

Bernáldez, A. *Historia de los Reyes Catolicos Don Fernando y Doña Isabel.* Sociedad de biliofilos andaluces. Sevilla, 1870.

Berwich y de Alba. *Autógrafos de Colón y papeles de América.* Madrid, 1892.

———. *Nuevos autógrafos de Colon y relaciones de Ultramar.* Madrid, 1902.

Biblia Latina (cum postillis Nicolai de Lyra). Venice, 1489.

Bibliografia Colombina. Enumeración de libros y documentos concernientes a Cristóbal Colón y sus viajes. Madrid, 1892.

Bleiberg, G., ed. *Dicciónario de Historia de España.* 3 vols. Madrid, 1969.

Boggs, R., et al. *Tentative Dictionary of Medieval Spanish.* 2 vols. Chapel Hill, 1946.

Buron, E. *The Imago mundi de Pierre d'Ailly . . . et des notes marginales de Christophe Colomb.* Paris, 1930.

Cancionero de Baena. Edited by Marquis de Pidal. Buenos Aires, 1949.

Cervetto, A. *Catalogo delle Opere componenti la Raccolta Colombiana della Civica Biblioteca Berio di Genova.* Genova, 1906.

Città di Genova. Genoa, 1931.

Chrysostom, J. *Opera omnia.* Edited by D. Bernardi de Montfancon. Paris, 1728.

Colón, C. *Libro de las profecías.* Biblioteca Colombina, Sevilla.

———. *Libro de las profecías.* Colección Tabula Americae, edited by F. Morales Padrón. Madrid, 1984.

Colón, F. *The Life of the Admiral Christopher Columbus.* Translated by B. Keen. New Brunswick, 1959.

Conti, S. *Un secolo di bibliografia Colombiana, 1880–1985.* Genova, 1986.

Cristoforo Colombo. Documenti e prove della sua appartenenza a Genova. Pubblicazione edita dal Comune di Genova, 1931.

De la Rosa y Lopez, S. *Libros y autógrafos de Cristóbal Colón.* Siviglia, 1891.

De Paoli, G., et al. *Contributi alla bibliografia colombiana.* Genova, 1980. De Lollis, C. *Scritti di Cristoforo Colombo.* In *Raccolta colombiana*, pt. I, vol. 2. Rome, 1892.

Douay Bible. New York, 1944.

Firmamentum trium ordinum intitulatur. Venice, 1511.

Gerson, J. *Opera omnia.* 3 vols. Basel, 1489.

Giraldo Jaramillo, G. *Bibliografia de bibliografias colombianas.* Bogota, 1960.

Giustiniani, A. *Polyglot Psalter.* Genoa, 1516.

Herrera Tordesillas, A. *Historia general de los hechos de las Castellanos.* Edited by P. Santiago. Santo Domingo, 1975.

Historia de los hechos de Don Rodrigo Ponce de León, Marqués de Cádiz. Colección de documentos ineditos para la historia de España. Madrid, 1893.

Huntington, A. *Catalogue of the Library of Ferdinando Columbus. Reproduced in Facsimile from the Unique Manuscript in the Columbine Library of Seville.* New York, 1905.

Isidore of Seville. *Etimologie e De Summo Bono.* Edited by Pietro Loslein de Langencen. Venice, 1483.

Jacob, E. *Christoph Columbus, Bordbuch, Briefe, Berichte, Dokumente, ausgewahlte, einleitete und erlautete.* Brema, 1956.

Knox, R. *The Holy Bible, a Translation from the Latin Vulgate in the Light of the Hebrew and Greek Originals.* New York, 1956.

Las Casas, B. *Historia de los Indias.* Edited by A. Carlo. Mexico City, 1951.

López de Gómara, F. *Hispania Victrix. Primera y segunda parte de la historia general de las Indias.* Biblioteca de Autores Espanoles. Madrid, 1852.

Martinez de Ampriés, M. *Libro del Antichrist.* Burgos, 1497.

Morison, S., ed. and trans. *Journals and Other Documents on the Life and Voyages of Christopher Columbus.* New York, 1963.

Mugridge, D. *Christopher Columbus: A Selected List of Books and Articles by American Authors Published in America, 1892–1950.* Washington, 1950.

de Navarette, F. *Colección de los viages y descubrimientos.* Madrid, 1825.

Obras escogidas de filosófos con un discurso preliminar del excelentísimo é ilustrímo Señor Don Adolfo de Castro. Edited by Adolfo de Castro y Rossi. Madrid, 1922.

Pérez Castro, F. *El manuscrito apologético de Alfonso de Zamora.* Madrid, 1950.

Peter Martyr Anglerius. *De orbe novo.* Edited by F. MacNutt. New York, 1912.

Raccolta di Documente e Studi Pubblicazione a cura della Regia Commissione Colombianna nel quarto centenario dalla scoperta dell'America. 6 parts in 11 volumes. Rome, 1892–94.

Rosa y Lopez, R. de la. *Biblioteca Colombina. Catálogo de sus libros impressos.* Seville, 1888.

Sancti Aurelii Augustini hipponensis episcopi opera omnia. Edited by J. Migne. Paris, 1841–1902.

Sancti Gregorii magni Homiliae in Hiezechihelem prophetam. Edited by M. Adriaen. Turnholti, 1971.

Serrano y Sanz, M. *El archivo colombino de la Cartuja de las Cuevos. Estudio histórico y bibliográfico, Cristóbal Colón y descubremiento de América.* Barcelona, 1945.

Streicher, F. "Die Kolumbus Originale: Eine Palaographische Studie." Munich. *Spanische Forschungen der Gorresgesellschaft* I. Munich, 1928.

———. "Las notas marginales de Colón en los libros de Pedro Alíaco, Eneas Silvio y Marco Polo, estudiadas a la luz de las investigaciones paleográficas." *Investigación y progreso* 3, nos. 7–8. Madrid, 1929.

Summula seu Breviloquium super Concordia novi et veteri Testamenti. British Library, Eg. 1150, n.d.

Terrero, A. *Diciónario de abreviaturas hispanas de los siglos XIII al XVII.* Salamanca, 1983.

Varela, C. *Cristóbal Colón: Textos y documentos completos.* Madrid, 1984.

✢ *Secondary Studies*

Agosto, A. "In quale 'Pavia' studió Colombo?" *Columbeis II.* Genoa, 1987.

Alba, R. "Acerca de Algunas particularidades de las Comunidades de Castilla tal vez relacionadas con el supriesto acaecer terreno del milenio igualitario." *Biblioteca de visionarios, Heterodoxos y Marginados.* Madrid, 1975.

Alexander, P. "Byzantium and the Migration of Literary Works and Motifs: The Legend of the Last World Emperor." *Medievalia et Humanistica* 2 (1971):47–82.

Almagiá, R. "Christophe Colomb et la science moderne." In *Les consequénces de la découverte de l'Amérique par Christophe Colomb.* Conférence faite au Palais de la Decouverte le 19 Mai 1951. Parigi, 1951.

Alvarez, F. "Cristóbal Colón y el estudio de la Sagrada Escritura." *Archivo hispánico* 17 (1952).

Alvarez Pedroso, A. *Cristóbal Colón. Hombre geniomistico.* L'Avana, 1937.

———. *Plan cientifico de Colón para el descubrimiento de América. Evolución de sus ideas cosmográficas.* L'Avana, 1942.

Anastos, M. "Pletho and Strabo on the Habitability of the Torrid Zone." *Byzantinische Zeitschrift* 44 (1951):7–10.

———. "Pletho, Strabo and Columbus." In *Mélanges Henri Grégoire, IV (Annuaire de L'Institut de Philologie et d'Histoire Orientales et Slaves XII),* pp. 13–18. Brussels, 1952.

André, M. *La Véridique aventure de Christophe Colomb.* Paris, 1927.

Antelo Iglesias, A. "Colón y la 'Casa Santa'." *El Faro a Colón* 9 (1958).

Atti I convegno internazionale di studi Colombiani. 3 vols. Genova, 1952.

Atti II convegno internazionale di studi Colombiani. Genova, 1974.

Atti III convegno internazionale di studi Colombiani. Genova, 1977.

Balbi, G. "La scuola a Genova e Cristoforo Colombo." *Columbeis II.* Genoa, 1987.

Ballesteros Beretta, A. *Cristóbal Colón y el descubrimiento de América.* Barcelona, 1945.

Bandin, M. "Introducción a los orígenes de la observancia en España. Las reformas en los siglos xiv y xv." *Archivo Ibero-Americano* 17, 2d ser. (1957).

Barzan, E. "Los Franciscanos y Colón." *Acta Ateneo de Madrid, April 4, 1892.* Madrid, 1892.

Bataillon, M. "Evagélisme et millénarisme au Nouveau Monde." *Courants religieux et humanisme a la fin du xve et au début de xvie siècle in colloque de Strasbourg.* Paris, 1957.

Baudot, G. *Utopía e historia en México.* Toulouse, 1977.

Bengoechea Izaguine, I. "La Virgen Maria en la vida y la obra de Cristóbal Colón." *Scripta de Maria* 3 (1980):427–76.

Benz, E. *Ecclesia Spiritualis.* Stuttgart, 1934.

Bignami-Odier, J. *Etudes sur Jean de Roquetaillade (Johanes de Rupescissa).* Paris, 1952.

Bignardelli, I. "Cristoforo Colombo e la scuola cartografica genovese." *Genova. Rivista Municipale* 38 (1961).

Bloomfield, M. "Recent Scholarship of Joachim of Fiore and His Influences." In *Prophecy and Millenarianism: Essays in Honour of Marjorie Reeves.* Edited by A. Williams. Essex, 1980.

Borigas i Balaguer, P. "Profecies Catalanes dels segles xiv–xv: Assaig bibliogràfic." *Bulletí de la Biblioteca de Catalunya* 6 (1920–32).

———. "La visión de Alfonso X y las 'profecías de Merlin'." *Revista de Filologia Española* 25 (1941).

Boscolo, A. "Fiorentini in Andalusia all'epoca di Cristoforo Colombo." *Saggi su Cristoforo Colombo.* Rome, 1986.

Braunwald, E. *Harrison's Principles of Internal Medicine.* New York, 1987.

Burr, D. "Olivi, Apocalyptic Expectations, and Visionary Experience." *Traditio* 41 (1985):273–88.

Caiazza, L. "Cristoforo Colombo ambasciatore di Dio. Luci ed ombre di una grande impresa." In *Conferenca in occasione del Columbus Day.* Florence, 1968.

Callacy, F. "Les idées mystico-Politiques d'un Franciscian spirituel." *Revue d'historire ecclésiestique* 11 (1910).

Caraci, G. "Quando cominci Colombo a scrivere le sue 'postille'?" In *Scritti Geografici in onore di Carmelo Colamonico.* Naples, 1963.

———. "Un elemento di base per la datazione delle postille colombiane." In *Tra scopritori e critici.* Rome, 1963–64.

———. "A proposito dell 'postille' colombiane." *Pubblicazioni dell'Istituto di Scienze Geografiche della Facoltà di Magistero dell'Università di Genova* 13 (1971).

Caraci, G., and L. Caraci. "Il latino di Colombo." *Atti del II Convegno Internazionale di Studi Americani.* Genova 1976.

Careras y Artau, J., and T. Careras y Artau. *Historia de la filosofiá española: filosofiá cristiana de los siglos xiii al xv.* Madrid, 1939.

Castro, A. *Aspectos del vivir hispánico: espiritualismo, mesianismo y actitud personal en los siglos xv al xvi.* Santiago, Chile, 1949.

Cervetto, L. *L'album della città di Siviglia e il libro delle Profezie di Colombo.* Milano, 1892.

Cessi, R. "Il misticismo di Cristoforo Colombo." *Atti convegno internazionale di Studi Colombiani.* Genova, 1952.

Chiappelli, F. *First Images of America: The Impact of the New World on the Old.* 2 vols. Berkeley and Los Angeles, 1976.

Chiareno, O. "Recenti studi sulla lingua scritta di Colombo." *Atti convegno internazionale di Studi Colombiani.* Genova, 1976.

Coll, J. *Colón y la Rábida.* Madrid, 1892.

Conti, S. "Le postille di Cristoforo Colombo alla 'Naturalis Historia' di Plinio il Vecchio." In *Temi colombian: Scritti on onore del prof. Paolo Emilio Taviani.* Genova, 1986.

Cuartero Huerta, B. *Historia de la Cartuja de Santa Maria de las Cuevas de Sevilla y de su filial de Cazalla de la Sierra.* 2 vols. Madrid, 1950–54.

Cummins, J. "Christopher Columbus: Crusader, Visionary and Servus Dei." In *Medieval Hispanic Studies Presented to Rita Hamilton.* Edited by A. Deyermond. London, 1976.

Davies, A. "Origins of Columbian Cosmography."

Atti convegno internazionale di Studi Colombiani. Genova, 1952.

———. "The 'miraculous' Discovery of South America by Columbus." *The Geographical Review* 44 (1954).

De Rachewiltz, I. *Prester John and Europe's Discovery of East Asia.* George Morrison Lecture, 32. Canberra, 1972.

Dillon, J. "A Dominican Influence in the Discovery of America." *American Historical Society of Philadelphia* 41 (1930).

Doussinague, M. *La politica internacional de Fernando el Catolico.* Madrid, 1944.

Dubois, E. "León Bloy, Paul Claudel and the Revaluation of the Significance of Columbus." In *Currents of Thought in French Literature: Essays in Memory of G.T. Clapton.* Oxford, 1965.

Durlacher-Wolper, R. "The Identity of Christopher Columbus." In D. Gerace, ed., q.v., pp. 13–32.

Edgerton, S. "Florentine Interest in Ptolemaic Cartography as Background for Renaissance Painting, Architecture, and the Discovery of America." *Journal for the Society of Architectural Historians* 33 (1974).

Eijan, S. *Hispanidad en Tierra Santa-Actuacion diplomatica.* Madrid, 1943.

Elliot, J. *The Old World and the New, 1492–1650.* Cambridge, 1970.

Evans, G. *The Language and Logic of the Bible: The Earlier Middle Ages.* Cambridge, 1984.

Fasce, S. "Colombo, il Paradiso terrestre e Mircea Eliade." In *Columbeis I.* Genova, 1986.

Fernández-Armesto, F. *Before Columbus: Exploration and Colonization from the Mediterranean to the Atlantic, 1229–1492.* Philadelphia, 1987.

Flood, D. *Peter Olivi's Rule Commentary.* Wiesbaden, 1972.

Fraker, C. *Studies on the Cancionero de Baena.* Chapel Hill, 1966.

———. "Prophecy in Goncalo Martínez de Medina." *Bulletin of Hispanic Studies* 43 (1966):81–97.

Galliano, G. "Forma e dimensioni della terra nelle postille colomiani." *Miscellania I.* Genoa, 1986.

García Franco, S. "La geografía astronomica y Colón." *Revista de Indias* 4 (1943).

Gaztambide, G. *Historia de la Bula de la Cruzada in Espana.* Vitoria, 1958.

Gerace, D. ed. *Proceedings from the First San Salvador Conference: Columbus and His World.* San Salvador Island, Bahamas, 1987.

Gil, J. *Mitos y utopías del Descubrimiento: Colón y su tiempo.* Madrid, 1989.

———. "Colón y la Casa Santa." *Historiografia y bibliografia Americanistas* 21 (1977):125–30.

———. "Los franciscanos y Colón." *Actas-del I congresso Internacional sobre Los Franciscanos en el Nuevo mundo.* Madrid, 1987.

———. "Pedro Mártir de Angleria, intérprete de la cosmografia colombina." *Anuario Estud Colon* 39 (1982).

Gil, J., and C. Varela, *Temas Colombinos.* Seville, 1986.

Gillett, W., and C. Gillett. "The Religious Motives of Christopher Columbus." *Papers of the American Society of Church History* 4 (1892).

Goldstein, T. "Geography in the Fifteenth-Century Florence." In *Merchants and Scholars: Essays in the History of Exploration and Trade.* Edited by J. Parker. Minneapolis, 1965.

Grendler, P. *Schooling in Renaissance Italy: Literacy and Learning, 1300–1600.* Baltimore, 1989.

Gribaudi, P. *Il Padre Gaspare Gorricio di Novara, amico e confidenti di Cristoforo Colombo.* Scritti di varia Geografia. Torino, 1955.

Harrisse, H. *Notes on Columbus.* New York, 1866.

Heathcote de Vaudrey, N. "Christopher Columbus and the Discovery of Magnetic Variation." *Science Progress* 27 (1932):82–96.

Herrera Tordesillas, A. *Historia general de las hechos de las Catellanos.* Edited by P. Santiago. Santo Domingo, 1975.

Humboldt, A. von. *Cristóbal Colón y el descubrimiento de América.* Buenos Aires, 1946.

Iriarte, L. *Franciscan History.* Chicago, 1983.

Jos, E. *El plan y le genésis del descubrimiento.* Valladolid, 1980.

Jourdain, C. de. *L'influence d'Aristote et de ses interprétations sur la découverte du Nouveau Monde.* Parigi, 1888.

Lee, H., M. Reeves, and G. Silano. *Western Mediterranean Prophecy: The School of Joachim of Fiore and the Fourteenth-Century Breviloquium.* Toronto, 1989.

Lenhart, J. *History of Franciscan Libraries in the Middle Ages.* Washington, 1954.

Linden, H. "Alexander VI and the Demarcation of the Maritime and Colonial Domains of Spain and Portugal, 1493–94." *American Historical Review* 22 (1916).

Lopez, P. *Fr. Juan Pérez y Fr. Antonio de Marchena, protectores de Cristóbal Colón y de los Pinzón.* Santiago de Compostela, 1938.

Loughran, E. "Did a Priest Accompany Columbus in 1492?" *Catholic Historical Review* (1930).

Ludlum, D. "Early American Hurricanes, 1492–1870." In American Meteorological Society, *The History of American Weather.* Boston, 1963.

Lunardi, E. "L'importanza del Monastero di Santa Maria de la Rábida nella genesi della scoperta d'America." *Atti convegno internazionale di Studi Colombiani.* Genova, 1952.

McAuster, L. *Spain and Portugal in the New World, 1492–1700.* Minneapolis, 1985.

McGinn, B. *The Calabrian Abbot: Joachim of Fiore in the History of Western Thought.* New York, 1985.

———. *Visions of the End: Apocalyptic Traditions in the Middle Ages.* New York, 1979.

Madariaga de, S. *Christopher Columbus: Being the Life of the Very Magnificent Lord Don Cristóbal Colón.* New York, 1940.

Mahn-Lot, M. *Christophe Colomb.* Parigi, 1960.

Manselli, R. *La 'Lectura super Apocalypsim' de Pietro de Giovanni Olivi: Ricerche sull'escatologismo medioevale.* Rome, 1955.

———. "La religiosità di Arnaldo da Villanova." *Bulletino dell'Istituto Storico Italiano per il Medio Evo* 63 (1951).

Manzano y Manzano, J. *Cristóbal Colón—Siete años decisivos de su vida 1485–1492.* Madrid, 1964.

Maravall, J. "La Utopía politíco-religiosa de los franciscanos en Nueva Espana." *Estudios Americanos,* 2:199–277. Madrid, 1949.

Markham, C. *Life of Christopher Columbus.* London, 1892.

Marquis de Pidal, ed. *Concionero de Baena.* Buenos Aires, 1949.

Martín, A. *Los Recogido: Nueva vision de la mistica española (1500–1700).* Madrid, 1975.

Martini, D. *Cristoforo Colombo. Tra Ragione e Fantasia.* Genova, 1986.

Menendez Pidal, R. *La lengua de Cristóbal Colón.* Madrid, 1958.

———, "La lengua de Cristóbal Colón." *Bulletin Hispanique* 42 (1940).

Milhou, A. *Colón y su mentalidad mesiánica en el ambiente franciscanista español.* Valladolid, 1983.

Milina, V. *The Written Language of Christopher Columbus.* Buffalo, 1973.

Molinari, D. *Notas sobre el saber astronómico y geográfico en la epoca del descubrimiento de América.* Buenos Aires, 1925.

Moorman, J. *A History of the Franciscan Order.* Oxford, 1969.

Moretti, G. "Nec sic terris ultima thule (La profezia di Seneca sulla scoperta del Nuovo Mondo)." In *Columbeis I.* Genova, 1986.

Morison, S. *Admiral of the Ocean Sea: A Life of Christopher Columbus.* 2 vols. Boston, 1942.

Mulhern, P. "Gifts of the Holy Spirit." *New Catholic Encyclopedia.* New York, 1967.

Newcome, M. "Drawings by Tavorone." *Paragone,* no. 375, pp. 44–52. Florence, 1981.

Nunn, G. *Geographical Conceptions of Columbus.* New York, 1924.

Oberman, H. *Forerunners of the Reformation: The Shape of Medieval Thought.* Philadelphia, 1981.

O'Gorman, E. *The Invention of America.* Bloomington, 1961.

Oliger, L. "De relatione inter observantium Quaerimonias constantienses (1415) et Ubertini Casalensis quoddam scriptum." *Archivum Franciscanum Historicum* 9 (1916):3–14.

Ortega, F. *La Rábida—Historia documental y critica.* Siviglia, 1925–26.

Pardo Bazán, E. *Los Franciscanos y Colón.* In *Nuevo Teatro Critico.* Madrid, 1892.

Pastor, J. *La ciencia y la técnica en el descubrimiento de América.* Buenos Aires, 1945.

Perez de Tudela y Bueso, J. *Mirabilis in Altis: Estudio critico sobre el origen y significado del proyecto descubridor de Cristóbal Colón.* Madrid, 1983.

Phelan, J. *The Millennial Kingdom of the Franciscans in the New World.* Berkeley and Los Angeles, 1970.

Phillips, J. *The Medieval Expansion of Europe.* Oxford, 1988.

Pidal, R. "La lengua de Cristóbal Colón." *Bulletin Hispanique* 42 (1940):1–28.

Pietsch, K. "The Madrid Manuscript of the Spanish

Grail Fragments." *Modern Philology* 17 (1920–21):591–96.

Pike, R. *Enterprise and Adventure: The Genoese in Seville and the Opening of the New World.* New York, 1966.

Pittaluga, S. "Il 'vocabulario' usato da Cristoforo Colombo (Una postilla all '*Historia rerum*' di Pio II e la lessicografia medievale)." In *Columbeis I*, pp. 107–15. Genova, 1986.

Portigliotti, G. "Per una biografia psicologica di Cristoforo Colombo: I. Le idee messianiche. II. I vaticini profetici." *Annali dell'Ospedale Psichiatrico della Provicia di Genova* (Cogoleto) 3 (1932).

Pou y Martí, J. "Visionarios, Beguinos y Fraticelos Catalanes, siglos xiii–xv." *Archivo Ibero-Americano* 18–21 (1922–24).

Quinet, E. *L'Ultramontanisme, Oeuvres complètes.* Paris, 1857.

Ragghianti, L. "Lazzaro Tavarone disegnatore." *Critica d'Arte* 5 (1954):439–44.

Ravelli, P. *Cristoforo Colombo e la scuola cartografica genovese.* Stabilimenti Italiani Arti Graphichi. Genoa, 1937.

———. "A proposito del '*Libro de las profecías*' di Cristoforo Colombo." *Atti dell'Accademia Nazionale dei Lincei.* Rome, 1951.

———. "L'italianità di Cristoforo Colombo." *Atti convegno internazionale di Studi Colombiani.* Genova, 1952.

Reeves, M. *The Influence of Prophecy in the Later Middle Ages: A Study in Joachimism.* Oxford, 1969.

———. "The Development of Apocalyptic Thought: Medieval Attitudes." In *The Apocalypse in English Renaissance Thought and Literature.* Edited by C. Patrides and J. Wittreich. Ithaca, 1984.

Reeves, M., and W. Gould. *Joachim of Fiore and the Myth of the Eternal Evangel in the Nineteenth Century.* Oxford, 1987.

Ricard, R. *La 'Conquete spiritual' du Mexico.* Paris, 1933.

Roselly de Lorgues, A. *L'Ambassadeur de Dieu et le Pape Pie IX.* Paris, 1874.

———, *Mémoire pour solliciter la béatification of Christophe Colomb.* Paris, 1870.

Rumeu de Armas, A. *El cosmógrafo Fray Antonio de Marchena amigo y confidente de Colón.* Siviglia, 1966.

———. *La Rábida y el descubrimiento de América. Colón Marchena, Fray Juan Pérez.* Madrid, 1968.

———. *Colón y la Rábida.* Madrid, 1972.

Sackur, E. *Sibyllinische Texte und Forschungen. Pseudo-Methodius Adso und die triburtinische Sibylle.* Halle, 1898.

Salembier, L. "Pierre d'Ailly and the Discovery of America." *Historical Records and Studies of the U.S. Catholic Society* 7 (1914).

Sarton, G. *Introduction to the History of Science.* 2 vols. Baltimore, 1931.

Severi, P. *L'ordine dei frati minori. Lezioni storiche.* 3 vols. Milan, 1942–60.

Shiels, W. *King and Church: The Rise and Fall of the Patronato Real.* Chicago, 1961.

Singleton, C. "Stars Over Eden." *Annual Report of the Dante Society* 75. Cambridge, 1957.

Sweet, L. "Christopher Columbus and the Millennial Vision of the New World." *The Catholic Historical Review* 72 (1986):369–82.

Sylvest, E. *Motifs of Franciscan Mission Theory in Sixteenth-Century New Spain Province of the Holy Gospel.* Washington, 1975.

Taviani, P. "Las Bocas del Orinoco: El Segundo gran Descubrimiento." *Boletín de la Academia Nacional de la Historia.* Caracas, 1985.

———. *La Genovesità di Colombo.* Genoa, 1987.

———. *Cristoforo Colombo: la genesi della grande scoperta.* Istituto Geografico de Agostini. 2 vols. Novara, 1974.

———. "Perché Cristoforo Colombo non parlava in italiano?" *Epoca.* Milano, 1972.

———. *Christopher Columbus: The Grand Design.* London, 1985.

Taylor, E. "Idée Fixe: The Mind of Columbus." *Hispanic American Historical Review* 11 (1931).

Thacher, J. *Christopher Columbus, His Life, His Work, His Remains.* 3 vols. New York, 1903.

Ullman, W. *The Origin and Development of Humanistic Script.* Rome, 1960.

Varela, C. "Aproximación a los escritos de Cristóbal Colón." *Jornadas de Estudios, Canarias-America* 3–4 (1984).

Verlinden, C. *Cristoforo Colombo. Visione e perseveranza.* Rome, 1985.

Vidal, A. "Un ascete du sang royal: Philip de Morque." *Revue de questions historique* 88 (1910).

Vignaud, H. *Toscanelli and Columbus: The Letter and Chart of Toscanelli.* London, 1902.

Watts, P. "Prophecy and Discovery: On the Spiritual Origins of Christopher Columbus's 'Enterprise of the Indies.'" *American Historical Review* 90 (1985).

Webster, J. "Nuevas apotaciones a los estudios Examinanos-Francisc Examenis, OFM: su familia y su vida." *Archivo Ibero-Americano* 39 (1979):429–38.

Weckmann, L. "Las esperanzas milenaristas de los franciscanos de la Nueva España." *Historia Mexicana* 32 (1982):89–105.

Weissmann, G. *They All Laughed at Christopher Columbus: Tales of Medicine and the Art of Discovery.* New York, 1987.

West, D. *Joachim of Fiore in Christian Thought: Essays on the Influence of the Calabrian Prophet.* 2 vols. New York, 1975.

———. "The Reformed Church and the Friars Minor." *Archivum Franciscanum Historicum* 64 (1971).

———. "Medieval Ideas of Apocalyptic Mission and the Early Franciscans in Mexico." *The Americas: A Quarterly Review of Inter-American Cultural History* 44 (1989).

———. "Wallowing in a Theological Stupor or a Steadfast and Consuming Faith: Scholarly Encounters with Columbus' *Libro de las profecias.*" In *Proceedings First San Salvador Conference: Columbus and His World.* Edited by D. Gerace. San Salvador Island, Bahamas, 1987.

Wright, J. *Human Nature and Geography.* Cambridge, 1966.

Young, F. *Christopher Columbus and the New World of His Discoveries.* London, 1906.

General Index

Scripture Index